Charting Transnational Fields

The volume provides a field-analytical methodology for researching knowledge-based sociopolitical processes of transnationalization. Drawing on seminal work by Pierre Bourdieu, we apply concepts of practice, habitus, and field to phenomena such as cross-national social trajectories, international procedures of evaluation, standardization, and certification, or supranational political structures. These transnational phenomena form part of general political struggles that legitimate social relationships in and beyond the nation-state.

Part 1 on methodological foundations discusses the consequences of Bourdieu's epistemology and methodology for theorizing and investigating transnational phenomena. The contributions show the importance of field-theoretical concepts for post-national insights. Part 2 on investigating political fields presents exemplary case studies in diverse research areas such as colonial imperialism, international academic rankings, European policy fields, and local school policy. While focusing on their research objects, the contributions also give an insight into the mechanisms involved in processes of transnationalization.

The volume is an invitation for sociologists, political scientists, and scholars in adjacent research areas to engage with reflexive and relational research practice and to further develop field-theoretical thought.

Christian Schmidt-Wellenburg is Assistant Professor at Potsdam University, Germany.

Stefan Bernhard is Senior Researcher at the Institute for Employment Research (IAB), Germany.

Routledge Research in Transnationalism

For more information: www.routledge.com/Routledge-Research-in-Transnationalism/
book-series/RRT

Charting Transnational Fields

Methodology for a Political Sociology of Knowledge

Edited by
Christian Schmidt-Wellenburg
and Stefan Bernhard

LONDON AND NEW YORK

First published 2020
by Routledge
2 Park Square, Milton Park, Abingdon, Oxon OX14 4RN

and by Routledge
52 Vanderbilt Avenue, New York, NY 10017

Routledge is an imprint of the Taylor & Francis Group, an informa business

British Library Cataloguing-in-Publication Data
A catalogue record for this book is available from the British Library

Library of Congress Cataloging-in-Publication Data
A catalog record for this book has been requested

ISBN: 978-0-367-22418-9 (hbk)
ISBN: 978-0-429-27494-7 (ebk)

Typeset in Times New Roman
by Apex CoVantage, LLC

Contents

Figures

Tables

Notes on contributors

Stefan Bernhard is Senior Researcher at the Institute for Employment Research (IAB), Germany. Research areas: qualitative methods, field analysis, the sociology of (labor) markets and European integration, social network analysis. Recent publications: "Analyzing Meaning Making in Network Ties – A Qualitative Approach", *International Journal of Qualitative Methods*, 2018; "Beyond Constructivism: The Political Sociology of an EU Policy Field", *International Political Sociology*, 2011.

Didier Bigo is Professeur de sociologie politique internationale (IPS) at Sciences Po Paris and Research Professor at the Department of War Studies, King's College London. He is also Directeur of the Centre d'études sur les conflits, la liberté, la sécurité (CCLS), and one of the editors of the new journal *Political Anthropological Research on International Social Sciences* (*PARISS*; Brill Publisher). His work concerns sociology of surveillance, policing, and borders. He co-edited *Transversal Lines* (with Tugba Basaran, Emmanuel-Pierre Guittet, and R.B.J. Walker), Routledge, 2016 and *Data Politics* (with Engin Isin and Evelyn Ruppert), Routledge, 2019.

Karim Fertikh is Associate Professor of Political Science at the University of Strasbourg, France. He is a researcher at the CNRS-Center Sociétés, acteurs et gouvernement en Europe (SAGE) and member of the Academic Institute of France. His current research focuses on the Europeanization and internationalization of social rights. He is the author of the monograph *L'invention de la social-démocratie allemande. Une histoire sociale du Bad Godesberg de la social-démocratie allemande*, éditions de la Maison des sciences de l'Homme, 2019, has edited a volume on *Social Europe*, Campus, 2018, and his articles have appeared in journals including the *Revue française de science politique*, *Genèses* and the *Austrian Journal of Historical Studies*.

Julian Go is Professor of Sociology at the University of Chicago, specializing in global historical sociology and social theory. His recent books include *Postcolonial Thought and Social Theory*, Oxford University Press, 2016, and *Global Historical Sociology* (co-edited with George Lawson), Cambridge University Press, 2017.

Julian Hamann is Postdoc at the Leibniz Center for Science and Society, Leibniz University Hannover, Germany. Research areas: sociology of science, higher education studies, and the sociologies of knowledge and culture. Recent publications: "The Making of Professors. Assessment and Recognition in Academic Recruitment", *Social Studies of Science*, 2019; "Gatekeeping in Cultural Fields" (with Stefan Beljean), *American Journal of Cultural Sociology*, 2019.

Sigrid Hartong is Senior Research Fellow at the Department of Education at the Helmut-Schmidt-University Hamburg, Germany. Research areas: global-local education reform dynamics, datafication and digitalization of education policy and practice. Recent publications: "Contextualizing the Datafication of Schooling – A Comparative Discussion of Germany and Russia", *Critical Studies in Education*, 2019; "Towards a Topological Re-Assemblage of Education Policy? Observing the Implementation of Performance Data Infrastructures and 'Centers of Calculation' in Germany", *Globalisation, Societies and Education*, 2018.

Niilo Kauppi is Research Professor at CNRS-Center Sociétés, acteurs et gouvernement en Europe (SAGE) and Visiting Professor at University of Helsinki in 2020–2021. Research areas: European integration, knowledge governance, social theory. Recent publications: "Rethinking Politicisation", *Contemporary Political Theory*, 2019 (with Hans-Jörg Trenz); "Waiting for Godot? On Some of the Obstacles for Developing Counter-Forces in Higher Education", *Globalizations*, 2019; *Max Weberin lukutapoja* (Reading Max Weber), SoPhi, 2018 (editor with Kari Palonen); *Toward a Reflexive Political Sociology of the European Union*, Palgrave, 2018.

Monika Krause is Associate Professor of Sociology at the London School of Economics. She is the author of *The Good Project: Humanitarian Relief NGOs and the Fragmentation of Reason*, Chicago University Press, 2014, and an editor of *Fielding Transnationalism: An Introduction*, Wiley, 2016 (with Julian Go). She was awarded the 2019 Lewis A. Coser Award for Theoretical Agenda-setting by the Theory Section of the American Sociological Association.

Frédéric Lebaron is Professor of Sociology at École normale supérieure Paris-Saclay, University Paris-Saclay and member of CNRS-Center Institutions et dynamiques historiques de l'economie et de la société. He specializes in economic and political sociology, methodology, and sociology of inequality. He recently co-edited *Empirical Investigation of the Social Space* (with Jörg Blasius, Brigitte Le Roux, and Andreas Schmitz), Springer, 2020.

Jens Maesse is Assistant Professor at Department of Sociology, University of Giessen. Research areas: discourse analysis, sociology of science, economic sociology, and political economy. His publications include: "Globalization Strategies and the Economics Dispositif. Insights from Germany and the UK", *Historical Social Research*, 2018; "Economic Experts. A Discursive Political Economy of Economics", *Journal of Multicultural Discourses*, 2015.

Tomas Marttila is Assistant Professor in sociology at the Vienna University of Economics and Business. His research interests include political economy, economic sociology, and sociology of education. He is the author of *The Culture of Enterprise in Neoliberalism*, Routledge, 2013 and *Post-Foundational Discourse Analysis*, Palgrave, 2015; and editor of *Discourse, Culture and Organization: Inquiries into Relational Structures of Power*, Palgrave, 2018.

Christian Schmidt-Wellenburg is Assistant Professor at Potsdam University, Germany. Research areas: sociology of economic knowledge and professions, field and discourse analysis. Recent publications: "There Is No Such Thing as 'the Economy'" (with Frédéric Lebaron), *Historical Social Research*, 2018; "Europeanization, Stateness, and Professions", *European Journal of Cultural and Political Sociology*, 2017.

Andreas Schmitz is Substitute Professor of Methodology at the University of Aachen (RWTH), Germany. Research areas: relational social theory, relational methodology, applied statistics, and generalized field theory. Recent publications: "Relational Sociology on a Global Scale: Perspectives from Field Theory on Cross-Cultural Comparison and the Re-Figuration of Space(s)", *Forum: Qualitative Social Research*, 2019 (in print, with Daniel Witte); *Empirical Investigation of the Social Space* (with Jörg Blasius, Frédéric Lebaron, and Brigitte Le Roux), Springer, 2020.

Daniel Witte is Interim Professor of Sociology with a focus on Sociological Theory and the History of Social Thought at the Institute of Sociology at Goethe University Frankfurt. He also serves as Research Coordinator at the Käte Hamburger Center for Advanced Study "Law as Culture" at University of Bonn. His research areas cover sociological theory, including classical social theory, differentiation theory, and relational sociology, sociology of law, sociology of religion, and political sociology. Recent publications: "Relational Sociology on a Global Scale: Perspectives from Field Theory on Cross-Cultural Comparison and the Re-Figuration of Space(s)", *Forum: Qualitative Social Research*, 2019 (in print, with Andreas Schmitz); "Post-socialist Constitutionalism in Central and Eastern Europe: Toward a Populist Constitutional Consensus?", in *Constitutional Cultures in Comparative Perspective*, ed. by W. Gephart & J.C. Suntrup, Frankfurt/M., 2020 (in print, with M. Bucholc).

Chapter I

How to chart transnational fields

Introduction to a methodology for a political sociology of knowledge*

Christian Schmidt-Wellenburg and Stefan Bernhard

Introduction

The main aim of this book is to explicate and exemplify a methodology for researching knowledge-based political processes of transnationalization from a field theoretical perspective. In our understanding, knowledge-based political processes of transnationalization refer to struggles over "common principles of vision and division" (Bourdieu, 1994a: 7) that involve "sustained cross-border relationships, patterns of exchange, affiliations and social formations spanning nation-states" (Vertovec, 2009: 2). Such processes bring about phenomena of different scale and scope. These include cross-national professional and life trajectories (Kelly & Lusis, 2006; Nedelcu, 2012); transnational procedures of evaluation, knowledge pooling, standardization, and generating statistics (Bruno, 2010; Bernhard, 2011); international educational certificates and diplomas (Wagner & Réau, 2015); and regional "supranational" institutions, such as the European Union (EU) (Favell & Guiraudon, 2011; Georgakakis & Rowell, 2013; Georgakakis, 2017). Transnationalization is not a new phenomenon. The fact that nation-states themselves – the entity that is literally *trans*cended – emerged from transnational arenas and models (Meyer, Boli, Thomas, & Ramirez, 1997; Sapiro, 2018), is a case in point. What has changed in recent decades is the increased visibility of transnational phenomena, which results from open contestations of national political scopes and boundaries in international, regional, and local contexts.

The complexity of transnationalism has made it necessary to introduce new ways of thinking as well as new ways of conducting empirical research (Amelina, Nergiz, Faist, & Glick Schiller, 2012; Go & Krause, 2016). We approach this challenge by focusing on transnational political knowledge processes and drawing on a vibrant research strand originating in Pierre Bourdieu's work on social fields. In recent years, field analysts have dealt with various processes beyond the nation-state, such as colonialism (Go, 2008; Steinmetz, 2008), transnational habitus (Nowicka & Cieslik, 2014), European security policy (Bigo, 2014; Berling, 2015), Europeanization of law (Vauchez & Witte, 2013), EU integration (Kauppi, 2005; Bernhard, 2010; Schmidt-Wellenburg, 2017), regional economic integration (Fligstein & Stone Sweet, 2002; Bernhard & Bernhard, 2016), transnational power elites (Kauppi & Madsen, 2013; Schneickert & Beri, 2016; Schmitz & Witte, 2017), international experts of state governance (Dezalay & Garth, 2002; Dezalay & Nay, 2015), academic internationalization (Marttila, 2014; Hartong, 2015; Hamann & Zimmer, 2017), transnational economic knowledge production (Schmidt-Wellenburg, 2014, 2018; Schmidt-Wellenburg & Lebaron, 2018; Maesse, 2018), worldwide central banking (Lebaron, 2010, 2013), global humanitarian relief (Krause, 2014), and cultural globalization (Sapiro, 2009; Buchholz, 2016).

Importantly, these studies share more than just a few theoretical terms and concepts. They share a common mindset, and a style of research with a distinct epistemology and methodology. In other words, they constitute a research program (Bernhard & Schmidt-Wellenburg, 2012). It is this research program that we build upon and develop further in this volume. In what follows, theory is never separate, prior, or superior to methodological and epistemological considerations, but rather deeply engrained in them. Theoretical concepts function as heuristics that guide researchers through the countless decisions, routines, reflections, and mistakes that they encounter during the research process. This is not a minor issue. In fact, one of the main deficits in many adaptions of Bourdieusian sociology is that it overlooks this mutual embeddedness – this relational co-constitution – of theory, methodology, and epistemology. One of the messages of this volume is that this deficit restricts too much of the potential of field analysis, which we should rather tap. To do so, we identify five foundational methodological principles of the field analytical research program and relate them to transnational phenomena.

Another preliminary remark is in place here: We use the term "transnational" to denominate a common feature of an otherwise vast and very heterogeneous set of (potential) research interests (or "objects"). In our understanding, *trans*national points to the continued relevance of nation-states in current knowledge-based political struggles. However, this relevance is purely empirical, i.e., nation-states are interesting to the degree that they are relevant contexts of contestations. They have no inherent ontological or epistemological qualities, nor are they containers (Wimmer & Glick Schiller, 2002). The methodological considerations in the first part of the book and the empirical studies in the second part are indebted to this kind of "post-nationalism" (Krause, Chapter 5). They illustrate how one can take nation-states seriously without reifying them. Field analysis characterizes knowledge-based transnational political processes as deeply conflictual, power-based, and "multi-sited" (Marcus, 1995). It shows that agents have vested interests, and that they defend these interests in struggles with and for scarce resources. The outcome of such struggles and hence, the degree and form of "trans-"nationalization, is constantly contingent.

In our introduction, we will start by giving an overview of recent work researching transnationalization from different theoretical angles. This approach is not restricted to perspectives labeled as transnational, but also includes work engaging with phenomena beyond the nation-state that is subsumed under other headings. We will complement the overview by discussing the vast variety of recent field analytical research in this area. Finally, we will exemplify our understanding of field theory as a vibrant research heuristic, outline five basic methodological principles that guide field analytical research practice, and conclude with a short summary of the contributions to this volume.

Researching transnational phenomena from different perspectives

In this section, we engage with the rich literature on transnational phenomena that can be roughly divided into two broad strands of research – one that starts from empirical research and focuses on transnational phenomena (research-driven approaches), and one that has more encompassing theoretical ambitions (theory-driven approaches). We are well aware that such an overview cannot do justice to the commendable, complex, and laborious extant research, but it allows us to position the merits and potentials of field analysis in contrast to other approaches.

From researching transnational phenomena to sociohistorical insights

The first strand of research we investigate starts from and centers on phenomena that transcend nation-state borders; it is called transnationalism studies, and since Phillip Jessup's pioneering work *Transnational Law* (1956), it has argued that the "diminishing importance of territoriality, the constraints on state sovereignty, [and] the role of non-state actors" (Waldinger, 2013: 758) have continually increased. In the 1970s, Joseph Nye and Robert Keohane picked up on this initial impulse in their rejection of neorealism (Waltz, 1959, 1979) and the associated turn toward "transnational relations", i.e., toward "contacts, coalitions, and interactions across state boundaries that are not controlled by the central foreign policy organs of governments" (Nye & Keohane, 1971: 331, q.v. 1977). In the wake of this programmatic work, political scientists increasingly moved their attention away from intergovernmental organizations and formal treaties and toward a diverse transnational landscape that is characterized by a blurring of the division between the "international" and the "domestic", private regulations, the increased importance of non-state actors, a shift toward new modes of rule making and rule enforcement, and a growing complexity of institutional interactions (Hale & Held, 2011: 6 ff.).

To tackle the growing complexity of these transformations, scholars such as Thomas Risse (Risse-Kappen, 1995; Risse, 2007) put more emphasis on the autonomous logic of international politics and its shaping of domestic state politics, turning international relations research into studying transnational governance. All approaches to transnational governance share an understanding of transnational phenomena as the outcome of a realm of contentious politics in its own right, but different approaches place varying emphasis on certain practices, agents, and institutional structures (Tarrow, 2001). Researchers from culturalist

and constructivist perspectives, for example, place at center stage political arrangements, politics, and ideas that actors see normatively or functionally as appropriate
(Ruggie, 2004). They investigate their production and dissemination by focusing
on the discourses that give meaning and legitimacy to transnational governance
institutions (Risse, 2007). Neo-institutional approaches recently proposed to use
the concept of field to account for "powerful structuring forces in the form of
cultural frames or patterns of meaning" (Djelic & Sahlin-Andersson, 2006b: 22)
or the concept of transnational communities (Haas, 1992; Djelic & Quack, 2010a,
2010b) to capture professionals' influence on transnational rule making and rule
shaping. In contrast to these perspectives, two more actor-centered approaches,
transnational networks (Keck & Sikkink, 1998) and transnational movements
(Tarrow, 2005; Tarrow & McAdam, 2005), concentrate on actors that are embedded in different national contexts and their manifest ties that span across borders.
The emergence of transnationally shared beliefs is explained by "multiple belong-
ings and flexible identities" of individuals (della Porta & Tarrow, 2005: 237).

We derive three main insights from these approaches of transnational governance. First, they see transnationalization as a change in the level of politics and in the
constellation of agents involved, leading to changes in the relationship between different sources of legitimacy that governance draws on (Djelic & Sahlin-Andersson,
2006a: 380). Second, they argue that processes of transnationalization involve an
institutional denationalization of states and regulatory power, and the creation of
private intermediary institutions that handle tensions between the global economy
and nation-states (Sassen, 2001). Third, they rebuke the idea that the relationship
between transnational and national politics is a zero-sum game, thereby acknowledging that not only transnational agents, but also many national agents, are
actively involved in building "the transnational" (Sassen, 2000).

Apart from political science, the concept of transnationalism flourished particularly within migration studies. In a prominent programmatic paper, Linda
Basch, Nina Glick Schiller, and Christina Blanc-Szanton (1994: 7) defined transnationalism as

> the processes by which immigrants forge and sustain multi-stranded social
> relations that link together their societies of origin and settlement. We call
> these processes transnationalism to emphasize that many immigrants today
> build social fields that cross geographic, cultural, and political borders.

In addition, the term "transmigrant" stresses that agents engage in home and
host societies alike when they create and sustain familial and economic relationships, as well as religious and political ones. The approach focuses not so much
on evolving social orders but stresses a bottom-up (non-state) impetus of the term
transnationalism, linking it explicitly to the movement of people and the boundary-
spanning activities that ensue from these movements. To this day, a plethora of
studies in migration research deal with all kinds of transnational aspects (Glick
Schiller, 2007). Among those are studies on the economic effects of migration

(Guarnizo, 2005); transnational families (Skrbis, 2008); transnational political action, identities, and citizenship (Bauböck, 2003); and transnational practices (Dunn, 2010). In sum, these studies paint a vivid picture of the manifold interdependencies between people across state boundaries.

At the same time, transnationalism, especially when understood as linked to transmigration, is not as omnipresent as proclaimed by its most fervent adherents, and it is commonly understood that further qualifications are needed (Portes, Guarnizo, & Landolt, 1999; Morawska, 2001). For example, not all migrants are able to engage in transnational practices to a similar extent due to differing economic resources and migration status (Al-Ali, Richard, & Koser, 2001), and states have to be taken into account as fostering or hampering cross-border relations (Waldinger & Fitzgerald, 2004). In recent years, the focus in migration studies has shifted from mere connectivity across borders, toward social spaces or fields (Levitt & Jaworsky, 2007: 131; Pries, 2008b). The focus is now on emergent qualities that originate from migrants' cross-border movements (Portes et al., 1999: 217) – for example, variants of transnational social spaces including small groups, issue networks, communities, and organizations (Pries, 2001; Faist, 2009). This research has begun to use social network analysis to operationalize structural patterns within such fields (Lubbers, Verdery, & Molina, 2018).

Both studies on transnational governance and studies on transnational migration focus on issues such as changes in rule making and enforcement; modes of governance or conflicts; and connectivity, movements, or identifications across borders. In so doing, both strands of research conceptualize transnational phenomena via social and political structurations. At the same time, studies in transnational governance, as well as studies in transnational migration research, do not deny the relevance of nation-states and national forms of societization. Moreover, recently, both substrands have explicitly referred to the concept of field to understand better these emergent structurations (Djelic & Quack, 2003; Levitt & Glick Schiller, 2004; Pries, 2008a; Faist, 2004, 2010). While this research provides valuable insights into relevant aspects of transnationalization, we argue that these studies do not go far enough when adopting field theory. Integrating methodological and epistemological axioms, such as relationalism and reflexivity, are valuable orientations that stipulate new perspectives on governance and mobility, as contributions to this volume show.

From theorizing transnational phenomena to general sociohistorical insights

Theory-driven approaches constitute a second broad strand of research into phenomena beyond national settings. They roughly fall into two substrands: approaches that elaborate general theoretical models of transnationalization, drawing on specific phenomena; and approaches that expand a general social theory to new scales. In both substrands, globalization (in a broad sense) is a key concept.

The first substrand concentrates on specific global phenomena as major objects of study and produces theoretical arguments that highlight their unique logic. Special emphasis is placed on "a transplanetary process or set of processes involving increasing liquidity and the growing multidirectional flows of people, objects, places and information as well as the structures they encounter and create that are barriers to, or expedite, those flows" (Ritzer, 2010: 2). Flows (Castells, 1996; Urry, 2001; Rey & Ritzer, 2010) are then contrasted with an age, or rather stage, of solidity in which analytical curiosity is captured by identities and barriers (Baumann, 2000). Transnational phenomena are seen as being neither fixed in time and space, as moving easily and being hard to stop, as roaming the globe and dissolving solids, such as nation-state boundaries, that stand in their way.

Connectivity over time and space, as well as transmogrification, are also at the heart of a set of concepts discussed in close proximity: glocalization, hybridization, and creolization (cf. Bhabha, 1994; Nederveen Pieterse, 1994; Robertson, 1995). Practices originating from one context become adapted to, integrated in, or connected with practices stemming from other contexts, making mélanges not an exception but the norm. Bricolage techniques such as sampling, collaging, and assembling explore relations and the simultaneous or mutual constitution of diversities. These approaches describe multiple ways the globe transforms, but at the same time, these analyses focus on very specific phenomena and neither aim at understanding overall societal processes, nor at providing more encompassing explanations.

Here, (post)colonial approaches have a more comprehensive take on globality in two ways. First, they focus on different flows and relations that persist between imperial powers and their subjects in a wider sense. Second, they engage in explaining how imperial powers are constructed, shaped, and reproduced in relations of colonialism up to the present day, creating global, regional, and national phenomena as well as shaping political, economic, and academic practices alike (Said, 1979). This opens up possibilities of critique, especially of the naturalization and universalization of the nation-state perspective in three ways: first, historically showing that teleological development of social order toward nation-stateness is specific only to a certain European period and needs to be analyzed by taking into account the imperial relationships of European agents to colonial subjects (Bhambra, 2018); second, focusing on the current situation and showing that we live in a postcolonial world in which the International Monetary Fund, World Bank, United Nations Organization (UNO), and EU have taken the place of former imperial powers (Go, 2017b); and third, laying open the discursive construction of legitimate and articulate subjects on the one hand and unarticulated subaltern subjects on the other (Spivak, 1988), and pushing for a reflexive turn on modernity as well as social sciences (Rodríguez Gutiérrez, Boatcă, & Costa, 2010; Seth, 2013; Go, 2017a; Connell, 2018).

The second substrand of theory-driven approaches "globalizes" theories of society and links transnationalization to modernity, evolution, and tendencies towards worldwide homogenization. In its most comprehensive version, all action or communication is seen as part of one world society (Luhmann, 1975, 1997), structured along the lines of the system of modern societies (Parsons, 1971) into functionally differentiated subsystems and integrated by exchange and symbolic generalized communication media. This evolutionary Parsonian heritage can also be found in more Weberian versions that analyze transnational phenomena as the outcome of not one but "multiple modernities" (Eisenstadt, 2000). Here, single societies or cultures are seen as developing units, rationalizing along distinct paths in a common direction, according to their specific cultural and structural prerequisites (cf. Münch, 1993). Even approaches that diagnose "reflexive modernity" and emphasize inverse and risk-laden consequences (Giddens, 1990; Beck, 2009) are indebted to the idea of modernization as a universal process, albeit in combination with a critique of methodological nationalism and a plea for cosmopolitanism (Beck & Grande, 2007, 2010).

The Weberian idea of rationalization and tackling negative consequences thereby produced also lies at the heart of world polity theory, as developed by the Stanford School. John Meyer (2000) argues that when acting, we all draw on a "generalized other" that stems from a currently globally shared meaning background, with the desire to be recognized as modern and hence "agentic" actors fueling an enactment of templates of rational agents (Meyer & Jeppersen, 2000). Empirical studies trace the worldwide spread of agency templates, such as common organizational forms (Boli & Thomas, 1999; Drori, Meyer, & Hwang, 2006), organizing politics in nation-states (Meyer et al., 1997), or practicing science in universities and research institutes (Drori, Meyer, Ramirez, & Schofer, 2003), and diagnose an increase in worldwide homogeneity – albeit with emphasis on local practical divergence (Alasuutari & Qadir, 2014).

In addition to these Weberian approaches, there is one prominent approach that starts from a distinct Marxian perspective: world systems theory (Chase-Dunn & Grimes, 1995; Wallerstein, 2000; Chase-Dunn, 2014). Here, the argument is turned around, and rationalization, modernity, and globalization are in effect analyzed as outcomes of economic development driven by specific modes of accumulation and the accompanying exploitation and changes in the population (Babones, 2015). World economic relations take the shape of relations of dependency between states, with the center being defined by the currently most effective mode of production, the periphery being exploited, and the semiperiphery breeding revolutionary tendencies aimed at toppling the center – which, in turn, stabilizes the world system by implementing hegemonic norms and values on a world political scale (Wallerstein, 1974).

Both substrands of research aim at theorizing general models of globalization, albeit differently, according to their object of research: on the one hand, theorizing focuses on a specific social phenomenon; on the other hand, the phenomenon in question is society. In both cases, overgeneralization of the model seems to be the danger, albeit with exactly contrary results. Ideas of global or world society end up with a simplified picture created due to the diffusion of the same content in the form of templates, structural morphologies, or cultural patterns, or by installing a homogenous set of relations. Ideas of glocalization, hybridity, and flows, on the other hand, overgeneralize one specific aspect of globalization, and tend to also lose the ability to differentiate between global and nonglobal tendencies.

In this situation, we propose to turn to concepts of relational and reflexive social thought inspired by the work of Bourdieu, that has been developed in a constant struggle against both these social scientific temptations. Field analysis offers a research style that marries theoretical concepts to empirical research in a way that is *uno actu* research driven and theory driven. Unlike other approaches to transnational phenomena, field analysis is a theory of practice that guides research routines and offers a tool to reflect upon them. This research aim amounts to a unique observer position that is simultaneously more involved in its research objects (by deliberately constructing them) and more detached from them (by using instruments to reflect upon and uncover relations of power).

Transnationalizing field analysis

At first sight, Bourdieu's theoretical approach might be considered an unlikely candidate for transnational analysis. He developed his sociology mostly on research questions closely linked to or originating in struggles with French institutions such as education (Bourdieu & Passeron, 1977), class structure (Bourdieu, 1984), state and government bodies (Bourdieu, 1992, 2013), elites (Bourdieu, 1994b), the housing market (Bourdieu, 2005), or the literary field (Bourdieu, 1996, 2008a). Moreover, when Bourdieu commented on transformations beyond the nation-state, he did so more as a public intellectual than as a sociologist (Bourdieu, 1999a; but see Bourdieu & Wacquant, 1999). However, the impression is misleading in at least two ways. First, Bourdieu's research was never confined to France or nation-state society. His studies on Kabyl life in Algeria in the 1960s (Bourdieu, 1979), his seminal theoretical work *Outline of a theory of practice* (Bourdieu, 1977), and his late work *The Weight of the World* (Bourdieu, 1999b) could be called transnational in the best sense, because the objects of research are constructed beyond nation-stateness, taking their distinct historical, social, and epistemological constitution seriously (cf. Heilbron & Steinmetz, 2018: 39, 41). Second, Bourdieu's heritage is not restricted to his own writings. His "équipe" at the Centre européen de sociologie et de science politique refined and developed the analytic and methodological tools of field analysis, and applied these tools to non-French settings (for more detail, see Wagner, 2005; Schultheis, 2018). In this context, field analysis proved to be a valuable tool to analyze complex interdependencies between social processes at different "scales" or, to be more precise, between social processes with different spatially connoted claims and resources. One of the reasons for this is that field analysis is sensitive to historical social processes, and this also holds in regard to analyzing the emergence of the nation-state as a dominant form of political organization (Bourdieu, 2014) – a development that has always been inherently transnational (Sapiro, 2009, 2013).

The field analytical research following in Bourdieu's footsteps has inspired a vast variety of studies on transnational phenomena, not only in France but also beyond. A first substrand of work focuses on the contextualized production of agents, ideas, practices, and worldviews in one national setting and their relocation into another setting, where they are recontextualized and "remade" (Bourdieu, 1999a). Well-known studies are Michele Lamont's work on the transatlantic construction of Jacques Derrida as a legitimate and dominant philosopher in France and the United States (1987); Pascale Casanova's study on the world literary field (Casanova, 2007); Yves Dezalay's and Brian Garth's research on lawyers and international arbitration (1996), as well as on the proliferation of Northern professional expertise in South American countries (2002); Loïc Wacquant's analysis of the transnational diffusion of a US-bred neoliberal punitive common-sense (e.g., Wacquant, 1999); or Richard Münch's study on the spread of academic capitalism (2014) and of neoliberalism in general (Bernhard & Münch, 2011).

A second substrand of research concentrates especially on European processes of how transnational fields are established and gain autonomy from nation-states as well as from each other, and this includes constituting transnational practices as opposed to a more national habitus and more national agents and institutions. This research envisages not only careers in transnational fields (Carlson, 2018) or the rise of European institutions and respective policy fields (Bernhard, 2011; Fertikh, chapter 9), but also the rise of a European bureaucratic and political field (Georgakakis & Rowell, 2013) populated by Europeanized agents such as members of the European parliament (Beauvallet & Michon, 2013), European bureaucrats (Georgakakis, 2017), or Brussels lobbyists (Lahusen, 2013; Laurens, 2018). With the establishment of European institutions of consecration such as the College of Europe, and institutionalized professional trajectories such as the Concours of the European Commission (Georgakakis, 2010), it can be argued that a transnational or EU habitus (Poehls, 2009) emerged and that transnational fields developed their own specific form of stateness (Schmidt-Wellenburg, 2017), radiating right into communal and regional administrations and their professionals (Büttner & Leopold, 2016). Recently, Niilo Kauppi (2018) integrated key insights of this political sociology of the EU from a Bourdieusian perspective.

A third substrand of field research takes a more global outlook and studies the colonial legacy of British, French, and German Empire (Go, 2008: Chapter 7; Steinmetz, 2008, 2016) and more recent US hegemony (Go, 2017b), opening up field analysis for ideas from (post)colonial and decolonization studies (Go, 2016). Other objects of research are transnationalization of migrants' habitus (Kelly & Lusis, 2006; Nedelcu, 2012; Nowicka & Cieslik, 2014), transnational capital accumulation in middle classes (Gerhards, Hans, & Carlson, 2017), the production and reproduction of transnational elites (Kauppi & Madsen, 2014), and transnationalization of social inequalities (Schneickert, 2018; Atkinson, 2019). Addressing these issues of power and inequality invites us to reflect on the question of how to construct the object of transnational research, e.g., the effects of struggles and differing constellations in a global field of power (Schmitz, Witte, & Gengnagel, 2017; Schmitz & Witte, Chapter 4) and taking the analysis into a "post-national" realm (Krause, Chapter 5).

A fourth substrand contributes directly to the development of an international political sociology. It puts emphasis on professional and disciplinary groups, such as lawyers (Dezalay & Madsen, 2012), judiciaries and transnational courts (Madsen, 2018), economic experts and regulation (Fourcade, 2006; Schmidt-Wellenburg, 2017; Suckert 2017; Maesse, 2018: Chapter 11), and experts in the areas of humanitarian relief (Krause, 2014), fields of art (Buchholz, 2016), security studies (Mérand, 2008; Bigo, 2014: Chapter 3), and terrorism (Stampnitzky, 2013). Here, close connections exist in research that looks into the transnationalization not only of certain disciplines but also more generally of science and education, such as the proliferation of a testing industry and related governance via the Organization for Economic Development's (OECD) Programme for International Student Assessment (PISA) (Münch, 2012; Hartong & Nikolai, 2017) or the EU's Bologna Process (Münch, 2014), the European Research Council (Gengnagel, Baier, & Massih-Tehrani, 2015), global academic rankings (Kauppi & Erkkilä, 2019; Hamann & Schmidt-Wellenburg, Chapter 8), or evidence-based governance of education (Marttila, Chapter 10), and the effects such developments have, for example, on national school reforms (Hartong, Chapter 12).

We argue that following the basic methodological traits inherent to the research just outlined in these four substrands enables us to construct the objects of research by confronting and challenging habitual, everyday, and academic perceptions that are taken for granted. One needs to avoid the temptations of empiricism as well as scholasticism, take agents' positions and their statements not as ontologically given but as relational effects that have a generative history, and last but not least, bring the academic, social, and political effects of research into a wider political debate (cf. Kauppi, Chapter 2).

Toward a methodology for transnational field analysis

In this section, we present the methodological principles of applied rationalism, oscillation between theoretical and empirical construction, relationalism, generative structuralism, and reflexivity. Together, these five principles constitute the core of a research program that intends to engage in theoretically informed empirical research processes.

Applied rationalism

Transnational phenomena seem well defined and marked off from national phenomena, as they have their own distinct existence. Our methodological approach advises against taking their existence for granted and against pursuing, as if these objects only need to be adequately recorded, either by quantitative measurement or qualitative documentation. We argue that the object under research needs to be actively constructed by the researcher as a scientific object, not simply adopted with all its societal implications and effects. There are two reasons why this is the case, which together constitute the methodological principle of applied rationalism.

First, we understand knowledge as a process of social construction evolving from the relationship between observer and object. In the case of scientific knowledge, this amounts to the insight that "for a scientific mind, all knowledge is an answer to a question. If there has been no question, there can be no scientific knowledge. Nothing is self-evident. Nothing is given. Everything is constructed" (Bachelard, 2002: 25). Hence, a scientific practice that pushes its reflexive potential cannot take scientific objects as self-evident. It needs to investigate them as specific scientific objects that have been constructed. This can be done using the concept of "epistemological rupture" that allows overcoming existing knowledge and facilitates creating new insights, and that has been deliberately initiated in scientific practice.

Second, we argue that this necessity for an epistemological rupture or break is especially virulent in the social sciences because, as Bourdieu (1991b) points out, we are constantly surrounded by spontaneous conceptions of the social interwoven into nonscientific meaning and power functions. Hence, we have to break with everyday perceptions and concepts of the social and consciously start to construct our scientific social objects. If not, we are reproducing not only the already existing categories of the social but also the politics inscribed in them, without being able to control the process. We need to actively put some distance between the standpoint of the scientific observer and the everyday cognition of the world, using the resource of "alienating" ourselves from our research objects in order to impregnate the sociological gaze against the danger of "going native" (Hartmann, 2012). However, epistemological rupture necessarily also involves a critique of the basic scholastic beliefs in a certain research area – a step much harder for researchers to take. Taken together, this means constructing the phenomena of interest as a scientific object, and reintroducing the subjective practical sense involved in the phenomena as part of the phenomenal reality that is able to irritate and control the scholastic view (Bourdieu & Wacquant, 1992; Champagne, Lenoir, Merllié, & Pinto, 1999).

What does this first principle of applied rationalism imply for researching transnational phenomena? Applied rationalism points to the necessity of distrusting everyday conceptions of the transnational as merely geo-spatial relocations of persons, objects, or ideas. Instead, we should ask whether and how *transnational practices* differ from national practices, and how they relate to one another. As Bigo (Chapter 3) points out, many national practices actually constitute themselves with reference to the transnational, and vice versa.

Focusing on agents, the question arises whether there is such a thing as *transnational habitus*, or if it exists only in the everyday perception as a caricature and empirically thin mirror image of national habitus. The indication of having lived abroad – in another "nation" – is not enough to define transnational habitus. Instead, we should pluralize the concept itself to include not only different class and (professional) field contexts, but also different "scopes": regional, local, national, international, and global contexts of habitus production, thereby abstaining from essentialism and taking the relationality of habitus seriously (Bourdieu,

1977; Witte, 2014). In such a reading, the everyday nationalist naturalism and essentialism is overcome in favor of a relational constructivism interested in the production – current and historical – of the scopes of habitus, practice, and field.

From a field analytical perspective, the production of such scopes is seen as an outcome of field struggles in which the national as well as the transnational are at stake: they are field effects, albeit not necessarily of a *transnational field*. We should not opt for a certain empirical type of field to be the specific one in which these struggles take place, such as bureaucratic fields, political fields, or religious fields. Instead, we argue that these struggles are a function that such fields may have more or less in relation to other fields. Some fields in comparison to others become places where struggles over the face of society and its processes of soci-etization are fought over, where "the social" and its "scope" become objectified and where their legitimacy and legitimate resources and agents are produced. At the same time, the open and observable struggles in such a "dominant" field are an effect of the underlying power and meaning within this field's relationship to other fields and vice versa.

Bourdieu describes this constellation as the field of power, the space that structures the struggles over the relationship between different fields and the dynamic relationship between different logics of symbolic and material domina-tion (Bourdieu, 2014; Schmitz & Witte, 2017). Therefore, it is not national poli-tics or international diplomacy alone where struggles about meaning and scope take place, albeit both are important catchment areas where certain agents have managed to historically monopolize material and symbolical power as they have engaged in these struggles. Instead, other fields, such as science and religion, also have to be taken into account, as they serve or have historically served a univer-salizing function and have contributed to certain legitimate visions of society and its divisions, that have managed to order fields and their relationships beyond the initial field where they were produced. Hence, researching transnational phe-nomena means becoming skeptical of everyday perceptions of the nation-state as the ultimate and unchallenged monopoly of symbolic and material power, and of functional differentiation as the only reasonable structure of field relations; instead, we are encouraged to take into account the possibility that other accre-tions of powers, forms of field relations, and scopes of social order may exist, and to research how they are produced.

Oscillation between theoretical and empirical construction

The second methodological principle spells out one of the consequences the first principle has for organizing the practice of social science research. Applied rationalism creates the necessity of constantly iterating between theoretical inter-pretation and abstraction on the one hand and empirical application of methods and data fabrication on the other hand, trying to realize theory-driven social research without imposing one's prejudicial preconstructions on the world and simultaneously creating empirically validated theoretical statements. As Bourdieu (1992: 225, 227) points out, the

> most 'empirical' technical choices cannot be disentangled from the most 'theoretical' choices. (. . .) It is only as a function of definite construction of the object that such a sampling method, such a technique of data collection and analysis, etc. becomes imperative.

At the same time, he warns not to interpret this relationship as a one-way road, calling to "try, in every case, to mobilize all the techniques that are relevant and practically usable, given the definition of the object and the practical conditions of data collection." Iterating between these two poles creates a research practice that is akin to a reflexive fitting process in which "grounded" sociological theory can be created through empirical theory building (Glaser & Strauss, 1967; Diaz-Bone, 2006: 79).

Such an approach to the practice of research entails dialectic research designs that reject (deductive or inductive) one-way reasoning. This indicates the necessity of using existing theories and theoretical insights to, on the one hand, devise research questions that structure the construction of research problems and, on the other hand, in a more self-reflexive theoretical thrust, to confront theories and practical theoretical reasoning with irritating empirical "evidence" to spark sociological, albeit not scholastic, puzzles that need mending. The second aspect reminds us to use methods against the grain in order to break the routine link between theoretical models, methodologically imagined empirical-sociological objects, and methods to generate and analyze these objects.

Relationalism

Field-analytical approaches to transnational phenomena are relational, not essentialist, meaning that the transnational character of a certain research object cannot be determined on its own but only with reference to other phenomena, their more or lesser transnational characteristics, and their associated spatial notions such as global, international, and regional, as well as national and local (Pries, 2008a). At the same time, these spatial notions refer to different proto-political authorities that make claims to prevalence, validity, and scope. These claims point to more or less well-established monopolies of power and the effects of symbolic domination. We thereby construct the transnationality of a scientific object by identifying some of its characteristics as backed by authoritative sources beyond the nation-state context, stabilizing its transnational scope. At the same time, we also need to specify – at least in the theoretical model – how these characteristics differ from more nationalized characteristics (and objects). Hence, the phenomenon under scrutiny is understood as a function of an abstract scientific model that involves more than one possible realization, and is relational in itself as well as to its empirical realization. When developing such models, we propose to use the three previously mentioned relational concepts: field, habitus, and practice.

Practice refers to the social processes in which agents actively relate to others through their engagement, whereas field and habitus are understood in relation to practice as two forms of its history – subjective and objective, which are structured over the course of time and which structure the present conditionality of practice at the same time. In addition, habitus and field also form a relation – not an opposition:

> they are not polarities, but 'limits'. [. . .] The habitus is a limit condition of the embodiment of the field. Field and habitus are both instruments to understand that collective and individualized are the single face of a Möbius strip seen from two angles, because society is a 'society of individuals' as Norbert Elias said before Bourdieu in order to describe specific historical figurations (Bigo, 2011: 238).

When researching transnational phenomena, a focus on *practices* triggers questions such as the following: Does the knowledge needed to engage in practices of different scope differ? How are differences in scope practically created and enforced? Do practices of a certain scope have an inner logic that excludes certain other practical logics? A major insight from relational sociology can be put to work here: Opposing aspects of relations do not cancel each other out, but may mutually condition each other. First, opposing scopes such as global and local often originate in the same practices, an insight that gave rise to the term "glocal" (Robertson, 1995). Second, practice is neither layered nor choppy but fluid and omnipresent; therefore, discontinuities between scopes and essences or hard cuts have to be researched as practically produced differences that are the effects of practices. Such a perspective challenges researchers to take "the other side" of relations into account: global effects appear only if there are also local effects, transnational effects imply national effects, and many structural effects that are perceived as opposing each other might actually originate from the same practice or from interlinked practices.

When we focus on the knowledge needed to engage in transnational practices – *habitus* – we should also take the principle of relationalism seriously; that is, there is no such thing as a transnational habitus, only more or less transnational versions in relation to other more or less national or otherwise scoped versions. All habitual dispositions are stances in the world, acquired in certain contexts and situations that differ in scope and are hence more or less linked to different sources of symbolic power. This nonessentialist conception allows us to use habitus as an attribute of individuals as well as of class in a double sense: Being more akin to certain agents and less to others due to one's dispositions and hence falling into a certain categorical class, but at the same time being classified as member of a specific social class because of differing dispositions and subsequently differing strategies due to one's position in relation to others (Bourdieu, 1985). A nonessentialist reading of habitus can then be combined with the multipositionality of agents in different fields in order to pose questions on the homology effects of certain habitus forms across different fields – or the occurrence of habitus cleavages, be it at the individual or collective level.

Using the concept of *field* to analyze transnational phenomena means conceptualizing them as field effects, albeit not necessarily of only one transnational field. Transnational fields, unlike national fields, are not restricted to the national scope in their (re)production of specific field practices, capitals, and habitus. This implies relative autonomy from other types of scopes in two dimensions: first, autonomy from nation-state politico-bureaucratic fields and, at the same time, links to likewise transnationally scoped politico-bureaucratic fields; and second, autonomy from other social fields scoped in a differing way, and linkages to transnationally scoped fields. Using these two dimensions creates an analytical grid in which relative "vertical" and "horizontal" autonomy (cf. Buchholz, 2016; Krause, 2018) from certain fields can be detected and at the same time understood as heteronomy in regard to other fields and scopes.

The relative autonomy of fields is created by field-immanent institutions of consecration (Bourdieu, 1996). They back certain practices as inherent to the field, as ways of gaining access, and as important steps in acquiring position and status, and they delimit others as not linked to the field or farther apart and needing "translational work". Transnational fields in the making often do not have strong immanent institutions of consecration, but instead rely on institutions more interwoven into other fields and their logics, and can hence be termed "weak fields" (Vauchez, 2011) in relation to "stronger", often national fields. However, such relations of autonomy are subject to sociohistorically specific conditions, as the relative "strength" of the field of transnational European nobility or of the Roman Catholic Church in former times shows, compared to "weak" European nation-states in the making (Elias, 1982; Bourdieu, 2014). At the same time, gradual differences in autonomy apply not only to the field as such but also to different areas in it: according to the practices enacted, the capital forms used, and agents that are more or less entangled in other fields, more autonomous field areas can be distinguished from more heteronomous field areas, and more transnationalized field areas can be distinguished from less transnationalized field areas.

Generative structuralism

If we take the third methodological principle of relationalism seriously, we cannot restrict thinking in relation to the dimensions of objects in space or social positions, but have to expand the notion to time and processes of becoming. Focusing on the generative characteristics of social phenomena is central to Bourdieu's concept of practice, which is not substantialist and hence not a theory of action, but a theory of agency. Following Émile Durkheim (2009), Bourdieu understands social practices as collective forms of thought and action. *Practices* are ever new becomings generated through agents engaging in life; they are a constant and changing flow that produces and shapes what social objects are. Here again, habitus is important, because it is the generative principle of regulated improvisation that shapes practice. Taking this conception of "generative structuralism" (Bourdieu, 1991a: 14) seriously leads to a radical sociohistorical contextualization of the constructed objects.

Turning to the analysis of transnational phenomena, questions arise about how transnational categories, practices, and habitus have historically developed, how they are constantly produced, how their relationships to nontransnational phenomena change – or not – and how they are connected to establishing not only normative orders in the Weberian sense, but also forms and relationships of authority beyond the nation-state setting. This in turn leads to the power-related questions, e.g., from where transnational orders draw their legitimation resources that had in recent centuries been concentrated in statist fields and institutions (Bourdieu, 2014).

The dynamic nature of the analysis allows us to address social order and change at the same time, and it paves the way to the relational idea of *habitus* advocated here. Social change is seen as a basic trait of social practice. In relation to practice, habitus becomes a source of social order, since it is the consolidated form of prior experiences. In relation to fields, habitus becomes a source of change, as it embodies experiences made in different fields and over time. Fields again are, in relation to each other, sources of constant irritation and hence, of change. In addition, habitus in itself can also be used for detecting changes in the form of trajectories that can not only be visualized over time though fields but also as trajectories of either individual lives as life-courses or of classes through social space as positional mobility.

Hence, in order to identify how transnationalism comes about, we have to follow two paths of investigation. First, we need to focus on the historic development of transnational dispositions and world relations that have a scope beyond the national. Second, we need to understand the individual socialization of the specific agents' habitus as equipped with either a more national or transnational outlook. In addition, we need to keep in mind all the other possible scopes interacting with the transnational scope. Finally, yet importantly, we have to be attentive to how the perceptions, judgements, and actions of agents change due to agents' changing positions in time and space vis à vis other agents.

If we want to discern which conditions are favorable of change toward "transnationalization", we need to turn to the concept of *field*. Fields are not solid social entities, but rather the product of agents engaging in practice, creating field effects according to their interrelatedness with other agents and their sociohistorically specific habitus. Institutions of consecration matter to this process of reproducing or changing certain field constellations, because they objectify certain positions, forms of capital, and habitus as legitimate and natural. Here, the question arises as to which institutions of consecration have historically existed and which scopes they had or were linked to. One prominent example is the Roman Catholic Church and its century-long dominance of fields as different as the arts, academia, and politics. In addition, the historical development of new institutions of consecration, such as the League of Nations, the UNO, or the EU institutions and their influence on existing fields and their scope – e.g., different legal and judiciary fields that had formally been closely scoped in the manner of a nation-state – becomes the center of interest. We need to investigate how different fields produce their own autonomy, hierarchies, and principles of differentiation using a variety of more or less internal institutions of consecration, and at the same time manage to draw on power monopolies beyond the field itself in order to universalize their claim of autonomy.

Reflexivity

According to Bourdieu, sociological knowledge – as with any other form of knowledge – is the result of a sociohistorically contextualized process of social objectification, structured by scientific field forces and stances in relation to other forms of knowledge. Bourdieu generalizes Durkheim's and Mauss's (1963) idea that all symbolic representations and moral judgments are social facts created by a specific socially embedded collective and serving a social function (Bourdieu, 1991b). At the same time, he draws on Karl Mannheim's (1960) thesis of the social determination of ideas (Vandenberghe, 1999: 57; Kögler, 1997) and argues, similar to Mannheim, that sociology does not need to discard the idea of objective knowledge for pure relativism (Bourdieu, 2004: 18 ff.). Two strategies are of help here. First, turning the methodological principle of reflexivity into self-reflexivity and objectifying one's own position, as Bourdieu has done himself as a scientific (Bourdieu, 1988) and, in a broader sense, social agent (Bourdieu, 2008b). Second, using the concept of field to analyze and determine which socialhistorical conditions are favorable of a high degree of autonomy that allows the production of objective scientific knowledge – albeit that this knowledge will always be in relation to a given state of society and in flux, thereby sociologizing Gaston Bachelard's epistemology (Bourdieu, 2004: 78 ff.). Social science is then at best a continuous reflexive and collective effort that has to be pursued repeatedly and will never be fully achieved, but yields the potential for new insights and scientific knowledge.

Why do we emphasize this methodological principle when researching transnational phenomena? When agents challenge national scopes and the dominance of national politico-bureaucratic fields, they need alternative resources and allies. Hence, researchers and whole disciplines that research transnational phenomena are seldom disinterested bystanders, but become sought-after experts and often comrades in arms in convincing the world that the phenomena in question do exist, are worth engaging, do make a difference, and are of universal importance. At the same time, scientists are themselves engaged in inner-disciplinary and interdisciplinary cognitive and power struggles to produce and legitimize transnational categories, ideas, and agents in the face of established research programs. New social science disciplines such as European or transnational studies start from the margins of existing disciplines, are transdisciplinary projects, and are closely linked to (if not personally interwoven with) the research objects they construct (Kauppi, 2010, 2018). In this configuration, social sciences gain practical influence. This makes a reflexive stance even more important and indispensable.

With respect to transnational phenomena and the question of scope, it becomes important to acknowledge that all practices are charged with certain indexicalities of scope, referencing legitimation contexts they draw on. The idea of an unfettered scientific access to reality is not only epistemologically undesirable but also ontologically unattainable; it needs to be substituted by a *reflexive scientific practice* that cautions against its own indexicalities of scope. Questions we desperately need to ask in our research practice are as follows: How do our everyday scientific practices contribute to the construction of categories, persons, objects, knowledge, and practices of the transnational, and which moments of symbolic violence are built into our research and objectification practices?

To perpetuate this methodological principle, we need to turn to the conditions of producing a *reflexive research habitus*, because without it, a reflexive scientific practice seems unattainable. Such a habitus does not simply exist and cannot be created out of thin air. Much to the contrary, it is in itself a social history and subjective effect of certain practical conditions of acquiring it. The five principles discussed here are the condensed and objectified prerequisites of such a habitus and can be used to highlight what is needed – albeit presented here in a pointed and at the same time scholastic way. Theoretical reflection and methodological guidance may only hope to irritate, but are bound to fail if applied only from the book in a top-down manner. As Bourdieu points out in his seminal work *The Craft of Sociology* (Bourdieu, Chamboredon, & Passeron, 1991), practical learning is necessary and can only be done by experiencing via one's own mind and body social research, including its pitfalls and dead ends, its unexpected and at times unwanted insights and stimulations; in the end it is a venture beyond one's own safe environment, albeit under scholarly guidance. What we need in transnational studies is a discussion about practical conditions that might be amenable or counterproductive for acquiring a reflexive research habitus.

This brings us to the conditions of the *scientific field* that favor the operation of such a *reflexive methodology*. Having the high material and high symbolic autonomy of the scientific field is advantageous, as it is derived not only directly from other social fields, such as the economic or political fields, but also in a broader sense from the field of power, be it national or transnational. The danger of being co-opted by transnationalist and/or nationalist political movements always exists. It goes much deeper than just a tit-for-tat exchange of economic or political capital for scientific capital in the form of "true" statements, as a homology of national versus transnational structures does exist in many fields; the relationship between positions of transnational researchers researching transnationalism, and nationally anchored researchers researching nationally framed phenomena, often mirror the relationship between positions of transnational political and economic agents in relation to nationally anchored colleagues (cf. Schmidt-Wellenburg, 2018;

Schmitz, Schmidt-Wellenburg, Witte, & Keil, 2019). Here, a possible coalition of interests to promote "the transnational" in its existence as a natural fact and outright influence on all other scopes may prevail, as it led in the 1990s and 2000s to a drive toward globalization as well as Europeanization in public discourse.

Only if it becomes possible to invest oneself in the game of academic pursuit, and to follow academic practices that aim to generate insights acknowledged as objective statements on the world that do not need to conform to the perspective of a certain scope, do we get the chance to truly construct and question transnational phenomena. This also holds for the field analytical methodology of a political sociology of transnational fields proposed here in relation to other possible approaches in analyzing transnational phenomena. It only stands a chance of contributing to the polycentric and competitive dynamic of producing scientific knowledge if it can secure a certain amount of symbolic and material autonomy in transnational studies as a whole. In addition, it will only be able to make a valuable contribution if it is alert to the need to constantly reflect on its own relationship – in resources (material) as well as categories (symbolic) – to the different sources of authority, their scopes, and aligned alliances. Hence, performing transnational field analysis means critically questioning one's involvement in fields via "academic" statements in political, economic, and other social processes of becoming, whether they are processes of transnationalization, nationalization, regionalization, or something else.

Overview of contributions

The contributions of this volume address two aspects of research on knowledge-based political processes. The first part, *Methodological foundations*, concentrates on the aspect of "charting" and presents methodological and theoretical contributions to the study of transnational processes in and across fields. The second section, *Investigating political fields*, contains contributions that address transnational phenomena in fields of different foci and scale.

Niilo Kauppi's contribution, *How many fields can stand on the point of a pin? Methodological notes on reflexivity, the sociological craft, and field analysis*, opens the first part of the book. He starts from the observation that Pierre Bourdieu's work has inspired social researchers all over the world. Countless books, articles, projects, and essays – including the present volume – draw on key concepts such as habitus, practice, and field. Such continuations are always adaptations that take place against the backdrop of social positions, individual trajectories, historical times, and cultural contexts. These factors inevitably influence how Bourdieu's concepts feed into research. Kauppi reflects on the reception of Bourdieu's sociology and its impact. Particularly in "mainstream" adaptations, he locates a tendency to abandon some of Bourdieu's most valuable insights. Turning against objectifying and realist reductionism, he reminds us that Bourdieusian field analysis constitutes a research program that offers heuristics for empirical research. It is a craft that guides a practice – the practice of doing social research.

Moreover, field analysis has normative implications that come from an effort to demystify "common-sense reality" and its underlying power relations. Researchers interested in transnational processes are well advised to bear Kauppi's argument in mind when constructing their research objects.

In his contribution, *Adjusting a Bourdieusian approach to the study of transnational fields: Transversal practices and state (trans) formations related to intelligence and surveillance*, **Didier Bigo** develops an analytical as well as an empirical argument. Analytically, Bigo argues that Bourdieu's conceptualization of sociogenesis, fields, and habitus cannot be a simple add-on to transnational studies, especially international relations. In contrast, he challenges the fundamental beliefs of these disciplines. He deconstructs the nation-state as a unitary actor and center of hierarchical decision making. Moreover, he views core distinctions, such as public versus private and national versus international, not as analytical elements employed by the researcher but as objects of the sociological analysis itself. Researching how these concepts are produced, legitimized, and used in transversal fields of state power needs to be the main task of a political sociology of transnationalization. Empirically, Bigo shows how national security has been reworked not only by states but also by a plethora of private agents, corporations, data experts, police, military, and secret services in recent years. He argues that the current realignment of national security together with the digitization of state reason has created a situation in which national intelligence services are no longer "national" but part of a transversal field. In times of crisis, they readily cooperate to produce a "state mission" focused on global protection against transnational threats and using prediction, prevention, and constant suspicion against those easy to target. The chapter illustrates the epistemological advances in research practice if one wholeheartedly adopts the basic relational and reflexive stance of Bourdieusian field analysis advocated here.

Andreas Schmitz's and **Daniel Witte**'s contribution, *National, international, transnational, and global fields: Theoretical clarifications and methodological implications*, taps the analytical potential of Bourdieu's field theory by an in-depth discussion of its relational theoretical foundation. The chapter reconstructs the epistemology of Bourdieu's sociology, describes how it links to field-analytical methodology, and theorizes "global" phenomena as effects of a global field of power. They take care not to identify their analytical framework prematurely with sociohistorical phenomena, such as the colonial nation-state or the UN, and thereby circumvent the danger of reifying traditional theoretical dichotomies such as micro versus macro, individual versus collective, or global versus local. This in turn opens the way toward a post-nationalized sociology: in their sociological construction of research objects, national, international, transnational, and global social phenomena have to be analyzed and understood as sociohistorical effects of a global field of power and meaning. The chapter thereby shows the potential a Bourdieusian relational and reflexive sociology holds for rethinking transnational research and theory alike.

Monika Krause deals with programmatic questions of field analysis beyond the nation-state in her conceptual contribution, *The post-national analysis of fields*. Against the backdrop of numerous empirical studies, she engages with inherent complexities of what she deliberately labels a "post-national" research object – complexities that emanate from intersections of fields at different scales. She argues in favor of a new vocabulary that revises and complements some of the field analytical vocabulary developed in national contexts. This theoretical move introduces terms such as "kinds of autonomy" (instead of degrees of autonomy) or "multiscalar fields", which open the way to new multiscalar questions about transnational fields. Thus, Krause's contribution is not only instructive for researchers engaging in empirical research, but also reflects on the field of field analysis and its dialogue with new research objects.

Frédéric Lebaron shows in his chapter, *European elites as (a)field(s): Reflections on the uses of prosopography and geometric data analysis based on three joint surveys of transnational objects*, the potentials and pitfalls that occur when researching transnational phenomena from a field analytical perspective by building prosopographical databases and investigating them using geometric data analysis (GDA). The contribution draws on experience gained during three large collective research projects on European elites: EU central bank governors in the global field of central bankers, the field of EU legal professionals, and the field of Eurocracy. He discusses the research logics behind constructing transnational objects, starting with the initial research design, data collection and limitations, followed by the assembly and management of the database, the use of GDA tools for the statistical investigation, and presentation of the results. His main emphasis lies on the methodological, epistemic, and sociological challenges that the construction of transnational research objects poses, the project-specific solutions found, and the more general insights that can be drawn from these experiences for further research. Lebaron's contribution is extremely valuable for all those who are currently engaging or might in the future engage with constructing transnational scientific objects themselves, because it does not conceal the difficulties one encounters when transferring the logics of field analysis into research practice.

The second part of the book begins with **Julian Go**'s chapter, *Global change: A field perspective on the end of empire*. Understanding and explaining social change is a key task of social science. Go addresses a fundamental shift in the global political field of the past century, the end of old colonialism. He grounds his historical perspective in a theory of change derived from Bourdieu's writings and, in particular, his conceptualization of fields as arenas of struggle over capital. Thus, the end of colonialism results from processes in and between several fields. The globalization of anti-colonial nationalism resulting from homologies in colonial fields was one of the mechanisms contributing to this development; the inter-imperial competition among the main actors on the global scale was another. The fundamental change brought about by these dynamics became visible when the British did not make Egypt a permanent colony after Nasser's announcement to nationalize the Suez Canal Company in 1956. The British decision not to subjugate the country permanently documented how much the "repertoire of power" had changed since the heyday of colonialism. The rules of the game had shifted in a way that still defines global politics today. From a theoretical point of view, Go's contribution demonstrates how some of Bourdieu's central ideas can be scaled up and used productively to understand post-colonial phenomena.

Valuation practices based on quantification are omnipresent phenomena in current societies. **Julian Hamann**'s and **Christian Schmidt-Wellenburg**'s contribution, *The double function of rankings: Consecration and disposif in transnational academic fields*, investigates how academic rankings rescope and transnationalize academic fields, often shifting the relation between existing power sources. Building on the extant literature, they identify key characteristics that make rankings a prevalent form of quantification in academia and an efficient instrument of power in transnational contexts. Integrating Foucault's concept of dispositif in their analysis, they proceed to argue that rankings serve a "double function": inside of academic fields, rankings impact the struggles of challengers and incumbents by giving preference to certain types of academic milieus, paradigms, agents, and strategies over others. Outside rankings open up boundaries of academic fields for lay audiences in economic, social, political, and mass media contexts. To the degree that academic fields become intelligible to these audiences, the dynamics within and around academic fields multiply and become further complicated. In pointing to these complexities, Hamann's and Schmidt-Wellenburg's study is an exemplary case of how internal rivalries, multiscalar settings, and renegotiated field, context, and relations intertwine in structuring transnational fields.

Farim Feritkh's empirical study, *A weak field of social policy? A transnational perspective on the EEC's social policymaking (from the 1940s to the 1970s)*, elaborates on a decisive development in EU integration – the entrenchment of a genuine European social policy. From a sociohistorical perspective, he meticulously reconstructs the multifaceted configuration of professionals, organizations, and venues that made the development of a "weak field" of EU social law possible. Opposing some commentators that question the significance of EU social policy, Fertikh stresses its remarkable achievements, most prominently the construction of new categories such as "deterritorialized social rights" and "social harmonization". To acknowledge such achievements, one must realize that transnational fields are multisited phenomena that evolve and settle in complex settings. Fertikh makes clear that the EU field did not materialize out of thin air, but was developed against the background of an international arena filled with players and resources that proved essential to its history. Thus, field analysis proves valuable for both unearthing the dynamics surrounding a field and recognizing its strengths and potentials.

Tomas Marttila's contribution, *The rise of a European field of evidence-based education*, shows that taking the development of transnational fields into account opens up the possibility to understand and explain change on a national and subnational level. Marttila argues that the introduction of the idea of evidence-based education to the field of education policy opened up national fields of education – that at the beginning of the twenty-first century, were dominated by national political and academic authority – to transnational agents, concepts, and strategies, reworking the practical logics of educational policy within the last two decades. Marttila is able to show that even in such an area as educational policy, that is absolutely central to the construction and reproduction of nation-state authority, certain expert communities have been able to construct a European imaginary using ideas of benchmarking and national competition to initiate a transnational field; these communities have created stakes and bound agents using their interests up to the degree to guarantee its relative autonomy. Marttila asserts that the European space of education is a "weak" field, with the European Commission acting as a dominant institution of consecration when appointing experts but subject to considerable influence by national and supranational academic and political agencies. Here, the wider global field of power does play a considerable role, equipping US-academic and OECD experts and expertise with particular symbolic power. Marttila highlights that developments in rather specialized policy areas are an important driver of governmental changes and contribute to the realigning and transnationalization of fields of state formation in a more general sense, rearranging what states and state authority are, and will be in times to come.

Jens Maesse's chapter, *The Euro crisis dispositif: Heterogeneous positioning strategies in polycentric fields*, shows that the different statements that agents have made in the Euro crisis can be best understood if we analyze them as the outcome of a transnational field seen as a complex and heterogeneous discursive positioning practice. The approach taken here argues that the conflict over economic policy is rooted in different but interrelated fields that are discursively drawn together into one transepistemic positioning arena. Combining Bourdieu's field theoretical approach with the Foucauldian discourse-theoretical concept of dispositif allows research on how the presentation or symbolic-imaginary visibility of social actors in their discursive practice relates to their institutionally sedimented modalities of existence. Maesse uses this theoretical framework to trace and analyze the discursive struggles are structured by different structural conditions in certain fields. This framework also allows us to show how new elements emerged in the crisis were used for strategic positioning in the transepistemic crisis dispositif, and opened up the possibility for change. Maesse reconstructs not only changes in the discursive struggles over the politico-economic order from a technocratic EU governance positioning toward new possibilities of critical democratic and more moderating positionings, but also changes in the institutional settings from which the discursive struggles draw, i.e., the different field contexts such as academic economics or Brussels bureaucratic institutions. He thereby not only offers an inspiring empirically grounded sociological theory of recent changes in EU crisis discourse, but also proposes a valuable concept for analyzing discursive change in transnational settings.

Sigrid Hartong shows in her contribution, *Tracing "the transnational" in the nationalization of school policy: The transformation of standards-based reform in the United States*, how standards-based reforms in school teaching, which have proliferated worldwide, changed school policy in the United States in the last 50 years. This is a prime example of a "national" policy issue and field created and developed not in isolation and entrenchment, but though the interconnectedness and varying linkages its agents hold beyond its imaged national confinement. Hartong argues that a hard distinction between national and international is of no real use to analyze such phenomena; instead, she opts for the concept of policy networks and transversal practices to trace the creation of a cast of new actors and organizations in this evolving policy space. Changing network constellations over 50 years have fabricated particular forms of reforms in which differing transnational imaginaries have played a significant role in shaping schooling practice. US school reform has hence been reconstructed as a US trans-state practice closely connected to developments in the worldwide production of standardized school performance data, best described in terms of heterarchical and topological connections spanning different scopes.

Note

* The present volume draws on the expertise of German, French, British, and American colleagues, most of whom are associated with the research network *Political Sociology of Transnational Fields*, which is funded by the German Research Foundation from 2017–2021. We would like to thank all members and workshop participants for the many lively discussions and fruitful collaborations, without which this volume would not have been possible. Christian Schmidt-Wellenburg would also like to thank the Käte-Hamburger Centre for Advanced Studies, Bonn, for the chance of spending a highly inspiring and productive half-year as fellow at the center, a stay without which this volume would not have flourished.

References

Al-Ali, N., Richard, B., & Koser, K. (2001). The Limits to 'Transnationalism': Bosnian and Eritrean Refugees in Europe as Emerging Transnational Communities. *Ethnic and Racial Studies, 24*(4), 578–600.

Alasuutari, P., & Qadir, A. (2014). *National Policy Making: Domestication of Global Trends*. London: Routledge.

Amelina, A., Nergiz, D., Faist, T., & Glick Schiller, N. (Eds.). (2012). *Beyond Methodological Nationalism: Research Methodologies for Cross-Border Studies*. London: Routledge.

Atkinson, W. (2019). *Bourdieu and After: A Guide to Relational Phenomenology*. London: Routledge.

Babones, S. (2015). What Is World-Systems Analysis? Distinguishing Theory from Perspective. *Thesis Eleven, 127*(1), 2–20.

Bachelard, G. (2002 [1938]). *The Formation of the Scientific Mind*. Manchester: Clinamen.

Basch, L., Glick Schiller, N., & Blanc-Szanton, C. (1994). *Nations Unbound: Transnational Projects, Postcolonial Predicaments, and Deterritorialized Nation-States*. Langhorne, PA: Gordon and Breach.

Bauböck, R. (2003). Towards a Political Theory of Migration Transnationalism. *The International Migration Review, 37*(3), 700–723.

Baumann, Z. (2000). *Liquid Modernity*. Cambridge: Polity Press.

Beauvallet, W., & Michon, S. (2013). MEPs: Toward a Specialisation of European Political Work? In D. Georgakakis & J. Rowell (Eds.), *The Field of Eurocracy: Mapping the EU Actors and Professionals* (pp. 16–34). Houndmills, Basingstoke: Palgrave Macmillan.

Beck, U. (2009). *World at Risk*. Cambridge: Polity Press.

Beck, U., & Grande, E. (2007). Cosmopolitism: Europe's Way out of Crisis. *European Journal of Social Theory, 10*(1), 67–85.

Beck, U., & Grande, E. (2010). Jenseits des methodologischen Nationalismus: Außereuropäische und europäische Variationen der zweiten Moderne. *Soziale Welt, 61*(3–4), 187–216.

Berling, T. V. (2015). *The International Political Sociology of Security: Rethinking Theory and Practice*. London: Routledge.

Bernhard, S. (2010). *Die Konstruktion von Inklusion: Europäische Sozialpolitik aus soziologischer Perspektive*. Frankfurt am Main: Campus.

Bernhard, S. (2011). Beyond Constructivism – The Political Sociology of an EU Policy Field. *International Political Sociology, 5*(4), 426–445.

Bernhard, S., & Bernhard, S. (2016). Do Anti-Discrimination Provisions Make a Difference? The Case of Wage Discrimination Against EU Foreigners in Germany. *Zeitschrift für Soziologie, 45*(1), 57–72.

Bernhard, S., & Münch, R. (2011). Die Hegemonie des Neoliberalismus: Ein gesellschaftstheoretischer Erklärungsansatz. *Sociologia Internationalis, 49*(2), 165–197.

Bernhard, S., & Schmidt-Wellenburg, C. (2012). *Feldanalyse als Forschungsprogramm* (2 vols.) Wiesbaden: Springer VS.

Bhabha, H. (1994). *The Location of Culture*. London: Routledge.

Bhambra, G. K. (2018). Colonialism, Postcolonialism and the Liberal Welfare States at the End of the Century. *New Political Economy, 23*(5), 574–587.

Bigo, D. (2011). Pierre Bourdieu and International Relations: Power of Practices, Practices of Power. *International Political Sociology, 5*(3), 225–258.

Bigo, D. (2014). The (In)Securitization Practices of Three Universes of EU Boarder Control: Military/Navy – Border Guards/Police – Database Analysts. *Security Dialogue, 45*(3), 209–255.

Boli, J., & Thomas, G. M. (Eds.). (1999). *Constructing World Culture: International Nongovernmental Organizations Since 1875*. Stanford, CA: Stanford University Press.

Bourdieu, P. (1977 [1972]). *Outline of a Theory of Practice*. Cambridge: Cambridge University Press.

Bourdieu, P. (1979 [1977]). *Algeria 1960*. Cambridge: Cambridge University Press.

Bourdieu, P. (1984 [1979]). *Distinction: A Social Critique of the Judgement of Taste*. Cambridge, MA: Harvard University Press.

Bourdieu, P. (1985 [1984]). Social Space and the Genesis of Groups. *Theory and Society, 14*(6), 723–744.

Bourdieu, P. (1988 [1984]). *Homo Academicus*. Stanford, CA: Stanford University Press.

Bourdieu, P. (1991a). *In Other Words: Essays Towards a Reflexive Sociology*. Stanford, CA: Stanford University Press.

Bourdieu, P. (1991b). Meanwhile, I Have Come to Know All the Diseases of Sociological Understanding. In P. Bourdieu, J.-C. Chamboredon & J.-C. Passeron (Eds.), *The Craft of Sociology: Epistemological Preliminaries* (pp. 247–260). Berlin: De Gruyter.

Bourdieu, P. (1992). The Practice of Reflexive Sociology. In P. Bourdieu & L. Wacquant (Eds.), *An Invitation to Reflexive Sociology* (pp. 217–260). Chicago, IL: University of Chicago Press.

Bourdieu, P. (1994a [1993]). Rethinking the State: Genesis and Structure of the Bureaucratic Field. *Sociological Theory, 12*(1), 1–18.

Bourdieu, P. (1994b [1989]). *The State Nobility: Elite Schools in the Field of Power*. Oxford: Oxford University Press.

Bourdieu, P. (1996 [1992]). *The Rules of Art: Genesis and Structure of the Literary Field*. Stanford, CA: Stanford University Press.

Bourdieu, P. (1999a [1997]). The Social Conditions of the International Circulation of Ideas. In R. Shusterman (Ed.), *Bourdieu: A Critical Reader* (pp. 220–228). Oxford: Blackwell.

Bourdieu, P. (1999b [1993]). *The Weight of the World: Social Suffering in Contemporary Society*. Stanford, CA: Stanford University Press.

Bourdieu, P. (2004 [2001]). *Science of Science and Reflexivity*. Cambridge: Polity Press.

Bourdieu, P. (2005 [2000]). Principles of an Economic Anthropology. In N. J. Smelser & R. Swedberg (Eds.), *The Handbook of Economic Sociology* (pp. 75–89). Princeton, NJ: Princeton University Press.

Bourdieu, P. (2008a [1999]). A Conservative Revolution in Publishing. *Translation Studies, 1*(2), 123–153.

Bourdieu, P. (2008b [2004]). *Sketch for a Self-Analysis*. Chicago, IL: University of Chicago Press.

Bourdieu, P. (2013). De la méthode structurale au concept de champ. *Actes de la Recherche en Sciences Sociales, 200*, 12–37.

Bourdieu, P. (2014 [2012]). *On the State: Lectures at the Collège de France, 1989–1992*. Cambridge: Polity Press.

Bourdieu, P., Chamboredon, J.-C., & Passeron, J.-C. (1991 [1968]). *The Craft of Sociology: Epistemological Preliminaries*. Berlin: De Gruyter.

Bourdieu, P., & Passeron, J.-C. (1977 [1970]). *Reproduction in Education, Society, and Culture*. London: Sage.

Bourdieu, P., & Wacquant, L. (1992). *An Invitation to Reflexive Sociology*. Cambridge: Polity Press.

Bourdieu, P., & Wacquant, L. (1999). On the Cunning of Imperialist Reason. *Theory, Culture and Society, 16*(1), 41–58.

Bruno, I. (2010). From Integration by Law to Europeanisation by Numbers: The Making of a 'Competitive Europe' Through Intergovernmental Benchmarks. In J. Rowell & M. Mangenot (Eds.), *A Political Sociology of the European Union: Reassessing Constructivism* (pp. 185–205). Manchester: Manchester University Press.

Buchholz, L. (2016). What Is a Global Field? Theorizing Fields Beyond the Nation-State. *The Sociological Review Monographs, 64*(2), 31–60.

Büttner, S., & Leopold, L. M. (2016). A 'New Spirit' of Public Policy? The Project World of EU Funding. *European Journal of Cultural and Political Sociology, 3*(1), 41–71.

Carlson, S. (2018). Intra-European Mobility and the Formation of a European Society? German Mobile Graduates' Early Careers in Trans-/National Professional Fields. *Innovation: The European Journal of Social Science Research, 31*(4), 464–483.

Casanova, P. (2007 [1999]). *The World Republic of Letters*. Cambridge, MA: Harvard University Press.

Castells, M. (1996). *Information Age: Vol. 1: The Rise of the Network Society*. Malden, MA: Blackwell.

Champagne, P., Lenoir, R., Merllié, D., & Pinto, L. (1999). *Initiation à la pratique sociologique: 2ᵉ édition entièrement revue et augmentée*. Paris: Dunod.

Chase-Dunn, C. (2014). Continuities and Transformations in the Evolution of World-Systems. *Journal of Globalisation Studies, 5*(1), 11–31.

Chase-Dunn, C., & Grimes, P. (1995). World Systems Analysis. *Annual Review of Sociology, 21*, 387–417.

Connell, R. (2018). Decolonizing Sociology. *Contemporary Sociology, 47*(4), 399–407.

della Porta, D., & Tarrow, S. (Eds.). (2005). *Transnational Protest and Global Activism.* New York, NY: Rowman & Littlefield.

Dezalay, Y., & Garth, B. G. (1996). *Dealing in Virtue: International Commercial Arbitration and the Construction of a Transnational Legal Order.* Chicago, IL: University of Chicago Press.

Dezalay, Y., & Garth, B. G. (2002). *The Internationalization of Palace Wars: Lawyers, Economists, and the Contest to Transform Latin American States.* Chicago, IL: University of Chicago Press.

Dezalay, Y., & Madsen, R. M. (2012). The Force of Law and Lawyers: Pierre Bourdieu and the Reflexive Sociology of Law. *Annual Review of Law and Social Science, 8*(1), 433–452.

Dezalay, Y., & Nay, O. (2015). Le marché des savoirs de réforme: circulations de l'expertise de gouvernement et reproduction des hiérarchies internationales. In J. Siméant (Ed.), *Guide de l'enquête globale en science social* (pp. 173–196). Paris: CNRS Éditions.

Diaz-Bone, R. (2006). Die interpretative Analytik als methodologische Position. In B. Kerchner & C. Schneider (Eds.), *Foucault: Diskursanalyse der Politik* (pp. 68–85). Wiesbaden: Springer VS.

Djelic, M.-L., & Quack, S. (2003). Conclusion: Globalization as a Double Process of Institutional Change and Institution Building. In M.-L. Djelic & S. Quack (Eds.), *Globalization and Institutions: Redefining the Rules of the Economic Game* (pp. 302–333). Cheltenham: Edward Elgar.

Djelic, M.-L., & Quack, S. (2010a). Transnational Communities and Governance. In M.-L. Djelic & S. Quack (Eds.), *Transnational Communities: Shaping Global Economic Governance* (pp. 3–36). Cambridge: Cambridge University Press.

Djelic, M.-L., & Quack, S. (2010b). Transnational Communities and Their Impact on the Governance of Business and Economic Activity. In M.-L. Djelic & S. Quack (Eds.), *Transnational Communities: Shaping Global Economic Governance* (pp. 377–413). Cambridge: Cambridge University Press.

Djelic, M.-L., & Sahlin-Andersson, K. (2006a). Institutional Dynamics in a Reordering World. In M.-L. Djelic & K. Sahlin-Andersson (Eds.), *Transnational Governance: Institutional Dynamics of Regulation* (pp. 375–397). Cambridge: Cambridge University Press.

Djelic, M.-L., & Sahlin-Andersson, K. (2006b). Introduction: A World of Governance: The Rise of Transnational Regulation. In M.-L. Djelic & K. Sahlin-Andersson (Eds.), *Transnational Governance: Institutional Dynamics of Regulation* (pp. 1–28). Cambridge: Cambridge University Press.

Drori, G. S., Meyer, J. W., & Hwang, H. (Eds.). (2006). *Globalization and Organization: World Society and Organizational Change.* Oxford: Oxford University Press.

Drori, G. S., Meyer, J. W., Ramirez, F. O., & Schofer, E. (Eds.). (2003). *Science in the Modern World Polity.* Stanford, CA: Stanford University Press.

Dunn, K. (2010). Embodied Transnationalism: Bodies in Transnational Space. *Population, Space and Place, 16*(1), 1–9.

Durkheim, É. (2009 [1900]). Die Soziologie und ihr Wissensbereich (1900). *Berliner Journal für Soziologie, 19*(2), 164–180.

Durkheim, É., & Mauss, M. (1963 [1903]). *Primitive Classification.* Chicago, IL: University of Chicago Press.

Eisenstadt, S. N. (2000). Multiple Modernities. *Daedalus, 129*(1), 1–29.

Elias, N. (1982). *The Civilizing Process: State Formation and Civilization*. Oxford: Basil Blackwell.

Faist, T. (2004). Towards a Political Sociology of Transnationalization: The State of the Art in Migration Research. *Archives Européen de Sociologie, 45*(3), 331–366.

Faist, T. (2009). Making and Remaking the Transnational: Of Boundaries, Social Spaces and Social Mechanisms. *Journal of Global Studies, 1*(2), 66–88.

Faist, T. (2010). Towards Transnational Studies: World Theories, Transnationalisation and Changing Institutions. *Journal of Ethnic and Migration Studies, 36*(10), 1665–1687.

Favell, A., & Guiraudon, V. (Eds.). (2011). *Sociology of the European Union*. Houndmills, Basingstoke: Palgrave Macmillan.

Fligstein, N., & Stone Sweet, A. (2002). Constructing Polities and Markets: An Institutionalist Account of European Integration. *American Journal of Sociology, 107*(5), 1206–1243.

Fourcade, M. (2006). The Construction of a Global Profession: The Transnationalization of Economics. *American Journal of Sociology, 112*(1), 145–194.

Gengnagel, V., Baier, C., & Massih-Tehrani, N. (2015). Zur Transnationalisierung des akademischen Feldes: Das 'europäische Projekt' als Ordnungsanspruch im Feld der Macht am Beispiel des European Research Councils (ERC). *Berliner Journal für Soziologie, 25*(4), 55–74.

Georgakakis, D. (2010). The Deconsecrated Administration: EU Civil Servants from Mission to Management. *Working Paper, European Group on Public Administration Meeting*, August 26, 2010, Toulouse.

Georgakakis, D. (2017). *European Civil Service (in Times of) Crisis*. Cham: Palgrave Macmillan.

Georgakakis, D., & Rowell, J. (Eds.). (2013). *The Field of Eurocracy: Mapping the EU Actors and Professionals*. Houndmills, Basingstoke: Palgrave Macmillan.

Gerhards, J., Hans, S., & Carlson, S. (2017). *Social Class and Transnational Human Capital: How Upper and Middle Class Parents Prepare Their Children for Globalization*. London: Routledge.

Giddens, A. (1990). *Consequences of Modernity*. Cambridge: Polity Press.

Glaser, B. G., & Strauss, A. L. (1967). *The Discovery of Grounded Theory: Strategies for Qualitative Research*. Chicago, IL: Aldine.

Glick Schiller, N. (2007). Beyond the Nation-State and Its Units of Analysis: Towards a New Research Agenda for Migration Studies: Essentials of Migration Theory. *COMCAD Working Papers, 33*, 1–42.

Go, J. (2008). Global Fields and Imperial Forms: Field Theory and the British and American Empires. *Sociological Theory, 26*(3), 201–229.

Go, J. (2016). *Postcolonial Thought and Social Theory*. Oxford: Oxford University Press.

Go, J. (2017a). Decolonizing Sociology: Epistemic Inequality and Sociological Thought. *Social Problems, 64*(2), 194–199.

Go, J. (2017b). Myths of Nation and Empire: The Logic of America's Liberal Empire-State. *Thesis Eleven, 139*(1), 69–83.

Go, J., & Krause, M. (2016). Fielding Transnationalism: An Introduction. *The Sociological Monographs, 62*(2), 6–30.

Guarnizo, L. E. (2005). The Economics of Transnational Living. *The International Migration Review, 37*(3), 666–699.

Haas, P. M. (1992). Introduction: Epistemic Communities and International Policy Coordination. *International Organization, 46*(1), 1–35.

Hale, T., & Held, D. (2011). Editor's Introduction: Mapping Changes in Transnational Governance. In T. Hale & D. Held (Eds.), *Handbook of Transnational Governance: Institutions and Innovations* (pp. 1–36). Cambridge: Polity Press.

Hamann, J., & Zimmer, L. M. (2017). The Internationality Imperative in Academia: The Ascend of Internationality as an Academic Virtue. *Higher Education Research & Development, 36*(7), 1418–1432.

Hartmann, E. (2012). Der Forscher als Exot: Fremdheit als Ressource praxeologischer Feldforschung. In S. Bernhard & C. Schmidt-Wellenburg (Eds.), *Feldanalyse als Forschungsprogramm 1: Der programmatische Kern* (pp. 243–264). Wiesbaden: Springer VS.

Hartong, S. (2015). Global Policy Convergence through 'Distributed Governance'? The Emergence of 'National' Education Standards in the US and Germany. *Journal of International and Comparative Social Policy, 31*(1), 10–33.

Hartong, S., & Nikolai, R. (2017). Observing the 'Local Globalness' of Policy Transfer in Education. *Comparative Education Review, 61*(3), 519–537.

Heilbron, J., & Steinmetz, G. (2018). A Defense of Bourdieu. *Catalyst, 2*(1), 35–49.

Jessup, P. (1956). *Transnational Law*. New Haven, CT: Yale University Press.

Kauppi, N. (2005). *Democracy, Social Resources and Political Power in the European Union*. Manchester: Manchester University Press.

Kauppi, N. (2010). The Political Ontology of European Integration. *Comparative European Politics, 8*(1), 19–36.

Kauppi, N. (2018). *Toward a Reflexive Political Sociology of the European Union: Fields, Intellectuals and Politicians*. Cham: Palgrave Macmillan.

Kauppi, N., & Erkkilä, T. (2019). University Rankings and the Europeanisation of Higher Education. In R. Harmsen & N. Kauppi (Eds.), *The Europeanisation of Higher Education and Research Policy: The Bologna Process, the Lisbon Agenda and Beyond* (forthcoming). Rodopi: Brill.

Kauppi, N., & Madsen, R. M. (Eds.). (2013). *Transnational Power Elites: The New Professionals of Governance, Law and Security*. New York, NY: Routledge.

Kauppi, N., & Madsen, R. M. (2014). Fields of Global Governance: How Transnational Power Elites Can Make Global Governance Intelligible. *International Political Sociology, 8*(3), 324–329.

Keck, M. E., & Sikkink, K. (1998). Transnational Advocacy Networks in the Movement Society. In D. S. Meyer & S. G. Tarrow (Eds.), *The Social Movement Society: Contentious Politics for a New Century* (pp. 217–238). Lanham, MD: Rowman & Littlefield Publishers.

Kelly, P., & Lusis, T. (2006). Migration and the Transnational Habitus: Evidence from Canada and the Philippines. *Environment and Planning A, 38*(5), 831–847.

Kögler, H.-H. (1997). Alienation as Epistemological Source: Reflexivity and Social Background After Mannheim and Bourdieu. *Social Epistemology, 11*(2), 141–164.

Krause, M. (2014). *The Good Project: Humanitarian Relief NGOs and the Fragmentation of Reason*. Chicago, IL: University of Chicago Press.

Krause, M. (2018). How Fields Vary. *British Journal of Sociology, 69*(1), 3–22.

Lahusen, C. (2013). Law and Lawyers in Brussel's World of Commercial Consultants. In A. Vauchez & B. de Witt (Eds.), *Lawyering Europe: European Law as a Transnational Social Field* (pp. 177–194). Oxford: Hart Publishing.

Lamont, M. (1987). How to Become a Dominant French Philosopher: The Case of Jacques Derrida. *American Journal of Sociology, 93*(3), 584–622.

Laurens, S. (2018). *Lobbyists and Bureaucrats in Brussels: Capitalism's Brokers*. London: Routledge.

Lebaron, F. (2010). European Central Bank Leaders in the Global Space of Central Bankers: A Geometric Data Analysis Approach. *French Politics, 8*(3), 294–320.

Lebaron, F. (2013). ECB Leaders: A New European Monetary Elite? In D. Georgakakis & J. Rowell (Eds.), *The Field of Eurocracy: Mapping the EU Actors and Professionals* (pp. 87–104). London: Palgrave Macmillan.

Levitt, P., & Glick Schiller, N. (2004). Conceptualizing Simultaneity: A Transnational Social Field Perspective on Society. *The International Migration Review, 38*(3), 1002–1039.

Levitt, P., & Jaworsky, N. B. (2007). Transnational Migration Studies. *Annual Review of Sociology, 33*, 129–156.

Lubbers, M. J., Verdery, A. M., & Molina, J. L. (2018). Social Networks and Transnational Social Fields: A Review of Quantitative and Mixed Methods Approaches. *The International Migration Review*, Online First. https://doi.org/10.1177/0197918318812343

Luhmann, N. (1975). Die Weltgesellschaft. In N. Luhmann (Ed.), *Soziologische Aufklärung 2: Aufsätze zur Theorie der Gesellschaft* (pp. 51–71). Opladen: Westdeutscher Verlag.

Luhmann, N. (1997). *Die Gesellschaft der Gesellschaft*. Frankfurt am Main: Suhrkamp.

Madsen, R. M. (2018). Who Rules the World? The Educational Capital of the International Judiciary. *UC Irvine Journal of International, Transnational, and Comparative Law, 3*(1), 97–118.

Maesse, J. (2018). Globalization Strategies and the Economics Dispositif: Insights from Germany and the UK. *Historical Social Research, 43*(3), 120–146.

Mannheim, K. (1960). *Ideology and Utopia*. London: Routledge.

Marcus, G. E. (1995). Ethnography in/of the World System: The Emergence of Multi-Sited Ethnography. *Annual Review of Anthropology, 24*, 95–117.

Marttila, T. (2014). Die wissensbasierte Regierung der Bildung: Die Genese einer transnationalen Gouvernementalität in England und Schweden. *Berliner Journal für Soziologie, 24*(2), 257–287.

Mérand, F. (2008). *European Defence Policy: Beyond the Nation State*. New York, NY: Oxford University Press.

Meyer, J. W. (2000). Globalization: Sources and Effects on Nation States and Societies. *International Sociology, 15*(2), 233–248.

Meyer, J. W., Boli, J., Thomas, G. M., & Ramirez, C. (1997). World Society and the Nation-State. *American Journal of Sociology, 103*(1), 144–181.

Meyer, J. W., & Jeppersen, R. L. (2000). The 'Actors' of Modern Society: The Cultural Construction of Social Agency. *Sociological Theory, 18*(1), 100–120.

Morawska, E. (2001). Structuring Migration: The Case of Polish Income-Seeking Travelers to the West. *Theory and Society, 30*(1), 47–80.

Münch, R. (1993). *Die Kultur der Moderne* (2 vols.) Frankfurt am Main: Suhrkamp.

Münch, R. (2012). Das PISA-Regime: Zur Transnationalisierung des Bildungsfeldes. In S. Bernhard & C. Schmidt-Wellenburg (Eds.), *Feldanalyse als Forschungsprogramm 1: Der programmatische Kern* (pp. 405–425). Wiesbaden: Springer VS.

Münch, R. (2014). *Academic Capitalism: Universities in the Struggle for Excellence*. New York, NY: Routledge.

Nedelcu, M. (2012). Migrants' New Transnational Habitus: Rethinking Migration Through a Cosmopolitan Lens in the Digital Age. *Journal of Ethnic and Migration Studies, 38*(9), 1339–1356.

Nederveen Pieterse, J. (1994). Globalisation as Hybridisation. *International Sociology*, *9*(2), 161–184.

Nowicka, M., & Cieslik, A. (2014). Beyond Methodological Nationalism in Insider Research With Migrants. *Migration Studies*, *2*(1), 1–15.

Nye, J. S., & Keohane, R. O. (1971). Transnational Relations and World Politics: An Introduction. *International Organization*, *25*(3), 329–349.

Nye, J. S., & Keohane, R. O. (1977). *Power and Independence: World Politics in Transition*. Boston, MA: Little, Brown.

Parsons, T. (1971). *The System of Modern Societies*. Englewood Cliffs, NJ: Prentice Hall.

Poehls, K. (2009). *Europa Backstage: Expertenwissen, Habitus und kulturelle Codes im Machtfeld der EU*. Bielefeld: transcript.

Portes, A., Guarnizo, L. E., & Landolt, P. (1999). The Study of Transnationalism: Pitfalls and Promise of an Emergent Research Field. *Ethnic and Racial Studies*, *22*(2), 217–237.

Pries, L. (2001). The Approach of Transnational Social Spaces: Responding to New Configurations of the Social and the Spatial. In L. Pries (Ed.), *New Transnational Social Spaces: International Migration and Transnational Companies in the Early Twenty-First Century* (pp. 3–33). London: Routledge.

Pries, L. (2008a). *Die Transnationalisierung der sozialen Welt: Sozialräume jenseits von Nationalgesellschaften*. Frankfurt am Main: Suhrkamp.

Pries, L. (2008b). Transnational Societal Spaces: Which Units of Analysis, Reference, and Measurement? In L. Pries (Ed.), *Rethinking Transnationalism: The Meso-Link of Organisations* (pp. 1–20). London: Routledge.

Rey, P. J., & Ritzer, G. (2010). Conceptualizing Globalization in Terms of Flows. *Current Perspectives in Social Theory*, *27*, 247–271.

Risse, T. (2007). Social Constructivism Meets Globalization. In D. Held & A. McGrew (Eds.), *Globalization Theory: Approaches and Controversies* (pp. 126–147). Cambridge: Polity Press.

Risse-Kappen, T. (1995). Democratic Peace – Warlike Democracies? A Social Constructivist Interpretation of the Liberal Argument. *European Journal of International Relations*, *1*(4), 491–517.

Ritzer, G. (2010). *Globalization: A Basic Text*. Malden, MA: Wiley-Blackwell.

Robertson, R. (1995). Globalisation or Glocalisation? *Journal of International Communication*, *18*(2), 191–208.

Rodríguez Gutiérrez, E., Boatcă, M., & Costa, S. (Eds.). (2010). *Decolonizing European Sociology: Transdisciplinary Approaches*. Farnham: Ashgate.

Ruggie, J. G. (2004). Reconstituting the Global Public Domain – Issues, Actors and Practices. *European Journal of International Relations*, *10*(4), 499–531.

Said, E. (1979). *Orientalism*. New York, NY: Vintage Books.

Sapiro, G. (Ed.). (2009). *L'espace intellectuel en Europe: De la formation des États-nations à la mondialisation XIXᵉ–XXIᵉ siècle*. Paris: La Découverte.

Sapiro, G. (2013). Le champ est-il national? *Actes de la Recherche en Sciences Sociales*, *200*, 70–85.

Sapiro, G. (2018). Field Theory from a Transnational Perspective. In T. Medvetz & J. J. Sallaz (Eds.), *The Oxford Handbook of Pierre Bourdieu* (pp. 161–182). Oxford: Oxford University Press.

Sassen, S. (2000). Territory and Territoriality in the Global Economy. *International Sociology*, *15*(2), 372–393.

Sassen, S. (2001). Global Cities and Developmentalist States: How to Derail What Could Be an Interesting Debate: A Response to Hill and Kim. *Urban Studies*, *38*(13), 2537–2540.

Schmidt-Wellenburg, C. (2014). Der Aufstieg der Beratung zur transnationalen Regierungsform im Feld des Managements. *Berliner Journal für Soziologie*, *24*(2), 227–255.

Schmidt-Wellenburg, C. (2017). Europeanisation, Stateness, and Professions: What Role Do Economic Expertise and Economic Experts Play in European Political Integration? *European Journal of Cultural and Political Sociology*, *4*(4), 430–456.

Schmidt-Wellenburg, C. (2018). Struggling Over Crisis: Discoursive Positionings and Academic Positions in the Field of German-Speaking Economists. *Historical Social Research*, *43*(3), 147–188.

Schmidt-Wellenburg, C., & Lebaron, F. (Eds.). (2018). Economists, Politics, and Society: New Insights from Mapping Economic Practices Using Field-Analysis. *Special Issue of Historical Social Research*, *43*(3). Köln: GESIS.

Schmitz, A., Schmidt-Wellenburg, C., Witte, D., & Keil, M. (2019). In welcher Gesellschaft forschen wir eigentlich? Struktur und Dynamik des Feldes der deutschen Soziologie. *Zeitschrift für theoretische Soziologie*, *8*(2), 245–276.

Schmitz, A., & Witte, D. (2017). Der Nationalstaat und das globale Feld der Macht, oder: Wie sich die Feldtheorie von ihrem methodologischen Nationalismus befreien lässt. *Zeitschrift für Theoretische Soziologie*, *6*(2), 156–187.

Schmitz, A., Witte, D., & Gengnagel, V. (2017). Pluralizing Field Analysis: Toward a Relational Understanding of the Field of Power. *Social Science Information/Information sur les sciences sociales*, *56*(1), 49–73.

Schneickert, C. (2018). Globalizing Political and Economic Elites in National Fields of Power. *Historical Social Research*, *43*(3), 329–358.

Schneickert, C., & Beri, S. (2016). Social Structure and Globalization of Political and Economic Elites in India. *Transcience: A Journal of Global Studies*, *7*(1), 115–130.

Schultheis, F. (2018). *Unternehmen Bourdieu*. Bielefeld: transcript.

Seth, S. (2013). 'Once Was Blind But Now Can See': Modernity and the Social Sciences. *International Political Sociology*, *7*(2), 136–151.

Skrbis, Z. (2008). Transnational Families: Theorising Migration, Emotions and Belonging. *Journal of Intercultural Studies*, *29*(3), 231–246.

Spivak, G. C. (1988). *Can the Subaltern Speak?* Basingstoke: Macmillan.

Stampnitzky, L. (2013). *Disciplining Terror: How Experts Invented Terrorism*. Cambridge: Cambridge University Press.

Steinmetz, G. (2008). The Colonial State as a Social Field: Ethnographic Capital and Native Policy in the German Overseas Empire Before 1914. *American Sociological Review*, *73*(4), 589–612.

Steinmetz, G. (2016). Social Fields, Subfields and Social Spaces at the Scale of Empires: Explaining the Colonial State and Colonial Sociology. *The Sociological Review Monographs*, *64*(2), 98–123.

Suckert, L. (2017). Unravelling ambivalence: A field-theoretical approach to moralised markets. *Current Sociology*, *66*(5), 682–703.

Tarrow, S. (2001). Transnational Politics: Contention and Institutions in International Politics. *Annual Review of Political Science*, *4*, 1–20.

Tarrow, S. (2005). *The New Transnational Activism*. Cambridge: Cambridge University Press.

Tarrow, S., & McAdam, D. (2005). Scale Shift in Transnational Contention. In D. della Porta & S. Tarrow (Eds.), *Transnational Protest and Global Activism* (pp. 121–150). Lanham, MD: Rowman & Littlefield Publishers.

Urry, J. (2001). *Sociology Beyond Societies: Mobilities for the Twenty-First Century*. London: Routledge.

Vandenberghe, F. (1999). 'The Real Is Relational': An Epistemological Analysis of Pierre Bourdieu's Generative Structuralism. *Sociological Theory, 17*(1), 32–67.

Vauchez, A. (2011). Interstitial Power in Fields of Limited Statehood: Introducing a 'Weak Field' Approach to the Study of Transnational Settings. *International Political Sociology, 5*(3), 340–345.

Vauchez, A., & Witte, B. D. (Eds.). (2013). *Lawyering Europe: European Law as a Transnational Field*. Oxford; Portland: Hart Publishing.

Vertovec, S. (2009). *Transnationalism*. London: Routledge.

Wacquant, L. (1999). *Prisons of Poverty*. Minneapolis, MN: University of Minnesota Press.

Wagner, A.-C. (2005). Pierre Bourdieu et le travail collectif de comparaison internationale. In G. Mauger (Ed.), *Rencontres avec Pierre Bourdieu* (pp. 347–354). Bellecombe-en-Bouges: Édition du Croquant.

Wagner, A.-C., & Réau, B. (2015). Le capital international: Un outil d'analyse de la reconfiguration de rapports de domination. In J. Siméant (Ed.), *Guide de l'enquête globale en science social* (pp. 33–46). Paris: CNRS Éditions.

Waldinger, R. (2013). Immigrant Transnationalism. *Current Sociology, 61*(5–6), 756–777.

Waldinger, R., & Fitzgerald, D. (2004). Transnationalism in Question. *American Journal of Sociology, 109*(5), 1177–1195.

Wallerstein, I. (1974). *The Modern World-System I: Capitalist Agriculture and the Origins of the European World-Economy in the Sixteenth Century*. New York, NY: Academic Press.

Wallerstein, I. (2000). Globalization or the Age of Transition? A Long-Term View of the Trajectory of the World-System. *International Sociology, 15*(2), 249–265.

Waltz, K. N. (1959). *Man, the State and War: A Theoretical Analysis*. New York, NY: Columbia University Press.

Waltz, K. N. (1979). *Theory of International Politics*. Reading: Addison-Wesley.

Wimmer, A., & Glick Schiller, N. (2002). Methodological Nationalism and Beyond: Nation-State Building, Migration and the Social Sciences. *Global Networks, 2*(4), 301–334.

Witte, D. (2014). Auf den Spuren der Klassiker: Pierre Bourdieus Feldtheorie und die Gründerväter der Soziologie. Konstanz: UVK.

Part I

Methodological foundations

Chapter 2

How many fields can stand on the point of a pin?

Methodological notes on reflexivity, the sociological craft, and field analysis*

Niilo Kauppi

The uses of undifferentiated collective concepts of everyday speech is always a cloak for confusion of thought and action.

(Weber, 1949: 110)

The preconstructed is everywhere.

(Bourdieu & Wacquant, 1992: 235)

The sociological craft

The concept of "field" has become a commonly used term in the toolkit of social scientists inspired by Bourdieu and the structural constructivist approach he pioneered (cf. for instance, Hilgers & Mangez, 2015). A closer look at the uses of the concept in the social scientific literature reveals that "field" is most often a substitute for concepts such as context, arena, sphere, or space. It is taken as an organized social space, with rules, institutions, and actors. From this perspective, by limiting the scope of research, scholars see the "field" as a convenient way of reducing the area of study, and thereby reducing the complexity of social reality to a manageable scale (the list of research would be too long; for recent studies, see for instance, Fligstein & McAdam, 2015 and Musgrave & Nexon, 2018; and for recent research in international relations (IR), see Nexon & Neumann, 2017). Other terms such as "habitus" or "strategy" seem to be more difficult to appropriate (for analysis of the formal diffusion of the terms, see Santoro, Gallelli, & Grüning, 2018: 40 f.; cf. also Kauppi & Swartz, 2015).

Typically, scholars have constructed fields as static and realist objects that exist "out there". Fields have mostly been national entities, or in recent research in IR "arenas of fields" or "the universe of fields in world politics" (Musgrave & Nexon, 2018: 599 f.), involving from the scholar no reflexivity over the perspective they engage and the instruments they use (for a refreshingly critical discussion, see Benson & Neveu, 2015; Neveu, 2018). Scholars have used field analysis more as a canon for applied empirical research than as a work in progress, to be theoretically developed as a critical social science perspective (for this, see for instance Swartz, 2013b; Bernhard & Schmidt-Wellenburg, 2014: 138; Gengnagel, 2014: 299). These appropriations have led to the diffusion of a simplified, objectifying understanding of field analysis that has forgotten structural constructivist ontological and epistemological presuppositions, most importantly the reflexive analysis of the social conditions of knowledge production. Consequently, certain key methodological problems, such as the link between pre-constructed reality and reality as a scholarly construction, and the scholarly status of the observer vis-à-vis the object of research, have not been dealt with in the literature. Field analysis has been incorporated into existing research frameworks such as that of social constructivism or power politics, and used unreflectively to legitimize institution building at the transnational level. A thorough discussion of these methodological questions is, however, necessary to adequately meet the research challenges posed by complex shifts of political and economic power to transnational and global fora, and to develop the structural constructivist theoretical framework (for some work in this vein, see Marginson, 2008; Bernhard, 2012; Kauppi, 2013, 2018a; Kauppi & Madsen, 2013; Bernhard & Schmidt-Wellenburg, 2014; Kull, 2018; Sapiro, 2018; Schmidt-Wellenburg & Lebaron, 2018).

In order to counter an expanding, formal understanding of field analysis, a discussion of the key methodological principles of structural constructivist research – a term that does not seem to have traveled outside of the European context – is necessary (for recent succinct English-language presentations, cf. for instance Swartz, 2013a; Benson & Neveu, 2015). The use of the term "structuralist constructivism", a concept used by Bourdieu himself to describe his research perspective (Bourdieu, 1989: 14), is motivated by a desire to develop the collective nature of the research program and the reflexive analysis of its historical and social embeddedness (cf. for the beginning of an analysis, for instance Kauppi, 1996, 2010; also Swartz, 2013a).

Bourdieu, Chamboredon, and Passeron's (hereafter, BCP) original 1968 research manual, *Le métier de sociologie*, was precisely intended to be a practical tool that aspiring researchers could use to create a scientific problématique (BCP, 1983, 1991: 253). The central element of this approach is the sociological construction of the scientific object. According to this point of departure, which is heavily based on Bachelardian epistemology (see for instance Bachelard, 1983), social reality is always pre-constructed using tools that are not scientific. At the same time, it is a world with which we are familiar. Echoing sociologists Berger and Luckmann (1966), BCP maintain that our social reflex is simply to reproduce it. In order to gain a more profound understanding of social reality, a break is needed from this pre-constructed world and taken-for-granted realities – a break made possible by adopting conceptual tools such as "field" that are especially designed for scholarly purposes (Bourdieu, Chamboredon, & Passeron, 1983: 27, cf. for a masterful analysis Bourdieu, 1983; see also Weber, 1949: 110 for a similar conceptual critique).

"Defamiliarization" (ostranenie), or making something familiar strange, was one of the methods theorized by Russian formalist art theorist Victor Shklovsky in the 1920s (Shklovsky, 1991). The playwright Berthold Brecht (2013) later picked it up with his concept of "Verfremdungseffekt". This idea resonates with Weber's remarks on theoretical valuation and "removal to a distance" (see Bruun, 1972: 110 for a discussion), and more broadly an anthropological posture of making the familiar exotic and the exotic familiar. The methodological position rimes with Claude Lévi-Strauss's distinction between the scientific approach of the engineer and the approach of the practitioner that he labels "bricolage" (1962). To use Bourdieu's more scholarly formulation, "the break necessary to establish a rigorous science of cultural worlds is something more and something other than a simple methodological enterprise. It implies a true conversion of the ordinary way of thinking and living the intellectual enterprise" (Bourdieu, 1993: 192).

For Bourdieu, the main task of a conceptual tool like "field" is to enable the scholar to construct a research problem by questioning the unproblematized building blocks of pre-constructed realities, and to take distance to those being constructed. He shared this demystifying (or rationalizing, to use Weber's term) perspective with sociologists like Peter Berger (1963). In this Socratic perspective, the enemy of knowledge is not so much ignorance but the belief that one knows. We believe certain things are true, and we take these for granted. This attitude and the spontaneous lay theories of social reality it produces have a disastrous effect on us, creating a sense of false nearness to the social world in which we live. For scholarly work, the constant danger is to "fall back" into reproducing this common-sense understanding of reality and the power interests embedded in it (Bourdieu & Wacquant, 1992). This theoretical interest is directly linked with scholarly claims for autonomy and the critical function of social scientific research.

In his research seminar at the Ecole des Hautes Études en Sciences Sociales (EHESS) in the second half of the 1980s, Bourdieu continuously emphasized the practical aspects of the scientific habitus, métier, or craft (for a recollection see Kauppi, 2018a). The pedagogical philosophy included appropriating through usage of specialized conceptual tools and following the master's advice in this process (for some of the students' works from that time, see Waser, 1989; Kauppi, 1990; Geay, 1991; Ghellab, 1997). The toolkit consisted of concepts such as field, habitus, strategy, homology, and dominant/dominated. These were to be used simultaneously, providing intellectual tools that enabled the student to make sociological sense of reality. Learning to use these tools on a specific object required time and training. Presenting one's work in the various research seminars; submitting written pieces for comments from Bourdieu and his closest collaborators of the time, Monique de Saint Martin and Louis Pinto; and learning from other students were some of the usual pedagogical techniques.

In order to be used to their full advantage, the tools required the student to acquire techniques of research and to develop through practice a certain perspective on reality. Acquiring the craft of the sociologist meant developing a sense of the materials (e.g., sources of information) and techniques used, a certain sociological sensibility which involved a systematic suspicion of so-called spontaneous knowledge. Spontaneous knowledge was a broad category that could include secondhand statistical information and data sets as well as scholarly works. In a way, the construction of the scientific object was the process of development of thinking habits. In competent use the tools are concealed to the user and precisely for that reason, their use is efficient. To paraphrase Kant, the hand is the visible part of the brain. Apart from the seminars of the staff of the Center for European Sociology and Bourdieu's seminars at the Collège de France, Ph.D. students had to follow Philippe Cibois's practical course on geometrical data analysis, held in the cellar of the Maison des sciences de l'homme, Boulevard Raspail (cf. Cibois, 1984).

This ontological understanding of the conceptual tool, and its use as a fusion of theory and empirics, is close to Heidegger's analysis of thinking of and working with tools in *Sein und Zeit*, of testing the limits of a tool and the construction of the subject and the object through action (Heidegger, 1962, for a sophisticated discussion see Siukonen, 2011). Instead of a linear process, acquiring sociological thinking techniques involves interaction between subject and object – changes in the perspective, in the definition of the problem, of "going around" the object of research, examining it from different points of view, etc. This intertwining of the craft of sociology and the habitus of the researcher stands in stark contrast to the unreflective practice according to which anybody can pick up any intellectual tool like "field" and just start using it as they see fit, without a potential transformative impact on either research subject (through socialization) or object (exploration of empirical complexity).

Field analysis is time consuming. To illustrate this process, for my sociological Ph.D. research on the French intellectual journal *Tel Quel*, I wrote two preliminary Finnish-language academic theses on the theoretical concepts developed by Julia Kristeva, a key member of the *Tel Quel* movement (Kristeva's semanalytical conception of ideology, 1986), and a 700-page study on the sociohistory of the journal, its networks, and its competitors (*Reproduction strategies in the French intellectual field: The case of Tel Quel*, 1988). From a methodological perspective, these were preliminary steps to a more thorough French-language sociological reconstruction of the power strategies of various actors in the French intellectual field (cf. Kauppi, 1990) in which the focus was more on networks and strategies than on textual strategies in the intellectual productions themselves, as in the 1986 and 1988 theses (cf. also Kauppi, 2010a for further analysis).

Break with the help of tools-in-use

There has been a lot of discussion in French and European social science on the nature of this epistemological break or scholarly conversion. Some, like Louis Althusser in his distinction between the young and the old Marx (Althusser, 1965), advocated a single, radical move from pre-construction to scholarly construction, from *illusio* to truth. Others emphasize the role of continual vigilance: the move from one to the other is a constant struggle that cannot be settled once and for all.

It requires never-ending readjustments and evaluation – in other words, reflexivity. Some, like BCP, are more ambivalent, as they emphasize the critical role of a radical break, but at the same time acknowledge that the break cannot be reduced to a single event that would guarantee the en bloc move from illusion to truth.

The structural understanding of meaning that BCP develop with the concept of "field" shifts the research problématique from the object itself to the context, or more precisely, the relevant relational network from which it receives its value – a topos familiar to linguists and to students of Weber (cf. for instance his exemplary relational analysis of the city, Weber, 1978: 1212 ff.). In this sense, defining the relevant context or, in other words, the reference category, is the crucial methodological move that will determine the value of the objects under study. Following this contextual understanding of meaning and social value, the classifications that are used to make sense of something are crucial. For example, a sports car in the category of sports cars will have a different meaning than a sports car in the category of family cars. Different properties are highlighted depending on the relevant characteristics of the reference category. The key methodological operation will consist of the definition of the relevant context or, in other words, the field in which a phenomenon is studied. While concepts like "context" or "strategic field" are loose enough to provide the beginning of a relational analysis, "field" refers to a more structured entity. In Bourdieu's conflict-theoretical approach, these are typically the main resources valued in the field and its dominant actors, a perspective that does not rule out cooperation between social actors. The dominant pole is the most structured part of the field, where accumulations and conversions of the valued capital are tightly socially controlled. This understanding is not necessarily far from Weber's idea of life spheres (Weber, 1991). The differences are well known: Bourdieu adds to this a dualistic model of analysis (dominant/dominated, etc.) and an analysis of inter-field relationships using linguistic concepts such as homology.

From a methodological point of view, a field analysis is not the end result of research – as many, eager to construct all kinds of fields, seem to believe. In a first research phase, it enables a distancing from the object of research, pointing to the main pertinent features of the object through analysis of its contextually relevant features. Following Bourdieu's holistic methodology, the outline of the building has to be drawn before placing the door and the windows. For instance, the structuration of a transnational field of higher education around two dimensions of academic and economic capital, and the strong correlation between the two (Kauppi, 2016, 2018b), is the starting point of an analysis of the social forces at play at the global level. The concentration of these resources testifies of global monopolization processes at work. This first step of objectification consists of taking distance to a non-scientific pre-constructed reality, of deconstruction and abstraction using a simple two-dimensional table, of highlighting certain elements and minimizing others. This process is followed by a reverse operation of reconstruction, of coming closer, of individualization, of controlled construction of sociological proximity, following the same principle of relationality. The second phase involves "subjectifying" or "substantiating" field analysis, but this time using interviews, field work, document analysis, archival work, or some other qualitative techniques.

One of the main methodological challenges and limits of field analysis is the reliance on previous scholarly work and the common-sense understanding of social reality that it conveys. Despite statements to the contrary, field analysis is often based on certain aspects of a common-sense understanding of the object under study. For instance, in his study of French literature, Bourdieu (1993) bases his definition of the French literary field on its established definition, on how literary scholars and manuals have defined it. In this sense, Bourdieu's conceptualization reinforces the standard, canonized definition of French literature, which marginalizes, for instance, regional literatures. Consequently, Bourdieu's definition of the French literary field reinforces a certain, dominant definition of literary value. In the same way, Daniel Gaxie defines the French political field as consisting of professional politicians involved in the definition of French politics (Gaxie, 1973). And my sociological reconstructions of the French intellectual field (1990, 1994, 1996) were based on a definition of the French intellectual field as a general reference point of the category "intellectuals" (see also especially Charle, 1990).

What this means is that a critique of pre-constructed reality does not necessarily liberate the observer from this pre-constructed reality. A competent analysis of reality always runs the danger of legitimizing what it focuses on. In other words, the dichotomy between pre-constructed and scientifically constructed is problematic, because even a scientific construction cannot totally disengage itself from pre-constructed reality. Rather than relying on a fictive break, rupture, or conversion, we should instead be aware of these structural and conjunctural limitations, and analyze degrees and forms of interdependency between pre-constructions and field-analytical constructions. Pre-constructions and field constructions are variably close on certain aspects, depending on available data and the perspective and interests of the observer. Field construction is not normatively neutral. It focuses on certain aspects of reality that differ from those of other perspectives, such as Foucaultian governmentality or Habermasian public sphere approaches (see for discussion Zimmermann & Favell, 2011).

Field analysis "in practice"

Since the 2010s, an increasing number of scholars have picked up some structural constructivist tools (for instance the influential book, Adler & Pouliot, 2011; Pouliot, 2017; for a critique, see Kauppi, 2017; Martin-Mazé, 2017; also Musgrave & Nexon, 2018). Many studies that present themselves as field-theoretical are little more than conventional IR power politics or hegemony analysis, or sociological studies jazzed up with terms like "strategic field" or "organizational field" (cf. for instance DiMaggio & Powell, 1983; Fligstein & McAdam, 2015). From a conceptual epidemiology perspective, the substitution of "context" with "field" has been especially successful in European studies and IR with labels of novelty such as the recent "practice turn" or "praxeology".

The problem is that research tools are used formally as external signs of scholarly distinction without deeper methodological reflection. Structural constructivist working methods are not found in the opus operatum. In other words, tools-in-use that fuse theoretical and empirical work do not structure the research from the inside out, so to speak, following structural constructivist methodology. Rather, tools are taken in a narrow object form, and are "imposed" a posteriori ("find and replace") from the outside in. They are separated from empirical work. This is visible in the ritualistic presentation of the concepts (field, habitus, strategy. . .), producing a parade effect followed by a disconnected empirical part peppered with the distinctive concepts. The main methodological idea and modus operandi, the construction of the object, and other principles such as the critical idea of analysis of conflict and of demystification of common-sense reality, are lost. The recent practice turn illustrates how this modality of formal appropriation and its spontaneous sociology waters down the perspective of the struggle for power that is characteristic of the structural constructivist approach. Instead of a critique of and distancing from pre-constructed realities, pre-constructed realities and official language are reproduced and legitimized in a disguised, scholarly form.

Creating a scholarly context that is not socially established is a trickier exercise. Here we enter into the problématique of the scholarly construction of many transnational fields (for examples, see for instance Dezalay & Garth, 1996; Georgakakis, 2012; Büttner, Leopold, Mau, & Posvic, 2015; Landorff, 2019). Most of the time, we are dealing with fields that are not canonized by practitioners or laymen, and which do not exist in bureaucratic categories. These social categories have not been symbolically and practically stabilized and legitimized. An example is the concept of "European political field". Its aim (Kauppi, 2003) as a transnational space of social action was to bring together in the analysis elements that are, in the established literature, separated from one another, but which in reality operate through the categories of perception and action of European politicians along the axis of supranational-national and executive-legislative. In other words, it was impossible to make adequate sense of European politics if the categories of analysis corresponded to national politics. Demonstrating the links between European and national levels and their constant, productive field effects challenges both the myth of the autonomy of national sovereignty and that of the supranational as being nothing more than the interaction between national fields. The evolving transnational field in question has instituting effects that cannot be reduced either to the national or European levels, but rather encompasses both by producing something new. For instance, the value of the position of Member of the European Parliament (MEP) in the emerging European political field unites analysis of the national political field and transnational levels, combining national levels to one another in new ways, for instance in terms of opening candidatures for politicians in other European Union (EU) member states. Unheard of developments, such as a Finnish politician running for the European Parliament on a French party list or MEPs like Marine Le Pen and Jean-Luc Mélenchon using European funds to finance national political activities, are now reality and make perfect sense in the context of an evolving European political field.

While attempting to break with a pre-constructed reality, the problem with a new category like "European political field" is that it does not necessarily have the social force to objectify the alternative reality it seeks to rationalize. A necessary preliminary step would require a deeper conceptual analysis of the uses of terms like "Europe", the "EU", "Euroskepticism", and "populism'. Data collection is a time-consuming and labor-intensive process. For field analysis to succeed in a longer term requires more than deconstructing a pre-constructed reality and its categories of legitimation following a scholarly rationale that obeys a theoretical interest, to use Kant's term. In the academic field, it demands backing from institutionally powerful social carriers. Beyond academia, it requires resonance with lay theories of political reality in the media as well as in government documents, ministerial reports, expert evaluations, etc. Some categories, like Ian Manners's "normative power Europe", have succeeded to a certain extent in linking to one another academic and policy discourses, but the price has been high (see Martin-Mazé, 2015 for analysis).

The uses and appropriations of certain concepts such as "field" leads us back to broader issues in the social sciences – the impact of social scientific concepts not only in the social sciences, but also beyond. While BCP were eager to present their sociological perspective as truly scientific, they also thought that theirs was not a normative approach. However, as this discussion has emphasized, field con-struction can be considered a normative process, as it legitimizes what it describes and sets apart its definition of reality from other definitions of reality. This hap-pens in the analysis of any field. While the transnational field of higher education or the global field of higher education highlights some relevant aspects of global process, at the same time the danger is that it legitimizes the processes it describes through their rationalization and objectification (Kauppi, 2016, 2018a).

Scholarly field construction should be seen as a perspective to reality that brings to the foreground certain aspects that the scholar deems important in relation to certain research questions. But undoubtedly, it also underlines the dominance of North American private universities by elevating some of them to the position of dominant pole of an evolving global field. Does this kind of objectification mean that the scholar legitimizes these power relationships? Not necessarily, if the analysis is inscribed in a reflexive social science that seeks in the process of rationalization of reality to objectify the scholar's perspective and tools (for attempts in this direction, see for instance Kauppi, 1996, 2000). To paraphrase Bourdieu, research should be practiced by scholars who reflect on their own prac-tice (Bourdieu, 1977). However, if it presents itself and is taken without taking into account the impact of the perspective and the tools used on both the subject and object of research, then the danger is that objectification turns into legitimiza-tion. Currently, as this reflexive dimension is missing, scholarly research turns in the name of analysis of "practices" into the uncritical legitimation of established political interests.

This leads us to defining what field analysis is.

Field dynamics

At a 2006 seminar in Montréal, Frédéric Mérand posed a pertinent, but unanswered, question to anyone working in a structural constructivist perspective: how many fields are there? Fields seem to pop up everywhere. Today we have, for instance, a literary field, a field of Eurocracy, of theoretical production, of immigration, of Middle East politics, and even "international sporting fields" (Musgrave & Nexon, 2018: 598). Tired of the multiplication of capital, Erik Neveu (2018) has argued that there are four forms of capital – economic, cultural, social, and symbolic – and not more, the rest being combinations of these fundamental types. The answer to the question will depend, to a certain extent, on the ontological position taken. It leads to other questions. What is a "field", exactly? Does it exist "out there", or in the head of the observer and their classification systems? Traditionally, realism and nominalism are distinguished. A realist position would correspond to the idea that fields exist independently of the observer, whereas a nominalist position à la Weber would argue that the perspective taken by the observer is crucial (see Palonen, 2017 for a defense of this position). This distinction captures some of the dimensions of Bourdieu's dichotomy between subjectivism and objectivism (see for instance Bourdieu, 1985: 85 ff.).

A realist might start calculating how many fields exist, an endless task that requires some conceptual divisions to be introduced. A preliminary division might be between primary and secondary fields (for an elaboration, see Kauppi, 2005: 37) – that is, between fields that are assumed to exist in all societies and fields whose number increases with the complexity of societies and the social division of labor. Primary fields could include the economic field, or some form of it, for instance. Its main capital (or more specifically some forms of it, like gold or cash) could be considered as forming a primary capital that can be used in all other fields as it is relatively portable, convertible, and fungible. Secondary capital would be more field-specific, less portable, and less convertible.

Certain commentators (Benson, 1998; Couldry, 2003; Davis & Seymour, 2010) seem to think that there would always be a one-to-one relationship between capital and field. This is not necessarily the case. For instance, symbolic capital can range across a variety of fields. Certain capital, like economic capital, can be a primary capital in an area of social activity – the economic field – and an important secondary capital in all other fields of social activity. Economic capital takes specific forms in different fields. Further, inter-field relations are not necessarily symmetrical. For instance, it could be argued that in certain aspects, the media field provides an important context for the political field (Couldry, 2003). That is, political action is always embedded in mediatized relationships. Political practices and media practices are intertwined. Of course, the political field as a whole cannot be reduced to the media field, as it has elements that are not reducible to media practices.

In contrast to this realist ontological position, which seems to be the dominant interpretation as the concept is mostly used to simplify and objectify reality, a nominalist ontological position would argue that the theoretical interest of the observer is key (Nietzsche, 1968). In this interpretation, the field is a scholarly instrument used to make something intelligible, to make sense of reality (Weber, 1991; BCP, 1983). The point of view creates the object of research, to paraphrase Saussure; or to quote Weber, "Concepts are primarily means of thought for the intellectual mastery of empirical data" (Weber, 2017: 106). Although Weber's take on this issue varied somewhat, one can say that for Weber the imagination of the scholar was a key aspect of the research process, this imagination not being "subjective" but also collective, relative to a historical period and social location (see for discussion Bruun, 1972: 121 ff.). Similarly, for BCP, the construction of the object of research is based on an ars invendi, a learned mental disposition (BCP, 1983: 17). But conceptual work and clarification has to be combined with empirical research. BCP and Weber share a critique of the positivist illusion according to which the scholar would be able to determine, independently of any theoretical presuppositions, what is "essential" and what is "accidental" in a social phenomenon (BCP, 1983: 149 ff.). On the contrary, the capacity to produce true statements is dependent on the interest and the capacity of the scholar to make sense of reality (Bourdieu, 1985: 42). The danger is to mix the model of reality, with reality.

While realism and nominalism are traditionally presented as being mutually exclusive, from a structural constructivist perspective these positions could be considered as being complementary. Scholarly inquiry is always developed from a certain position with certain interests in mind (nominalism), but it is aimed at a reality that is pre-existing, with a materiality, legitimacy, and solidity of its own (realism). An answer to Frédéric Mérand's question of how many fields "exist" might be: as many as it is legitimate (and convincing from the point of view of a scholarly community) to construct (Occam's razor). From this perspective, it makes little sense to talk about "weak" or "strong" fields, as if they would be in themselves weak or strong, as the capacity to analyze field effects will depend on the availability of empirical data, either from previous research or from the objects of research, and on the perspective taken and the formulation of the research problem. Saying that some people "belong to no field at all" (Couldry, 2003: 663) is equally problematic, as a field research on a specific question covers objects that are relevant for the study. This statement reflects the realist or objectivist interpretation of fields as entities that are not scholarly constructions, but rather have an existence of their own independent of the research question, the theoretical background, previous empirical studies, etc. A statement like "often several fields intersect or relate, but they are [still] relatively distinct" (Go & Krause, 2016: 10) is debatable for the same reason. Fields intersect if this intersection is relevant from the point of view of the formulated research question, and if the scholar can empirically demonstrate in a convincing way with appropriate empirical backing the relevance of this intersection.

Discussing the capacity for self-governance and the conditions of autonomy should start with analysis of the forms of dependency vis-à-vis external factors.

Autonomy can be formal; that is, guaranteed by institutional autonomy or legal regulations. It can also be substantial, relative to the kinds of goals and activities that are favored and rewarded in the field itself. Because the accumulation of specific capital cannot be isolated from the influence of various secondary capital, most notably economic capital, the economic basis of any specialized activity will influence the degree of self-governance of the field in question. Self-governance does not mean independence or freedom from dependency. Nothing is totally autonomous, and that is why advocating an Eliasian approach that is interested in forms of (in)dependency is more useful (Elias, 1985). Evaluating degrees of autonomy requires detailed empirical studies that would define what actors mean by autonomy in a specific field and at a specific point in time.

The complementarity of realist and nominalist ontological positions leads us to a series of questions that are of epistemic nature, but that have not been dealt with in the literature because scholars usually construct fields as static entities (recent exceptions include, for instance, the engaging studies in the edited volume Schmidt-Wellenburg & Lebaron, 2018). However, methodologically speaking, a deeper understanding of social action requires a temporal – or, to use Piaget's term, socio-genetic – perspective (see also Bourdieu & Wacquant, 1992: 90 f.). Like an experienced chess player, the scholar has to know the set of moves that precede a moment in the game or a constellation of power relationships in society, its dynamic topography (Kauppi, 2005: 14 f.; Djelic & Sahlin, 2009; Krause, 2018). This very labor-intensive process requires a lot of background work that will not be directly visible in the end product, the publishable article or book. Intellectual integrity and self-discipline are learned practices, and field analysis requires a lot of both. The research challenges include a critique of pre-constructed objects (including previous research and available data sets), collecting one's own data whenever possible (for instance prosopographic data), not mixing one's personal biases with the interpretation of the collected data, and sticking to what is relevant from the point of view of the research problem. This is all, of course, more easily said than done, requiring time and practice, not just theoretical knowledge.

A field is always in construction and is never finished. The scholar's job is to try to capture some of its empirical dynamics. Field dynamics can involve inter-field and intra-field dynamics related to issues of density, size, centrality, and fluidity. The level of social interaction will depend on the density of the field in question. Unless heavily internally segmented, high density equals a high level of interaction in a field between the different actors, which might correlate with difficulties in distinguishing between different kinds of capital – between personal relationships and professional relationships, for instance. This fluidity might signify a field characterized by a high level of conversion of capital. While in a certain field, field-specific capital dominate, but other capital such as economic capital might have a significant impact, blurring the lines between secondary field-specific capital and generic or primary capital. The size of a field will influence the likelihood that the field can provide enough symbolic and economic rewards for sustained social interaction. For instance, in France the literary field is large enough to enable some writers, journalists, and critics, for instance, to live from literature (Bourdieu, 1993). But this is less the case in Finland, for instance. In many European countries, the political field was traditionally manned by people who lived for politics, as they were either independently wealthy or had another occupation, and not off politics as today with professional politicians. Field development can then lead to an expansion of the size, which can also mean that professionalization develops.

The centrality of the field will have an impact on the value of its resources. The more central a field is in a constellation of fields, the higher its impact on other fields. For instance, in modern societies, the economic field has a significant impact on all other social fields. The conversion of economic capital – the capital of capital, to paraphrase Marx – into field-specific capital is a key question in all fields, creating forms of dependency that can jeopardize claims to autonomy. A field's momentum of change, the pace of expansion or contraction, will also directly affect the value of field-specific capital. A rapid contraction will mean a dramatic devaluation of its resources, and can lead to an outflow of actors. A contraction occurred in the philosophical field in France after World War II (Bourdieu, 1983; Fabiani, 1988). A rapid expansion, on the contrary, can correlate with an influx of external actors, as the mechanisms of social control loosen at the margins of the field and the value of the field's primary and secondary capital, and of its centrality in relation to other fields, increases. The conversion of French philosophers into other fields, such as the field of the social sciences, is an example in point (for this, see Fabiani, 1988; Kauppi, 1996, 2010a). This expansion is of course part of a broader development – the massification of tertiary education and the spectacular growth for a market for middle-brow intellectual goods (Pinto, 1984; Kauppi, 1990). In France, the number of university students tripled from approximatively 200,000 in 1960 to 600,000 in 1970, and the faculty from about 8,000 to 30,000.

The global field of higher education is another example of an expansive field developing with the increase in size of a global middle class, especially in China and East Asia (Marginson, 2008). As of this writing, there are 200 million students in tertiary education. Out of these 200 million, 5 million study outside of their home country. There has been an expansion of paying higher education following "Anglo-Saxon" models. Educational capital is increasingly conceptualized, through theories such as human capital theory and endogenous growth theory, as central to economic development and well-being. It is seen as central in many areas of social life. For these reasons, it can be argued that it is crucial to look at these developments from a field theoretical perspective to decipher the dominant values and the forms of social power, as well as the forms of the taken for granted knowledge that are being constructed. This global space of social action has been fabricated using quantitative tools, such as university rankings, that are problematic from a scholarly perspective but very powerful as mechanisms of coordination of higher education policies (for a discussion, see for instance Marginson, 2008; Kauppi, 2018b; Hamann & Schmidt-Wellenburg, Chapter 8).

If fields are everywhere, they are nowhere. Consequently, structural constructivist analysis has to have certain limits that have not been analyzed in the literature. Apart from the limits already discussed concerning the research perspective
and the availability of data (previous research, access to interviews, archives,
availability of statistics, etc.), a more generic limit might have to do with the
aspects of social reality that field analysis can capture. The distinction between
primary and secondary worlds might be useful in thinking about the limits of field
analysis. By definition, field analysis deals with contexts of human behavior that
can be characterized as forming secondary worlds in contrast to primary worlds
(for this distinction, see Berger & Luckmann, 1966). Primary worlds refer to contexts such as family, close intimate relationships, and the early human years of
existence. Developmentally speaking (a perspective largely missing in Bourdieu's
work; Kauppi, 2000: 93 ff.), secondary worlds follow these primary worlds. Secondary contexts such as school, work, hobbies, and activities, for instance, are
less developmentally necessary, less emotionally charged, more instrumental,
more politicized, and more specialized. In other words, primary and secondary
worlds have different ontological and epistemological properties (for a discussion
in another context and from a different perspective, see Searle, 1995). Primary
worlds are ontologically more central, and for this reason are more "shielded" or
"bracketed", to use a phenomenological term from instrumentalization (for analysis, see Kauppi, 2010b; see also Swartz, 2013b; and Bourdieu, 2016). Secondary
worlds can be expansive, with the development of the social division of labor and
the autonomization of spheres of social activity (compare to Lahire's interpretation, 2012).

The constant danger for structural constructivist research is that scientific construction becomes a mere recording of dominant, pre-existing social categories
and their power relations, a legitimation of these in a scholarly register. In cases
of strongly predefined realities that are linked to national political, economic,
and cultural structures but can also deal with legitimized supranational contexts
such as international organizations like the EU, a field approach can range from a
relabeling process whereby terms like "field" substitute "context" or "arena", to
a rarer field theoretical reconceptualization of the object that seeks to reveal the
hidden conditions of the construction of the pre-constructed object (BCP, 1991:
256). But even in the latter case, a clear detachment from predefined realities
cannot be assumed. For the relabeling process that we have seen, especially in
research in IR with the "practice turn", less theoretical work, and less distance to
a reality predefined by state and diplomatic practitioners, their official language
and political interests can mean a greater impact for certain types of research and
methodology. The danger for this is an uncritical legitimation of existing power
asymmetries and a methodologically less developed research. In contrast, for
more ambitious field theoretical reconceptualization, more theoretical work and
a longer distance to a predefined reality can mean less research impact. Because
structural constructivist discourse does not necessarily resonate with other theoretical interests, but competes with them and might not succeed in receiving the

backing of powerful opinion makers as well as lay theories outside academia, its impact can be low outside narrow research communities (for analysis of obstacles in higher education in Europe, see Kauppi, 2019).

Conclusion

The global diffusion of terms like "field" has been disconnected from the structural constructivist modus operandi. The original social context, which includes the web of ideas and the critical methodology that informed the terms, has not traveled. Until now, most "field analytical" constructions have been "mainstreamed" into the English-language literature and dominant realist methodology as either objectifying tools and/or a substitution game where "field" has taken the place of concepts such as "context" or "arena". These "quick fixes" have watered down the revolutionary potential and critical edge of structural constructivist methodology. In IR with "praxeology" and the "practice turn", field theoretical research has produced studies that merely supplement some aspects of existing approaches without questioning either their epistemological presuppositions or their links to established political and economic interests. This formal diffusion has not been accompanied by a deeper critical reflection on tools-in-use, on the interaction of theory and empirics in the research process, and the epistemological requirements of field theoretical research. Arguably the key elements of structural constructivist modus operandi, the systematic suspicion toward pre-existing knowledge, and the transformative effects of the research process itself on subject (the development of a research habitus and of a scholarly culture) and object (the impact on the definitions of social reality), have been absent in mainstreamed field theoretical endeavors.

From the point of view of research on transnational fields, field analysis as it has been practiced until now has often reified the national context and some of its legitimate value hierarchies as the privileged object of research. This has developed on the basis of available information and data, ranging from other scholarly work to government databases and lay theories of social reality in the media, that have backed the nation-centered and state-centered scholarly activity. The difficulty will be to further develop convincing field theoretical studies on transnational processes. This will require acquiring sufficient research funding as well as constructing adequate databases and other sources of information.

More than ever, it is now necessary to counteract with a more reflexive analysis of the social conditions of possibility of knowledge, including social scientific knowledge and the tools it uses. This should enable, by avoiding a sense of false nearness to social reality, methodological shallowness and unreflective legitimation of established scholarly approaches, as well as of dominant non-academic political and economic interests, the development of an epistemologically and methodologically better-armed analysis of symbolic domination in relation to current national and transnational transformations.

Note

* I wish to thank Stefan Bernhard, Christian Schmidt-Wellenburg, and David Swartz for constructive comments.

References

Adler, E., & Pouliot, V. (2011). *International Practices*. Cambridge: Cambridge University Press.

Althusser, L. (1965). *Pour Marx*. Paris: Plon.

Bachelard, G. (1983). *La Formation de l'esprit scientifique*. Paris: Vrin.

Benson, R. (1998). Field Theory in Comparative Context: A New Paradigm for Media Studies. *Theory and Society*, *28*, 463–498.

Benson, R., & Neveu, E. (2015). Introduction: Field Theory as a Work in Progress. In R. Benson & E. Neveu (Eds.), *Bourdieu and the Journalistic Field* (pp. 1–3). Abingdon: Routledge.

Berger, P. L. (1963). *Invitation to Sociology*. New York, NY: Doubleday.

Berger, P. L., & Luckmann, T. (1966). *The Social Construction of Reality*. Harmondsworth: Penguin.

Bernhard, S. (2012). Informationelles Kapital als transnationale Ressource. In S. Bernhard & C. Schmidt-Wellenburg (Eds.), *Feldanalyse als Forschungsprogramm 2: Gegenstandsbezogene Theoriebildung* (pp. 195–216). Wiesbaden: Springer VS.

Bernhard, S., & Schmidt-Wellenburg, C. (2012). *Feldanalyse als Forschungsprogramm 2: Gegenstandsbezogene Theoriebildung*. Wiesbaden: Springer VS.

Bernhard, S., & Schmidt-Wellenburg, C. (2014). Politische Soziologie Transnationaler Felder. *Schwerpunktheft des Berliner Journal für Soziologie*, *24*(2). Wiesbaden: VS Springer.

Bourdieu, P. (1977). *Outline of a Theory of Practice*. Cambridge: Cambridge University Press.

Bourdieu, P. (1983). *Homo Academicus*. Paris: Minuit.

Bourdieu, P. (1985). *Sosiologian Kysymyksiä*. Tampere: Vastapaino.

Bourdieu, P. (1989). Social Space and Symbolic Power. *Sociological Theory*, *7*(1), 14–25.

Bourdieu, P. (1993). *The Field of Cultural Production*. New York, NY: Columbia University Press.

Bourdieu, P. (2016). *La domination masculine*. Paris: Seuil.

Bourdieu, P., Chamboredon, J.-C., & Passeron, J.-C. (1983 [1968]). *Le métier de sociologue*. Berlin; New York, NY: Mouton.

Bourdieu, P., Chamboredon, J.-C., & Passeron, J.-C. (1991). *The Craft of Sociology: Epistemological Preliminaries*. Berlin; New York, NY: Walter de Gruyter.

Bourdieu, P., & Wacquant, L. (1992). *An Invitation to Reflexive Sociology*. Chicago, IL: University of Chicago Press.

Brecht, B. (2013). Alienation Effects in Chinese Acting. Retrieved from https://courses.cit.cornell.edu/ engl2080/208.scholia19.html

Bruun, H. H. (1972). *Science, Values and Politics in Max Weber's Methodology*. Copenhagen: Munksgaard.

Büttner, S. M., Leopold, L., Mau, S., & Posvic, M. (2015). Professionalization in EU Policy-Making? The Topology of the Transnational Field of EU Affairs. *European Societies*, *17*(4), 569–592.

Charle, C. (1990). *Naissance des 'intellectuels'*. Paris: Minuit.

Cibois, P. (1984). *L'analyse des données en sociologie*. Paris: PUF.

Couldry, N. (2003). Media Meta-Capital: Extending the Range of Bourdieu's Field Theory. *Theory and Society*, *32*(5–6), 653–677.

Davis, A., & Seymour, E. (2010). Generating Forms of Media Capital Inside and Outside a Field: The Strange Case of David Cameron in the UK Political Field. *Media, Culture & Society*, *32*(5), 739–759.

Dezalay, Y., & Garth, B. G. (1996). *Dealing in Virtue*. Chicago, IL: University of Chicago Press.

DiMaggio, P., & Powell, W. (1983). The Iron Cage Revisited: Institutional Isomorphism and Collective Rationality in Organizational Fields. *American Sociological Review*, *48*(2), 147–160.

Djelic, M.-L., & Sahlin, K. (2009). *Transnational Governance*. Cambridge: Cambridge University Press.

Elias, N. (1985). *La société de cour*. Paris: Flammarion.

Fabiani, J.-L. (1988). *Les philosophes de la république*. Paris: Minuit.

Fligstein, N., & McAdam, D. (2015). *A Theory of Fields*. Oxford: Oxford University Press.

Gaxie, D. (1973). *Les professionnels du politique*. Paris: PUF.

Geay, B. (1991). Espace social et 'coordinations'. *Actes de la Recherche en Sciences Sociales*, *86–87*, 2–24.

Gengnagel, V. (2014). Transnationale Europäisierung? *Berliner Journal für Soziologie*, *24*(2), 289–303.

Georgakakis, D. (2012). *Le champ de l'Eurocratie*. Paris: Economica.

Ghellab, G. S. (1997). *La transformation du système d'enseignement Italien*. Paris: L'Harmattan.

Go, J., & Krause, M. (2016). *Fielding Transnationalism*. Malden, MA: Wiley-Blackwell.

Heidegger, M. (1962). *Being and Time*. London: Blackwell.

Hilgers, M., & Mangez, E. (2015). *Bourdieu's Theory of Social Fields: Concepts and Applications*. Abingdon: Routledge.

Kauppi, N. (1990). *Tel Quel: La constitution sociale d'une avant-garde*. Helsinki: Finnish Society of Sciences and Letters.

Kauppi, N. (1994). *The Making of an Avant-garde: Tel Quel*. Berlin; New York, NY: Mouton de Gruyter.

Kauppi, N. (1996). *French Intellectual Nobility: Institutional and Symbolic Transformations in the Post-Sartrian Era*. Albany, NY: State University of New York Press.

Kauppi, N. (2000). *The Politics of Embodiment: Habits, Power and Pierre Bourdieu's Theory*. Frankfurt; New York, NY: Peter Lang.

Kauppi, N. (2003). Elements for a Structural Constructivist Theory of Politics and of European Integration. *Harvard University, Minda de Gunzburg Center for European Studies, Working Paper No. 104*. Retrieved from www.people.fas.harvard.edu/~ces/publications/docs/abs/kauppi104_abst.html

Kauppi, N. (2005). *Democracy, Social Resources and Political Power in the European Union*. Manchester: Manchester University Press.

Kauppi, N. (2010a). *Radicalism in French Culture: A Sociology of French Theory in the 1960s*. Abingdon: Routledge.

Kauppi, N. (2010b). The Political Ontology of European Integration. *Comparative European Politics*, *8*(1), 19–36.

Kauppi, N. (2013). *A Political Sociology of Transnational Europe*. Essex: ECPR Press.

Kauppi, N. (2016). Ranking and the Structuration of a Transnational Field of Higher Education. In R. Normand & J.-L. Derouet (Eds.), *A European Politics of Education: Perspectives from Sociology, Policy Studies and Politics* (pp. 92–103). Abingdon: Routledge.

Kauppi, N. (2017). À la recherche d'un langage de l'action. *Études Internationales, 48*(2), 219–229.

Kauppi, N. (2018a). *Toward a Reflexive Political Sociology of the European Union: Fields, Intellectuals and Politicians*. London: Palgrave.

Kauppi, N. (2018b). The Global Ranking Game: Narrowing Academic Excellence Through Numerical Objectification. *Studies in Higher Education, 43*(10), 1750–1762.

Kauppi, N. (2019). Waiting for Godot? On Some of the Obstacles for Developing Counter-Forces in Higher Education. *Globalizations, 16*(5), 1–6.

Kauppi, N., & Madsen, M. R. (2013). *Transnational Power Elites: The New Professionals of Governance, Law and Security*. Abingdon: Routledge.

Kauppi, N., & Swartz, D. L. (2015). Global Bourdieu. *Comparative Sociology, 14*(4), 565–586.

Krause, M. (2018). How Fields Vary. *British Journal of Sociology, 69*(1), 3–22.

Kull, M. (2018). *European Integration and Rural Development: Actors, Institutions and Power*. Abingdon: Routledge.

Lahire, B. (2012). *Monde pluriel*. Paris: Seuil.

Landorff, L. (2019). *Inside European Parliament Politics: Informality, Information and Intergroups*. London: Palgrave.

Lévi-Strauss, C. (1962). *La pensée sauvage*. Paris: Plon.

Marginson, S. (2008). Global Field and Global Imagining: Bourdieu and World-Wide Higher Education. *British Journal of Sociology of Education, 29*(3), 303–315.

Martin-Mazé, M. (2015). Unpacking Interests in Normative Power Europe. *Journal of Common Market Studies, 53*(6), 1285–1300.

Martin-Mazé, M. (2017). Returning Struggles to the Practice Turn. *International Political Sociology, 11*(2), 203–220.

Musgrave, P., & Nexon, D. H. (2018). Defending Hierarchy from the Moon to the Indian Ocean: Symbolic Capital and Political Dominance in Early Modern China and the Cold War. *International Organization, 72*, 591–626.

Neveu, E. (2018). Bourdieu's Capital(s): Sociologizing an Economic Concept. In T. Medvetz & J. Sallaz (Eds.), *The Oxford Handbook of Pierre Bourdieu* (pp. 347–374). Oxford: Oxford University Press.

Nexon, D., & Neumann, I. (2017). Hegemonic-Order Theory: A Field-Theoretic Account. *European Journal of International Relations, 24*, 662–686.

Nietzsche, F. (1968). *The Will to Power*. New York, NY: Vintage Books.

Palonen, K. (2017). *A Political Style of Thinking: Essays on Max Weber*. Colchester: ECPR Press.

Pinto, L. (1984). *L'intelligence en action*. Paris: Métailié.

Pouliot, V. (2017). La logique du praticable: Une théorie de la pratique des communautés de sécurité. *Etudes Internationals, 48*(2), 153–190.

Santoro, M., Gallelli, A., & Grüning, B. (2018). Bourdieu's International Circulation: An Exercise in Intellectual Mapping. In T. Medvetz & J. Sallaz (Eds.), *The Oxford Handbook of Pierre Bourdieu* (pp. 21–67). Oxford: Oxford University Press.

Sapiro, G. (2018). Field Theory from a Transnational Perspective. In T. Medvetz & J. Sallaz (Eds.), *The Oxford Handbook of Pierre Bourdieu* (pp. 161–182). Oxford: Oxford University Press.

Schmidt-Wellenburg, C., & Lebaron, F. (2018). Economists, Politics, and Society: New Insights from Mapping Economic Practices Using Field-Analysis. *Special Issue of Historical Social Research, 43*(3). Köln: GESIS.

Searle, J. (1995). *The Construction of Social Reality*. London: Penguin.

Shklovsky, V. (1991). *Theory of Prose*. Bloomington, IN: Dalhey Archive Press.

Siukonen, J. (2011). *Vasara ja hiljaisuus*. Helsinki: Kuvataideakatemia.

Swartz, D. L. (2013a). *Symbolic Power, Politics, and Intellectuals*. Chicago, IL: University of Chicago Press.

Swartz, D. L. (2013b). Metaprinciples for Sociological Research in a Bourdieusian Perspective. In P. S. Gorski (Ed.), *Bourdieu and Historical Analysis* (pp. 19–35). London; Durham, NC: Duke University Press.

Waser, A.-M. (1989). Le marché des partenaires: Etudes de trois clubs de tennis. *Actes de la Recherche en Sciences Sociales, 80*, 2–21.

Weber, M. (1949). *The Methodology of the Social Sciences*. New York, NY: The Free Press.

Weber, M. (1978). *Economy and Society* (Vol. 2). Berkeley, CA: University of California Press.

Weber, M., Gerth, H. H., & Mills, C. W. (1991). *From Max Weber: Essays in Sociology*. London: Routledge.

Zimmermann, A., & Favell, A. (2011). Governmentality, Political Field or Public Sphere? Theoretical Alternatives in the Political Sociology of the EU. *European Journal of Social Theory, 14*(4), 489–515.

Chapter 3

Adjusting a Bourdieusian approach to the study of transnational fields

Transversal practices and state (trans)formations related to intelligence and surveillance

Didier Bigo

Introduction

An important debate about the study of the practices of transnational groups of actors – be they called the 1 percent, transnational elites, a global class in formation, or transnational guilds – has arisen since the 1990s in different disciplines, and has recently created new interest in a more complex approach to state formation and transnational practices (Kauppi & Madsen, 2013). Human geography, political sociology, and cultural anthropology have challenged the reductionist views of traditional international political economy (IPS) about globalization, homogenization, and market democracies being the inescapable future of world politics (Robinson, 1998; Walker, 2009; Cerny, 2012).

But, despite these challenges, the Fukuyama-like analyses of globalization describing the end of the struggles for the meaning of the best forms of polities still resonate today, as the default position of many international relations (IR) professors and of the main leaders of the Western world. Globalization is still seen as a natural process of convergence, even if it has now encountered opponents and "ignorants", especially with the formation of "ultra-patriotist" parties, often called populists, and the fact that in some places – like the United States, the United Kingdom, Italy, and Hungary – they have succeeded at winning elections. These ultra-patriots accuse the global elites of having driven the world toward more inequalities and even toward its destruction, masking their vested interests with universal claims in proposing their visions of what is needed for a global, safe, and orderly political and economic order.

These discussions about globalization versus nationalistic "populism" are everywhere. Some are longstanding (Swank & Betz, 2003), while others are more recent (Berletm, 2011; Algan, Guriev, Papaioannou, & Passari, 2017; Rodrik, 2018). Unfortunately, they create a long series of analytical confusions by mimicking the analysis from the 1930s of the roles of the state, of leadership, and of representative democracy, saying these now operate at a global scale but without any serious inquiry about the terminology of "global". This assumption of having reached a "global" scale, of having a world "empire" with no outside border (Negri & Hardt, 2001), of having a "global field of power" integrating and swallowing the structural lines differentiating different state territories and regimes, has been criticized for its eschatology and for having generated its current antithetic discourse based on the opposition between global economic elites and sovereignist populists rooted locally (Go & Krause, 2016). It has been considered as one of the most damaging illusions of geopolitics and IR political science when they speak of international relations. It has also been a strong resource for both sides, used to support claims that a global (in)securitization process is at work and that prevention, protection, and prediction are central in such an environment. The development of a large group of scaremongers has unleashed the constraints on intelligence gathering and surveillance, and has turned these practices once reserved for espionage into a banal action.

This is why a discussion regarding seriously what transversal practices mean, and more importantly what they do, is so necessary. A theory of practices, and here a reflection on what have been called transnational practices, is a precondition for discussing how fields of power emerge, circulate, evolve, and structure the contemporary international set of problems, including the analysis of the collaboration between secret services and their relations with national security, sovereignty, and loyalty. This will lead us to discuss further the territorial and the digital, and how they affect the transformation of what counts for playing in the field of the state.

Transnational: what do you mean? the travel of a terminology from IPE to IPS

As any IR student knows, a certain tradition of IPE where the category of transnational is applied has the objective of first differentiating the levels of the national and the international, but with the strategy of reframing the specificity of the latter by insisting that the international is not restricted to governments representative of states. The international (as a level) is also populated by other actors, transnational ones – such as companies, non-governmental organizations (NGOs), intergovernmental organizations (IGOs), and churches – in opposition to the state actors, which possess or are constrained by the use of force and the necessity to act as sovereigns.

Krasner, Keohane, and Nye, as well as James Rosenau in the 1980s, participated in this elaboration of a category of "transnational actors" that is essentially different from state actors (Keohane & Nye, 1987; Krasner, 1999; Nye & Keohane, 1971; Rosenau, 1990). This logic of "bifurcation" transformed the verticality of strict hierarchical levels – Man-State and (international) War – into a logic of "stairs", allowing the attainment of a multilevel governance differently arranging (international) anarchy and (national) sovereignty by mediating them in a liberal way (Liesbet & Gary, 2003). According to this logic, the "global" is a terminology replacing the "international" to designate a process of governance undertaken by transnational actors and governments working together. The process of differentiation restructures the power of states and gives places to other actors, but *in fine* it functions as a melting pot, an integrative move toward a new higher level, the global. This narrative of a social whole in the making and of achieving the global without violence and struggles, but nevertheless with some disfunctions (Albert & Buzan, 2013), reproduces at another scale (the global world) previous narratives of the nineteenth century regarding the "homogenization" of society via its embrace by the state, and its slow transformation into an integrated body via functional differentiation. This meaning of a cosmopolitan global culture shared universally is in itself responsible, by its assimilation of progress, elites, bureaucracy, politics, and peace, for the emergence of the counter-narrative that is hostile to these ideas and endorses tradition, patriotism, national values, sovereignty, and revenge. Sometimes, in favor with writers unaware of the paradigm changes in IR and working in other disciplines, this meaning of transnational is still used, despite its unhelpful nature for a contemporary analysis of international problems. If it needs to be remembered, one may say, it is only to keep in mind its inopportune contribution of developing its inverse mirror image of ultra-patriotism and of perpetuating a dualist and essentialist vision of the world.

Fortunately, the contributions of different disciplines acting as critiques of the assumptions in US political sciences of the "global" and its "transnational actors" have reconfigured international relations today. After the crisis of IR that challenged its position as a political science capable of predicting the future of international politics via its knowledge of state behaviors and its pretense to have scientific laws for understanding conflict, exemplified by the incapacity of the discipline to understand what would happen before, during, and even after the end of the bipolarity of the late 1990s, it became obvious that the emergence of the epistemological debate interrogating the simulacrum played by a political science of IR to duplicate physics and the "hard" sciences was even more "actual" and necessary. The so-called third debate gives to historians, sociologists, and most of the disciplines which had already engaged in a constructionist, reflexive, and empirical approach, a possibility to reframe IR by a double move showing first the limits of narrow positivist accounts, and second the exaggerations of some trends of post-structuralism regarding processes of veridictions and appetence for novels and styles over in-depth research concerning historical transformations (Lapid, 1989). The section of the International Studies Association called International Political Sociology (IPS), and later the journal of the same name, along with other publications, have been the locus of a critique of some of the assumptions of the US political sciences concerning what was international relations, and the place for a convergence of researchers wanting to address the international as a crucial question to the world and the globe, urging each specialist to try to cross the boundaries of their own discipline and work collectively with others as a form of collective intellectual (Walker, 2009). This transdisciplinary perspective has been developed on redefining the international away from the dualism between an anarchist situation and a natural political order, insisting on the contrary on the logics of flows, of change, of different "scapes", of the heterogeneities and struggles of organizing a political process of transnationalization, different from a logic of globalization (Bigo, 2016b; Aradau & Huysmans, 2016; Basaran, Bigo, Guittet, & Walker, 2016; Guillaume, 2016; Huysmans & Nogueira, 2016; Gheciu & Wohlforth, 2018).

The authors of IPS, following a vision of a theory of historical change inspired by a Bourdieusian sociology, have reframed the notion of transnational practices and actors, not as a challenge and competitors to nation-states who would be immune from these transnational activities, but on the contrary as transversal practices affecting all actors, including the components of the states themselves, and redefining the latter in their claims of control over the boundaries of territory, identity, and violence (Gorski, 2013). These transversal practices deploy and (re)construct chains of interdependences and fields of power by opening new connections – violent or not – or by trying to reinforce boundaries, not necessarily territorially at the state borders, but through management at a distance of suspicion and use of digital technologies.[1] The maps of the different fields of power and their inscriptions into territories do not easily follow the traditional understanding of statist geopolitics. They describe networks organized in specific social spaces where all actors refuse to stay static and on the defensive, waiting for the mobile ones to spike them. Governmental actors are not reacting as dinosaurs against small mammals; they are themselves transnational, or more exactly, their bureaucracies have often constructed contact at a distance with their counterparts.

Transgovernmental networks and their status

To take into account this phenomenon, the notion of transgovernmentalism has been forged in IR with the objective to avoid the previous trap of reasoning, opposing old state actors and new transnational actors reduced to a mix of private companies, NGOs, and IGOs "free from sovereignty". This innovation including state bureaucracies in the transnational logic has nevertheless been limited because, for most authors of transgovernmentalism, like Hale and Slaughter, the impact of this reformulation was effective only at the margins of politics. They have considered in their research that these practices of collaboration and solidarity between branches of bureaucracies of different states do not touch the core of national security or social welfare, and can play only a role enabling technical solutions to emerge (Slaughter, 2004; Slaughter & Hale, 2010). Thus, for these authors, states continue to be regulated hierarchically and, despite the development of transgovernmental networks, maintain vertical lines of decision making while governments keep control of the national sphere and its reproduction. Transnational practices of bureaucracies are still dependent on the will of their governments. In this approach, transnational practices are circumventing the state and reorganizing spheres of expertise, but the state is, for the sake of the analysis, a centripetal force, concentrating power in a specific place of decision making – the government.

Therefore, if the image of a unified state is slowly deconstructed by the notion of transgovernmental networks, the state continues nevertheless to be conflated in the description with the government in charge, and transnationalist or transgovernmentalist authors continue to maintain the central illusion of traditional IR: the state is "acting" as a collective "persona" for all key decisions.

Consequently, if transgovernmentalism has partly destabilized the old vision of transnational actors opposed to state actors and shown that transnational networks construct transversal lines which affect all actors, including the actors composing parts of the state (judges, tax collectors, social security workers, and health providers), IPS authors have to go even further and think of the transversal lines as fracturing the bureaucracies themselves to find the set of dispositions of groups in relations, inside these bureaucracies, which drive them toward solidarities at a distance and enmity in proximity.

The added value of a Bourdieusian approach to understanding transnational practices: the transversal logic of practices

The central interest of taking into account the sociological work of Pierre Bourdieu, despite the fact that IR was not at the core of his research, is that, by all his conceptual problematization of sociogenesis, fields and habitus, trajectories and dynamics of change and reproduction, he reveals the assumptions and myths which are considered the pillars of the "discipline" of IR: actorness of the state, centrality of its "action", exclusivity of representation, belief in forms of hierarchical decision making, organization of a series of distinctions between private and public, inside and outside, welfare and warfare (Bourdieu, Wacquant, & Farage, 1994; Bourdieu, 2004, 2014).

Bourdieu is therefore crucial for understanding sociologically what the conditions are under which "transnational practices" embed almost all actors engaged in international politics. His approach is not a small add-on for solving an epistemic problem of idealist IR regarding security communities; it is a way to change a paradigm concerning state formation and transformation, transversal practices, and their intertwined relations deployed at a transnational scale. For that, Bourdieu begins with a very simple statement: the state is never an actor playing at a certain "superior" level called the interstate or the international arena. The division between an inside of the state and an outside of the state is not a way to analyze the situation, but the way by which the agents claiming to be part of the state bureaucracies justify a series of major distinctions: public–private, state–societal, citizen–foreigner, friend–enemy, chaos–order. Political science, by reproducing these categories as analytical categories, has a serious difficulty questioning the "power" of the state and its reproduction. A more historical and sociological understanding has to be used to give a more substantial "thickness" to the state and international relations (Buzan, 2004). The sociology of Max Weber, Norbert Elias, Charles Tilly, and many others has already paved the way for a history of coercion and capital, of city and space, as we will see, but Bourdieu has added a key element by insisting on the symbolic power by which the "magic" of the state is performed. The state, in this case, is the by-product of symbolic struggles to legitimate forms of domination, and each state has its own sociogenesis linked with the combination of different specific fields where their social structuration is simultaneously related not only to national institutions and to a dominant group of actors in a specific territory, but also to transversal networks of solidarity and antagonisms at a distance operating mainly through professional networks, recognition of shared know-how, and competitions around forms of knowledge.

On this topic of state formation, in his course on the state, Bourdieu himself borrows most of his analysis from Weber and Tilly. The latter has very often insisted on the internal-external dialectic forming a dynamic and a "helix" that is never reducible to a single path due to the construction of elites themselves. The making of the state is not the result of a program, as thought by those who consider the state as an "entity", an "essence" controlled by groups internally; its formation is affected by transversal forces, including war, demographic trends, and many other dimensions that the leaders did not want. States, from their origins, have therefore been the by-product not only of moments of struggle between dynasties in competition, but also of transversal trends (births, diseases, environmental elements). These dynamics have favored, in Europe, the institutional form of a national territorial state stabilized in its consecration into international law as the definition of stateness, against empires and leagues of cities. But when Bourdieu and Tilly met at the Collège de France, both insisted that this pseudo-stability and universality of the "national" state was partly illusionary and that forces are always evolving (Bourdieu, Christin, & Will, 2000). This is a characteristic that Bourdieu has nevertheless sometimes himself forgotten, by emphasizing the centripetal dynamics more than the centrifugal dynamics in state formation and by putting excessive weight on the role of "cultural capital", education, and therefore the boundary making of language and the struggles of social classes internally around welfare, perhaps because he wanted also to have a specific and stable frame of action to theorize his notion of symbolic power. In his model, it is not so much the territory as such that is important for state formation, but the conditions under which the relations and capacities of the actors in competition create some network connections and succeed at attracting them into a field – a field that already concentrates the powerful actors (or heirs) in a certain place related to the structure of their capitals, distinguishing them from the more marginal pretenders. This is how a homology between the objective positions, the dispositions, and the position-takings can emerge. States and markets are in some ways organized through these centripetal dynamics.

Nevertheless, in centrifugal dynamics generating fields based on professional solidarities, the concentration does not work, and mimetic rivalries about small distinctions can create more struggles between people who share almost the same places and social positions than between those with distant positions.

National and transnational state formation and transformations: reassembling the field of state power

The forms that the field of state power takes are the results of local and world-wide structural dynamics, acting in continuity and emerging from heterogeneous fields of power. Boundaries and limits of state powers are therefore not given by geography or ideology; they are always in a state of flux. They change with time, regardless of what the dominant actors want. This is why sociogenesis is so important as a methodology. Even the most stabilized field of power ends up with crucial changes, which can be abrupt or occur slowly. Boundaries may be fluid, or viscous like magma, but they are never walls that stand firm forever. By the same token, practices are not designed to work at a certain level, either local or national or international; their effects as practices come from the relations they are embedded into. The length of the chain of interactions will determine how a practice is seen as local, national, or international by commentators and their scripts of the relations.

Political processes of transnationalization or transversalization refer therefore (c.f. here Schmidt-Wellenburg & Bernhard, Chapter 1) to a series of struggles over "common principles of vision and division" (Bourdieu et al., 1994: 7), and they are an inherent part of the national and social construction of the state by also organizing the boundaries and limits of "what is national in the state field" and what is "beyond" it, or "across" it. As Bourdieu insisted, "Research also needs to take into consideration changes in the forms and boundaries of power in places other than the territorial state", and he suggested looking more at the "extra-territorial" forms of power and their jurisdictions by arbitration and/or courts mechanisms and struggles (Bourdieu to Bastien, in Bourdieu, 2012: Discussions). In practice, this means that the national territory does not bind the state. Rather, boundary making depends on the chains of interdependencies of the state's bureaucracies inside and outside the territory (Gorski, 2013). Boundaries of loyalty and territory are the constructs resulting from mechanisms of stabilization of flows and changes "traversing" institutions, fragmenting them through the struggles for organizing them in order to orient the direction of their stream. Politics of visas, readmissions, and denials of citizenship are examples of this intuition and of the limitations of the theories that do not take into account the projections of state bureaucracies abroad. The question of the "force of the law" and its relations with the use of force is therefore coming back (Derrida, 1994). The mystical foundation of authority is questioned even more at the territorial border than anywhere else when it becomes obvious that inequality, discrimination, and inhumanity lead to practices of violence in the name of sovereignty and survival of a group that is not in danger. Following the sociological work of Bourdieu, more recent works about the role of the profession of lawyers have insisted on this central element of symbolic power via the law (Madsen, 2011a, 2011b; Dezalay & Madsen, 2012; Kauppi & Madsen, 2013). These authors have analyzed the sociogenesis of the role of legists by looking at the crystallization of boundaries limiting the number of actors entering into the competition for having the "last" word and a position of sovereign, while other scholars have analyzed their current role in the transformations occurring following this pretense to be sovereign affected by the reconfiguration of rule of law, sovereignty, security, and universal claims, along the lines of the positions, dispositions, and interests of the lawyers and law professors contributing to the building of different international European laws and courts (Dezalay, 2004; Cohen, Dezalay, & Marchetti, 2007; Vauchez, 2008; Georgakakis & Weisbein, 2010; Bigo & Madsen, 2011; Cohen, 2011; Kauppi, 2013; Georgakakis & Rowell, 2013). Implicitly reproducing the distinction between the levels of the national and the transnational and looking for a unique field, some have suggested that in this case because of the span of the intermediations, fields are weaker and are less coherent in terms of capitals, but in my view fields are not weak or strong as such. Fields are made of networks of relations which are polarized by certain stakes, but the number and the frequency of the relations depend on the degree of autonomy of each field and its power of attraction. Some fields have intense or sparse relations inside the main group of actors; others are more connected between them by multipositioned actors filtering the different stakes along territorial or linguistic lines, often along their own interests as "translators" or "parasites". So transversal practices are "specific" and often fluid and transnational, but sometimes they may solidify via a specific international "organization". They "pierce" the network of relations and stich it differently. They are therefore crucial, but they are not a "total social fact", an "entity", a bubble, or a form of order. They interconnect (via contradictions); they traverse and reframe by their actions, all the dynamics making the reproduction and transformation of the different nation-states themselves.

This approach to stateness as a specific "field of power" that is not exclusively national, and that is not only the use of force and the pretense to have a monopoly on it, reframes our understanding of the international today. It also reframes the way states have evolved as configurations including, in addition to the political class and public bureaucracies, different emergent powerful actors – like major internet companies, conglomerates of banks, including central banks, and financial institutions, as well as their relations with specific sectors of bureaucracies, especially signal and internet intelligence services and military forces interested in space and cyberspace.

It seems that the field of stateness has evolved and it is, in my view, the best angle from which to discuss the current relations between transnational practices and state formation, as well as their current reproduction and transformations. Stateness is no longer constituted only around coercion by public actors in a specific territory where they can legitimately apply a criminal justice system regulating the use of violence and illegalities. The current dynamics exist more around the conduct of conducts at a distance, beyond and across many territories with an expansion of number and a span on the strength of the chains of interdependence. These chains have expanded considerably from the development of quicker technologies of travel and the advent of a digital age. They have allowed more travel to happen at a higher speed, and doing so they have compressed distance and time (Harvey, 2005), creating the conditions of possibility for solidarity at a distance and indifference in proximity. Transversal practices have changed in terms of impact because of the speed of the diffusion (contagion, virality) of their contents and the reduction of the spatial distance they can cover by creating the feeling of the instantaneity of events. They reconfigure what the boundaries of the state are and the economy of forces of the field of power, especially in the places where transmission and reproduction of positions has been routinized.

Intelligence data about citizens, consumers, travelers: assembling differently welfare and warfare in the name of predictive suspicion

The current stateness is, especially in the so-called advanced democracies, a dis-assembling of the public, especially of welfare, and a movement toward a gamble on the future played by private actors and a reassembling around suspicion, pre-vention, and prediction of all the organizations, both private and public, acting on the extraction of information and personal data for commercial and surveillance purposes.

As we will see, this shift in stateness and the creation of an articulation of suspicion and surveillance organized around a politics of fear and emergency has given to the Signals-Intelligence(SIGINT)-internet intelligence services a spe-cific importance, and explains in some way their self-appreciation that they can "connect the dots" and anticipate the future. At least if the politicians admit that they have to give them the technology, the money, and the workforce necessary to transform haphazard and vague elements into weak signals having a specific meaning in terms of suspicion. The intelligence services are cleft between the ones that refuse to change their role from informing politics, letting politicians decide and be responsible for failures, and the ones that have the ambition to build total information awareness. Correlated with these opposing stances on the social use of technology and the belief that prediction can emerge from big data, I have shown with Laurent Bonelli that the relations between the deep state of the dif-ferent secret services and the politicians are subject to huge variations, according to the degree to which the intelligence services are connected or not with their foreign counterparts, as this determines their dispositions toward a preference for national security and obedience to their politicians; or on the contrary, their primary allegiance to the services abroad with whom they collaborate (Bigo & Bonelli, 2019). A practical logic is at work and connects the sense to play the same game, the relations to the national politicians, the vision of global threats beyond the national realm, and the dispositions toward collaboration between agencies operating on the same domain. Intelligence services populated by police-men (the Federal Bureau of Investigation (FBI) and Drug Enforcement Adminis-tration (DEA) in the United States; Direction Générale de la Sécurité Intérieure

(DGSI) in France; Military Intelligence 5 (MI5) and Secret Intelligence Service (SIS) in the United Kingdom) continue to follow a traditional behavior, even if they use massively digital techniques. On the contrary, the SIGINT and internet intelligence services (National Security Agency [NSA] in the United States; Government Communications Headquarters [GCHQ] in the United Kingdom; Australian Signals Directorate [ASD]; Canadian Security Intelligence Service [CSIS]; New Zealand Government Communications Security Bureau [GCSB]; but also the Swedish Försvarets Radioanstalt [FRA]; and the Direction Technique of the Direction Générale de la Sécurité Extérieure [DGSE] in France) have very strong transnational links (the Five Eyes plus network), and their transnational exchanges and activities generate a transversal field which challenges strongly the national state field (often represented by a national security office, theoretically coordinating the activities of all national intelligence services). The loyalty to this transversal field even gains supremacy over the national when a service prefers sending secret information to a foreign agency about national suspects than to respect the loyalty they have, in theory, regarding all their national politicians and citizens. The affair around the German Bundesnachrichtendienst (BND) revealed by the leaks of the NSA documents by Edward Snowden demonstrates that the BND agents were spying on their own citizens and even politicians when asked by the NSA, and without the other national services knowing their activities (Bauman et al., 2014; Schulze, 2015). This does not mean that in other cases the national imperative is not successful against foreign collaboration if sensitive matters (industrial secrets, for example) are at stake, but it seems that the government defends better its national companies than its national citizens.

In sum, this digitization of the reason of state, which is distributed between transnational actors first (and not by national or international coordination structures), shows a more important stake for international political sociology in who participates today in the field of the national state. So, beyond the findings of our research on the Five Eyes and their relations with intelligence organizations of continental Europe, what is revealed is the strong transformation of what national security and state agents mean today in a transnationalized, digitized world where private companies have the capacity to resist, merge with, or constrain states if necessary.[2]

Therefore I suggest that the dimensions of suspicion and security which include intelligence policing, and even criminal justice towards "preventive, predictive" logics are part of a more general trend concerning the field of the state and its polarization between warfare and welfare: polarization that is now changing after a trend in favor of welfare immediately after World War II, into a new logic of warfare characterized by suspicion and surveillance.

Loïc Waquant proposed seeing this transformation of the field of the state (and the balance between the two hands of the state, coercion and redistribution) via the decline of the welfare state and the rise of a renewed penal state through the punitive regulation of poverty in a neoliberal age (Wacquant, 2009). He considered rightly the transformation from taking charge of poverty from the public with the idea of creating a safety net for the poor, toward a private logic of poverty organizing a society of debtors and the possibility for private companies to make money from the poor, and to participate in the prevention of their disobedience by punishing them more for what they are than for what they have done. He has therefore concentrated his analysis on the reorganization of the criminal system, followed also by Bernard Harcourt, who insisted on the predictive dimension related to a preventative regime of justification (against transnational and global threats) (Harcourt, 2006). Wacquant and Harcourt, along with other criminologists (Loader, 1997; Zedner, 2010; Aas, 2012; Hudson & Ugelvik, 2013), have shown how the preventative argument has modified the current logic of criminal justice regarding presumption of innocence, access to justice, and certainty of penalty. I have also, with Mireille Delmas-Marty, insisted on this reorganization of the state around evaluation and suspicion, about virtual violence which is not actualized but generates anxiety and fear as a state of mind, reinforced by diverse politics of unease (Bigo, 2002; Delmas-Marty, 2010; Bigo & Delmas-Marty, 2012).

All these works are testimony of the current limitation of the use of physical violence, even if it does not disappear, and a strong increase in the use of forms of symbolic power reinforcing surveillance and control at a distance. They are also complemented by research on how military, police, border guards, and intelligence services have ensured their position in this state field of power not only through their use of force, but also through their use of "secrecy" and arguments of forecasting and predicting future threats (Sayad & Bourdieu, 1991; Bourdieu, 1993; Mérand & Pouliot, 2008; Mérand, 2010; Berling, 2012; Bigo, 2012; Paulle, van Heerikhuizen, & Emirbayer, 2012; Martin-Mazé, 2017). The existence of a field of power that does coincide with the interstate map of the international with neat territorial borders separating the actors in national containers, which become the main stock exchange of the different forms of capital the actors possess, has never existed. This is not an evolution of the world, but a difficulty of understanding the transversal practices of field societies, groups, and individual relations spanning across territorial borders.

Transversal practices at the core of stateness: reading differently the SIGINT-internet intelligence services collaboration

To make the argument of this co-constitution of transversal practices and national state formation and transformations, I want to illustrate it with the example of the secret services, considered as the very core of the state – the deep state structuring the multiplicities of its activities and specialized bureaucracies. Even there, despite the discourse of national security, national sovereignty, national interest, and the supposedly vertical line of decision making and command, solidarity and loyalty between actors are not always driven by the proximity of their structural positions inside the national state. Despite all the narratives about the exclusive loyalty to their respective "nation" by all the different intelligence services, the national security exclusivity narrative has been destabilized, and the role of a transnational "community" of intelligence has been emphasized. To temper the paradox of the transnational acquisition of information for national security, it has been justified on different bases after the end of the Cold War with the rise of a narrative by Western states of global threats (terrorism, transnational organized crime) imposed by a larger "community" of states than the Anglophone Five Eyes supposedly inherited from World War II. The argument was the necessity to collaborate against terrorism while pursuing national interests on other topics, and it has created the terminology of co-opetition (cooperation and competition simultaneously) to justify the collaboration while maintaining the idea of national security first. But this transversal network between services abroad has *de facto* reinforced the tensions between military secret services and police intelligence services, and given rise to the autonomization of technological ones. The will of politicians to speak in terms of coordination created by fusion centers, or by coordination structures, is in some way the result of this competition between the services and the difficulty to maintain a proximity between the heads of states and the executives of the top agencies. Our research has shown that each time a crisis arises, the different secret services cooperate better with their counterparts abroad than with their national "fellows", and this disrupts the so-called community of national security in each country. During the extraordinary rendition saga of the Central Intelligence Agency (CIA), its first opponents came from the FBI and the branch of the military lawyers, and its first supporters were the SIS (Military Intelligence 6 [MI6]) of the United Kingdom, the Polish military intelligence services, and those in Romania, Thailand, and many other places that were *de facto* relying on funds from the CIA for their present and future, and were trained to act completely outside their own legal regime (Guild, Bigo, & Gibney, 2018). The fact of pertaining to a certain informal transnational guild of extraction of information, considering that the services inside this network have a specific know-how and their own rules and ethics, different from the public, seems to be the crucial criterion for collaboration between them, even if it may create tensions with the national government itself. In the case of the disclosures by Edward Snowden of the practices of the NSA and its collaborators (the so-called Five Eyes, which are now more surely nine, if not twelve), it has been clear also that the NSA shared its little secrets about personal data of suspects with its counterparts abroad (English GCHQ, Canadian CSE, French DGSE, Swedish FRA, Australian ASD) to elaborate from a large-scale logic of data interception a transnational map connecting the dots and willing to trace the networks of suspects by differentiating them from the "normal" public and the non-risky travelers (Bigo, 2016a, 2019a, 2019b). It went as far as asking the German BND to put some German citizens under surveillance, including some in the political class, and to send back the information only to the NSA. At the same moment the NSA, which was justifying its operation in the name of counterterrorism, did not share information with the FBI or even the CIA. What makes no sense in the traditional framework of intelligence studies following the distinction between state and non-state actors' behaviors, and is easily considered as an aberration both in ethical and in statistical terms, makes on the contrary a lot of sense if the fetishism of the national security community is considered not as a routine in terms of practice, but as a constant necessity to remind the agents that they have to be "patriotic" and serve as an indigenous category of theoretical practice (Bonditti & Olsson, 2016).

Some authors of intelligence studies have already used the term "transgovernmental networks analysis" to discuss the practices of cooperation between different services (Aldrich, 2009), but they have not dared to analyze the intelligence services of the global North as a specific field of power challenging their own professionals of politics. They have preferred to continue to consider that, in normal times, intelligence services have no initiative and obey the orders of the politicians. It is only when such politicians become "rogue", like Bolsonaro the current Brazilian president, that the services that have formed an alliance try to "rationalize" them, to act along their own appreciation of the situation as a guild of professionals.

In fact, to clarify who has the most chance of opposing politicians with a certain level of success, it seems from my analysis of the types of capitals of each intelligence service, which are important in the field of management of sensitive information, that the first criterion is the modification in time of allocation of resources between the different services to the advantage of those using technological tools, and especially those in charge of internet surveillance, and the detriment of those continuing the policing practices of human infiltration. It has reinforced the move against criminal justice and anti-terrorist logics related with the traditional military and police services, and it has been rearticulated in favor of the previous service providers, the SIGINT-internet intelligence services, which have imposed their vision in terms of preventative-predictive-algorithmic suspicion and counterterrorist logics of operating preventatively and at a distance. They have used this not only against the other services, but also against some of their own national politicians.

The second element to have in mind is the necessity of seriously reassessing the story of the Five Eyes as a "community" sharing common values between intelligence agencies among Anglo-Saxon countries, and that these "bonds" have created the necessary conditions for a form of mutual trust to develop between political leaders and agency actors. Instead of this cultural analysis, with Laurent Bonelli, we have collected interviews from intelligence professionals and later employed a structural analysis of the space in which the selected intelligence agencies are situated. We have related their exchange of information to a series of defining characteristics of the agencies (type of missions conducted, supervisory authority, territory of action, staff numbers, technological capital, etc.).

Constructing a multiple correspondence analysis (MCA) has allowed us to rigorously visualize the space of institutional positions. In making connections between these objective positions and the discourses of actors regarding their practices and the meaning of intelligence, we were able to identify homologies as well as divergences that structure cooperation and data exchanges between agencies. The positions have generated a transnational space where the logic of transversal practices was organized along three universes of competition and solidarity depending not only on their number of personnel, their capacity to have private contractors and links with the major internet companies and data brokers, and their capacity to have innovative software or specific positioning regarding the internet cables, but also on their ability to be a credible voice in the competition over the symbolic power related to the modes of reasoning (indicial-algorithmic) which are involved in their tools and resources, and to have the support and belief of other fields like artificial intelligence specialists in their efficiency in terms of the prediction of human behaviors (Bigo & Bonelli, 2019).

From this research, it became clear that the "national" factors of identity and "community" do not create a common position or solidarity; on the contrary, the national is not the logic of the field, and nationalism seems outdated. This has obliged all the services to put an emphasis not on national interest (espionage, self-interest), but on shared interest in global risk and threats (dangers): terrorism or trafficking where a majority of citizens are at risk and a very small minority of criminals is acting. This change in the regimes of justification is the most obvious and palatable sign of the modification of patterns affecting all secret services, and simultaneously the sign that the development of practices of exchange is displacing loyalties and of the limits of what democracies can do.

All these transversal practices are therefore modifying the composition of what was called the "deep state" itself: that is, its very core with its secret intelligence services running for the state and their missions to protect national security. Certainly some services continue to subsist only as national actors both in terms of position and narratives, but if they are more implicated in active foreign policy and advocate a global struggle against terrorism, their connections through a centripetal dynamic are contradicted by the opposite direction, which creates allegiance at a distance with foreign services and introduces also private actors, internet companies, and data brokers as mediators into the field of stateness. This is especially the case for the collaboration between SIGINT-internet intelligence services, which are nowadays more powerful than ever in the competition for funds with the other services, and which play a key role by reorganizing the full equilibrium between the different secret services and the politicians of each national state. Their centrifugal dynamics have given to the SIGINT internet collaboration of the Five Eyes plus a dispersed but very effective field of power, which reinterprets state missions along the idea of a global protection against vulnerability and a focus on the suspicion of travelers, minorities, and especially those who are also poor and fragmented, i.e., easy to target.

Transversal lines: how many angels can dance on the head of a pin? how many fields traverse a single agent?

Despite all the demonstrations given by researchers who have observed transversal practices and refused to present them in an inside-outside binary model, complemented by a vertical scale going from man to state (and the global), this form of blindness about the transformations of stateness is still strongly present in academia. This explains why the myth of national security is still performative in certain areas of politics and geopolitics and continues to be the doxa of some sociologists. We therefore have to come back to this question of stateness through time. How do we avoid essentialism and nominalism? How can we analyze in a sociogenetic way the *longue durée* of the state as a field of actors, and simultaneously as a certain frame of the world which has imposed itself as evidence for quite a long time? Have we ever been "modern", asked Bruno Latour (2012)? Have we ever had the capacity to escape the sacrality of the state and its rituals, without creating an international separating states into territories and recognizing their claims of sovereignty? The theological empire and global neoliberalism surround by their verticality the world of sovereign states, theoretically equal. It is not sure we can jump from the transversal relations of our deep state agents to the reformulation of contemporary practices of the actors who claim to be part of the field of the state and international, but it is nevertheless necessary to be reflexive on the legitimacy of the practices of the intelligence services that we analyze. Are they the future actors organizing our life in the fields of states we still recognize as such, as long as they claim to be ruled by democratic imperatives?

Rob Walker has insisted that believing that we can resolve the international of the states by arguing about the global as a new totality encompassing homogeneity and equality, is *de facto* a reconstruction of the imperial logic of verticality ending up with a god position, and the end of a sublunar world of humanity. Erasing this verticality is not easy, and the visions of multiple levels of governance are so seductive for the experts that they reappear in many different forms. But if we are serious enough with the notion of transversality, this approach supposes thinking reflexively about a world of equality that no natural hierarchy has already constructed (Walker, 2017).[3] Transforming the actors into their data doubles, in depriving them of actions, and treating them as "angels" and/or as "data subjects", is a temptation of current bureaucracies. But this transformation of actors into non-actors, into subjects which are only the support of their data, is always a way to try to fragment the individuals, to dissociate them into small parcels that can be piled up vertically and organized into the categories of danger and suspicion. The philosophical question of the number of angels on the head of a pin can obsess us, and can certainly resonate with the surveillance by big data, but, as Bourdieu and Yves Dezalay explained many times, in this flat world, an analysis of practices begins by dispelling the ghost of institutional autonomy and the imaginary of the spokespersons who construct them by concentrating the analysis on the struggles in which the agents are engaged because they live at the very same scale (Dezalay, 2004).

A certain kind of critique developing the fears of a dystopic future is therefore sometimes complicit with this vision of a new sense of history leading towards a global empire to come, by evoking the resistance of the multitude against a global unifier instead of analyzing the transversal lines at work (Negri & Hardt, 2001).

The authors following this kind of critique dismiss the international of the states and pray for a machinic global, but their research of levels depending still on geographical-territorial scale is a non-sense: the bigger size is not the best fitted form of power.

To say it differently, transversal practices are not hierarchized in vertical levels and becoming bigger and bigger. They are not a pathway to the global. They are fragmented, and may be transversal but minuscule. A unique global field cannot exist and subsume the other ones. Fields exist when they are populated by certain specific groups which have specific interests at stake. For example, the European field of bureaucracy described by Didier Georgakakis is certainly a field of transversal practices, but it is not a "larger" or "superior" field than the different national bureaucratic fields, as some have (wrongly) interpreted (Georgakakis & Rowell, 2013). Fields exist through the trajectories of the actions of the persons interested in the games they play, and they always play many games simultaneously, because of multiple dispositions which are activated or not by the constraints of each game.

Bernard Lahire has deconstructed the simplified view of one habitus per person or their interlocking like a Russian doll that some followers of Bourdieu, in search of scientific prediction, wanted to maintain (Lahire, 2001, 2012). He has shown that split habitus(es) are not an exception but the rule. Unfortunately, he has sometimes introduced a psychological language which is not necessary to express his view. In my understanding, this is certainly not a reduction toward an individualization of the collective relations and an IR approach reduced to the everyday and its banality, which will help us to understand the diversity of habitus(es). On the contrary, a strong understanding that all actors play in a series of multiple games by doing one act only is necessary. They are structurally "double agents" and cannot strategize all the effects of their actions and the chains of interdependence in which these actions are inserted (Dezalay & Garth, 2002). Some of these multiple agents hit their targets, but most do not. Most actions in a chain of interdependences with multiple paths and bifurcations are so dispersed that they reach unwanted territories and cross boundaries.

The transversal practices are therefore not all driven by "vector-forces" that polarize the actions towards a center. They cannot be strategic all along their effects. On the contrary, what is central is understanding that the struggles inside and between fields of power and politics do not always polarize; they escape, stretch, disjunct, diffract, or intermingle on overlapping subjects. This is a vision that we share with sociolinguists when they analyze everyday interactions (C. Charalambous, P. Charalambous, Khan, & Rampton, 2016; Rampton, 2016). The way forms of insecuritization travel from fields to fields and look "unbound" is also an example of this diffraction, or translation, which does not end up as a binary fight with identified actors.

Their local proximities of positions, determined often by the types of resources they can mobilize, exist at the same moment and space that their transversal solidarities and struggles at a distance (be they geographical and/or digital) act. If the first ones are easily captured by the centripetal dynamics of state making and even market making which concentrate power in specific centralized loci, it is more difficult for traditional apparatuses or *dispositifs* of states and markets, even jointly, to control the centrifugal dynamics of transversal-transnational practices at a distance, which plays with more indeterminacy and freedom, hazard of encounters, reduction of space boundaries, and acceleration of time units (Bigo, 2016b, 2018).

Centripetal and centrifugal dynamics of power: the trajectories of transversal practices

Reading the Five Eyes intelligence collaboration differently is certainly important for analyzing the fragile boundaries of the democratic oversights of intelligence services, but it is also through this analysis of the "deep state" that we can reflect better on a reframing of the theory of state formation and transformation by beginning with the transversal practices of the various actors. Understanding the dynamics, the trajectories, and their diffractions is central to avoiding reducing the fields to spaces looking like miniature territories with strong borders. Fields are always open to many circulations, and their policing is very complex. The spaces of these more or less invisible relations which constitute transversal practices are crossing or avoiding territorial boundaries, but they are also constitutive of the boundaries of the national state today; and these two elements are certainly not to be opposed or to be seen as complementary, but are strongly embedded into the very same logic. State formation and transformation is in itself a transversal-transnational practice.

However, the trajectory may differ depending on the dynamics of these practices (Bigo, 2016c).[4] Therefore, do they converge and create centripetal dynamics concentrating in proximity the most powerful actors, or do they diverge and create centrifugal dynamics dispersing the most powerful actors who continue to play together but at a distance? The model of a national state whose actors capture transversal forces to help them to control the value of the different forms of capital inside a territory, and differentiating strongly an inside from an outside, is not always successful. The building of fences delimiting an enclosed territory is rare in practice, even if it has colonized the Western political imagination with the reinvention of the myth of an effective Chinese "great wall" and the idea of transposing it to the southern border of the United States. Contrary to a clear enclosure in the form of a circle, it is better to think about boundaries as the apparent two faces of a Möbius strip, which may look different at first sight but which are in fact one single line producing intersubjectively for the observers the idea of borders objectively separating two things, but where the inside and the outside vary in function of the position of the observer (Bigo, 2000). People who have been in waiting zones of airports, detained inside while being considered outside the territory by the border guards, understand this specific geometry.

This is also the form of a Möbius strip that digital documents more and more often have. They are constructed by private companies with our personal data and delivered to bureaucracies in a time–space zone which is no longer the physical space of the territorial border. Public and private have mixed, while still looking different. State agents work at a distance, via the exchange of information through the interoperability of databases managed by public and private actors, far from the "gates" of their border guards' territory, and these "new" agents are more informed by intelligence data suspicions than by criminal evidence at the territorial border. Stateness is therefore more complex and fragile than supposed and more subject to fluctuation, and it is not immune from transversal practices because they are part of what constitutes it.

Conclusion: transversal practices and regimes of justification

These processes of transversal practices have constituted state making itself, as Tilly explains in detail, and they are at work if one wants to analyze the transformations of stateness today. But these practices are also, intimately, theoretical practices, folk theories coming from the most authoritative agents of the moment, and processes of justifications which refer to the mythical origins and the current strategies of legitimization of actors who claim to speak in the name of the national state, even if they are neither public nor territorial (Tilly, 1990).

For example, the field of power is now frequently constituted by relations where the capacities (capital) of certain private companies like Google, Apple, Facebook, and Amazon to voice that they represent the state and protect national security better than the "old public bureaucracies" allow them to play against the political class of their country of origin, which is accused of being incompetent. This is also what regional and international organizations do by claiming that they have access to a universal point of view more reasonable than nationalist sovereign claims enacted by the politicians of a specific territorial state, as informed by the rhetoric between the European Union Commission or the United Nationals General Secretariat and US President Donald Trump.

To show this importance of the symbolic power in the construction of the boundaries of state actorness, and the rules of who is forbidden to enter into this transversal field, is crucial and changes the perspectives we have on the world (political order). It allows us to look at the most traditional institutions of the state – ministries of the interior, welfare organizations, armies, secret services – as forms of transnational guilds, as transversal actors who act across boundaries and territories (Bigo, 2016c). The metaphor of the two arms of the state and of this Janus-like form has to be abandoned. The field of the state is always a polymorph, a pulp more than a man.

In this vision of the transnational, the field of the state is therefore not "internalized" into a territory; the state exists beyond its own borders and its own public agents. We certainly have difficulty believing and understanding concretely what this means as it works against our doxa, but this difficulty to reflect may also be productive if, thanks to a reflexive move, it allows us to propose an alternative narrative or a different script in which the national state is not one nation, one homogeneous entity. The different public and private bureaucracies always act transversally, and they are not obedient or constrained by ministries of foreign affairs deciding on the practices abroad of state agents. Assemblages of actors in networks both public and private claim that they are the "real" state, that they follow the national interest of a population badly represented by the national politicians. They may call themselves a coalition for ecological survival or a collaboration of the silent "deep state" agents when reason escapes the professionals of politics. Anchored in a long tradition of a territorial logic of representative democracies, the boundaries of what is a state are de-essentialized by the formulations of these claims. They are desacralized from the territory as the ultimate distinction between illegitimate violence and the use of force to reestablish order, and they refer also and sometimes mainly to the practices of actors in networks, who may live outside the territory, as for example diasporas, or across different polities and languages, as "frontaliers", or members of international organizations considering they have to be distant from an egoist national interest but always loyal to the "values" of the state in which they were born and of which they are citizens.

In conclusion, the terminology of "transnational" is therefore used by the authors developing an IPS with a precise meaning of "transversal lines" crossing, traversing national-societal fields (Basaran et al., 2016). Transnational refers neither to a transition towards the global, an in-between place between the national state belonging to the past and the global not yet achieved, nor to a specific "level" gathering exclusively specific actors which would be called "regional" actors, as particular members of non-governmental and/or bureaucratic organizations beyond (above) the national level.

Transnational is therefore neither an intermediary "level", a path towards homogenization and the global, nor a specific set of actors playing a specific game in a particular arena. It is on the contrary a set of "transversal lines", of relational practices of power structuring the ways by which actors struggle to impose their own views of what is claimed to be the "common principles of vision and division of a specific set of practices in the social world" (Bourdieu et al., 1994: 8). But the specificity of the stakes gives to each field its "autonomy", its "originality". Fields are sets of relations and processes; they do not belong to a group or an institution. They cross, enmesh, entangled. These practices and their regimes of justification cut through and coexist on the same (horizontal) plane as the local, the national, and the international.

Far from opposing transnational actors to state actors, a transversal approach insists on the central element of transgovernmentalism and the fact that the different components of the "state" have never been one actor, but a set of actors fighting for a specific capital allowing the imposition of a final word on the quarrels over hierarchizing the allocation of values. Beyond the differentiation of the left and the right hands of the state opposing welfare and warfare, a transnational approach will show that in all "sectors", the practices of some groups inside bureaucracies are structurally opposed to other groups in the national game in which they have to participate, but often strongly attached to foreign bureaucracies doing the same kind of tasks as them and generating solidarities at a distance, and an even stronger loyalty to their "foreign natural correspondents" than to their "national governments which include their opponents" (Bigo, 2016b).

Thinking transnational practices therefore dismantles the implicit verticality of ordered levels and the correlative creation of prosopopeia, of the "artificial conscience" of the state or the community of states acting as "persons" with a specific will and strategy. This horizontalization is necessary to escape from the verticality of traditional IR and their "actors" who play in a shadow theatre (of puppets whose agencies are given only by their creator-writer). Analyzing transversally is the way to rediscover the dynamics of power between groups of individuals playing multiple games simultaneously. This approach (or script) for a different narrative of the transnational desacralizes the superiority of international or state levels over local and "individual in relation" practices. All practices are collective and in the very same sublunar world. The false transcendence of a certain type of US political science of IR reproducing the verticality of different levels to organize thoughts justifying order and obedience to the state (and God) cannot continue to be the guide of the research and to have the canonical definition of terminologies. Our fragmented world is a pluriverse deployed in many different dimensions, but its understanding comes from us only.

Notes

1 Transversal and transnational: In the most general terms, the terminology of transversal lines seeks to present a problematization that cuts across conventional planes of scholarship, both theoretically and empirically. Empirically transnational is often the terminology used to describe these crossings and multidimensional scapes (see the following, and for more details see Basaran et al., 2016).
2 The ANR research UTIC on the uses of technologies for communication surveillance that Laurent Bonelli, Sébastien Laurent, and myself have conducted from 2015 to 2019 is available at www.sciencespo.fr/ceri/en/content/uses-technologies-communications-surveillance-utic. The main results can be found in Bigo, 2019a, 2019b; Bigo & Bonelli, 2019.
3 As Rob Walker explains in his book in the first chapter, "One great difficulty posed by the modern international in this context is that it (modern international) arguably emerged historically precisely as an alternative to imperial forms of hierarchical authority, sometimes theologically ordained, and as an affirmation of principles of pluralism, autonomy and even self-determination; or at least this is has become our standard retrospective understanding of what must have happened at some rather elusive point. Like the modern state and modern nation, the modern international expresses ambitions for secular principles of liberty and equality rather than hierarchy and subordination. Whatever we might suppose we refer to when using the concept of an international, it is not a universal empire, though it has certainly provided opportunities for many universalizing empires" (2017: 19).
4 For a discussion of centripetal and centrifugal dynamics, see Bigo, 2016c.

References

Aas, K. F. (2012). (In)Security-at-a-Distance: Rescaling Justice, Risk and Warfare in a Transnational Age. *Global Crime*, *13*(4), 235–253.

Albert, M., & Buzan, B. (2013). International Relations Theory and the 'Social Whole': Encounters and Gaps Between IR and Sociology. *International Political Sociology, 7*(2), 117–135.

Algan, Y., Guriev, S., Papaioannou, E., & Passari, E. (2017). The European Trust Crisis and the Rise of Populism. *Brookings Papers on Economic Activity,* 2017(2).

Aradau, C., & Huysmans, J. (2016). Performing Methods. In T. Basara, D. Bigo, E.-P. Guittet, & R. B. J. Walker (Eds.), *International Political Sociology: Transversal Lines* (pp. 126–144). Abingdon: Routledge.

Basaran, T., Bigo, D., Guittet, E.-P., & Walker, R. B. J. (Eds.). (2016). *International Political Sociology: Transversal Lines*. Abingdon: Routledge.

Bauman, Z., Bigo, D., Esteves, P., Guild, E., Jabri, V., Lyon, D., & Walker, R. B. J. (2014). After Snowden: Rethinking the Impact of Surveillance. *International Political Sociology, 8*(2), 121–144.

Berlet, C. (2011). Taking Tea Parties Seriously: Corporate Globalization, Populism, and Resentment. *Perspectives on Global Development and Technology, 10*(1), 11–29.

Berling, T. V. (2012). Bourdieu, International Relations, and European Security. *Theory and Society, 41*(5), 451–478.

Bigo, D. (2000). When Two Become One: Internal and External Securitisations in Europe. In M. C. Williams & M. Kelstrup (Eds.), *International Relations Theory and the Politics of European Integration, Power, Security and Community* (pp. 171–205). London: Routledge.

Bigo, D. (2002). Security and Immigration: Toward a Critique of the Governmentality of Unease. *Alternatives: Global, Local, Political, 27*(Supplement 1), 63–92.

Bigo, D. (2012). Analysing Transnational Professionals of (In)security in Europe. In R. Adler-Nissen (Ed.), *Bourdieu in International Relations: Rethinking Key Concepts in IR* (pp. 114–136). London: Routledge.

Bigo, D. (2016a). Digital Surveillance and Everyday Democracy. In L. Weber, E. Fishwick & M. Marmo (Eds.), *The Routledge International Handbook of Criminology and Human Rights* (pp. 496–510). London: Routledge.

Bigo, D. (2016b). International Political Sociology: Rethinking the International Through Dynamics of Power. In T. Basaran, D. Bigo, E.-P. Guittet & R. B. J. Walker (Eds.), *International Political Sociology: Transversal Lines* (pp. 24–48). Abingdon: Routledge.

Bigo, D. (2016c). Sociology of Transnational Guilds. *International Political Sociology, 10*(4), 398–416.

Bigo, D. (2018). Dramaturgy of Suspicion and the Emergence of a Transnational Guild of Extraction of Information by Torture at a Distance. In E. Guild, D. Bigo & M. Gibney (Eds.), *Extraordinary Rendition: Addressing the Challenges of Accountability* (pp. 30–52). London: Routledge.

Bigo, D. (2019a). Shared Secrecy in a Digital Age and a Transnational World. *Intelligence and National Security, 34*(3), 379–394.

Bigo, D. (2019b). Beyond National Security, the Emergence of a Digital Reason of State(s) Led by Transnational Guilds of Sensitive Information: The Case of the Five Eyes Plus Network. In B. Wagner, M. C. Kettemann & K. Vieth (Eds.), *Research Handbook on Human Rights and Digital Technology* (pp. 33–52). Cheltenham: Edward Elgar.

Bigo, D., & Bonelli, L. (2019). Digital Data and the Transnational Intelligence Space. In D. Bigo, E. Isin & E. Ruppert (Eds.), *Data Politics: Worlds, Subjects, Rights* (pp. 100–122). London: Routledge.

Bigo, D., & Delmas-Marty, M. (2012). *Prédiction et Prévention: Conversation at the New York Library*. New York, NY: New York Public Library.

Bigo, D., & Madsen, M. R. (2011). Introduction to Symposium 'A Different Reading of the International': Pierre Bourdieu and International Studies. *International Political Sociology, 5*(3), 219–224.

Bonditti, P., & Olsson, C. (2016). Violence, War and Security Knowledge: Between Practical Theories and Theoretical Practices. In T. Basara, D. Bigo, E.-P. Guittet & R. B. J. Walker (Eds.), *International Political Sociology: Transversal Lines* (pp. 228–253). Abingdon: Routledge.

Bourdieu, P. (1993). Esprits d'Etat: Genèse et Structure du Champ Bureaucratique. *Actes de la Recherche en Sciences Sociales, 96*(1), 49–62.

Bourdieu, P. (2004). From the King's House to the Reason of State: A Model of the Genesis of the Bureaucratic Field. *Constellations, 11*(1), 16–36.

Bourdieu, P. (2012). *Discussions on "Sur l'Etat: Cours au Collège de France1989–1992"*. Website for persons attending the course Bastien. Retrieved August 1, 2016, from www.dialogus2.org/BOU/votredefinitiondeletat.html

Bourdieu, P. (2014). *On the State: Lectures at the Collège de France 1989–1992*. Cambridge: Polity Press.

Bourdieu, P., Christin, O., & Will, P.-E. (2000). Sur La Science de l'État. *Actes de la Recherche en Sciences Sociales, 133*(1), 3–11.

Bourdieu, P., Wacquant, L. J. D., & Farage, S. (1994). Rethinking the State: Genesis and Structure of the Bureaucratic Field. *Sociological Theory, 12*(1), 1–18.

Buzan, B. (2004). *From International to World Society? English School Theory and the Social Structure of Globalisation*. Cambridge: Cambridge University Press.

Cerny, P. G. (2012). Globalization and the Transformation of Power. In M. Haugaard & K. Ryan (Eds.), *Political Power: The Development of the Field* (pp. 185–213). Toronto: Barbara Budrich Publishers.

Charalambous, C., Charalambous, P., Khan, K., & Rampton, B. (2016). Security and Language Policy. In J. W. Tollefson & M. Pérez-Milans (Eds.), *The Oxford Handbook of Language Policy and Planning* (pp. 633–653). Oxford: Oxford University Press.

Cohen, A. (2011). Bourdieu Hits Brussels: The Genesis and Structure of the European Field of Power. *International Political Sociology, 5*(3), 335–339.

Cohen, A., Dezalay, Y., & Marchetti, D. (2007). Esprits d'État, entrepreneurs d'Europe. *Actes de la Recherche en Sciences Sociales, 166–167*(1), 5–13.

Delmas-Marty, M. (2010). *Libertés et Sûreté Dans Un Monde Dangereux*. Paris: Le Seuil.

Derrida, J. (1994). *Force de Loi: Le 'Fondement Mystique de l'Autorité'*. Paris: Galilée.

Dezalay, Y. (2004). Les Courtiers de l'International: Héritiers Cosmopolites, Mercenaires de l'Impérialisme et Missionnaires de l'Universel. *Actes de la Recherche en Sciences Sociales, 151–152*(1), 4–35.

Dezalay, Y., & Garth, B. G. (2002). *The Internationalization of Palace Wars: Lawyers, Economists, and the Contest to Transform Latin American States*. Chicago, IL: University of Chicago Press.

Dezalay, Y., & Madsen, M. R. (2012). The Force of Law and Lawyers: Pierre Bourdieu and the Reflexive Sociology of Law. *Annual Review of Law and Social Science, 8*, 433–452.

Georgakakis, D., & Rowell, J. (2013). *The Field of Eurocracy: Mapping EU Actors and Professionals*. London: Springer.

Georgakakis, D., & Weisbein, J. (2010). From Above and from Below: A Political Sociology of European Actors. *Comparative European Politics, 8*(1), 93–109.

Gheciu, A., & Wohlforth, W. C. (2018). *The Oxford Handbook of International Security*. Oxford: Oxford University Press.

Go, J., & Krause, M. (2016). Fielding Transnationalism: An Introduction. *The Sociological Review*, *64*(Supplement 2), 6–30.

Gorski, P. S. (2013). *Bourdieu and Historical Analysis*. Durham, NC: Duke University Press.

Guild, E., Bigo, D., & Gibney, M. (2018). *Extraordinary Rendition: Addressing the Challenges of Accountability*. London: Routledge.

Guillaume, X. (2016). *Routledge Handbook of International Political Sociology*. London: Routledge.

Harcourt, B. E. (2006). *Against Prediction: Profiling, Policing, and Punishing in an Actuarial Age* (New ed.). Chicago, IL: University of Chicago Press.

Harvey, D. (2005). *A Brief History of Neoliberalism*. Oxford: Oxford University Press.

Hudson, B., & Ugelvik, S. (2013). *Justice and Security in the 21st Century: Risks, Rights and the Rule of Law*. London: Routledge.

Huysmans, J., & Nogueira, J. P. (2016). Ten Years of IPS: Fracturing IR. *International Political Sociology*, *10*(4), 299–319.

Jensen, C. J. III, McElreath, D. H., & Graves, M. (2018). *Introduction to Intelligence Studies*. London: Routledge.

Kauppi, N. (Ed.). (2013). *A Political Sociology of Transnational Europe*. Essex: ECPR Press.

Kauppi, N., & Madsen, M. R. (2013). Postscript: Understanding Transnational Power Elites, Understanding Europe in the New World Order. In N. Kauppi & M. R. Madsen (Eds.), *Transnational Power Elites: The New Professionals of Governance, Law and Security* (pp. 207–212). London: Routledge.

Keohane, R. O., & Nye, J. S. (1987). Power and Interdependence Revisited. *International Organization*, *41*(4), 725–753.

Krasner, S. D. (1999). *Sovereignty: Organized Hypocrisy*. Princeton, NJ: Princeton University Press.

Lahire, B. (2001). *Le Travail Sociologique de Pierre Bourdieu*. Paris: Seuil.

Lahire, B. (2012). *Monde Pluriel: Penser l'Unité des Sciences Sociales*. Paris: Seuil.

Lapid, Y. (1989). The Third Debate: On the Prospects of International Theory in a Post-Positivist Era. *International Studies Quarterly*, *33*(3), 235–254.

Latour, B. (2012). *We Have Never Been Modern*. Cambridge, MA: Harvard University Press.

Liesbet, H., & Gary, M. (2003). Unraveling the Central State, but How? Types of Multi-Level Governance. *American Political Science Review*, *97*(2), 233–243.

Loader, I. (1997). Policing and the Social: Questions of Symbolic Power. *The British Journal of Sociology*, *48*(1), 1–18.

Madsen, M. R. (2011a). *La genèse de l'Europe des droits de l'homme: enjeux jruidiques et strategies d'etat (France, Grande-Bretagne et Pays Scandinaves, 1945–1970)*. Strasbourg: Presses Universitaires deStrasbourg.

Madsen, M. R. (2011b). Reflexivity and the Construction of the International Object: The Case of Human Rights. *International Political Sociology*, *5*(3), 259–275.

Martin-Mazé, M. (2017). Returning Struggles to the Practice Turn: How Were Bourdieu and Boltanski Lost in (Some) Translations and What to Do About It? *International Political Sociology*, *11*(2), 203–220.

Mérand, F. (2010). Pierre Bourdieu and the Birth of European Defense. *Security Studies*, *19*(2), 342–374.

Mérand, F., & Pouliot, V. (2008). Le Monde de Pierre Bourdieu: Éléments pour une Théorie Sociale des Relations Internationales. *Canadian Journal of Political Science, 41*(3), 603–625.

Negri, A., & Hardt, M. (2001). *Empire*. Cambridge, MA: Harvard University Press.

Nye, J. S., & Keohane, R. O. (1971). Transnational Relations and World Politics: A Conclusion. *International Organization, 25*(3), 721–748.

Paulle, B., van Heerikhuizen, B., & Emirbayer, M. (2012). Elias and Bourdieu. *Journal of Classical Sociology, 12*(1), 69–93.

Rampton, B. (2016). Foucault, Gumperz and Governmentality: Interaction, Power and Subjectivity in the Twenty-First Century. In N. Coupland (Ed.), *Sociolinguistics: Theoretical Debates* (pp. 303–328). Cambridge: Cambridge University Press.

Robinson, W. I. (1998). Beyond Nation-State Paradigms: Globalization, Sociology, and the Challenge of Transnational Studies. *Sociological Forum, 13*(4), 561–594.

Rodrik, D. (2018). Populism and the Economics of Globalization. *Journal of International Business Policy, 1*(1–2), 12–33.

Rosenau, J. N. (1990). *Turbulence in World Politics: A Theory of Change and Continuity*. Princeton, NJ: Princeton University Press.

Sayad, A., & Bourdieu, P. (1991). *L'Immigration Ou Les Paradoxes de l'Altérité*. Brussels: De Boeck Université.

Schulze, M. (2015). Patterns of Surveillance Legitimization: The German Discourse on the NSA Scandal. *Surveillance & Society, 13*(2), 197–217.

Shapiro, M. J. (2002). Bourdieu, the State and Method. *Review of International Political Economy, 9*(4), 610–618.

Slaughter, A.-M. (2004). *A New World Order*. Princeton, NJ: Princeton University Press.

Slaughter, A.-M., & Hale, T. N. (2010). Transgovernmental Networks and Multi-Level Governance. In H. Enderlein, S. Walti & M. Zürn (Eds.), *Handbook on Multi-Level Governance* (pp. 358–369). Cheltenham: Edward Elgar.

Swank, D., & Betz, H.-G. (2003). Globalization, the Welfare State and Right-Wing Populism in Western Europe. *Socio-Economic Review, 1*(2), 215–245.

Tilly, C. (1990). *Coercion, Capital, and European States*. Malden, MA: Blackwell.

Vauchez, A. (2008). The Force of a Weak Field: Law and Lawyers in the Government of the European Union (for a Renewed Research Agenda). *International Political Sociology, 2*(2), 128–144.

Wacquant, L. (2009). *Punishing the Poor: The Neoliberal Government of Social Insecurity*. Durham, NC: Duke University Press.

Walker, R. B. J. (2009). *After the Globe, Before the World*. London: Routledge.

Walker, R. B. J. (2017). Only Connected: International, Political, Sociology. In T. Basara, D. Bigo, E.-P. Guittet & R. B. J. Walker (Eds.), *International Political Sociology: Transversal Lines* (pp. 13–23). Abingdon: Routledge.

Zedner, L. (2010). Security, the State, and the Citizen: The Changing Architecture of Crime Control. *New Criminal Law Review: An International and Interdisciplinary Journal, 13*(2), 379–403.

Chapter 4

National, international, transnational, and global fields

Theoretical clarifications and methodological implications

Andreas Schmitz and Daniel Witte

Introduction

In recent times, the analytical potential of Bourdieusian theory has been impressively exemplified by research on numerous phenomena both "across" and "beyond" the nation-state (e.g., Vauchez, 2008; Kauppi & Madsen, 2013; Buchholz, 2013; Schneickert, 2015; Go & Krause, 2016; Schmidt-Wellenburg, 2017). As a whole, the ever-expanding body of work indicates that this approach might enable sociology to transcend the division of labor in contemporary theorizing, which treats globality either as a horizon of the diffusion of meaning (e.g., in Luhmann, 1982, 1997) or as a structure of power and domination (e.g., in Wallerstein, 1974, 2004). Yet the very proliferation of empirical studies inspired by Bourdieusian space/field theory may considerably overburden the theory in its original form (Wacquant, 1996: 151; cp. Buchholz, 2016; Schmitz & Witte, 2017; Atkinson, 2019). In order to reveal this theory's full analytical strength, we shall contribute a systematic discussion of the foundations upon which recent works rely when empirically investigating international, transnational, and global phenomena. For the purpose of remedying the restrictions that are inherent to Bourdieu's concepts, we shall neither resort to orthodox interpretations nor to eclectic accounts; we will instead apply a comprehensive strategy by rigorously adhering to the fundamental theoretical and methodological premise immanent in Bourdieusian theory, namely *relationalism* (cp. Witte et al., 2017). Relational reasoning rejects *traditional dichotomies* (micro versus macro; power versus meaning; global versus national, etc.) that haunt (social) sciences, in favor of a genuinely anti-essentialist approach to knowledge production. Against this backdrop, we will develop a generalized analytical framework for research that refers to the concepts of field and space (cp. Schmitz, Witte, & Gengnagel, 2017) and address its core methodological implications for future empirical research.

Theoretical foundations

Epistemology

Space/field theory, first and foremost, means an *epistemological stance, namely to apply the notions of space or field to an aspect* of (social) reality that is assumed to exist, or *as a perspective* on (social) reality, thereby constructing the aspect itself (which, at its core, represents an analytical distinction between a more positivist and a more constructivist notion).[1] In both cases, the concepts of "field" or "space" serve as a priori for the production of (scientific) knowledge. Based on this premise, we may interpret and use the field-theoretical perspective in a rather positivistic way, in a radical-constructivist style, or in any manner that tries to moderate between these ideal-typical poles. This minimal consensus is important for our subsequent elaborations, as the particular conception of "field" or "space" varies between different researchers (and, in fact, "within" different researchers). Unspoken, hidden differences in the specific usages of the concept, however, are at the root of countless and sometimes severe misunderstandings.

It therefore follows that an epistemological understanding of the concept of field represents the most general usage of the term: It forms the basis from which all other notions can be derived, and which (logically and empirically) contains all other perspectives. This is a significant insight, as well as a point of departure for a generalized field theory: It curbs cognitive laziness, e.g., eclectically stating that different authors "simply have a different understanding of the concept of field", which can result in important theoretical issues being neglected. Such discussions, however, are not merely abstract: They allow and actually force us – as individual researchers and as scientific collectives – to reflect on the limitations of particular research designs and to systematically identify relevant aspects that have previously been ignored.

At this point, we shall specify the notion of space/field in its epistemological sense: *"Field" and "space" signify the attribution of a specific form and logic – relationality – to (social) reality.* By using the concept of field (or space), basically, the observer relates entities of any kind to one another and assumes a latent structure that empirically frames and integrates these entities (including processes of structured disintegration). Seen from this standpoint (which is the most general and, hence, most comprehensive one, thereby also *including* "realistic" or reifying notions of fields), neither subjects or objects, nor actors or structures, constitute the starting point of sociological thinking, but *the very idea of relationality and the corresponding operation of "relating"* (cp. Vandenberghe, 1999; Martin, 2003; Witte, Schmitz, & Schmidt-Wellenburg, 2017).

Moreover, field analysis implies *the objectification of space/field structures* and the identification of mechanisms that are characteristic for the particular field or space in question. Yet, if we apply a constructivist notion, the *extent* to which a certain field or space actually relates particular entities, i.e. the question of its degree of "fieldness" or "spaceness", is brought to the fore. Thus, *the very existence or non-existence of a "field" or "space" itself is a relational question.* Just like social classes, which both exist and do not exist at the same time (Bourdieu, 1987a), social fields and spaces are constructions, yet constructions that are – in varying degrees – well founded in reality.[2]

Social space, the field of power, and the generalized field of power

In order to derive a comprehensive analytical approach to the realm of the "global" and of global phenomena, we shall now discuss, elaborate, and refine the structure of Bourdieu's theoretical framework. In this approach, the concept of "social space" is used as the equivalent to a notion of *society at large*. Its purpose is to conceptualize the overarching structures of society, especially in the sense of (national) capital distributions and class relations. The objective structures of social space inscribe themselves in the cognitive structures of actors, who perceive the social world through these structures and contribute to their transformation and reproduction by way of their practice. Bourdieu conceives of these phenomena as relations of symbolic power between actors that underlie both the reproduction and transformations of the social world. The concept of "field" refers to the construction or assumption of a differentiated, distinct social sphere which displays a certain *degree of ("relative") autonomy*, which is structured along a number of distinct dimensions (capital forms), and which comprises and, potentially, partially integrates ("*einbeziehen*") a set of entities (e.g., human actors), as well as their practices and effects. The field's relative autonomy indicates the operation of a certain *nomos*, which is associated with a certain field-specific interest and a corresponding *illusio*. The interrelation between social spaces (in the sense of societal totalities) and social fields (in the sense of societal segments) has, for the most part, been neglected or discussed unsystematically (cp. Witte, 2014: 93 ff.; Schmitz et al., 2017). This is all the more problematic in the context of Bourdieu's second notion for society at large, namely the *field-theoretical* concept that he proposed to analytically frame not only social fields separately, but – crucially – with regard to their interrelations.

While the social space functions as a concept for "society" from the perspective of social inequalities and class structures, *the field of power has an analogous function from the perspective of field theory*. Following Bourdieu, the first step of field analysis consists in locating the field in question within the field of power (Bourdieu & Wacquant, 1992: 104). This field of power comprises three aspects that can be analytically differentiated in Bourdieu's works: It is 1) defined as the sphere of encounter, interaction, or interdependence of different field elites; 2) equated with the nation-state; or 3) conceived of as a "meta-field" in which power balances between differentiated fields are negotiated. With regard to the *first* usage, it comprises phenomena and processes that are of particular relevance for the sociology of elites (Kauppi & Madsen, 2013; Schneickert, 2015), thus functioning as a more differentiated term for the Marxist concept of a "ruling class" (Wacquant, 1993). This, however – and in contrast to Bourdieu's relational concept of "power" – tends to neglect other actors such as those belonging to dominated classes (and thereby large parts of those very actors that are included in the social space concept) (cp. Schmitz et al., 2017). The *second* notion, in turn, allows for the state to be conceptualized as a contested battlefield, yet it simultaneously limits the concept of the field of power to the analysis of the state and its (bureaucratic) institutions and, hence, – again – to a narrow set of research questions. Considering these limitations, the *third* understanding appears to be the broadest and theoretically most promising one: As a comprehensive meta-field, the field of power is thought of as a frame for all social fields and their interrelations. However, even in this form, this meta-field is conceptualized as a national space by Bourdieu: just like class relations are framed by national social spaces, field relations are almost naturally located within national fields of power. Thus, a strong emphasis on the nation-state prevails: for Bourdieu, it seems to represent the key setting for central mechanisms of guaranteeing, maintaining, and reproducing social order. Shaped by the sociohistorical contexts in which his own research questions were located, the ensemble of administrative and bureaucratic fields is thought of as possessing the monopoly on legitimate symbolic violence and the power to render it universal (Bourdieu & Wacquant, 1996). In the last instance, thus, it is the nation-state which guarantees the relative autonomy of social fields, but which is also constitutive for field-internal processes. Ultimately, the state is even constitutive for the cognitive and moral integration of societies, hence operating as a functional requirement for the field of power (Riley, 2015: 263) as well as for Bourdieu's social space concept (cp. Schmitz & Witte, 2017).

However, and given the vast amount of empirical research "beyond the nation-state", *both conceptualizations – the national social space and the national field of power – are deficient*. The field of power is conceptualized via the limits and borders of the nation-state – as is the social space (Weiss, 2005), rendering the concepts nation-state, social space, and "society" virtually identical – thus making it susceptible to criticisms of methodological nationalism (Wimmer & Glick Schiller, 2002; Beck & Grande, 2010). The assignment of core theoretical functions to the nation-state (or to a national social space) obscures those processes and phenomena that may take place between, below, above, or beyond nation-states. The national framing of the field of power and the social space seem thus to neglect the *historical implications of societalization*. We may highlight two ideal-typical examples here: The birth of the nation is often associated with the Treaty of Westphalia, the result of the great European war between different empires, religions, and ethnicities.[3] Whether one accepts this epochalization or not (cp. Steinmetz, 2016), it is plain to see that societies, social classes (or groups), and even (some of) the social fields that we focus on nowadays were indeed related – and ultimately even integrated – *before* the emergence of the nation-state. In fact, the Roman Empire can be said to have been fulfilling some of the core functions that Bourdieu assigned to the modern nation-state, and principally, the same applies to developments of societies in late modernity. If, for example, the United States and China today are labeled as modern empires rather than nation-states, they still can be understood as national fields of power (cp. Go, 2011). Furthermore, an overly strong focus on nation-states and/or other national actors tends to neglect *the ever-increasing relevance of other types of entities* such as international organizations, corporations, networks, or political movements (cp. Bourdieu, 2005: 223 ff.). Similarly, important processes such as, inter alia, migration, global communication, or global class formation, may easily be claimed and observed, but constitute severe problems for an overly orthodox conception of either the field of power or the social space. Ultimately, *the very epistemological foundations of space/field theory run the risk of disintegration* by devoting themselves to this approach: Schinkel (2015) rightfully characterizes the nation-state as an epistemic guarantee, even, for Bourdieu's theory, as it is assumed to be so pivotal for the construction of symbolic orders and social realities which the sociologist, then, tries to transcend by taking a "meta-meta" position. Empirically, however, there is ample evidence that the categories of thinking today are (and, in fact, always have been) provided by more instances than merely the nation-state, just as the material resources crucial for scientific autonomy and practice are provided not only by nation-states but also by a plurality of other fields.

Obviously, for the purpose of systematically addressing phenomena across and beyond the nation-state, Bourdieu's concepts are insufficient (at least when used in an overly orthodox way). In light of the prevailing empirical phenomena, as well as the theoretical problems outlined, categorically identifying the field of power (or *meta-field*) with the nation-state, and identifying the social space with national societies, conflicts with the current requirements of social sciences, which profess to investigate transnational and global phenomena. Consequently, in light of the fundamental restrictions that Bourdieusian theory in its original form exhibits, a more theoretically abstract concept – an analytically functional equivalent to the national social space and the national field of power – is needed. At the same time, such a concept should be able to clarify the relationship between the two concepts of the social space and the field of power.

In order to address these problems, two general theoretical conditions of the concept of the field of power shall be discussed. 1) The plurality of fields is a crucial element of the overall theoretical architecture: social fields do not possess a *relative autonomy* as such, but always *in relation* to other fields (i.e., ultimately, to the social space). As social fields always also entail *relative heteronomies*, we can derive by definition that they are also affected and structured by other fields (or even by "extra-social" factors). Thus, *heteronomy has to be regarded a basic condition for both the operation and structure of a particular field*, and for its reconstruction by the sociological observer. In a fundamental sense, a field (say, science) can be understood as being *embedded in all other fields* and (to an extent which has to be determined by research) as potentially *structured by all other fields*, just as the field can be a structuring instance within the field of power.

2) *Defining a field by its "natural" actors* (e.g., "scientists *are situated in* the field of science", or "the field of science *consists of* scientists") *is a problematic approach:* Any field comprises a plurality of actors that are associated with other fields (e.g., bureaucrats, economic agents, etc.) but who (for that very reason) are relevant to the field's structure and functioning. A more general and theoretically stringent definition is the one that Bourdieu and Wacquant (1992: 100) have given, thereby providing us

with an important orientation: *the boundaries of a field are to be localized where its field effects cease*. This issue of boundaries is also of consequence for the definition of actors themselves: Given the ineluctable role that the logics of relationality and heteronomy play for field theory, any empirical entity, as "pure" as it may appear, has to *be treated as principally "hybrid"*. Whereas this argument is not reserved to (human) actors, their hybridity constitutes one important example for the interrelation between the field of power and the social space within our framework.

It is against this backdrop that we have defined the field of power as a field of fields, i.e. as a general "perspective on the social space which focuses on field effects and field-specific practices in the context of their interdependencies" (Schmitz et al., 2017: 69). The field of power, in this generalized sense, is an actual and effective meta-field, as no single social field is seen as the ultimate frame of reference, but rather the relational interdependency between social fields as such. Whereas the term "power" may suggest a rather narrow understanding of the nature of the social, it is worth remembering here that social fields are to be described not only by their power relations, but at the same time by their internal structures of meaning; the generalized field of power, accordingly, is always and necessarily also a field of meaning relations.

As a consequence, the social space concept is "harmonized" with field theory in general and with the field of power in particular: firstly, since the epistemological relation between both concepts has been revealed and defined; secondly, insofar as the generalized field of power comprises the same range of entities (such as human actors) as the social space does; and thirdly, because it paves the way for systematically integrating concepts of field theory and social space theory (such as field effects on the social space, class effects on social fields, the relation between certain capital forms and social fields, etc.).

From the nation-state to the global space and the global field of power/meaning

According to the specific empirical questions under investigation, the generalized field of power and the social space can take different forms. As we shall argue, the generalized field of power, as a meta-field, can be translated into the analytical forms necessary for a) (re)thinking the nation-state, b) analyzing international fields or spaces, and c) examining supranational and subnational fields or spaces. In a final step, we will discuss the widest possible system of reference, namely (d) the "global field of power/meaning" and its relation to a concept of "global social space".

Rethinking the nation-state

After several decades of sociological debate over "transnationalization" and the "global age", the question still remains open as to how to systematically think of the empirical and analytical role of the nation-state as a structured and structuring principle in world society (with some authors having already dismissed it almost entirely, and others maintaining it as a still ineluctable – and often even unquestioned – point of reference). In this context, our previous considerations *bear important consequences*, as a given nation-state (say, France) may not only be understood as an embedding instance that has the function of framing the field of power/meaning, but also as being itself embedded into it. The nation-state, in this sense, just as science or any other field, must be understood as a field *within* the field of power/meaning and, by implication, needs to be understood as being affected and structured by different social fields. Depending on the case at hand, it may then appear as a strongly dominated social field (think of states that are described as, e.g., "failed", "religiously dominated", or "dynastically struc-tured"). As a result of our approach, however, a wide variety of different forms of statehood has to be acknowledged beyond the narrow "Western" notion of the nation-state, which – just as any form of societal organization – emerged from a particular figuration of social fields (such as a relatively autonomous field of law and a religious field with weak autonomy). An essentially normative, Western stance, however, tends to blur the latent structural similarities between Western European states strongly affected by a powerful legal corps and, for example, the state of Iran that is "problematically" and "inadequately" dominated by religious actors (not even to mention the "natural" legitimacy that the economic field's impact has in capitalist societies). Thus, and from a formal point of view, ascrip-tions such as "failure", "weakness", or "dysfunctionality" can be understood as exertions of symbolic power in that they reject specific forms of influence over the nation-state while accepting or naturalizing others.

As a result, the nation-state can no longer be conceived of as the exclusive guar-antor of symbolic order, but rather as one competing principle (with a *state doxa*, a *state nomos*, and a *state illusio*, even a *national habitus* in this specific sense, etc.) amongst others. The (or: *a*) nation-state, then, constitutes an important field that affects, structures, and maybe sometimes even dominates other fields. Yet, this relation is in fact subject to change. For example, scientific fields today are at the same time (perhaps even to a larger extent) affected by the economic field, just as they had once been specifically structured by the religious field, render-ing the impact of the nation-state a merely relative one (Gengnagel, Schmitz, & Witte, 2016).

From the arguments of heteronomy, plurality, and historicity it further follows that the field of the nation-state *cannot be reduced to purely "national" or "stat-ist" traits* (such as in a reductive definition of the state as a bureaucratic ensem-ble). On the contrary, what can be perceived as a nation-state is at the same time affected and structured by different social fields such as economy, science, etc., which ultimately cannot be defined as nationally bounded entities themselves. We may accordingly contend that social fields, when defined via the extent of their effects, are already by definition "transnational" in the sense that their *effects* do not simply cease to exist at national borders. Certainly, there may be many empirical cases in which a nation-state can defend its *plural (geographic, insti-tutional, cultural, etc.) boundaries* against external influences to a great extent.

However, such defense is never fully realized (for instance, even North Korea is affected by the global economy and culture). *Empirically*, one may then examine how globally circulating entities (Bourdieu, 2002; cp. Atkinson, 2019) are incorporated, translated, or transformed in particular ways that could be labeled as "cultural patterns (or mechanisms) of appropriation". At the same time, mechanisms of keeping heteronomous influences outside of a field or of translating them into the field's specific structuring principles cannot only be observed in nation-states. On the contrary, *every* social field can (and usually tries to) at least partially block external influences, just as it may (partially) exert its own logic (i.e., nomos and doxa) on field-external goods, symbols, norms, etc. In such processes, they often may become constitutive parts of a given field, which are more or less refracted by the field's inner logic. *Analytically*, one crucial lesson for the sociology of transnational fields can be drawn from this shift of perspective: in a certain sense, fields are always, and have always been, "transnational" – not only regarding their effects, but also with regard to the external influences they experience and internalize, influences that cannot be said to be purely or even largely "national". Consequently, as a field that is affected and structured by a plurality of other fields which cannot themselves be defined via national borders, even the nation-state itself might be understood – at least in a certain sense – as a "transnational" entity from the outset. At the same time, and because the nation-state's very own effects do not end at the official ('territorial") borders either, the nation-state can also be treated as "transnational" in its consequences. To repeat this counterintuitive insight: *With regard to both its structuration and its effects, the nation-state itself constitutes a transnational field.*

By rethinking the state along these lines, *the concept of the nation-state, in comparison to Bourdieu's own version, is "generalized" even further*: as this field cannot be reduced to its elites and main institutions, as Bourdieu tends to do, we should also take into account the "field of consumption of national goods", i.e., the citizens and "national laymen" who – by way of their self-conceptions and/ or by way of the normative power of national inclusion – are equally part of the national field of power. This is *not* to say that we define the field via its actors, as criticized above. Rather, we emphasize the trivial fact that a particular nation-state "consists" of effects that involve and affect a population much larger than political and institutional elites alone.[4]

The question, then, is *to what extent actors can be described in terms of being affected by national fields.* Let us name but a few examples: An inhabitant of a colonialized society is surely affected by the colonializing national field; but the military representative of this field will also have a high chance of being affected by it, as the national field is likely to have contributed to the structure of his habitus and *doxa* (this is precisely what Bourdieu, 2014 labels "state-thinking"). Similarly, the heretic German "Reich Citizens' Movement" (*Reichsbürger*)[5] questions the legitimacy of the modern-day German Federal Republic while at the same time referring to the German nation and constitution (or to some nations within Germany), thereby constituting what could be understood as a heterodox pole in the national field. Thus, to say that actors live in the territory of a nation-state or are part of its people does not necessarily entail the actors' strong belief in (or cathexis towards) this field.[6] By implication, field theory should analytically distinguish between national fields and state fields, which, among other things, allows us to conceptualize processes by which ethnic groups autonomize themselves from an overarching state field, or processes of subjugation of ethnic minorities under the dominance of an emerging state.

Based on our elaborations, it is now also possible to differentiate between the various external references against which a nation-state tries to define and defend its (physical and social) borders, on the one hand, and the varying degrees to which it is capable of doing so, on the other. For example, Bourdieu (1985) raised the question as to whether a Belgian field of literature "existed" at all. Of course one could analyze a Belgian field of literature, because literature is produced in Belgium and by writers of Belgian origin – just as a Belgian bureaucracy, a Belgian football league, or a Belgian army "exists", so does Belgian literature which, hence, can also be assessed in terms of a field. However, what Bourdieu illustrates is that French-speaking Belgian writers are oriented towards French culture and markets to such an extent that no autonomous Belgian field could be said to "exist" in the sense that no sufficient national autonomy of the Belgian field of literature can be "observed" (i.e., constructed) which, in turn, shows that the (Belgian) nation-state does not structure all social fields to the same extent. This in itself may not be an overly surprising finding, but – as the state of Belgium may well control other spheres more efficiently (such as the military field) – it exemplifies the fact that a certain "national" field can be described in terms of its diverging capabilities to secure its various field borders. In a more general way, this culminates in examining the extent to which a nation-state field succeeds in enforcing its own *nomos*, i.e., in imposing its boundaries on other fields and establishing a certain level of congruency between them (i.e., "homology"), while other nation-state fields (say, Afghanistan) may be dominated by different (trans-) national fields to such an extent that they can hardly control any geographical and institutional areas beyond some sections of their capital city.

This, in turn, leads to important ramifications: In the debate over "transnationalization", a recurring question deals with the "existence" or "nonexistence" of transnational fields (or, for that matter, transnational habitus, etc.). Such questions, based on a deeply engrained essentialist *doxa, misconstrue the relational principles as well as the constructivist potential of field theory.* Consequently, we would be well-advised to replace such problem formulations with questions such as: *In which sense –* or: *to what degree –* "is" a field X (say, economy) national *and* transnational, respectively (i.e., to what degree can it be treated as such)? A field (but also, e.g., a discourse or network), in this sense, "is" (i.e., can be treated as) transnational to the extent to which it possesses strong autonomy relative to a) a certain national field, or b) any national field, or c) the field of nation-states. From this perspective, we may, for example, identify national and transnational poles of a field and analyze their antagonistic interdependence, or assess the most relevant reference systems (i.e., fields) that structure their corresponding internal and external habitual conditions of practice. By shifting the focus in this way, one may identify many cases of habitus being strongly structured by mechanisms that are often subsumed under the term "transnationality": beginning with practices and ideas that are dominantly transnational (such as certain patterns of consumption or communication), to an internalized belief in the value of the "transnational" (which often goes hand in hand with the devaluation of the national), and to a *doxa* which may even replace "state thinking" with "global thinking" (this, ultimately, has become known as "cosmopolitanism" in a certain sense). Here, an old motive proposed by Elias (1996) can be revived in this light and may be integrated into Bourdieu's theory, namely the concept of "national habitus". At the same time, it should have become clear by this point that neither "nationality" nor "transnationality" is essentialized within our framework: a certain habitus may incorporate more or fewer national or transnational dispositions, but it is never an entirely transnational or global habitus, just as it is never exclusively a national, a female, or an economic habitus. The epistemological clarifications provided above are pivotal here: of course, we may construct (or reconstruct) the specificities of an "academic habitus", for example to describe the differences between two actors from different social classes or in order to elaborate the ideal-typical logic of the scientific field – and the same holds true, of course, for the question of whether a given actor's habitus is dominantly characterized by either "national" or "transnational" dispositions. However, pragmatic arguments for the reduction of complexity in concrete research projects should not be confused with exhaustive statements about theoretical (axiomatic) fundamentals. The simplest example can be found in the academic habitus again: The dispositional systems of two randomly chosen professors will probably differ to a considerable extent, depending on their class background and trajectories, on their gender, age, subject area, positions in various fields (including, yet not limited to, the academic field), etc. (cp. Bourdieu, 1991). Certainly, the same can be said about national or transnational habitus: the extent, the form, and the degree to which "nationality" and "transnationality" are sedimented in a given habitus, and the answer to the question as to the different fields from which these dispositions stem, are a matter of research rather than of a priori definition.

International, supranational, and subnational fields and spaces

As it turns out, the nation-state, when conceptualized properly, may still prove a valuable point of reference for a political sociology of transnational fields. Yet, further questions remain with regard to the conceptualization of international, supranational, or subnational fields within this framework. To begin with, *"internationality"* here refers to a field of nations or national entities that can be constructed as relatively autonomous. We have to take into account, however, that this definition allows for at least three different approaches: 1) To treat and construct nations as (national) actors in an international field; 2) to treat and construct national fields in the traditional Bourdieusian way, in which their respective elites encounter and interact in an international field of power (i.e., a field of national or state elites); or 3) to treat and construct national fields, as previously outlined, in a consistently relational way, with national and state elites as well as national and state "laymen" interacting in an international field of power. It must be emphasized that all three approaches can be put into practice within the framework of a generalized field theory and that they all, indeed, represent valuable perspectives. For instance, Schmitz, Heiberger, and Blasius (2015) apply a field-theoretical approach, interpreting the international field of nation-states as an empirical outcome of the global field of power/meaning. Applying multiple factor analysis, they analyze an integrated data set from different social fields on country level and demonstrate that this international field can be described by two dimensions: meta-capital, and internal functionality or institutional capital. A core insight here is that the very applicability of the unit "nation-state" varies over this international field of power/meaning: Some countries (those with low meta-capital and low institutional capital) are nation-states in name only,[7] whereas others possess meta-capital and institutional capital on such a scale that they resemble empires more than nation-states in the classical sense.

Turning from relations between national fields to entities "above" and "below" the nation-state now, a *supranational* entity could be interpreted as a substitute for national fields of power in the Bourdieusian sense, so the "European field of power", for example, would take the role of these previously assumed national fields. Again, this would be one possible construction within generalized field theory as outlined here; however, the aforementioned problems regarding the narrow definition of the nation-state would merely be reproduced this way. How and why would we use the geographic and institutional borders of "Europe" as the definitional criterion? Are we not, in doing so, reproducing definitions and boundaries which were established in the political and juridical field, and which must instead be understood as field effects themselves? How could we then conceptualize in a systematic fashion the fact that the European Union is, in turn, affected and structured by other fields? Thus again, the most general approach is to analytically localize and relate a field of such supranational qualities to all other fields. Regarding the example of the European Union, this would motivate empirical questions for the actual *extent* of its autonomy as well as for the respective *references* of autonomy such as the economic field, cultural fields, but also national fields – the latter in at least two regards: firstly with respect to the concrete autonomy from those states that form the European Union, as well as from those that are outside this state coalition; and secondly with regard to autonomy from the abstract idea (*nomos, doxa*) of the nation-state, with low autonomy meaning the attempt here to merely form a "higher-level nation-state" out of the European Union.

The previous argumentation also paves the way for a reconsideration of the conceptualization of *sub-national* fields. Analytically, these could be differentiated into 1) sub-fields of a given nation and/or state field, 2) apparats of the nation-state field with little autonomy, and 3) local fields with a high degree of autonomy from the nation-state. This autonomy can empirically emerge in different ways: as the legally institutionalized autonomy of certain regions, in symbolic forms that may or may not correspond to political structures, or as a mere claim to autonomy that is entrenched in the habitus of the inhabitants of a region, etc. In any case, the degree of this autonomy has to be assessed in empirical research rather than by merely claiming it.

Global space and the global field of power/meaning

So far, we have used generalized field theory in order to conceptualize a range of (possible) empirical phenomena that cannot be framed within the idea of national social spaces or national fields of power in the orthodox sense. Yet, from the viewpoint of relationalism, the crucial question is how to define the field of power/ meaning if not via the nation-state or spontaneous substitutes that simply reproduce existing, well-known theoretical pitfalls. We hold that a solution to this task would also allow us to locate the aforementioned national, international, supranational, and subnational fields within a single analytical framework.

As we have previously argued, the nation-state (as well as the field of national elites) is too narrow a reference system, leading to a first important step, which was to reconceptualize the field of power as a "field of fields", i.e., as the system of reciprocal embedding of social fields in their totality. However, no single, contingent social field can be specified that would embed all other social fields. This can be derived from the definition given above: the meta-field – from a systematical point of view – is the sum of relations itself. Furthermore, as fields are defined by the range and scope of their effects, the boundaries of the field of power/meaning and the social space are congruent with the ones of (global) society. Accordingly, the field of power/meaning can no longer be conceptualized convincingly by drawing on any sort of geographic or institutional limitations; its effects – by definition – operate at any place in geographic space, as they reach as far as the effects of the different fields involved. *The field of power, by implication, has to be conceptualized as a global field in the last instance*, if one does not intend to assume that these field effects take place outside of society. Thus, the term "global" actually transports a twofold meaning here, referring to the globe (Earth) itself as well as to the widest possible reference that one could take into account when studying any phenomenon in question. If we remind ourselves of the basic propositions of generalized field theory, *the global field of power can now be understood as the field-analytical perspective on the global social space;* or, in other words: the global field of power and the global social space are merely two different perspectives on the same social reality. Empirical phenomena that one might traditionally conceptualize in terms of social space and class structures – such as "international classes" and classes of nation-states, etc. – can be re-conceptualized and thus analytically augmented by way of identifying those social fields that are involved in each case (the economic field, the field of nation-states, scientific fields, etc.). Yet, the same also applies in the opposite direction: For example, any analysis that may refer to a specific global field (again, say, economy) can and in fact must be understood in relation to structures of the global social space (e.g., as the extent to which the world population can be described as structured by class is both cause and consequence of the dynamics of global economy and a variety of other fields).

The global field of power, hence, can be regarded as a *true global meta-field*, i.e., as a field that does express relations of power *and* meaning, practice *and* structure, locality *and* globality, in equal measure. This is not to say that any phenomenon always has to be (or even could be) explained by referring to all other phenomena – it rather specifies the (epistemo)logically *widest possible frame of reference for space/field analysis*. Thus, the aforementioned aspects – "nation-states", "international fields", "supranational fields", etc. – can analytically be located *within* the global field of power/meaning (and, thus, within the global social space). Likewise, transnational fields (e.g., Go & Krause, 2016), trans-national movements (e.g., della Porta & Tarrow, 2005), transnational networks (e.g., Lubbers, Verdery, & Molina, 2018), transnational organizations (e.g., Djelic & Quack, 2003), transnational discourses (Mitchell, 1997), etc., in the last instance, are all *analytically embedded in the global field of power/meaning and the global social space*. In theoretical terms, they can thus be connected to a more systematic concept when compared with Bourdieu's original "sketch". Far from being a mere scholastic abstraction, our approach has far-reaching consequences for the conceptualization of current and future research. For example, it invites researchers to combine field theory with other concepts (such as "discourse" or "network"), thus providing them with a systematic yet flexible "search space" for the derivation of further research questions (e.g.: In what ways are transnational discourses involved in the constitution of transnational fields? How do transnational networks span national fields and contribute to their stability? How do discourses of globalization diffuse and reconstitute transnational networks? etc.). In doing so, "nationality", "internationality", "globality", etc., must no longer be thought of as logical and mutually exclusive opposites: We may easily think of national, anti-national, local, or any other traits that could be constitutive for any field in question. Eventually, considerations of this kind lead to questions of methodology and method that shall be discussed in the next section.

Questions of methodology

Our contribution pursued a twofold purpose: 1) to free Bourdieusian theory from restricted understandings of society "beyond", "below", and "across" nation-states; and 2) to thereby provide current empirical research with an integrative framework that – if understood relationally – motivates an entire set of further research perspectives. While the elaborations that were outlined here focus on issues of foundational theory, they also imply consequences relevant to methodology and empirical research.

First of all, the fact that we approach a certain ("transnational", "global", etc.) empirical phenomenon does anything but suspend the *principles of relational reasoning*; on the contrary, relational methodology is a scientific modus operandi that seems particularly suitable to such phenomena. Generalized field theory, as it turns out, redresses traditional dichotomies such as "meaning versus power", or "culture versus structure". This basic insight is of particular interest when we enter the global sphere, because both traditional and more current discourses on global sociality evidently reproduce these classical dichotomies. For instance, sociological accounts of transnationalization and globality often either rely on one-sided bottom-up *or* top-down approaches, thus focusing on *either* local practices *or* global structures. Likewise, while some authors tend to overemphasize the aspect of meaning, culture, and diffusion (Luhmann, 1982, 1997; Meyer, Boli, Thomas, & Ramirez, 1997; Meyer & Jeppersen, 2000), others one-sidedly focus on power, material resource structures, and conflict (e.g., Wallerstein, 1974, 2004). A generalized field theory, in contrast, allows us to transcend such false dichotomies: relational reasoning can enable sociology to gain a more integrated account of scientific knowledge than comparable theoretical projects that systematically obstruct themselves through self-imposed analytical restrictions.

While other contemporary paradigms in the social sciences seem to possess a remarkable a priori knowledge about the character of the social, in space/field theory, social structures and their underlying principles are (often) unknown before investigation, even in "traditional" analyses of nation-specific phenomena. The same, however, applies to research on international, transnational, or global spaces and fields: While the social space perspective can be effectively mobilized for analyses beyond national spaces, its empirical results cannot be simply transferred from context A (say, 1960s France) to context B (today's Uganda). This fallacy would lead to the charge that Bourdieu's theory is "empirically false", as Ugandan society may not be structured by the same capital forms as French society (of the time). Any extension of the social space concept to phenomena beyond the nation-state – be it in the sense of international comparisons, in the sense of transverse spaces that transcend national barriers, or in the sense of an overarching social space – requires a relational rather than essentialist account of traits and practices within different cultures (e.g., the meaning of specific practices or goods in different contexts). This may seem trivial, yet a dominant practice in quantitative comparative sociology can be found in the attempt to "harmonize" both the entity of the "nation-state" and the entity of the "citizen" across a maximum of constructs and indicators. Here, solutions that may work well in certain parts of the world (especially Western Europe and the United States) are indiscriminately imposed on all cultures and regions of the globe in order to distinguish those entities based on the doxic belief in the nation-state, and along indicators that seem to be objective from the subjective point of view of researchers (who can be objectively located in certain regions – in a double sense – of the global field of power/meaning). As a consequence, "harmonization" as the cardinal error of this dominant type of current comparative empirical research may be understood as a veritable act of symbolic violence on the global scale; it turns out to be a comprehensive euphemism for processes of unification and differentiation alike.

Accordingly, the comparison of social fields in different (regional) contexts – say, European and Asian legal fields – requires us to construct these different fields with different indicators that are appropriate to their respective (local, cultural, etc.) conditions.[8]

The principles of *relational methodology* provide us with useful toolkits when field theory is practiced "on the global scale". It must be emphasized, however, that this neither suggests to simply apply the same methods as used in national contexts, nor that it necessarily forces us to (re)invent new techniques. Relational methodology on a global scale still will involve techniques of objectification. Indeed, this can be achieved – in principle and given the availability of adequate data – within the framework of geometric data analysis (GDA). Relational methodology stresses that a certain technique (such as multiple correspondence analysis, MCA) may not be a one-size-fits-all solution, but that its basic principle of relational objectification still constitutes a core task for the construction (or reconstruction) of fields "beyond the nation-state".[9] A crucial problem that can be derived from the concept of the generalized field of power/meaning is represented by *multiple entities*, making it necessary to analyze, for instance, actors such as organizations, nation-states, and individual human persons simultaneously.[10]

Not only (but also) because we need to keep in mind that the global field of *power* is at the same time a global field of *meaning*, questions of qualitative research are just as relevant as they have ever been. Even without regard to specific qualitative designs, revealing meaning structures in global society – i.e., the relationality of world-views, semantic structures, ideas, etc. – poses specific challenges for field-theoretical methodology. First and foremost, any hermeneutic approach to these structures, especially one that "knows the necessity and pitfalls" of objectification (Dreyfus & Rabinow, 1983), necessarily would have to take this global field's objective heterogeneity into account in order to avoid forcing specific concepts or accounts on objects which, in and of themselves, are structured according to other principles ("epistemic violence").

As ever, the constructing subject (the sociologist) has to be *reflexive about the categories they use*, about the consequences of their scientific practice, and about their relation to the phenomenon under investigation (and construction). When it comes to the sociology of knowledge, the sociology of science, or political sociology, for example, this always involves the necessity of locating one's own (material, ideological, etc.) position within the fields in question. These challenges of reflexivity demand a fundamentally historical approach to seemingly "natural" phenomena. One key to understanding Bourdieu's deconstruction of "state thinking" in *On the State* lies in the methodological approach presented and demonstrated in these lectures, namely "genetic structuralism" (Bourdieu, 2014: 84 ff.). This approach allows for an "epistemic rupture" by reconstructing the genesis of the state both as a field-structure and as a mindset, that is, "by bringing back into view the conflicts and confrontations of the early beginnings and therefore all the discarded possibilities" (Bourdieu, 1998: 40). The concept of the global field of power/meaning (or global meta-field) goes one step further, as it aims not only to discard the hidden epistemology of "state thinking" (which prevails, for example, when researchers project the formalism of state thinking onto "higher-level" fields), but likewise to discard the structural conditions and forms of comparable epistemologies, some of which can be empirically observed today: global thinking, internationalist thinking, taken-for-granted cosmopolitanism, etc. By contextualizing such principles of vision and division, it articulates a caveat – to be wary about declaring a new "epochalist" stance when facing a seemingly "new" phenomenon such as globalization. Simply substituting the previously dominant "state thinking" with a new ideology of "world thinking", in order to follow the well-founded call to abandon "methodological nationalism", would mean replacing one essentialist stance with another and, in doing so, restricting oneself anew to a too-narrow understanding of processes of societalization. Generalized field theory, in contrast, invites researchers to analyze how different social fields in the broadest sense are involved in the creation and abolition of real existing constructions such as nation-states, nationality, transnationality, regionality, or globalization. Especially for a *political* sociology of (international, transnational, global) fields, this consideration is of major relevance, as it prevents us from making hasty and lopsided (yet powerful) judgments about the analytical form that is to be applied to present-day society. The way we look at the world that we live in, in this sense, is always structured by certain distinctions and principles of vision and division, some of which may become hegemonic for reasons amenable to sociological reasoning. One core task of a political sociology of transnational fields – and thus its critical, even emancipatory power – lies in exposing and demystifying these "natural" principles, and the relations of power and meaning that they stem from. In fact, being reflexive about these principles' arbitrary character, instead of actually reproducing them by way of spontaneous (pre-)sociological discourse, represents a key challenge for any field-theoretical approach to (national, transnational, and global) society.

Ultimately, this kind of reflection should entail the localization of any research and collaborative (e.g., network) projects within overarching (field and space) structures, as well as the localization of oneself as a researcher within these research networks and the overarching structures. In turn, this reflexivity includes an awareness of whether it is a doctoral student, a postdoctoral researcher, or a tenured faculty member who is working with the notion of "field" in a particular way. In a world of academic capitalism, postdoctoral researchers, for example, rarely have enough time to work on the systematic use of terminology; neither are there many strategic incentives to do so, because it costs time and overshadows the uniqueness of one's own research. Accordingly, it is the field's very structure that often prevents thorough and unprejudiced theorizing, whereas the basic premises of field theoretical thinking – relationality and reflexivity – at least allow us to recognize and question the obstacles that any form of collective scientific practice faces.

Notes

1 It is in this sense that, from the perspective of field theory, "[t]he antinomy between constructivism and realism does not exist" (Bourdieu, 1992: 46).
2 In fact, this question of varying degrees of "fieldness", which comprises the idea of "emerging" and "vanishing" fields, was identified and productively implemented by Bourdieu, e.g., in the context of the field of art (1996), the field of law (1987b), and, especially, the field of the nation-state (1994).
3 Despite widespread interpretations in parts of the secondary literature, historicity, social change, processes of structuration, and the emergence of new social forms are at the center of (Bourdieusian) relational theory, which emphasizes the complexity of social reality and the myriad reciprocal influences it expresses.
4 Thus, we also contend that the generalized field of power/meaning can indeed grasp what Bourdieu expressed with the social space concept, namely society at large.
5 To a certain extent, the "Reichsbürgerbewegung" might be compared to the US "sovereign citizen movement".
6 A similar point could be made for other fields: Actors who spend most of their time in academic contexts, for example, do not *necessarily* feature an "academic" habitus in the narrow sense, i.e., one that is significantly structured by the autonomous pole of the scientific field.
7 Again, the fact that some units are treated as "deficient" nation-states according to a hegemonic Western model must be put into the context of the relations of (symbolic) domination between different countries.
8 Still, apart from the hermeneutic problems of deriving indicators that are adequate to the cases in question, researchers should also try to use common indicators (derived from different fields and cultural perspectives) in order to develop meaningful, relational references.
9 Consequently, it should be emphasized that these statistical approaches share the same foundational properties (such as identifying latent dimensions, constructing spatial relations, decomposing matrices for those purposes, etc.).
10 Another relevant problem, well-known from traditional research endeavors, is to accept that the construction of a field can always fail – not because of personal shortcomings, but due to the mere fact that calling something a "field" may simply rest on inadequate assumptions.

References

Atkinson, W. (2019). *Bourdieu and After: A Guide to Relational Phenomenology*. London: Routledge.

Beck, U., & Grande, E. (2010). Varieties of Second Modernity: The Cosmopolitan Turn in Social and Political Theory and Research. *British Journal of Sociology*, *61*(3), 409–443.

Bourdieu, P. (1985). Existe-t-il une littérature belge? Limites d'un champ et frontières politiques. *Études de lettres*, *3*, 3–6.

Bourdieu, P. (1987a). What Makes a Social Class? On the Theoretical and Practical Existence of Groups. *Berkeley Journal of Sociology*, *32*, 1–17.

Bourdieu, P. (1987b). The Force of Law: Toward a Sociology of the Juridical Field. *Hastings Law Journal*, *38*(5), 814.

Bourdieu, P. (1991). *The Political Ontology of Martin Heidegger*. Cambridge: Polity Press.

Bourdieu, P. (1992). Thinking About Limits. *Theory, Culture & Society*, *9*(1), 37–49.

Bourdieu, P. (1994). Rethinking the State: Genesis and Structure of the Bureaucratic Field. *Sociological Theory*, *12*(1), 1–18.

Bourdieu, P. (1996). *The Rules of Art: Genesis and Structure of the Literary Field*. Stanford, CA: Stanford University Press.

Bourdieu, P. (1998). *Practical Reason: On the Theory of Action*. Stanford, CA: Stanford University Press.

Bourdieu, P. (2002). Les conditions sociales de la circulation internationale des idées. *Actes de la recherche en sciences sociales, 145*(5), 3–8.

Bourdieu, P. (2005). *The Social Structures of the Economy*. Cambridge: Polity Press.

Bourdieu, P. (2014). *On the State: Lectures at the Collège de France, 1989–1992*. Cambridge: Polity Press.

Bourdieu, P., & Wacquant, L. (1992). *An Invitation to Reflexive Sociology*. Chicago, IL: University of Chicago Press.

Buchholz, L. (2013). *The Global Rules of Art*. New York, NY: Columbia University, Doctoral dissertation.

Buchholz, L. (2016). What Is a Global Field? Theorizing Fields Beyond the Nation-State. *The Sociological Review Monographs, 64*(2), 31–60.

della Porta, D., & Tarrow, S. (Eds.). (2005). *Transnational Protest and Global Activism*. New York, NY: Rowman & Littlefield.

Djelic, M.-L., & Quack, S. (Eds.). (2003). *Globalization and Institutions: Redefining the Rules*. Cheltenham: Edward Elgar.

Dreyfus, H. L., & Rabinow, P. (1983). *Michel Foucault: Beyond Structuralism and Hermeneutics*. Chicago, IL: University of Chicago Press.

Elias, N. (1996). *The Germans: Power Struggles and the Development of Habitus in the Nineteenth and Twentieth Centuries*. New York, NY: Columbia University Press.

Gengnagel, V., Schmitz, A., & Witte, D. (2016). Die zwei Gesichter der Autonomie: Wissenschaft im Feld der Macht. In V. Gengnagel, J. Hamann, A. Hirschfeld & J. Maeße (Eds.), *Macht in Wissenschaft und Gesellschaft: Diskurs- und feldanalytische Perspektiven* (pp. 381–421). Wiesbaden: Springer VS.

Go, J. (2011). *Patterns of Empire: The British and American Empires, 1688 to the Present*. Cambridge: Cambridge University Press.

Go, J., & Krause, M. (Eds.). (2016). *Fielding Transnationalism*. Malden, MA: Wiley-Blackwell.

Kauppi, N., & Madsen, M. R. (Eds.). (2013). *Transnational Power Elites: The New Professionals of Governance, Law and Security*. London: Routledge.

Lubbers, M. J., Verdery, A. M., & Molina, J. L. (2018). Social Networks and Transnational Social Fields: A Review of Quantitative and Mixed-Methods Approaches. *The International Migration Review*, OnlineFirst. https://doi.org/10.1177/0197918318812343

Luhmann, N. (1982). The World Society as a Social System. *International Journal of General Systems, 8*(3), 131–138.

Luhmann, N. (1997). Globalization or World Society? How to Conceive of Modern Society. *International Review of Sociology, 7*(1), 67–79.

Martin, J. L. (2003). What Is Field Theory? *American Journal of Sociology, 109*(1), 1–49.

Meyer, J. W., Boli, B., Thomas, G. M., & Ramirez, F. O. (1997). World Society and the Nation-State. *The American Journal of Sociology, 103*(1), 144–181.

Meyer, J. W., & Jeppersen, R. L. (2000). The 'Actors' of Modern Society: The Cultural Construction of Social Agency. *Sociological Theory, 18*(1), 100–120.

Mitchell, K. (1997). Transnational Discourse: Bringing Geography Back in. *Antipode, 29*(2), 101–114.

Riley, D. (2015). The New Durkheim: Bourdieu and the State. *Critical Historical Studies*, *2*(2), 261–279.

Schinkel, W. (2015). The Sociologist and the State: An Assessment of Pierre Bourdieu's Sociology. *The British Journal of Sociology, 66*(2), 215–235.

Schmidt-Wellenburg, C. (2017). Europeanisation, Stateness, and Professions: What Role Do Economic Expertise and Economic Experts Play in European Political Integration? *European Journal of Cultural and Political Sociology, 4*(4), 1–27.

Schmitz, A., Heiberger, H., & Blasius, J. (2015). Das globale Feld der Macht als 'Tertium Comparationis'. *Österreichische Zeitschrift für Soziologie, 40*(3), 247–263.

Schmitz, A., & Witte, D. (2017). Der Nationalstaat und das globale Feld der Macht, oder: Wie sich die Feldtheorie von ihrem methodologischen Nationalismus befreien lässt. *Zeitschrift für Theoretische Soziologie, 6*(2), 156–189.

Schmitz, A., Witte, D., & Gengnagel, V. (2017). Pluralizing Field Analysis: Toward a Relational Understanding of the Field of Power. *Social Science Information/Information sur les sciences sociales, 56*(1), 49–73.

Schneickert, C. (2015). *Nationale Machtfelder und globalisierte Elite*. Konstanz: UVK.

Steinmetz, G. (2016). Social Fields, Subfields and Social Spaces at the Scale of Empires: Explaining the Colonial State and Colonial Sociology. *The Sociological Review Monographs, 64*(2), 98–123.

Vandenberghe, F. (1999). 'The Real Is Relational': An Epistemological Analysis of Pierre Bourdieu's Generative Structuralism. *Sociological Theory, 17*(1), 32–67.

Vauchez, A. (2008). The Force of a Weak Field: Law and Lawyers in the Government of the European Union. *International Political Sociology, 2*(2), 128–144.

Wacquant, L. (1993 [1989]). From Ruling Class to Field of Power: An Interview With Pierre Bourdieu. *Theory, Culture, and Society, 10*(1), 19–44.

Wacquant, L. (1996). Reading Bourdieu's 'Capital'. *International Journal of Contemporary Sociology, 33*(2), 151–170.

Wallerstein, I. (1974). *The Modern World-System I: Capitalist Agriculture and the Origins of the European World-Economy in the Sixteenth Century*. New York, NY: Academic Press.

Wallerstein, I. (2004). *World-Systems Analysis: An Introduction*. Durham, NC: Duke University Press.

Weiss, A. (2005). The Transnationalization of Social Inequality: Conceptualizing Social Positions on a World Scale. *Current Sociology, 53*(4), 707–728.

Wimmer, A., & Glick Schiller, N. (2002). Methodological Nationalism and Beyond: Nation – State Building, Migration and the Social Sciences. *Global Networks, 2*(4), 301–334.

Witte, D. (2014). *Auf den Spuren der Klassiker: Pierre Bourdieus Feldtheorie und die Gründerväter der Soziologie*. Konstanz: UVK.

Witte, D. (2017). Passing the Torch: From Durkheim's Statism to Bourdieu's Critique of the State. In W. Gephart & D. Witte (Eds.), *The Sacred and the Law: The Durkheimian Legacy* (pp. 229–262). Frankfurt am Main: Klostermann.

Witte, D., Schmitz, A., & Schmidt-Wellenburg, C. (2017). Geordnete Verhältnisse? Vielfalt und Einheit relationalen Denkens in der Soziologie. *Berliner Journal für Soziologie, 27*(3–4), 347–376.

Chapter 5

The post-national analysis of fields*

Monika Krause

Introduction

Scholarship in the last 20 years has successfully shown that the concept of field can be useful to analyze transnational as well as national cases. Early work analyzing transnational social spaces as fields has focused on commercial lawyers (Dezalay & Garth, 1995, 1996, 2002a, 2002b), human rights lawyers, and "good governance professionals" more broadly speaking (Guilhot, 2005; Hagan, 2005; Dezalay & Garth, 2006). The European Union has attracted early and consistent attention (e.g., Bigo, 2000, 2007; Vauchez, 2008, 2011; Cohen, 2011; Mudge & Vauchez, 2012; Büttner & Mau, 2014).

Economists (Fourcade, 2006) have been followed by other social scientists as the subject of field-theoretical studies, which paid attention to transnational or global dynamics (Steinmetz, 2007, 2008; Heilbron, Guilhot, & Jeanpierre, 2008). We now have studies also of management consultants (Schmidt-Wellenburg, 2014), humanitarian relief (Krause, 2014; Dromi, 2016), art (Buchholz, 2016), and religion (McKinnon, Trzebiatowska, & Brittain, 2011; Petzke, 2016) in this vein.

Building on this work, this chapter asks what we can learn from this attention to transnational cases for the general theory of fields, and more particularly for the formal description of fields.

I will argue that, when we abandon assumptions about the national as the natural container of social life, we begin to notice transnational cases, yes; but we also notice the complex ways in which any given field coexists with other fields on different scales. In this way, as I will try to show, attention to transnational fields encourages us to ask new questions about fields on any scale.

Developing the language for the formal description of fields is a particular agenda within field theory, one I have explained and justified at greater length elsewhere (Krause, 2018). I should briefly spell out here two of my presuppositions. By pursuing the language for the formal description of fields, I firstly put value on developing concepts through specifying their dimensions as a meaningful aspect of social scientific work, which deserves time and attention relatively independently of our ability to measure these dimensions. I put value on description as an end in itself and as a prerequisite for other aims, such as critique or (different kinds of) explanation (Krause, 2016).

In the context of discussions within the Bourdieusian tradition I should also emphasize, secondly, that pursuing the language for the formal description of fields means pursuing an analysis of fields in relative isolation from questions about habitus and practice, despite Bourdieu's insistence on the ways these concepts are linked.

The chapter will first review some of the theoretical presuppositions of work on transnational fields in the tradition established by Pierre Bourdieu. I will then review some of the advantages of fields as a tool and insights, which case studies of transnational fields have provided. I will argue that abandoning the assumptions of methodological nationalism and empiricizing scale highlights the complex ways in which any given field coexists with other fields on different scales. This allows us to ask new questions about fields on any scale; I will here focus on the questions we can ask about national fields and transnational fields, particularly concerning the specific form a field's autonomy takes and the way a field is structured symbolically.

Transnationalizing fields

Based on a casual reading, one might accuse Bourdieu, one of the founders of the social scientific study of fields, of methodological nationalism: Bourdieu's own studies have mostly been of fields organized on the national level. The seminal study *The Rules of Art* is a study of the French field of art. *Homo Academicus* is a study of the French academic field (Bourdieu, 1995). Bourdieu has also delivered studies of the French legal field (Bourdieu, 1987) and of the French religious field (which is mostly a study of the Catholic Church) (Bourdieu, 1991; Bourdieu & de Saint Martin, 1982).

There are reasons, however, why Bourdieu's work offers significant resources for a social science that seeks to escape methodological nationalism and, with that, seeks to overcome the a priori divide between the national and the international toward a more open investigation into patterns of the world (Sapiro, 2013; Bernhard & Schmidt-Wellenburg, 2014; Go & Krause, 2016). The main advantage of Bourdieu's work is a simple feature of his methodological approach: as a relational approach, field theory does not start from entities, but from relationships and calls for establishing relevant research objects empirically based on observed relationships, rather than assuming isolated units of analysis such as individuals or nation-states as the starting point of the investigation.

Among relational sociological approaches (Emirbayer, 1997; Martin, 2003; Hilgers & Mangez, 2014), field theory focuses specifically on relationships between actors – individual or corporate – that take each other into account (di Maggio & Powell, 1983; Powell & di Maggio, 1991; Fligstein, 2001; see also White, 2002), either explicitly or through shared orientation toward a field-specific capital or the stakes of the field. This specifies the invitation to start from relationships rather than entities, such as individuals or nation-states: field theory invites researchers to ask empirically what kind of other actors, and what stakes are important for actors. These stakes might be construed on a local, national, regional, or global scale.

We can in principle include all such relationships under the term; that is, for example, speak of the field of kinship, or the field of sexual relations (Martin & George, 2006), or speak of organizations or social movements as fields (Fligstein & McAdam, 2011, 2012). Among field-theoretical approaches, Bourdieu invites us to inquire specifically into actors who are oriented toward shared stakes with regard to specific professional or specialized practices.[1] He sees fields like art, science, or religion as not only shaped by meanings and competition for status in general, but also as more specifically marked by competition for a specific type of symbolic capital, and he sees them marked by a certain structure to the symbolic differentiation among positions.

Some advantages of field as a tool

Drawing on a sociological theory developed for the analysis of national contexts, field theorists have entered a lively interdisciplinary conversation about social order in a globalized world. Political scientists and scholars in international relations had been concerned with the "international" much more consistently than sociologists; for them the challenge was to come to terms with the seemingly new role of a range of non-state actors. I would highlight two advantages of "field" as a conceptual tool in the context of a debate, which in IR has been shaped by a strong dualism between approaches that emphasize interests and approaches that emphasize values and meanings.

Firstly, in contrast to idealist approaches, field theory encourages us to take values seriously but link an account of values to concrete actors and how they are related to other actors through institutional arrangements. Bourdieu directs us to inquire how interests are interpreted and how values get articulated through mediating spaces, such as fields. This allows us to raise questions that go beyond the assumptions of homogeneity and consensus associated with the notion of "world culture". Values are contested, and are the object of struggle at every level, not just at the point of reception or diffusion (Go & Krause, 2016).

In my study of humanitarian relief non-governmental organizations (NGOs), for example, I argue that neither a focus on stated values nor a focus on state's interests can fully explain what these organizations do and do not do; or the role these organizations play (Krause, 2014). Rather, since the late 1960s a relatively autonomous field of relief organizations has emerged that mediates the relationship between Western publics and Western states on the one hand, and distant suffering on the other hand. This shared social space, in which actors are oriented towards shared stakes, produces assumptions that are common across agencies. It also produces the debates that agencies have with each other over what it means to be a "humanitarian". Humanitarianism is contested among humanitarians themselves in a way that reflects but is not reducible to broader divisions.

Secondly, in contrast to interest-driven accounts, fields are conceptualized as relatively autonomous areas of social life and thus enable an analysis of the complex ways in which power relationships are institutionally mediated. Fields organize practices through at least some orientation toward shared stakes, or a shared field-specific capital. Resources from other fields also matter, but there is usually a cost associated with converting resources associated with one field into another. This notion of relative autonomy allows us to see a special role for the field of states (Go, 2008) or various national political fields without denying the politics of other areas of practice. Because of this, field theory opens up questions about how power is mediated through specific logics of practices, specific forms of symbolic capital, and different kinds of actors. This contrasts with accounts of imperialism based on discourse analysis or accounts of governmentality, which despite Foucault's explicit statements to the contrary, risk overestimating the coherence of governmentality (as O'Malley, Weir, & Shearing, 1997 have also argued). The European Central Bank, for example, could be described as an expression of neoliberal ideology or a tool of German hegemony. But as Mudge and Vauchez (2016) show, we can better understand its role if we also inquire into the specific ways in which it is and is not integrated into the field of professional economists, and if we also consider it as an actor in the European political field competing for capital (Mudge & Vauchez, 2016; see also Fourcade, 2006, 2009; Lebaron, 2008, 2010).

From transnational cases to a post-national perspective

In what follows I offer some questions we can ask of fields when we study them from a post-national perspective. I want to be clear that a post-national perspective for me does not entail the claim that nation-states and the national as a scale on which stakes are constructed no longer matter. It also does not entail the claim that nation-states and stakes on a national scale matter less now than they did at any other time: It is important to emphasize that one of the conclusions of globalization research in the 1990s was that there is no zero-sum relationship between the national and the global (Sassen, 2006).

I take "post-national" to mean "having abandoned the problematic assumptions of methodological nationalism" (see Wallerstein, 1997; Wimmer & Glick Schiller, 2003; Sassen, 2016). That is, it means not taking the national for granted as a natural unit of social life and as a natural unit of analysis. In field-theoretical terms, it is an empirical question of what kinds of other actors are important, whether they are local, national, regional, or global. On what scale are stakes that are relevant to actors articulated? What are the range of responses to scale relevant stakes? How do these change? This reminds us that the emergence of field dynamics on any scale is a puzzle, including on the national level. We can learn about empiricizing scale by looking at the history of the national itself: the national as a scale is itself the result of specific struggles.

Building on the classical sociological tradition, and in line with much of historical sociology, Bourdieu already makes the nation-state an explicit target of his analysis (Bourdieu, 1994). He develops a historical account of how states and national fields have formed, which enables questions about other possible forms that the political orders may take. State formation as a project is successful when stakes are constructed on the national scale; that is, when elites become oriented toward stakes on the national level (Bourdieu, 1994).

This was not always the case, but has a specific history: the European aristocracy, for example, was not traditionally oriented towards national stakes. Norbert Elias (1994) describes the aristocracy's international outlook: aristocrats were oriented towards aristocrats across Western and Eastern Europe, holidaying in the same resorts, using French as their shared language. They were also to some extent interested in the fields of their own locality, comprising tenants, clergy, and local competitors. In France, the king's court was one step towards producing a national field. In England, noblemen were more firmly embedded in their local contexts (Mennell, 1996). In Germany and in many other contexts, it was ultimately a project of the up-and-coming bourgeoisie to restrict relevant competitors to those tied to language and territory (Elias, 1994).

We can further note that different ties matter at the same time. When some aristocrats started buying into the stakes of the emerging national fields, this did not mean that the international aristocratic field ceased to exist, or that local fields ceased to matter. Similarly, global fields may coexist with national fields in the present. I would argue that relationships on different scales might matter to actors at the same time: local, national, and global fields of the same kind, such as art or science, can coexist (Kuipers, 2011; Buchholz, 2016). Post-national analysis thus (along with other motives) pushes us to consider the coexistence of fields and how they relate to each other.

One other point is worth emphasizing in order to move more fully toward an empirical investigation of scale. When studying field formation on different scales, we should take the study of transnational fields out of the study of "globalization", which can be shaped by historicist and teleological assumptions.

We should not assume, as the term "globalization" can be taken to imply, that we know which scale "comes first". The term globalization might lead us to focus on the globalization of national fields, but it is very clear that not all fields were national before they were global. Science, for example, was a transnational set of relationships before it was nationalized in the nineteenth century (Gingras, 2002). The same argument can be made about religion (Petzke, 2016) and politics (Albert, 2016).

We should be open to reconsidering the historical relationship between the global and the national, but also be wary in general of assumptions of a shift from "smaller" to larger sets of linkages: Among professional economists, to take an example from the twentieth century, "global" links preceded regional, intra-European ones. Economists from different national fields in Europe started to network on a European level after the United States had emerged as a shared privileged point of reference (Fourcade, 2006). Because historicism continues to shape the social sciences with an assumption of a direction from local towards more circumscribed scales, case studies that explore examples of early global stakes and resurgent national stakes can be expected to yield high theoretical dividends.

Post-national questions about national fields

Starting from a post-national perspective, we can ask new questions about national fields as well as about transnational fields. We can more closely examine the autonomy of a specific field, as well as its symbolic structure.

Kinds of autonomy

I have argued that we benefit from asking in more detail not just about the degree of autonomy of a field, but also its kind of autonomy (Krause, 2018). Bourdieu has an argument about autonomy as a variable in his explicitly historical writings: according to him, fields have developed as contingent outcomes of processes we might call modernization in the nineteenth and early twentieth centuries. When fields emerge, they become more autonomous. Others have followed both with accounts of field emergence (Chalaby, 1998; Ferguson, 1998; see also Armstrong, 2002, 2005) and loss of field autonomy (Maton, 2005; McQuarrie, 2010, 2013; Strand, 2011).

While much of the discussion analyzes autonomy in terms of "more" or "less", we can distinguish different forms of autonomy based on different positions a field as a whole might have in the overall architecture of fields that make up social order. This argument was originally developed by Rodney Benson, who compared the journalistic fields in France and the United States, and suggested that the French field was more autonomous from the market or economic field, and the American field was more autonomous from the political field, and less autonomous vis-à-vis the market (Benson, 2005, 2013).

Considering national fields from a post-national perspective, we can ask how a national field's autonomy is shaped by its relationship not only with other fields of other kinds in its context but also, firstly, with fields of its own kind in other contexts and, secondly, with fields of its own kind on other scales.

This means, staying with the case of journalism, for example, we can ask not only how the French field of journalism relates to the French political field and the French economic field, but also how the French field of journalism relates to the Belgian field of journalism or the American field of journalism. Bourdieu has hinted at some of the asymmetries we might investigate in his essay *Is there a Belgian field of literature?* (Bourdieu, 1985), highlighting the struggle of Francophone Belgian writers to succeed in Paris, or be content in Brussels.

Angele Christin has addressed related issues in her comparative ethnographic study of a French and an American news site (Christin, 2016). She shows that the

French journalists are very well informed about their American counterparts, as well as about the American media market more generally, whereas the American journalists know very little about French journalism. I would read these findings as suggesting that the American field of journalism is more autonomous from the French field of journalism, than the French field of journalism is from the American field of journalism.

Distinguishing between intra-national and cross-national dimensions of field autonomy also allows us to make sense of findings from the sociology of science. Sociologists of science have noted that the American social sciences are very autonomous with regard to non-American social science: American social scientists rarely cite non-American work, and recognize foreign degrees in recruitment only in exceptional cases. In this type of horizontal autonomy, American social science is more autonomous than German or Argentinian social science, which highly values publications in American journals. But that does not necessarily mean that American sociology, for example, is more autonomous from American political or economic forces than Argentinian or German sociology is from Argentinian or German political or economic forces (Gingras, 2002; Beigel, 2014a, 2014b).

We can also ask questions about how any given field relates to fields of its own kind on other scales. Larissa Buchholz has addressed this using the example of the field of art (Buchholz, 2008, 2016): Recognizing the relevance of transnational ties, and acknowledging that these need not supersede national ties, Buchholz suggests that we ask about the autonomy of the French field of art from the global field of art, and vice versa. Buchholz (2016) has coined the term "vertical autonomy" to describe this aspect of field autonomy.

Field structure

Considering national fields from a post-national perspective allows us to ask new questions about a field's autonomy. It also allows us to ask new questions about a field's symbolic structure. Bourdieu draws on the structuralist philosophy of language to analyze the symbolic oppositions that structure the ways that positions within fields are differentiated from each other. It is commonly emphasized in the tradition that there is one autonomous pole high in field-specific capital, and a heteronomous pole high in other forms of capital, resulting in two-dimensional maps.

But some later studies indicate that the kind of oppositions that structure symbolic competition can vary, depending on the type and range of field-external resources that play a role (Hjellbrekke et al., 2007; Denord, Hjellbrekke, Korsnes, Lebaron, & Le Roux, 2011; Vauchez, 2011; Krause, 2014, 2018; see also Gorski, 2013). We should thus be asking empirically how the heteronomous pole, or heteronomous poles, are construed in each field.

For any national field, we can ask to what extent access to resources from fields on other scales plays a role in the symbolic oppositions that differentiate positions.

For the late twentieth and early twenty-first centuries, we may find that national fields may be divided between globalizers and their opponents. Scale here becomes a stake in the competition within a field. Marion Fourcade, for example, discusses how international links have played a role in national fields among economists in peripheral countries. The Chilean field of professional economics, for example, is divided between those with American degrees who advocate internationalization and others who insist on local standards and signs of recognition (Fourcade, 2006).

International influence also plays a role in structuring national fields in core countries (Fourcade, 2006; see also Bockman & Eyal, 2002). American social scientists can use recognition from abroad as a resource when competing against each other. In a related analysis, Ulrich Best has argued that the debate critiquing Anglo-American hegemony in geography has been driven by those seeking to bolster elite positions in national European fields by investing into a European field of geography (Best, 2009).

National political fields are also shaped by a division between "national" and "international" loyalties. This tension is not new: When national fields emerged in the late eighteenth and nineteenth centuries, we can presume that an orientation towards international elite ties remained a source of heteronomy. For the case of Germany, we could also consider the struggle over the influence of the Catholic Church in the late nineteenth century on these terms.

The division between those oriented toward national stakes, and those with access to resources from fields on other scales, seems particularly salient in recent years. It does, for example, play an important role in the politics of countries that see themselves as on the periphery of the European Union (Zawadewicz, 2015).

Multiscalar questions about transnational fields

Scholars who analyze transnational fields by definition have abandoned some of the assumptions of methodological nationalism; evidence about transnational stakes continues to undermine assumptions about the national as the natural container of social life. Yet the study of transnational fields can be pushed further by consistently abandoning also the assumptions associated with the term "globalization". An analysis of transnational fields in the context of globalization can invite assumptions about a zero-sum game between the national and the global, and it can invite assumptions of direction, of a gradual shift from the national to the global, and more generally, from links on a smaller scale to links on a larger scale.

I have suggested that the formal description of national fields can gain from considering the way national fields do not just coexist with other fields in their national context, but coexist with fields in other contexts and fields on other scales. The formal description of transnational fields can also gain by considering how transnational fields remain embedded in a multiscalar architecture, and are to some extent precarious in the context of this multiscalar architecture. Here too, we have an opportunity, firstly, to discuss how the specific kind of autonomy we see in a field is related to other fields, including other transnational fields and fields of the same kind on a different scale. Secondly, we can discuss how the symbolic structure of a transnational field is shaped by resources from the range of other fields it coexists with.

This again raises questions about "vertical autonomy" (Buchholz, 2016). Larissa Buchholz has argued that the global field of art is only relatively autonomous from important national fields of art. Considering another example, the global field of science coexists with various national and regional fields, and it is not fully autonomous from the American field of science (Gingras, 2002). Many national forms of evaluation use indicators that privilege success publishing in Anglo-American journals.

Regarding the analysis of symbolic structure, the analysis of transnational fields can also consider a broader range of symbolic oppositions. Instead of assuming an opposition between an autonomous pole and a heteronomous pole, we can examine each field with a view to asking what forms of heteronomy play a role. That means asking what resources from other fields play a role in the symbolic oppositions that differentiate positions (Krause, 2018).

Because transnational fields in many cases coexist with regional, national, or local fields, asking about access to resources from other fields as a dimension of structuring a field's position includes asking about resources from fields on other scales. We can ask how resources from national fields create symbolic divisions within global fields.

There is some evidence that resources from different national fields matter in national fields, and that resources from different national contexts carry different kinds of symbolic value within global fields, creating an opposition between hegemonic and anti-hegemonic positions. In the global field of humanitarian relief, for example, resources associated with some governments, such as Sweden or Norway, are seen as purer than others, such as the United States (Krause, 2014). This reflects the hegemonic position of the United States within the field of power, but also the strategies of smaller Western countries to invest in strategies of purity.

Conclusion

The surge of interest in transnational cases presents important opportunities for the development of field theory as a general theory of a specific kind of social form. By highlighting the complex ways in which any given field coexists with other fields on different scales, attention to transnational fields encourages us to ask new questions about fields on any scale. I have here focused on the questions we can ask about national fields as well as transnational ones, particularly concerning the specific form a field's autonomy takes and the way a field is structured symbolically. In studying the kind of relative autonomy associated with a field, and in studying the symbolic divisions that structure it, we need to situate it in the context of other fields on its own scale, and fields on other scales.

I have discussed on what abandoning methodological nationalism offers for developing the language for the description of fields, which is only one goal of field analysis. Distinguishing between different kinds of fields is an important foundation for recasting descriptive questions as well as for pursuing other ends, such as explanation or critique.

We can ask, for example, descriptive questions about change as a change in field properties. We can research globalization as a question of a shift in field autonomy in particular cases. The globalization of science is then the gain in autonomy of global science from any national field of science, the globalization of politics as the emergence of a relatively autonomous global political field.

Hegemony can be conceptualized as an unreciprocated relationship of heteronomy between two fields. "US-American hegemony" can be traced in terms of the autonomy of other national fields vis-à-vis US-American fields and a global field that may (or may not be) dominated by the United States.

Distinguishing between different kinds of fields can also help us explain outcomes that we care about. Different field properties might enable different types of political forms, for example. We can examine which field properties are required for national political fields to sustain a liberal democratic political system. If contestation about transnational resources becomes a major cleavage, they might hinder a field's capacity to play out other lines of symbolic oppositions. There is some indication of this dynamic in Estonia, Hungary, and Poland, and to some extent in Italy, Spain, Greece, and the United Kingdom.

We can ask how field properties affect the distribution of practices. Field-specific practices, such as "reporting" in the case of journalism, or handing out supplies according to need in the case of humanitarian relief, depend on a field's relative autonomy (Chalaby, 1998; Krause, 2011), and the implications of different kinds of autonomy on the distribution of practices has not been fully explored in comparative work.

We can also treat field properties as an outcome, and try to explain why a specific field has specific properties in a given context. Formalizing the description of fields is compatible with different approaches to explanation. Explaining field forms can consider particular historical contexts, as well as examine conditions in the environments of fields more formally.

Notes

* The chapter draws on earlier arguments by the author (Go & Krause, 2016; Krause, 2018). I thank the members of the Network Political Sociology of Transnational Fields funded by the German Research Foundation, the editors, and the International Relations Theory Workshop at the LSE for useful discussions and feedback.

1 See McCall (1992) and McNay (1999) for an analysis of the association between field formation and the emergence of the public/private division; they raise the question to what extent field analysis mirrors the exclusion of the private rather than examining it.

References

Albert, M. (2016). *A Theory of World Politics*. Cambridge: Cambridge University Press.

Armstrong, E. (2002). *Forging Gay Identities: Organizing Sexuality in San Francisco, 1950–1994*. Chicago, IL: University of Chicago Press.

Armstrong, E. (2005). From Struggle to Settlement: The Crystallization of a Field of Lesbian/Gay Organizations in San Francisco, 1969–1973. In G. Davis, D. McAdam, W. Scott & M. Zald (Eds.), *Social Movements and Organization Theory* (pp. 161–187). Cambridge: Cambridge University Press.

Beigel, F. (2014a). Current Tensions and Trends in the World Scientific System. *Current Sociology, 62*(5), 617–625.

Beigel, F. (2014b). Publishing from the Periphery: Structural Heterogeneity and Segmented Circuits: The Evaluation of Scientific Publications for Tenure in Argentina's CONICET. *Current Sociology, 62*(5), 743–765.

Benson, R. (2005). Mapping Field Variation: Journalism in France and the United States. In R. Benson & E. Neveu (Eds.), *Bourdieu and the Journalistic Field* (pp. 85–112). Cambridge: Polity Press.

Benson, R. (2013). *Shaping Immigration News: A French American Comparison*. Cambridge: Cambridge University Press.

Bernhard, S., & Schmidt-Wellenburg, C. (2014). Politische Soziologie transnationaler Felder. *Schwerpunktheft des Berliner Journals für Soziologie, 24*(2). Wiesbaden: Springer VS.

Best, U. (2009). The Invented Periphery: Constructing Europe in Debates About 'Anglo Hegemony' in Geography. *Social Geography, 4*, 83–91.

Bigo, D. (2000). Liaison Officers in Europe: New Officers in the European Security Field. In J. W. E. Sheptycki (Ed.), *Issues in Transnational Policing* (pp. 67–100). London; New York, NY: Routledge.

Bigo, D. (2007). *The Field of the EU Internal Security Agencies*. Paris: Centre d'études sur les conflits/l'Harmattan.

Bockman, J., & Eyal, G. (2002). Eastern Europe as a Laboratory for Economic Knowledge: The Transnational Roots of Neoliberalism. *American Journal of Sociology, 108*(2), 310–352.

Bourdieu, P. (1985). Existe-il une literature belge? *Etudes de Lettres, 4*, 3–6.

Bourdieu, P. (1987). The Force of Law. *Hastings Law Journal, 38*(5), 805–853.

Bourdieu, P. (1991). Genesis and Structure of the Religious Field. *Comparative Social Research, 13*, 1–44.

Bourdieu, P. (1994). Rethinking the State: Genesis and Structure of the Bureaucratic Field. *Sociological Theory, 12*(1), 1–18.

Bourdieu, P. (1995). *The Rules of Art: Genesis and Structure of the Literary Field*. Stanford, CA: Stanford University Press.

Bourdieu, P., & de Saint-Martin, M. (1982). La sainte famille: l'episcopat français dans le champ du pouvoir. *Actes de la recherche en sciences sociales, 44–45*, 1–53.

Buchholz, L. (2008). Feldtheorie und Globalisierung. In B. von Bismarck, T. Kaufmann & U. Wuggenig (Eds.), *Nach Bourdieu: Visualität, Kunst, Politik* (pp. 211–238). Vienna: Turia and Kant.

Buchholz, L. (2016). What Is a Global Field? Rethinking Bourdieu's Field Theory Beyond the Nation-State. *Sociological Review, 64*(2), 31–60.

Büttner, S., & Mau, S. (2014). EU Professionalismus als transnationales Feld. *Berliner Journal für Soziologie, 24*(2), 141–167.

Chalaby, J. K. (1998). *The Invention of Journalism.* Basingstoke: Macmillan.

Christin, A. (2016). Is Journalism a Transnational Field? Asymmetrical Interactions and Symbolic Domination in Online News. *The Sociological Review, 64*(2), 212–234.

Cohen, A. (2011). Bourdieu Hits Brussels: The Genesis and Structure of the European Field of Power. *International Political Sociology, 5*(3), 335–339.

Denord, F., Hjellbrekke, J., Korsnes, O., Lebaron, F., & Le Roux, B. (2011). Social Capital in the Field of Power: The Case of Norway. *The Sociological Review, 59*(1), 86–108.

Dezalay, Y., & Garth, B. G. (1995). Merchants of Law as Moral Entrepreneurs: Constructing International Justice from the Competition for Transnational Business Disputes. *Law and Society Review, 29*(1), 27–56.

Dezalay, Y., & Garth, B. G. (1996). *Dealing in Virtue: International Commercial Arbitration and the Construction of a Transnational Legal Order.* Chicago, IL: University of Chicago Press.

Dezalay, Y., & Garth, B. G. (2002a). *Global Prescriptions: The Production, Exportation, and Importation of a New Legal Orthodoxy.* Ann Arbor, MI: University of Michigan Press.

Dezalay, Y., & Garth, B. G. (2002b). *The Internationalization of Palace Wars: Lawyers, Economists, and the Contest to Transform Latin American States.* Chicago, IL: University of Chicago Press.

Dezalay, Y., & Garth, B. G. (2006). From the Cold War to Kosovo: The Rise and Renewal of the Field of International Human Rights. *Annual Review of Law and Social Science, 2,* 231–255.

Di Maggio, P., & Powell, W. (1983). The Iron Cage Revisited: Institutional Isomorphism and Collective Rationality in Organizational Fields. *American Sociological Review, 48*(2), 147–160.

Dromi, S. (2016). For Good and Country: Nationalism and the Diffusion of Humanitarianism in the Late Nineteenth Century. *Sociological Review, 64*(2), 79–97.

Elias, N. (1994 [1939]). *The Civilizing Process.* Oxford: Blackwell.

Emirbayer, M. (1997). Manifesto for a Relational Sociology. *American Journal of Sociology, 103*(2), 281–317.

Ferguson, P. (1998). A Cultural Field in the Making: Gastronomy in Nineteenth Century France. *American Journal of Sociology, 104*(1), 597–641.

Fligstein, N. (2001). Social Skill and the Theory of Fields. *Sociological Theory, 19*(2), 105–125.

Fligstein, N., & McAdam, D. (2011). Toward a General Theory of Strategic Action Fields. *Sociological Theory, 29*(1), 1–26.

Fligstein, N., & McAdam, D. (2012). *A Theory of Fields.* Oxford: Oxford University Press.

Fourcade, M. (2006). The Construction of a Global Profession: The Transnationalization of Economics. *American Journal of Sociology, 112*(1), 145–195.

Fourcade, M. (2009). *Economists and Societies: Discipline and Profession in the United States, Britain and France, 1890s–1990s*. Princeton, NJ: Princeton University Press.

Gingras, Y. (2002). Les formes spécifiques de l'internationalité du champ scientifique. *Actes de la recherche en sciences sociales, 141–142*, 31–45.

Go, J. (2008). Global Fields and Imperial Forms: Field Theory and the British and American Empires. *Sociological Theory, 26*(3), 201–229.

Go, J., & Krause, M. (2016). Fielding Transnationalism: An Introduction. *Sociological Review Monographs, 64*(2), 6–30.

Gorski, P. S. (2013). Bourdieusian Theory and Historical Analysis: Maps, Mechanisms, and Methods. In P. S. Gorski (Ed.), *Bourdieu and Historical Analysis* (pp. 327–367). Chapel Hill, NC: Duke University Press.

Guilhot, N. (2005). *The Democracy Makers: Human Rights and International Order*. New York, NY: Columbia University Press.

Hagan, J. (2005). Crimes of War and the Force of Law. *Social Forces, 83*(4), 1499–1534.

Heilbron, J., Guilhot, N., & Jeanpierre, L. (2008). Toward a Transnational History of the Social Sciences. *Journal of the History of the Behavioral Sciences, 44*(2), 146–160.

Hilgers, M., & Mangez, E. (2014). *Bourdieu's Theory of Social Fields*. London: Routledge.

Hjellbrekke, J., Le Roux, B., Korsnes, O., Lebaron, F., Rouanet, H., & Rosenlund, L. (2007). The Norwegian Field of Power Anno 2000. *European Societies, 9*(2), 245–273.

Krause, M. (2011). Reporting and the Transformations of the Journalistic Field: US News Media, 1890–2000. *Media, Culture, and Society, 33*(1), 89–104.

Krause, M. (2014). *The Good Project: Humanitarian NGOs and the Fragmentation of Reason*. Chicago, IL: University of Chicago Press.

Krause, M. (2016). The Meanings of Theorizing. *British Journal of Sociology, 67*(1), 23–29.

Krause, M. (2018). How Fields Vary. *British Journal of Sociology, 69*(1), 3–22.

Krause, M., & Robinson, K. (2017). Charismatic Species and Beyond: How Cultural Schemas and Organisational Routines Shape Conservation. *Conservation and Society, 15*(3), 313–321.

Kuipers, G. (2011). Cultural Globalization as the Emergence of a Transnational Cultural Field: Transnational Television and National Media Landscapes in Four European Countries. *American Behavioural Scientist, 55*(5), 541–557.

Lebaron, F. (2008). Central Bankers in the Contemporary Global Field of Power: A 'Social Space' Approach. *Sociological Review, 56*(1), 121–144.

Lebaron, F. (2010). European Central Bank Leaders in the Global Space of Central Bankers: A Geometric Data Analysis Approach. *French Politics, 8*(3), 294–320.

Martin, J. L. (2003). What Is Field Theory? *American Journal of Sociology, 109*(2), 1–49.

Martin, J. L., & George, M. (2006). Theories of Sexual Stratification: Toward an Analytics of the Sexual Field and a Theory of Sexual Capital. *Sociological Theory, 24*(2), 107–132.

Maton, K. A. (2005). A Question of Autonomy: Bourdieu's Field Approach and Policy in Higher Education. *Journal of Education Policy, 20*(6), 687–704.

McCall, L. (1992). Does Gender Fit? Feminism, Bourdieu and Conceptions of Social Order. *Theory and Society, 21*(6), 837–867.

McKinnon, A., Trzebiatowska, M., & Brittain, C. C. (2011). Bourdieu, Capital, and Conflict in a Religious Field: The Case of the 'Homosexuality' Conflict in the Anglican Communion. *Journal of Contemporary Religion, 26*(3), 355–370.

McNay, L. (1999). Gender, Habitus and the Field. *Theory, Culture and Society*, *16*(1), 95–117.

McQuarrie, M. (2010). Nonprofits and the Reconstruction of Urban Governance: Housing Production and Community Development in Cleveland, 1975–2005. In E. Clemens & D. Guthrie (Eds.), *Politics and Partnerships in American Governance* (pp. 237–268). Chicago, IL: University of Chicago Press.

McQuarrie, M. (2013). Urban Governance and the End Civil Society: Community Organizations in the Rust Belt from Populism to Foreclosure. *Politics and Society*, *41*(1), 73–101.

Mennell, S. (1996). *All Manners of Food: Eating and Taste in England and France from the Middle Ages to the Present*. Champaign, IL: University of Illinois Press.

Mudge, S. L., & Vauchez, A. (2012). Building Europe on a Weak Field: Law, Economics and Scholarly Avatars in Transnational Politics. *American Journal of Sociology*, *118*(2), 449–492.

Mudge, S. L., & Vauchez, A. (2016). Fielding Supernationalism: The European Central Bank as a Field Effect. *The Sociological Review Monographs*, *64*(2), 146–169.

O'Malley, P., Weir, L., & Shearing, C. (1997). Governmentality, Criticism, Politics. *Economy and Society*, *26*(4), 501–517.

Petzke, M. (2016). Taken in by the Numbers Game: The Globalization of a Religious 'Illusio' and 'Doxa' in 19th-Century Evangelical Missions to India. *Sociological Review*, *64*(2), 124–145.

Powell, W., & di Maggio, P. (1991). *The New Institutionalism in Organizational Analysis*. Chicago, IL: University of Chicago Press.

Sapiro, G. (2013). Le champ est-il national? La theorie de la differenciation sociale au prisme de l'histoire globale. *Actes de la recherche en sciences sociales*, *200*, 70–86.

Sassen, S. (2006). *Territory, Authority, Rights: From Medieval to Global Assemblages*. Princeton, NJ: Princeton University Press.

Sassen, S. (2016). The Global City: Enabling Economic Intermediation and Bearing Its Costs. *City & Community*, *15*(2), 97–108.

Schmidt-Wellenburg, C. (2014). Der Aufstieg der Beratung zur Transnationalen Regierungsform im Feld des Managements. *Berliner Journal für Soziologie*, *24*(2), 227–255.

Steinmetz, G. (2007). *The Devil's Handwriting: Precoloniality and the German Colonial State in Qingdao, Samoa, and Southwest Africa*. Chicago, IL: University of Chicago Press.

Steinmetz, G. (2008). The Colonial State as a Social Field: Ethnographic Capital and Native Policy in the German Overseas Empire Before 1914. *American Sociological Review*, *73*(2), 589–612.

Strand, M. (2011). Where Do Classifications Come From? *Theory and Society*, *40*(3), 273–313.

Vauchez, A. (2008). The Force of a Weak Field: Law and Lawyers in the Government of the European Union (for a Renewed Research Agenda). *International Political Sociology*, *2*(2), 128–144.

Vauchez, A. (2011). Interstitial Power in Fields of Limited Statehood: Introducing a 'Weak Field' Approach to the Study of Transnational Settings. *International Political Sociology*, *5*(3), 340–345.

Wallerstein, I. (1997). Eurocentrism and Its Avatars: The Dilemmas of Social Science. *New Left Review*, *226*, 93–108.

White, H. C. (2002). *Markets from Networks: Socio-Economic Models of Production*. Princeton, NJ: Princeton University Press.

Wimmer, A., & Glick Schiller, N. (2003). Methodological Nationalism, the Social Sciences, and the Study of Migration: An Essay in Historical Epistemology. *The International Migration Review*, *37*(2), 576–610.

Zawadewicz, B. (2015). The Impact of Symbolic Political Cleavages on the Elites' Strategies in Divided Societies: The Case of Bosnia and Ukraine. Retrieved December 22, 2019, from www.gsi.uni-muenchen.de/lehreinheiten/le_ps1/le_verg_ps_oe/bogdan_zawadewicz/index.html

Chapter 6

European elites as (a) field(s)

Reflections on the uses of prosopography and geometric data analysis based on three joint surveys of transnational objects

Frédéric Lebaron

Introduction

Based on several collective studies focusing on Europe's elite (the field of Eurocracy in the broadest sense, Georgakakis & Rowell, 2013), we reflect on and analyze the issues and problems encountered at different phases of these surveys by highlighting the tools used and the potentialities of geometric data analysis (GDA). We focus on the design of the approach, the data collection process, the management of the biographic database, and the statistical analysis of the data.[1]

We will thus adopt a "methodological", epistemological, and purely sociological approach to reflect on the process that leads to the use of prosopographic databases in the framework of transnational studies. This process is already part of a rich tradition of studies undertaken in the field of the internationalization of elites (Broady, Palme, & de Saint-Martin, 1995).[2] This reflection, which is only partly personal,[3] has been nourished by long-term collective experiences implemented by different teams with distinct perspectives. These teams, however, all share the same theoretical references, research problems, and ways of conceiving the sociological approach.

In particular, they have all adopted a relational analysis perspective resumed by Pierre Bourdieu's (1989) concept of "field". This concept has continued to fuel debate. For an overview see, for instance, the edition of the *Actes de la recherche en sciences sociales* journal devoted to the "field" published in December 2013 (Bourdieu, 2013).

In the three cases analyzed, the statistical and visual representation of the field emerged as a central phase in formalizing and operationalizing the concept. It also allowed us to identify the issues specific to each survey in a more specific manner.

Analyzing a transnational field is not without its challenges: on a purely national level, the training and selection system and the recognition authorities in any given field are relatively unified and easy to identify. It is thus easier to build ties between different positions (for instance social, institutional, etc.) given that the "metrics" – with the exception of the currency – are relatively more homogeneous. In the transnational context, notably the European context, we posit that the spaces analyzed are relatively unified, albeit on a less established base. We will see that in some cases, however, the process of the homogenization of trans-national elites can be rather advanced (as reflected, for example, by the European Central Bank [ECB]).

Backed by a quantitative sociological approach based on GDA, the perspective adopted also involves more "qualitative" elements.[4] The analysis of individual trajectories, based on either interviews or direct observations and using various archival documents, is indeed inseparable from the relational approach to transnational fields. Mixing qualitative and quantitative approaches makes all the more sense because, rather than reflecting on "groups" (institutions, other groups) from the outset, focus is placed on restoring the complexity of biographical trajectories (primarily academic and professional in our case).

The surveys

The Central Bank survey (BANQCENT, 1999)

This prosopographic study (Lebaron, 2008, 2010, 2012, 2015) focused on central bank leaders (governors, deputy governors, members of councils) and paid special emphasis to the ECB, specifically the Board of Governors. The approach, which evolved over time, was developed within the framework of personal research projects I undertook following my doctoral thesis and which were later developed thanks to technical collaborations, in particular with the Master's students enrolled in the Science and Techniques/Computer Science and Statistics applied to Humanities and Social Sciences (MST/ISASH) Program at the Paris Descartes University. I also worked alongside Karin Darin, a postdoctoral fellow at the Academic Centre for Research on Public Policy, Politics, Epistemology and Social Sciences (CURAPP-ESS) and, more recently, with Aykiz Dogan, a Ph.D. student in sociology at the Institute for the Analysis of Economic and Social Development (IEDES) at the Panthéon-Sorbonne University. The objective of the study was to compare the trajectories of central bank leaders around the world, analyze the specificity of Central European bankers, and examine the relationship between their positions and their trajectories on the one hand and their points of view on the other (monetary, budgetary orthodoxies, etc.). There was an almost "natural" unity here, because the Governing Council is the central body that determines the monetary policy of the euro area.

Survey on the space of legal "professions" in Europe (POLILEXES, 2009)

Driven by sociologists of law and legal professions, this project sought to analyze the space legal "professions" have occupied in Europe since the 1957 Treaty of Rome. Its objective was to understand how the legal field contributed to the making of Europe. Funded by the French National Agency of Research (the law and lawyers in the European government project led by Guillaume Sacriste of the Panthéon-Sorbonne

University), the survey began in 2009. Antonin Cohen, Guillaume Sacriste, and Antoine Vauchez were the key members of the team. Frédéric Lebaron, Antoine Mégie, and Jérôme Pacouret also participated in the more methodological aspects of the project. The project involved regular discussions that allowed progressive development over a period of several years, and resulted in several conferences and some preliminary publications (Mégie & Sacriste, 2009). As technical adviser, I was involved in data collection and its statistical analysis using GDA tools.

Surveys in the field of Eurocracy (EUROCRATIE, 2014)

This project built on studies undertaken within the framework of the Groupe de sociologie politique européenne/politique, religion, onstitutions et sociétés: mutations européennes (GSPE/PRISME) in the 2000s. The GSPE/PRISME project that began in the 2000s and was led by Didier Georgakakis and Marine de Lassalle, brought together several other members of the GSPE/PRISME group such as Willy Beauvallet, Vincent Dubois, Philippe Juhem, Valérie Lozac'h, Michel Mangenot, and Sébastien Michon (see Georgakakis & de Lassalle, 2007). It resulted in the setting up of a prosopographic database on staff across Europe. These surveys made it possible not only to document the existence of European capital, but also to describe the field of Eurocracy. Beauvallet and Michon (2013) applied GDA methods to European parliamentarians.

Working with Didier Georgakakis, we launched a survey on a smaller scale in 2014 focusing on the changes in the social and professional recruitment of high-ranking officials in Brussels (managing directors, deputy directors, etc.), and paid special attention to the most recent changes. We sought to analyze the rise of the sub-field of economic governance within the scope of European power in order to understand, in particular, the maintenance of fiscal austerity policies in a context of mass unemployment and a decline in economic dynamism. Data entry was carried out by Florent Parruite (a Ph.D. student in political science at the Paris-Ouest-Nanterre-La-Défense University) in 2014 and 2015 (Georgakakis & Lebaron, 2015, 2018).

The design of the survey approach

Surveys usually begin with preliminary research questions before stating – as clearly as possible – their main empirical objectives. In the three cases analyzed, the major sociological or historical issues had already been developed prior to the "prosopographic" survey, in relation to the highly established field of European studies and international political sociology. This strongly marked the study's orientation, with regard to the individuals surveyed and the information deemed relevant to respond to specific questions.

As mentioned earlier, the idea behind the central bank survey was to analyze the relationship between professional trajectories, social characteristics, and "viewpoints". Europe was only one among many other possible levels of observation. The survey, which fell under the (sub-) field of the Governors of the ECB, primarily sought to identify the specificities of the European space from a "global" perspective in order to analyze internal specializations and their consequences for monetary policy guidelines (Lebaron, 2014). The ECB was perceived as a subspace within a more global transnational space.

The objective of the POLILEXES survey was to question how law has shaped the making of Europe. It focused on the historical characteristics and evolution of biographical trajectories taking shape within Europe. From the outset, the survey presented a strong sociohistorical and biographical dimension. It paid great interest to trajectory changes, the forms of heteronomy, plural and hybrid trajectories, and the complex structuring of the field, which shifted from a phase of the juxtaposition and connection of autonomous national histories to a more clearly Europeanized space, due in particular to the rise of community law.

This ongoing study in the field of Eurocracy aims to build on a comparative analysis of the characteristics of certain groups of administrative actors of the European Commission (directors, deputy directors, etc.) according to various criteria. It seeks to further reinforce, from an empirical perspective, the subfield of European economic governance within a larger context and within the background of an Europeanization process to which the "permanent" members of Europe contribute (Georgakakis & Rowell, 2013). The POLILEXES survey privileges two periods, namely, the early 2000s and the early 2010s – unlike the GSPE/PRISME survey, in which the historical perspective and the systematic analysis of trajectories was more clearly defined and career-related data was coded on a yearly basis. This implies that economic institutions must analyze the concept of reinforcement in line with the crisis and relative stability of the structure of European careers.

Data collection and the delimitation of the area studied

Data collection choices are often initially guided by a theoretical dimension that tends to overlook the specialists in a particular field. Defining the limits of the area or field analyzed is undoubtedly the most debated and critical issue. Indeed, this process leads to a shift away from the relative uncertainty of concepts, which relates to the existence of symbolic struggles about definitions, and guides the first phase of operationalization, which is also a radical empirical test. It is possible to highlight the problems posed by this phase in each survey analyzed, the common point being that these choices, insofar as they largely "calibrate" the empirical potentialities of data, are both theoretical and practical in nature.

One of the challenges in the three studies presented is to affirm the existence of a European space that is not only sufficiently autonomous from the distinct national spaces, but is also sufficiently specific compared to the global space: making this double distinction is never easy because while some fields may be characterized by strong national autonomy, others are characterized by a genuine "global" insertion. Rather than undertake endless discussions about the games played at different levels or through multilevel relationships, we will characterize the degree of autonomy of each relevant level analyzed.

One of the key challenges encountered in the central bank study revolves around the definition of the very notion of *leadership* (or governance) of a central bank. By extending the definition of the relevant sub-field of governors to sub-governors and members of monetary policy councils, we sought to emphasize the institutional criteria that gives monetary policy advice true "sovereignty" over the issue. The actors selected were directly involved in the decision-making process, i.e., they either "voted" or at least took an official stance on monetary decisions. The highly centralized, highly formalized, and highly standardized nature of the sector makes this separation possible, particularly with regard to the administrative directors of the Central Bank, who are thus considered here, rightly or wrongly, as "implementers". The specificity of the ECB leads us to pay special attention to the subspace constituted by the European Executive Board in monetary matters, i.e., the Board of Governors composed of members of the management board and the governors of national central banks. The survey, which began in 1999 and is still ongoing, is global. The base currently comprises 700 individuals. Certain areas have been covered far less than others and the list of board members has not always been easy to obtain, which implies a permanent reflection on potential biases of the sample. Moreover, members' CVs, which are unevenly available and have been filled in diverse ways, were also difficult to get.

Although the POLILEXES survey was restricted to legal professionals, it included a relatively broad number of professionals: judges of the various courts, law clerks, parliamentarians specializing in law (determined by their membership of the legal committees of the European Parliament), and legal officers of the EC since the Treaty of Rome. Three major periods (defined by each "major enlargement" before the 2004 enlargement) were taken into account. One of the recurring problems encountered was that although lawyers were not taken into account as such, they were present when they occupied (or had occupied) one of the positions analyzed. Given the absence of comparable sources and for practical reasons, this large group was not integrated into the study in its current state (N = 530). We found that analyzing European unity was problematic over a relatively long historical perspective. Indeed, European history is marked by increasingly large "groups of countries", which justified our decision to stop the analysis in 2004, i.e., after the 2004 enlargement that most clearly challenged the homogeneity of the entire European Union (EU) setup.

In the EUROCRATIE survey, we focused on the directors, members of staff, and the senior management of the various European institutions. We paid special attention to the so-called "economic" directorates, which led to debate around the management of the budget in particular. Although it was a difficult choice, we decided to ignore national "economic" directorates below the governor level in the Finance Ministries or the national central banks. We thus focused on comparing two periods (2001 and 2012–2013) and on the "administrative" core of

Eurocracy (N = 410). We also focused on the most "strictly European" section of European elites, insofar as this section does not belong to a national administration. This choice was justified to a large extent by the increased autonomy of the field of Eurocracy, whose momentum contributes in part to the momentum of European dynamics.

Our data thus covers a very large scope and corresponds to many different forms: number of variables, with approximately 40 for BANQCENT (which is closely linked to the sources), more than 500 for POLILEXES (which may be explained by duplications within three separate periods and the quest to collect comprehensive professional information), and only 30 variables for EUROCRATIE (the idea was to work with a small model and to avoid exaggerating the degree of accuracy of the biographical information necessary to analyze the structures).

The organization and division of scientific activities also differed across surveys. These ranged from the most creative and individual (BANQCENT) to the most standardized and collective (POLILEXES) survey, and from the most "undivided" (BANQCENT) to the most segmented (POLILEXES). These differences resulted in differences in temporalities (artisanal research being slower), potential cumulativeness (a single study is theoretically less powerful than a set of comparative sub-studies), and the nature of the "*outputs*" (number of published articles, etc.).

The making and management of the database

Various sources provided the data used in these three surveys: directories, websites, etc. The EUROCRATIE survey has so far primarily relied on the *Trombinoscope*, a yearbook listing biographical information on most EU policy agents (Trombinoscope, 2001, 2013). There is a fundamental need to compare sources and an almost endless production of information, which risks provoking researchers' exhaustion and frustration, as has been witnessed in some of the surveys.

Transnational biographic sources are not easy to manipulate: while one may choose to stick to international directories (such as official directories, The International Who's Who, Trombinoscope, etc.), which are relatively standardized and easy to use to code data, these data are also relatively superficial. A different option may be to use the maximum amount of national information, with varying degrees of precision depending on regions, institutions, etc. In particular, access to information on family and social origin is often difficult to obtain even though one may imagine that the characteristics produced from the primary *habitus* of individuals in cultural matters (multilingualism, familiarity with transnational institutions, etc.) greatly influences their experiences.

Manual procedures undertaken collectively were used in the three surveys. These procedures were often not performed at one moment in time and sometimes delegated to people not involved in the initial elaboration of the surveys (BANQCENT and EUROCRATIE, for example). The automation of the information production has increasingly taken advantage of the generalization and ease of access to digital tools (as has been shown by the studies undertaken by Denord, Lagneau-Ymonet, & Thine, 2011).

Specific subpopulations present an additional difficulty. One must thus deal with contrasting situations in terms of access to information according to the group and the region of the world. Many "non-responses" (missing responses) are commonly encountered by researchers in the field of contemporary prosopography, and this is particularly true in the transnational context. This explains the significance of methods such as the analysis of specific multiple correspondences which allow researchers to address the issue of non-responses in a simple and refined manner.

The first basic sorting reveals variables with many categories with low or very low values. This reflects the quasi-ethnographic richness of the information collected by specialists attentive to the subtle variations within a given field. However, the large number of low-frequency categories in the variables collected implies the presence of coding-related issues and problems. Interpreting the structure of the spaces highlighted will thus require a shift from a qualitative to a geometric model-based analysis, before returning to a qualitative analysis.

Lastly, "viewpoints" and "discourses" remain an important issue in the construction of biographical data. How may they be integrated into the data collection process? We believe that researchers must first code information as one would code more "objective" information, i.e., by constantly remaining alert to the characteristics of viewpoints: their contextual nature, their variability, the difficulty of interpreting discourses, etc. We may draw in part on the approaches used in network analysis, for instance, to allow a co-citation analysis of articles (Callon, Courtial, & Pénan, 1993).

Big Data success will undoubtedly allow researchers to deal with much larger databases more exhaustively in the future. This, however, will not help resolve any fundamental methodological and scientific problems mentioned in this chapter: the many "empty spaces" and the heterogeneity encountered in the data collected will indeed accentuate the issue of sociological relevance already caused by the cumbersome and meandering nature of prosopographic work.

This is an ongoing process involving the collection, coding, and initial processing of data and, in some respects, appears an endless quest (Schmidt-Wellenburg & Lebaron, 2018; Schmidt-Wellenburg & Bernhard, Chapter 1). The example of POLILEXES helped us regularly assess the limits of any ambitious database: through "surprises" and detected "errors", which were often a result of coders' application of standards not set out before and thus not fully harmonized, a new desire for harmonization emerged alongside some form of relativization of the numerical data produced.

It thus rapidly emerges that while coding is required for modeling, it is also a process through which information may be lost, albeit temporarily, when structuring and representing the results. The quality of the statistical analysis, notably geometric analysis, is strongly dependent on the quality of the coding schemes used, which largely depends on the expertise of the experts, who alone can determine, for instance, appropriate divisions concerning the space occupied by academic institutions.

In practice, it is possible to compare subpopulations based on specific indicators (sex ratio, proportion of different age groups, etc.). This heuristic approach also serves as a tool for verifying the quality of the data collected. A systematic comparison of transnational populations is important, specifically because it disessentializes these populations by characterizing them using ordinary and immediately comparable traits such as sex ratio, the proportion of Ph.D. holders, the proportion of disciplines in initial training programs, the presence of "compulsory experiences" in one's career, etc. Inspired by a sociodemographic approach (Fouquet & Vinokur, 1996), reasoning in terms of subpopulations therefore complements the fundamentally biographical approach associated with GDA.

GDA as a framework for the analysis of transnational spaces

Cleaning up the database is only the first step in a systematic research process, and it is not one which need necessarily be carried out by the original designers (Lebaron, 2006). Obtaining basic descriptive statistics is always a decisive phase. In all the three cases analyzed, a first set of results is presented in the form of summary information about a population (see, for example, the tables on European Central bankers in the articles quoted). Contingency tables help refine the comparisons between subpopulations and produce results that are easy to communicate and interpret.

A wide variety of "multivariate" analyses can then be carried out on this type of database. These may include methods that help construct categories, depending on trajectories: hierarchical agglomerative clustering (HAC), extending multiple correspondence analysis (MCA), sequence analysis, etc. The co-affiliation data allows the construction of social network graphs and the interpretation of, for instance, central and intermediate points.

We favored the use of GDA as a tool for the geometric modeling of social spaces (Lebaron, 2006; Lebaron & Le Roux, 2015). The first phase involved responding to the research questions of the survey designers or to the questions that the data enabled us to start addressing. The construction of a space is only one phase of sociological analysis, making it primarily possible to replace vague questions with systematic operationalization. This calls for discussions around fundamental choices and requires researchers to calibrate their analyses, both in terms of the significance of effects and variations as well as with regard to the "dividing principles" that affect all social environments. In the context of the study of transnational spaces, this approach makes it possible to replace abstract entities that remain at risk of becoming *sui generis* essences with multidimensional spaces that rely on the statistical relationship established across the relevant statistical properties of individuals.

This heuristic and pragmatic approach does not mean that one should abandon the rigor of formalization and statistical practice. Rather, it means that these should be conceived as instruments of the progressive construction of the scientific object, likely to use more "qualitative" observations to foster dialogue and to refine interpretative or "modeling" strategies.

To illustrate this, we present three examples of the construction of space, with special emphasis on their heuristic nature, the issues raised, and the limitations.[5]

Example 1. The case of innovations within the ECB

We will begin by presenting "innovations" within the ECB. The key objective of the exploratory study is to show the heuristic potentialities of this approach in terms of the analysis of viewpoints in a specific subfield.

The participants comprised 38 members of the Board of Governors of the ECB present between January 2010 and December 2014. In addition to sociodemographic variables, the "economic and monetary" style of the Board members was coded on the basis of their explicit and public positions and the comments and codes developed by ECB watchers on their websites.

A specific MCA was applied to 12 active issues and 31 active categories in order to geometrically model the Council's social space across this period: age, gender, position at the ECB between 2010 and 2014, education level, discipline, dominant career, stints in politics, the Central Bank, academia, public service, and finance.

An analysis of eigenvalues reveals a strong first axis followed by two axes of lesser "importance" as sums of the data (i.e., a modified rate of approximately 75%). This study will focus on the first two axes.

Figure 6.1 shows the cloud categories (the 30% with the highest contribution) in the foreground. On the right is one of the highest contributing categories: "Main career in administration", holds an MA degree, was a member of the Management Board between 2010 and 2014 ("was a member of the Executive Board at a moment during the period 2010–2014"), women, law, administration, and politics. On the left are opposite categories (academia, private sector, no stints in administration).

Table 6.1 BANQCENT Eigenvalues, gross variance rates, and modified rates

Axis	Eigenvalue	Gross variance rate	Cumulative gross variance rate	Modified variance rate	Cumulative modified rate
1	0.254	16.0	16.0	45.1%	45.1%
2	0.178	11.2	27.1	17.3%	62.3%
3	0.160	10.1	37.2	12.8%	75.1%
4	0.149	9.4	46.6	10.3%	85.4%
5	0.121	7.6	54.1	5.1%	90.5%

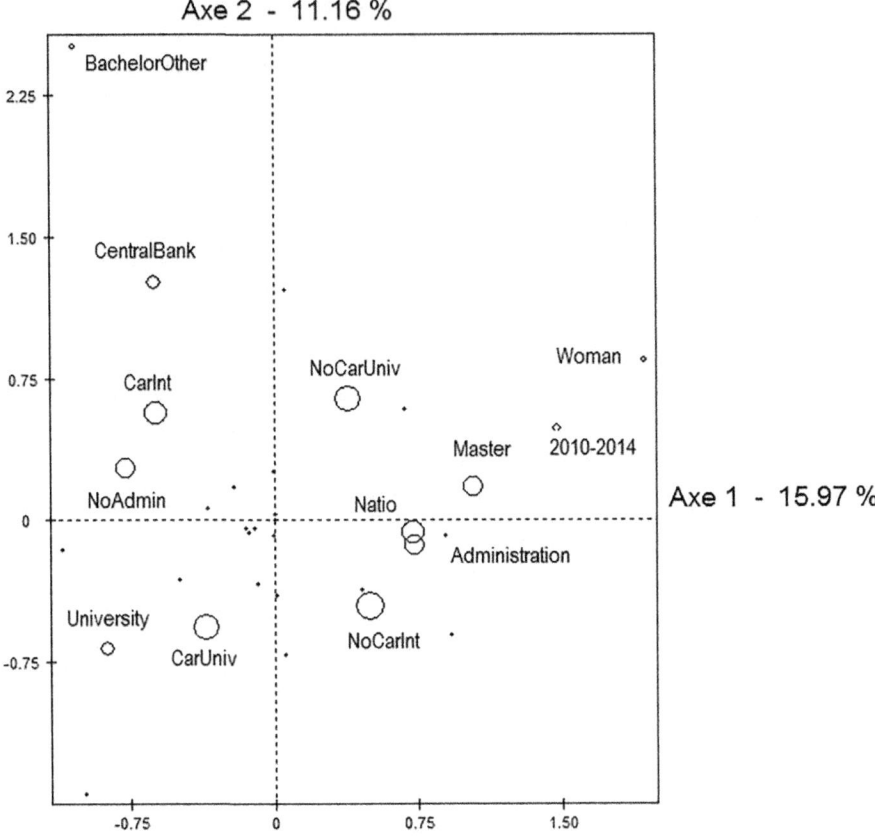

Figure 6.1 BANQCENT Plain 1–2 most contributory categories (30% of all active categories)

The first axis therefore pits political and administrative careers against academic, private, or internal careers at the Central Bank. It is a political and bureaucratic capital axis, linked to the presence of youth within the Board of Governors and thus to a generational and gendered process.

The second axis contrasts external careers in both the private sector and academia to internal careers at the Central Bank, reflecting a clear principle of distinction within the space.

The projection of additional elements (Figure 6.2) shows that the first axis is descriptively linked to an opposition between "hawks" (hostile to monetary easing and to innovation) and "moderates" to the right, and "doves" (favorable to monetary easing) who are more clearly to the left (with a standard deviation of 0.59, which may be read directly using the coordinates in the cloud categories, between the two extreme categories). The lack of political and bureaucratic capital and the

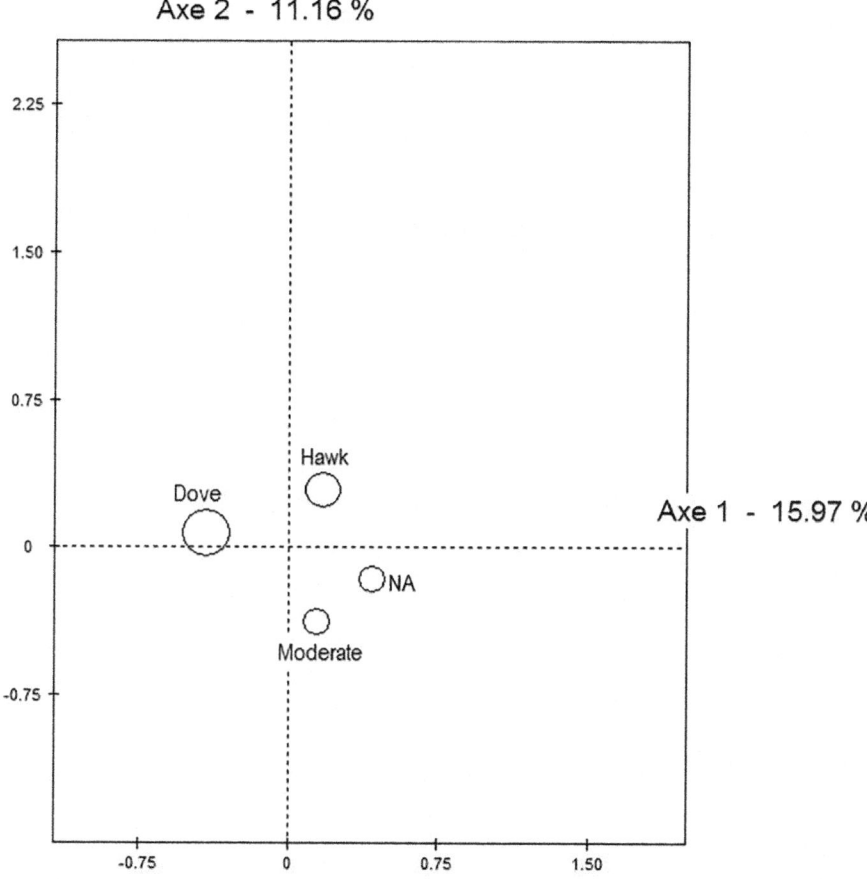

Axe 2 - 11.16 %

Axe 1 - 15.97 %

Figure 6.2 BANQCENT Plain 1–2 "doves" versus "hawks" (additional elements in the cloud categories)

relationship with the private sector and the university seem to be broadly associated with a more "innovative", "moderate", or "pragmatic" orientation.

This division provides insight into the reasons for the internal difficulties encountered by the Governing Council and the strong support for Mario Draghi's "innovative" orientation, a rather heterodox view and practice of monetary policy, with regard to monetary matters. Through his own hybrid trajectory, Draghi illustrates a mixed structure of capital and a pragmatic conception of monetary policy.

The cloud of individuals (Figure 6.3) also shows a strong dispersion within each of the two sub-groups of "hawks" and "doves" and strong divisions within the political and bureaucratic capital. The most "recent" members of the Management Board, irrespective of whether they are doves (B. Coeuré) or hawks (S. Lautenschläger), are clearly on the right on the first axis. One may expect them to have a strong political "influence".

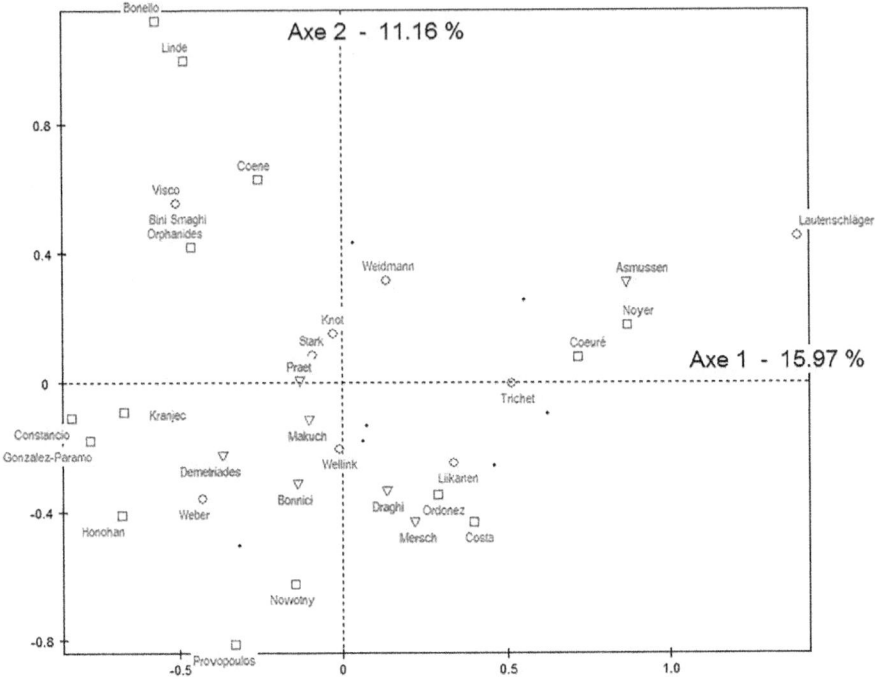

Figure 6.3 BANQCENT Plain 1–2 Clouds of individuals and their viewpoints (squares: "doves", circles: "hawks", triangles: "moderates")

Lastly, the study shows the internal political divisions among the Board of Governors that are linked to the social and professional characteristics of its members. On the side of resistance to innovation, one may notably find German central bank actors (but not all of them, because individuals, for example Jörg Assmussen, are primarily doves) and other members of a "German Coalition" within the Council, such as Yves Mersch from France or Erkki Liikanen from Finland. On the other side, the group supporting Mario Draghi through statements and votes, is led by a small group of actors with strong bureaucratic and political capital. It is also led by a majority (which is silent on many subjects) comprising national governors who are more often from academia and the private sector. In periods of high monetary and financial instability, building and maintaining a majority is critical within the Council.

It is worth mentioning that these results are based on very few participants, which implies that they need to be extended through the use of inference procedures, in particular combinatorial inference, which prevents the use of overly rigid "assumptions" (Le Roux & Rouanet, 2004).

Rather than study the impact of the national variable alone, the analysis thus establishes the significance of the attributes of trajectories defined at central bank level in Europe.

Example 2. The space of European legal professions from 1950 to 2004

Based on the information about individuals with regards to the issues analyzed above, we decided to construct a space of European legal professions from 1950 to 2004. We sought to analyze the extent to which the general structure of a European space thus constructed relates to variables such as the period of activity, the positions occupied, or any other information in the database. This phase enabled us to identify some important results by revealing a global dynamic of the internationalization of training that was more pronounced in some sectors within the space than in others. It also allowed us to highlight the major polarizations internal to this sphere, as has been found by various studies on the subject (Cohen, 2006; Mégie & Sacriste, 2009; Cohen & Vauchez, 2010; Vauchez & de Witte, 2012).

The European space analyzed comprised 442 individuals and was constructed on the basis of 15 active questions and 45 active categories relating to three areas:

- Two questions (four active categories) relating to sociodemographic identity: gender (two categories) and type of country (two categories: big and small);
- Six questions (13 active categories) relating to the academic and educational trajectory: qualification level (five categories, including two passive categories*: Ph.D., master's, bachelor's, university entrance qualifications*, and missing*), location where education qualifications were obtained (four categories, including two passive categories*: partly abroad, completely national, completely abroad*, missing*), university in the United States (two categories), the College of Europe (two categories), Universities of Paris (two categories), Oxbridge (two categories);
- Seven questions on the career path (28 active categories): age one first joined a European institution (30 categories, including one passive category*: before age 30, 30–39, 40–49, 50–59, 60 and above, missing*), sector of the first professional activity (six categories: academic, administrative, economic, judicial, political, other [association, journalism]), sector of the last professional activity (seven categories, including two passive categories [other and missing*]), number of sectors across the entire career (four categories: 1, 2, 3, and 4–5 sectors]), number of positions in European institutions (five categories, including one passive category*: 1, 2, 3–4, 5 and more, missing*), stint in the private sector (two categories), stint in politics (two categories).

This space was thus primarily constructed based on the indicators of academic and, notably, professional trajectories. This is perfectly in line with our research objectives, which focus on the differentiation of professional paths within the European legal framework. To enable a comparison, the study assumes that there is at least some homogeneity across the active variables selected. It also assumes that the differentiations relating to these variables are meaningful at the European level.

Based on the results of a specific MCA, we selected four axes. We will only focus on the first two axes retained (highest contributing 30% of active categories were analyzed for each axis). Axis 1 is predominantly an axis of career and school trajectories. It contrasts, on the right, no stint in the political sector (11.6%), national and foreign education (9.7%), university in the United States (7.8%), College of Europe (5.8%), one sector throughout the career (5%), entry before age 30 (3.7%), with, on the left, prior political profession (11.7%), stint in the political sector (10.4%), strictly national education (4.1%), entry into institutions between 50 and 59 years (3.1%).

This axis is thus strongly influenced by the relationship to both politics and academic trajectories privileged by some countries and international institutions on the one hand, or is "strictly national" on the other. It therefore contrasts the national academic capital to some form of international academic capital, and the political capital to the other types of capital.

Axis 2 distinguishes between different types of professional trajectories. It contrasts, at the bottom of the graph, private sector (12.2%), prior profession in economics (7.8%), master's degree (7.8%), Oxbridge (7.4%), first profession in the legal sector (5.1%), first profession in economics (3.8%), with, at the top of the graph, no private sector (16%), Ph.D. (5.8%), first profession in academics (5.7%), two European positions (3.2%), first profession in the administration sector (2.6%), prior last profession in the administrative sector (2.5%), first profession in an association/journalism (2.4%). Axis 2 clearly contrasts a private and economical cluster at the bottom with a public and academic/administrative cluster at the top.

It is also relatively easy to interpret axes 3 and 4, not presented visually here. Axis 3 represents European capital positioning, on the one hand, a strong European capital, associative, journalistic, or administrative trajectories, training in the College of Europe, and early entry into European institutions, against, on the

Table 6.2 POLILEXES Eigenvalues, gross variance rates, and modified rates

Axis	Eigenvalue	Gross variance rate	Cumulative gross variance rate	Modified variance rate	Cumulative modified rate
1	0.184	9.1	9.1	49.8%	49.8%
2	0.124	6.1	15.2	14.1%	63.9%
3	0.110	5.4	20.6	8.8%	72.7%
4	0.107	5.3	25.9	7.9%	80.5%
5	0.100	4.9	30.8	5.8%	86.3%

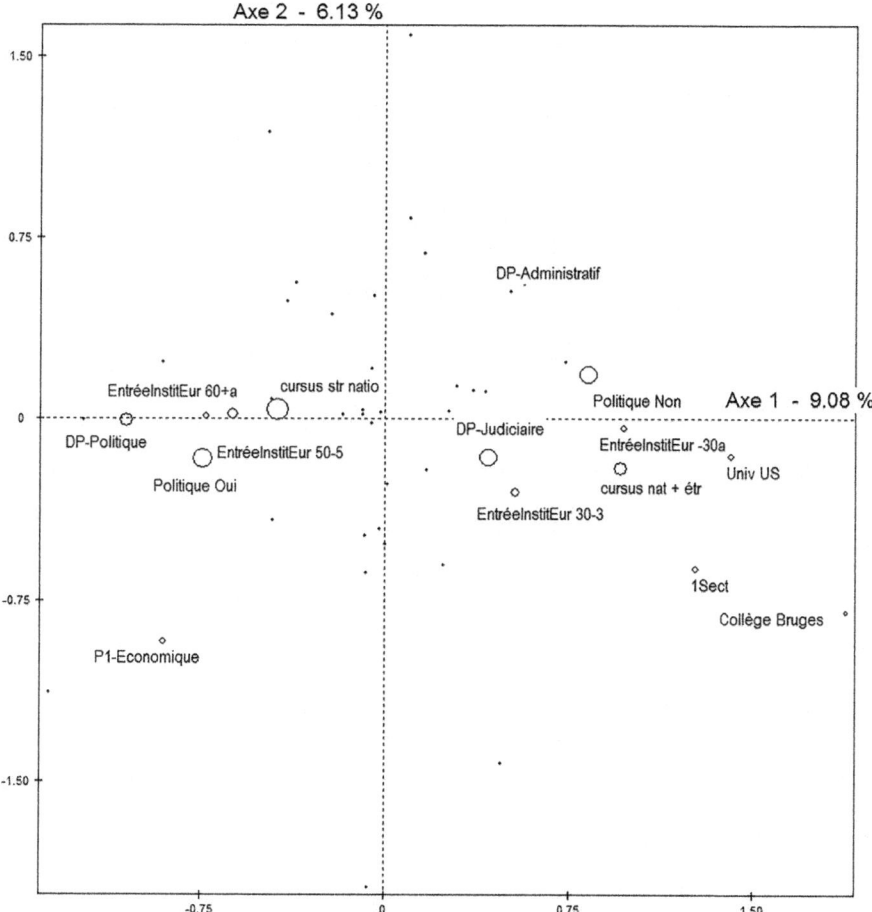

Figure 6.4 POLILEXES Axis I most contributory categories (30% of all active categories)

other hand, trajectories in the judicial sector and individuals who joined the field rather late. Axis 4 contrasts multi-sectoral trajectories, often linked to academic and economic worlds, with mono-sectoral trajectories, more often linked to the political world.

The cloud of individuals reveals "paragon" individuals, characteristic of the different poles of the space. The first axis reveals a clear opposition between the parliamentarians on the left, law clerks, members of legal services and, on the right, members of the Civil Service Tribunal, with judges occupying an intermediate position. An opposition between judges (top) and members of the Civil

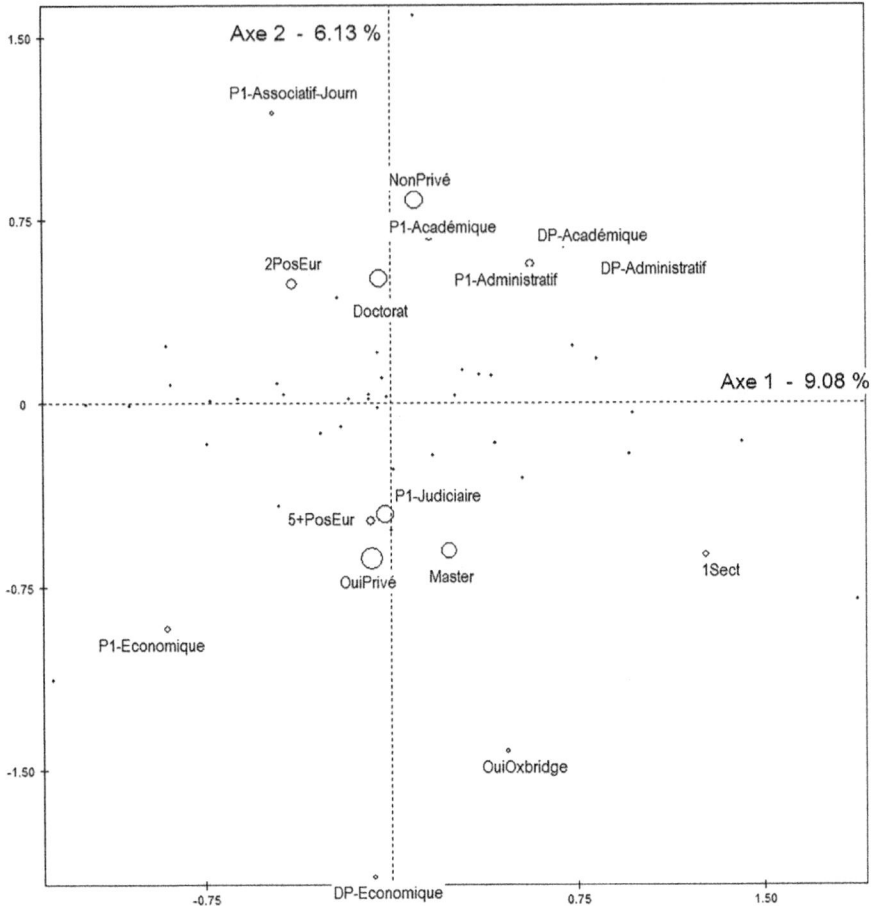

Figure 6.5 POLILEXES Axis 2 most contributory categories (30% of all active categories)

Service Tribunal (bottom) appears on axis 2. For the others, there are minor differences between the various "populations" just named in this regard. These populations have been selected at the beginning of the research, and include judges and legal secretaries at the different European courts, members of a legal committee at the European Parliament, and law advisers at the European Commission and other European institutions.

Philippe de Villiers (on the left of axis 1) is a French politician, who was a member of the European Parliament on the basis of strong anti-European "pro-sovereignty" position takings; whereas Gaëlle Bontinck (on the right)

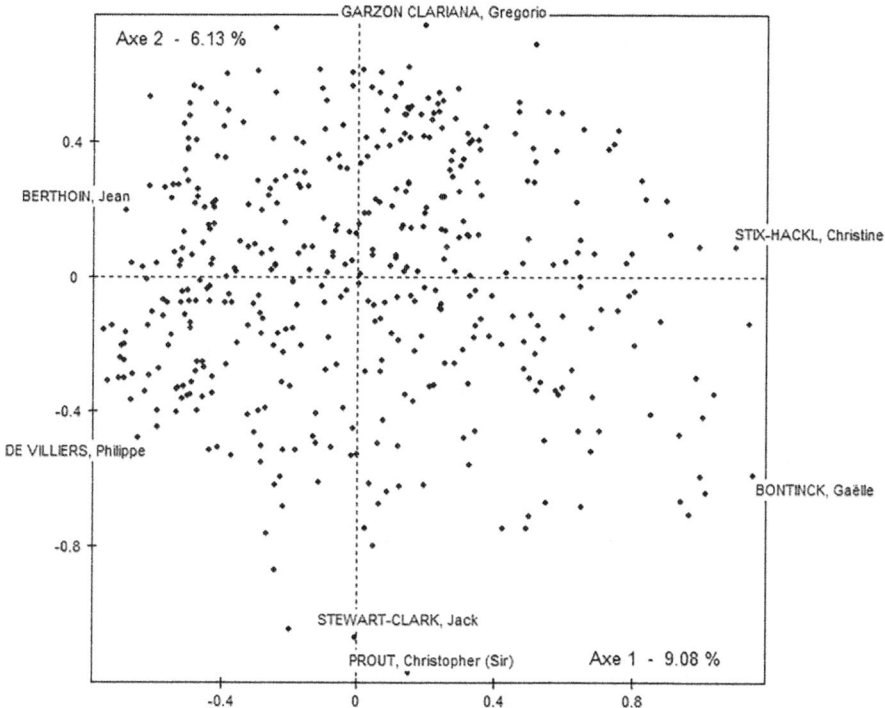

Figure 6.6 POLILEXES Plain 1–2 cloud of individuals

is an internationally trained law professional, having worked as a legal secretary at the Court and well inserted in the global judicial field. Down below on axis 2, Christopher Prout (Lord Kingsland) was a British barrister and politician, who served as the leader of Conservatives at the European Parliament and had a clear pro-European orientation inside the Tories; whereas Gregorio Garzon Clariana was Legal Counsel and Director-General of the Legal Service at the European Parliament, and is now a professor of European Law in Barcelona.

The analysis thus allows us to better specify the relational properties of the subpopulations identified as components of a European legal field. These properties were defined based on the systematic differences of individual trajectories, meaning that they simply represent the averages of individual properties and may thus be dispersed. Naturally, the construction of the European field is undoubtedly partial and only provides a heuristic representation of a multidimensional transnational space, thus surpassing the fixed and juxtaposed representations of the different groups.

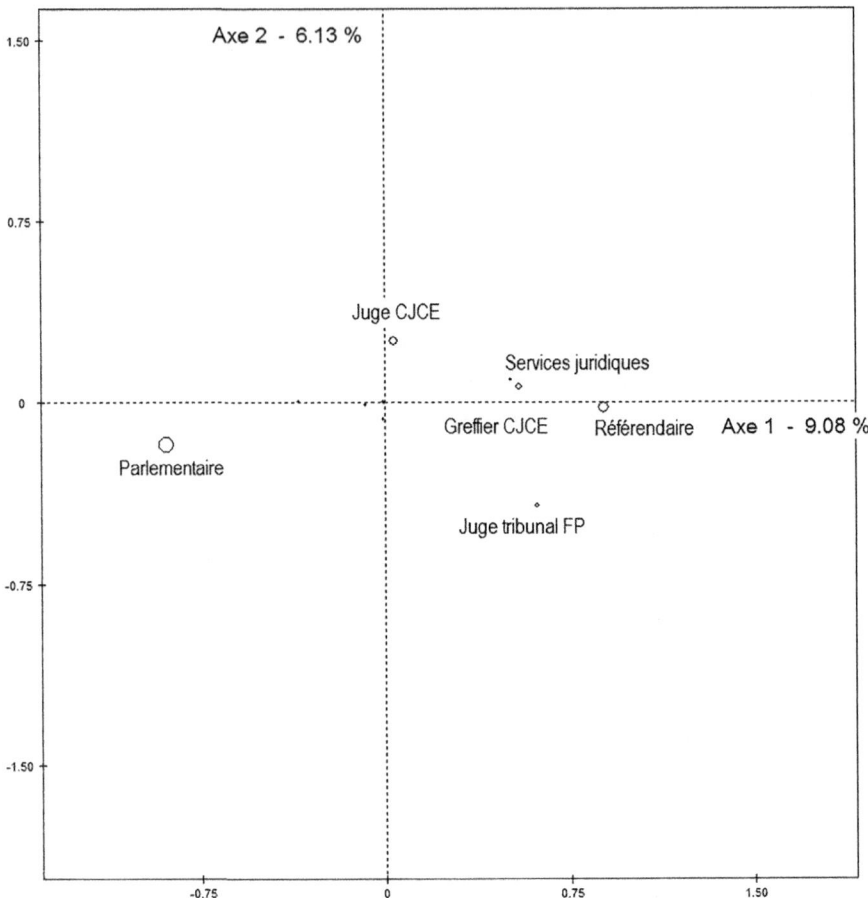

Figure 6.7 POLILEXES Plain 1–2 different "professional populations" (passive categories)

Example 3. Outline of field of European economic governance

We applied a specific MCA to analyze the structure of this European area, selecting the following 14 variables as active variables, grouped in three areas:

*   Socio-demographic properties (two variables, five categories): gender (two categories), age at the time of publication of the notice (three categories: less than 45 years/45–60 years/60 years and above);
*   Academic trajectory (eight variables, 19 categories): main location of training (three categories), location where the last diploma was obtained

(three categories), education level (three categories), economics (two categories), law (two categories), management (two categories), political sciences/public administration (two categories), sciences (two categories);

- Career (four variables, nine categories): previous experience in an administration position (two categories), was a member of cabinet (three categories), sectoral mobility (two categories), held a horizontal position (two categories).

Given the eigenvalue decay, we retained three axes. Only the first two axes will be analyzed here. Axis 1 contrasts the left (negative values): economy, no law, and national administration, with the right: the cabinet of the commissioner, law, no economy, European administration, multi-sectoral mobility, etc. There is thus a clear opposition between the capital linked to economics, which has an American component but is also linked to national administration, and legal capital, which appears to be more specific to the European institutions ("Brussels") themselves. There is therefore a differentiation according to the level of Europeanization of the capital held, which is inversely proportional to capital holding in economics.

Axis 2 is primarily determined by issues relating to careers and contrasts (at the top) the absence of horizontal mobility, experience in a cabinet, sectoral mobility, European administration, and training in a major US-American university, with (at the bottom) experience in a leadership firm, horizontal and multi-sectoral mobility, national administration, the sciences, and the political sciences.

Here we have an axis of positional differences (it increases as one descends along the axis), of political capital (with experience in a cabinet of a political leader), including at the national level (experience in the national administration), with diplomas in the political sciences.

There is a close relationship between the capital held and the institutional positions occupied in the sub-field of economic governance that shows in the positions of passive categories used. This confirms that it is somewhat futile to compare

Table 6.3 EUROCRATIE Eigenvalues, gross variance rates, and modified rates of the first five axes

Axis	Eigenvalue	Gross variance rate	Cumulative gross variance rate	Modified variance rate	Cumulative modified rate
1	0.176	12.9	12.9	55.6%	55.6%
2	0.105	7.7	20.7	11.1%	66.6%
3	0.102	7.5	28.2	9.8%	76.4%
4	0.095	7.0	35.1	7.4%	83.8%
5	0.089	6.5	41.7	5.6%	89.4%

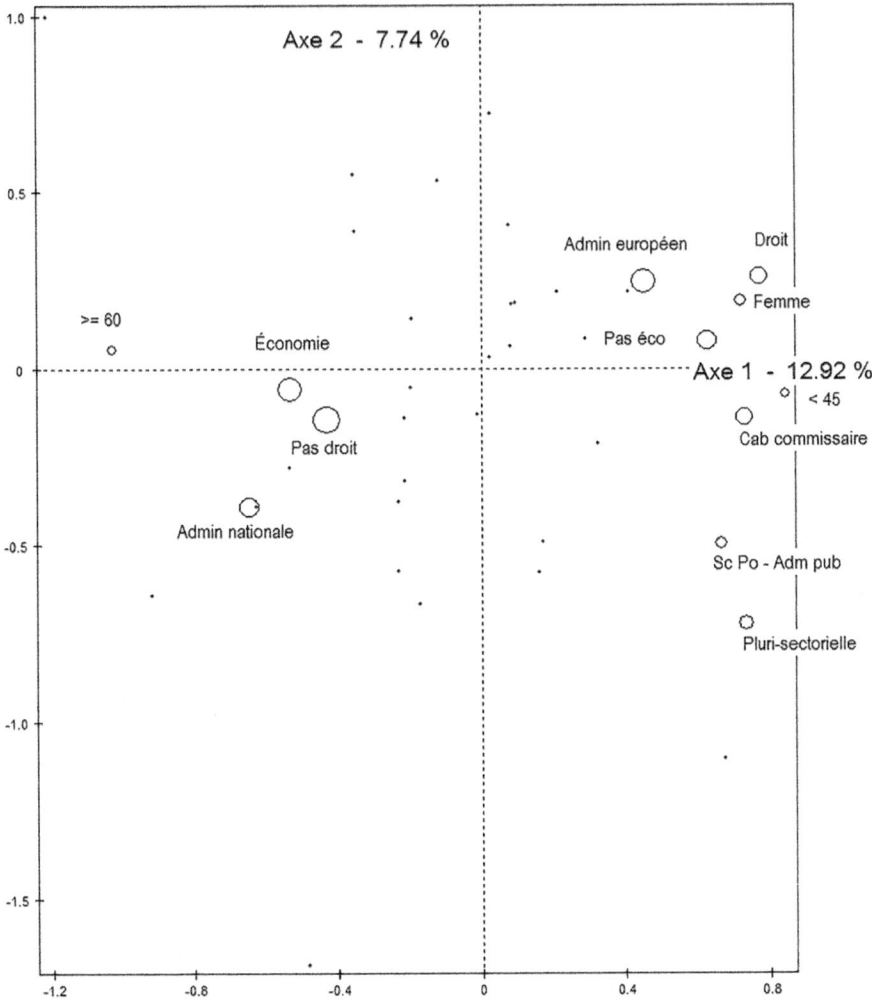

Figure 6.8 EUROCRATIE Axis I most contributory categories (30% of all active categories)

the resources held by an individual with the effects of their official (institutional) position. Indeed, the two elements interact strongly with each other, and the characteristics "incorporated" in a specific trajectory help determine the meaning, effectiveness, and authority of the position, the position itself being a fundamental resource of the individual's concrete action.

Axis 1 contrasts the positions within the ECB to the left, with the positions of the heads and members of the cabinet to the right; the most specific

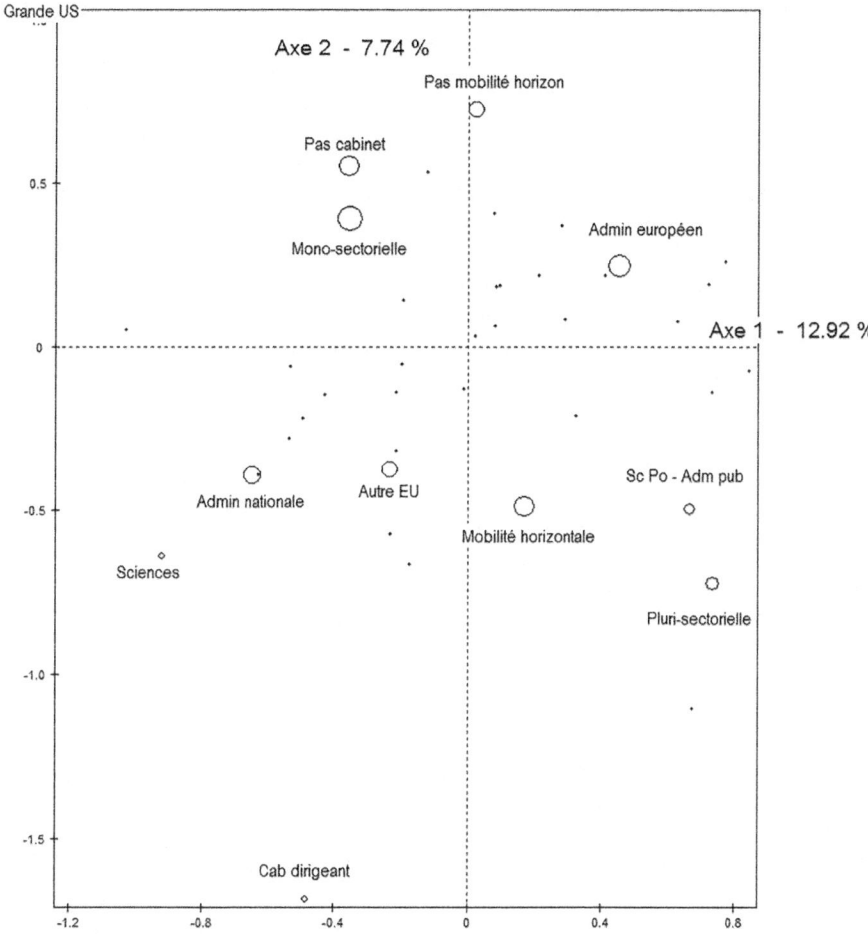

Figure 6.9 EUROCRATIE Axis 2 most contributory categories (30% of all active categories)

positions are to the left of the most "European" positions on the right. Thus, at this level, there is already a strong relationship between the capital of the actors and the institutions, which insulates the special ECB universe ("Frankfurt") on the left. Axis 2 clearly contrasts positions dominated by politics (at the bottom), such as the EU Secretary-General and Commissioner, with the "purely" administrative positions (at the top), such as those held by directors.

In institutions, the space is clearly divided (axis 1) between a cluster associated with economics, embodied by the ECB and by Eurostat. It is also embodied, albeit to a lesser extent, by the Directorate-General (DG) for Economic and Financial Affairs

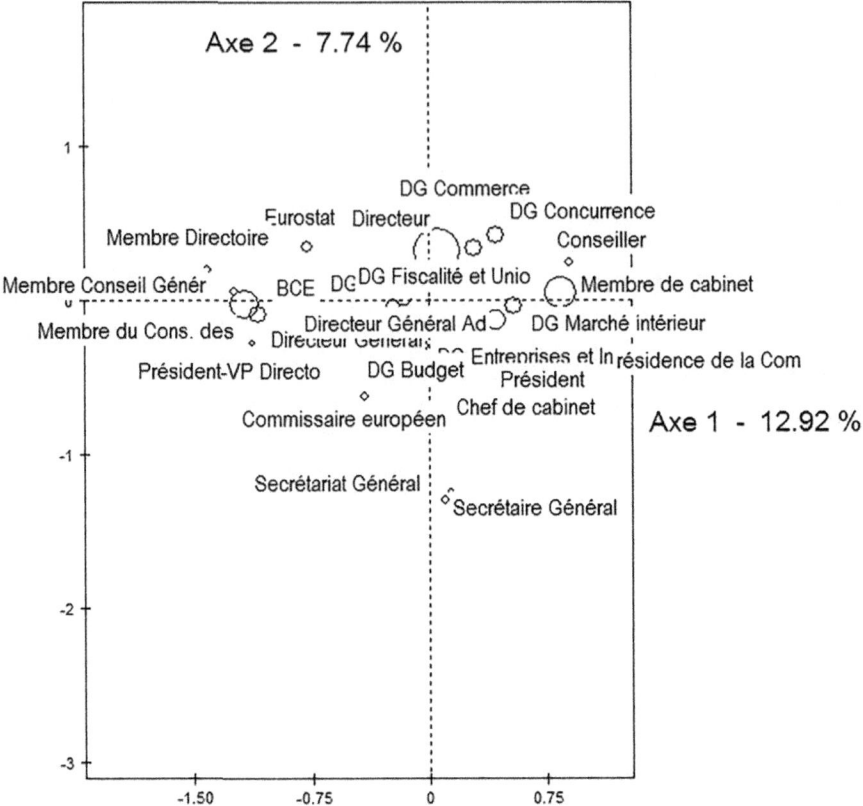

Figure 6.10 EUROCRATIE Plain 1–2 positions and institutions (supplementary categories)

(DG ECFIN) and by the most "legal" directorates within the sub-field of economic governance, such as the DG Internal Market. Axis 2 isolates (at the bottom) the General Secretariat of the Council of the EU and, to a lesser extent, the chairmanship of the Commission, where the greatest political surface, circulation, and capital resides.

Once again, the space thus created makes it possible to situate any individual in the population analyzed from a relational perspective: institutions are distributed throughout this multidimensional space, in which the common factor is that it is made up of actors who hold economic governance positions. The cloud of individuals reveals the positions occupied by the actors rather than by institutions, enabling us to overcome the artificial distinction between the level of individual and institutional actors.

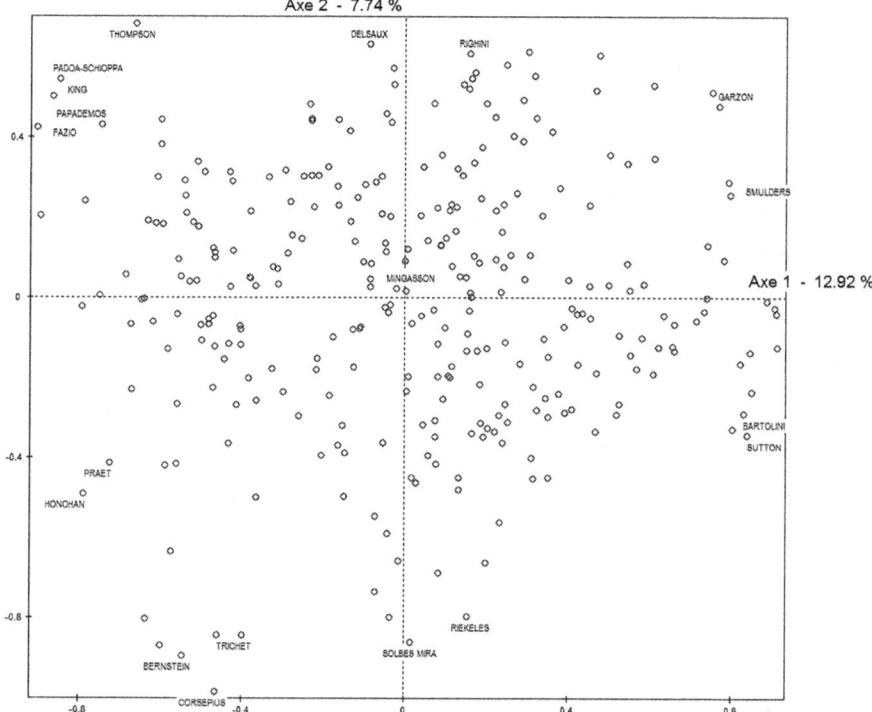

Figure 6.11 EUROCRATIE Plain 1–2 cloud of individuals

Conclusion

Analyzing transnational fields using GDA methods is a long and rather thank-less task, especially during the complex data development phase. However, these methods propose many heuristic potentials that make it possible to explore com-plex social spaces when used alongside more qualitative methods or approaches that focus on the analysis and interpretation of personal careers.

Such an analysis involves considerable investments in terms of budget, time, and scientific rigor. It also requires individual and collective commitment. Indeed, the scientific impact of GDA methods is still relatively underestimated, in particu-lar because these methods call for collaborative research dynamics that appear to be increasingly necessary in transnational spaces. Moreover, while relying on observations at the individual level, they pave the way for new ways of comparing macro-social or meso-social structures.

Different scales and different levels of information are possible, ranging from the individual "small base" to the large collective base, from the base resulting from a thesis or from major transnational research programs partially exploited by one or more researchers.

This perspective implies that researchers must adopt a relational approach, i.e., they must think in terms of the social space and the objects studied, meaning that it may be used for both qualitative and quantitative analyses (Bigo, 2007; Dezalay, 2007: 67 ff.; Vauchez, 2008; Fligstein & McAdam, 2013). In particular, it may allow the systematic development of structural or relational biographies, making it possible to avoid some of the limitations of classical biography and, especially, "the biographical illusion". Lastly, the perspective provides a means through which to test the empirical scope of theoretical concepts and refine the theory on specific questions the data is expected to answer.

This research perspective is particularly relevant in the analysis of transnational spaces for various reasons highlighted in this chapter: the temptation to reify collective entities is all the stronger when, at the transnational level, relatively abstract spaces are analyzed. This is why it is important to represent complex and highly multidimensional spaces – which actors often overlook – in a relational and synthetic manner, by placing the individual actors within these spaces.

By defining these spaces based on simple biographical characteristics that are sufficiently comparable to be meaningful within these spaces, one may thus draw on concrete trajectories of transnational actors to "repopulate" sociological analyses. This would make it possible to consolidate the analyses and assumptions developed by the analysis of the biographies of individual actors and by the analysis of the "careers" of institutions and organizations.

Notes

1 This chapter builds on a paper originally presented at King's College London at a seminar organized by Didier Bigo in 2014. It was developed at the Moulin D'Andé as part of the thematic summer school organized by D. Georgakakis, J. Rowell, and A. Vauchez in June 2015.
2 The collection by Broady et al. (1995) presents a good overview, resulting from an international conference presenting work carried out at Bourdieu's Centre de sociologie de l'éducation et de la culture (renamed again Centre de sociologie euopéene at the end of the 1990s). The research presented in the volume was the first of a series of many prosopographic studies undertaken in the 1990s in different national contexts such as Brazil, Russia, Sweden, etc.
3 We would like to thank all the colleagues who sparked different reflections and who contributed to the progress of these studies.
4 With regard to the "qualitative" approach, we focus in particular on the reflections developed by Olivier de Sardan (2008). For an in-depth historical and epistemological reflection of the ethnographic approach employed, see e.g. Weber (2015).
5 The analyses were all performed using the SPAD8 software and the modified rates were calculated using Macro Excel developed by Flora Chanvril.

References

Beauvallet, W., & Michon, S. (2013). MEPs: Toward a Specialisation of Euroepan Political Work? In D. Georgakakis & J. Rowell (Eds.), *The Field of Eurocracy: Mapping the EU Actors and Professionals* (pp. 16–34). Houndmills, Basingstoke: Palgrave Macmillan.

Bigo, D. (2007). *The Field of the EU Internal Security Agencies*. Paris: L'Harmattan.

Bourdieu, P. (Ed.). (2013). *Théorie du champ: Actes de la recherche en sciences sociales, No. 200*. Paris: Seuil.

Bourdieu, P. (1989). *La noblesse d'État: grandes écoles et esprit de corps*. Paris: Minuit.

Broady, D., Palme, M., & de Saint-Martin, M. (Eds.). (1995). *Les élites, Formation, Reconversion, Internationalization*. Paris: Centre for the Sociology of Education and Culture, EHESS.

Callon, M., Courtial, J. P., & Pénan, H. (1993). *La scientométrie*. Paris: PUF.

Cohen, A. (2006). L'Europe en constitution: Professionnels du droit et des institutions entre champ académique international et champ du pouvoir européen. In A. Cohen, B. Lacroix & P. Riutort (Eds.), *Les formes de l'activité politique: Éléments d'analyse sociologique, du xviii ᵉ siècle à nos jours* (pp. 297–315). Paris: PUF.

Cohen, A., & Vauchez, A. (2010). Sociologie politique de l'Europe du droit. *Revue française de science politique, 60*(2), 223–226.

Denord, F., Lagneau-Ymonet, P., & Thine, S. (2011). Le champ du pouvoir en France. *Actes de la recherche en sciences sociales, 190*, 24–57.

Dezalay, Y. (2007). De la défense de l'environnement au développement durable: L'émergence d'un champ d'expertise des politiques européennes. *Actes de la recherche en sciences sociales, 166–167*, 67–79.

Fligstein, N., & McAdam, D. (2013). *A Theory of Fields*. Oxford: Oxford University Press.

Fouquet, A., & Vinokur, A. (1996). *Démographie socio-économique*. Paris: Dalloz.

Georgakakis, D., & de Lassalle, M. (2007). Genèse et structure d'un capital institutionnel européen: Les très hauts fonctionnaires de la Commission européenne. *Actes de la recherche en sciences sociales, 166–167*, 38–53.

Georgakakis, D., & Lebaron, F. (2015). Le champ de la gouvernance économique européenne et les politiques d'austérité (2010–2015): Premières esquisses. Conference paper presented at *The Economic Crisis and the Reconfiguration of European Actors*, November 4, 2015, Strasbourg.

Georgakakis, D., & Lebaron, F. (2018). Yanis (Varoufakis), the Minotaure and the Field of Eurocracy. *Historical Social Research, 43*(3), 216–247.

Georgakakis, D., & Rowell, J. (Eds.). (2013). *The Field of Eurocracy: Mapping the EU Actors and Professionals*. Houndmills, Basingstoke: Palgrave Macmillan.

Lebaron, F. (2006). *L'enquête quantitative en sciences sociales: Recueil et analyse des données*. Paris: Dunod.

Lebaron, F. (2008). Central Bankers in the Contemporary Global Field of Power: A 'Social Space' Approach. In M. Savage & K. Williams (Eds.), *Remembering Elites* (pp. 121–144). Oxford: Blackwell.

Lebaron, F. (2010). European Central Bank Leaders in the Global Space of Central Bankers: A Geometric Data Analysis Approach. *French Politics, 8*(3), 294–320.

Lebaron, F. (2012). A Universal Paradigm of Central Bankers? An Inquiry Based on Biographical Data. *Social Glance, 1*(1), 40–58.

Lebaron, F. (2014). Banquiers. In E. Lambert-Abdelgawad & H. Michel (Eds.), *Dictionnaire des acteurs de l'Europe*. Strasbourg: Larcier.

Lebaron, F. (2015). A Sociological Take on Central Bank Innovation. *ECPR General Conference*, August 28, 2015, Université de Montréal.

Lebaron, F., & Le Roux, B. (Eds.). (2015). *La méthodologie de Pierre Bourdieu en action: Espace culturel, espace social et analyse des données*. Paris: Dunod.

Le Roux, B., & Rouanet, H. (2004). *Geometric Data Analysis: From Correspondence Analysis to Structured Data Analysis*. Dordrecht: Kluwer.

Mégie, A., & Sacriste, G. (2009). Polilexes: Champ juridique européen et polity communautaire. *Politique européenne*, *28*(2), 57–162.

Olivier de Sardan, J.-P. (2008). *La rigueur du qualitative: Les contraintes empiriques de l'interprétation socioanthropologique*. Louvain-La-Neuve: Bruylant.

Schmidt-Wellenburg, C., & Lebaron, F. (2018). There Is No Such Thing as 'The Economy': Economic Phenomena Analysed from a Field-Theoretical Perspective. *Historical Social Research*, *43*(3), 7–38.

Trombinoscope. (2001). *Le trombinoscope: Union européenne 2001–2002*. Neuilly-sur-Seine: Huveaux politique.

Trombinoscope. (2012). *Le trombinoscope: Union européenne 2012–2013*. Neuilly-sur-Seine: Huveaux politique.

Vauchez, A. (2008). The Force of a Weak Field: Law and Lawyers in the Government of the European Union. *International Political Sociology*, *2*(2), 128–144.

Vauchez, A., & de Witte, B. (2012). *The European Legal Field*. Oxford: Hart Publishing.

Weber, F. (2015). *Brève histoire de l'anthropologie*. Paris: Flammarion.

Part II

Investigating political fields

Chapter 7

Global change

A field theory perspective on the end of empire*

Julian Go

Introduction

As the present volume and other works show, Bourdieu's field theory has been increasingly deployed to understand global and transnational politics and struggles.[1] But how might it be used to account for change on a global scale? In this chapter, I deploy Bourdieusian field theory to account for one of the most monumental modern transformations of the global political field: the end of colonial empires. For centuries, colonial empires had dominated the globe, but today, formal colonies or dependencies can scarcely be found. True, *informal* empires persist – empires by which a state exerts power or influence over a string of nominally independent but nonetheless subordinate or client states. We also see temporary military occupations and war of all sorts. But colonial or *formal* empire – consisting of long-term colonial occupations, whereby a foreign state declares permanent sovereignty over another society – is over and done with. The *United Nations Resolution 1514* in 1960 formalized this. Known as the *Declaration on the Granting of Independence to Colonial Countries and Peoples*, it announced that "the subjection of peoples to alien subjugation, domination and exploitation constitutes a denial of fundamental human rights, is contrary to the *Charter of the United Nations* and is an impediment to the promotion of world peace and co-operation." Given this, even if a powerful state were to annex new territory and turn it into a subordinate dependency, it would have a lot of justifying to do.

How and why did the dominant political form of three or four centuries (at least) suddenly end? At issue, to be clear, is not the decolonization of the old empires. Various studies have shown how and why decolonization happened. At issue rather is the fact that *formal colonization has been excised from the repertoire of global power*. How and why did this happen? To address this question about the end of colonialism as a dominant political form, we must not only ask why older empires fell and nation-states emerged, but also why great powers did not colonize or recolonize territory. Existing scholarship offers some possible clues, but has not directly addressed this specific question. This chapter shows how Bourdieu's field theory can help.[2] Accordingly, I begin by sketching the basic contours of field theory and extending its principles to theorize change, before turning to the particular empirical issue on the table.

Global fields and their transformation

Fields as arenas of struggle over capital

Bourdieu did not claim that all social relations are "fielded". Fields only exist when social actors compete or struggle with each other over different forms of capital.[3] Without competition or struggle, there are no fields. Therefore, unlike other approaches to global relations that highlight cohesion and consensus (e.g., Meyer, 2010), Bourdieu's field theory emphasizes struggle, competition, and conflict over capital (Bourdieu & Wacquant, 1992: 17). On the other hand, field theory is not reducible to international relations (IR) realism. Fields do not imply a state of anarchy, nor are fields devoid of culture and meaning. A field is structured by the objective relations between actors (the field of positions) and the subjective and cultural forms of those relations. The latter include, among other things, the "rules of the game" that the "players" agree upon and that may be taken for granted – part of the field's *doxa* – or formally codified as law. Fields are not reducible to lower-level units like individuals or states (Bourdieu, 1989: 19). Furthermore, unlike either realism or constructivism, multiple "species" of capital can be stake. Economic capital, cultural capital, spiritual capital – all of these can exist, depending upon the type of field in question (Bourdieu & Wacquant, 1992: 97; Verter, 2003).

In this sense, Bourdieu would find no utility in disputes between world-systems or realist IR theories that emphasize materialism and naked interests on the one hand and, on the other, constructivists or world polity proponents who focus on meanings and norms. Culture is not opposed to hierarchy and power: to the contrary, they are intertwined (Swartz, 1997: 92). For instance, Bourdieu claims that field hierarchies are sustained and reproduced through cultural processes – not least, legitimation. Bourdieu theorizes this as "symbolic capital". Those who are dominant in the field, Bourdieu avers, legitimate their monopoly over capital by adopting a particular "stance" of worthiness. Symbolic capital is thus a type of prestige that accrues to the dominant and gives them the privilege of dominating (Bourdieu, 1977a: 197, 1977b).

The final relevant point about Bourdieu's field theory is its *relationality*. For many scholars, Bourdieu's field theory is exemplary of relationalism, and so it nestles easily within relationality in IR (Jackson & Nexon, 1999; Martin, 2003; Hilgers & Mangez, 2015). One of the analytic advantages of this relationalism in field theory is that it helps recognize that even powerful actors in fields are constrained and shaped by the field. All actors strategize, maneuver, and struggle in relation to all others; their "position-takings" or stances in the field (i.e., their self-presentation and strategies) are shaped by what everyone else does (Bourdieu, 1992: 231 ff.). Powerful dominant players in the field are no exception (Bourdieu, 1984, 1985: 738; Go, 2008). As we will see, this relational approach is an important part of the explanation for how and why norms change.

A global political field

While Bourdieu's main body of work examines fields *within* nations, it can be scaled in different ways. Bourdieu does not insist upon a singular field or sole "system": there can be multiple cross-cutting fields along different spatial scales. Furthermore, field boundaries are not stable; they can expand or contract. It follows that fields do not always coincide with the territorial boundaries of nation-states (Sapiro, 2013: 71 f.). In addition, the types of actors in fields might be individuals or corporate actors like states (even as most of Bourdieu's work addresses individuals). Field theory, therefore, can be used to address global relations between and across nation-states (Bourdieu, 1991a; Sapiro, 2013; Buchholz, 2016; Go & Krause, 2016).

Consider the "global political field" (Go, 2008). This is a field of political actors competing on a global scale, having its own "rules" for struggle ("norms") and distinct types of capital: economic capital, political capital (such as allies), cultural capital (recognition), symbolic capital (legitimacy) or what Go (2008) calls "security capital", and so on. Other actors populate this field too, such as corporations or non-governmental organizations, but unless these come into direct competition with states, these other actors most likely occupy other fields that overlap with this field; for instance, a field of humanitarian organizations (Krause, 2014). In turn, fields might change over time. Before the twenty-first century, for instance, key actors in the field were not nation-states but empires, constituting an inter-*imperial* field rather than an inter-*national* one. In this inter-imperial field, empires competed with each other for various forms of capital, including colonies that provided economic or security capital. Colonization of foreign societies was an accepted part of inter-imperial competition. It was a doxic rule. Another part of that doxa was a set of racialized assumptions about who could or who could not govern themselves: colonized peoples were assumed to be incapable and inferior in terms of their civilizational status (Jackson, 1993: 116 ff.). Furthermore, symbolic competition was part of this struggle. Great Britain or the United States portrayed themselves as "exceptional" or superior to other empires, like the German or Japanese (and vice versa) (Howe, 2002; Go, 2011).

Theorizing change

But how exactly might fields change? While Bourdieu has often been thought of as theorist of reproduction, the possibility of change is built into the very nature of fields (Calhoun, 2006; Gorski, 2013; Hilgers & Mangez, 2015: 11 f.). Still, Bourdieu never systematically sketched a clear theory of change. Doing so, I suggest, requires elaborating upon his basic concepts to highlight: a) struggle and its different types, and b) different relations between fields.

Regarding the first, while struggle is built into the very definition of fields, it is important to note that it can take different forms (Bourdieu, 1991b: 25, 1992: 126).

One is a "succession" struggle: "challengers" contend with dominant groups (or "incumbents") to accumulate more capital and essentially seek to replace them (Bourdieu, 1992: 124; Swartz, 1997: 125). The other form of struggle is a "subversion" struggle: challengers compete with incumbents for capital, but they do so in part by challenging the principles of the field that had been functioning to maintain the existing field hierarchy. They challenge which capitals are valued, what constitutes symbolic capital, or even the very rules of the game (Bourdieu, 1992: 121). In various works, Bourdieu shows how this happens in fields like religion or art, when dominant actors' very "monopoly over symbolic power" is often challenged by "heretics" who propose "heterodox" principles to undo the established "orthodoxy" (Bourdieu, 1991b: 25, 1992: 72 ff.) "Every field is the site of a more or less openly declared struggle for the definition of the legitimate principles of division of the field" (Bourdieu, 1991c: 242).

By these subversion struggles, not everything is challenged. Some elements of the *doxa* subtending oppositions in the field – which Bourdieu calls the "illusio" – do survive (Bourdieu, 1992: 227 f.). But subversion struggles do much more than lead to the replacement of one group with another at the top. They can transform what should count as capital in the first place, overthrowing the very principles by which capitals had been distributed in the field and hence, the premise of the existing hierarchy. The "principles of hierarchical differentiation" in the field are potentially overthrown, and in turn "the very shape and divisions of the field become a central stake" (Bourdieu, 1992: 17 f., 127).

But what impacts the outcomes of these struggles? Here is where the *relations between fields* become important: the dynamics of one field can be affected by struggles in other fields and make change more likely. There are at least two types of such relations between fields. The first is what Bourdieu calls variously "correspondence" or "homology". Fields are autonomous from each other, but they can be structurally homologous. This facilitates alliances between challengers across the different fields "on the basis of a homology of position" (Bourdieu, 1991c: 244; see also 1983: 322, 1988: 165 f., 1991b: 26, 1992: 251). The second is nesting or intersection. Fields can exist within fields (nested fields) or cross other fields (intersection) such that some actors, particularly powerful ones, simultaneously occupy dominant positions in multiple fields at once. They have to contend with challengers below, but also rivals horizontally (Bourdieu, 1984: 233, 1991b: 26 f.).

These different interfield relations are important because they can impact the outcome of struggles between incumbents and challengers by strengthening the latter and/or by weakening the former (Bourdieu, 1992: 27). As field homologies facilitate alliances among subordinated groups, the balance of power can lean toward the latter. Challengers receive support (Bourdieu, 1992: 252 f.). Or, through the intersection of fields, incumbents find themselves caught in multiple struggles. Dominant actors in any given field face competition from challengers below, but also competition from other powerful groups. Pressures upon incumbents can thus be multiplied, and this might weaken them to the point of overturning them. Or, faced with such overwhelming pressures, dominant actors may have to adopt new "conservation" strategies that unintentionally alter the field. This is where field theory's relationalism is paramount. Because actors in field struggles are always strategizing and maneuvering in relation to each other, powerful players facing multiple struggles will have to adjust, re-strategize, or adopt new tactics in face of the pressures. And if challengers had been adopting a subversion strategy, dominant players might be compelled to respond by joining the critical chorus and incorporate the new heterodox principles into their own stances (Bourdieu, 1992: 157; Swartz, 1997). While this would be merely an attempt by the dominant group to hold on to their position through cultural incorporation, it may nonetheless induce "deep transformations of the symbolic relations of force" (Bourdieu, 1992: 27; Gartman, 2002: 259 f.). I now show how something similar happened in the global political field in the twentieth century, spelling the death of empire.

Changing fields

Anti-colonialism as heterodoxy

The transformation in the global field spelling the end of empire as the dominant form did not begin as a global movement. Rather, it began as a series of localized field struggles for succession. By the early twentieth century, local colonized political elites across different colonies and empires had begun to compete with state officials from the metropole for more control over government. These elites represented a rising middle-class of westernized intellectuals, lawyers, and bureaucrats who sought higher positions of power and privilege.[4] Yet, as metropoles continually frustrated these movements, these struggles for succession eventually became struggles of *subversion* whose main form was *anti-colonial nationalism*: political movements demanding replacement of colonialism with national independence.

There were two waves of anti-colonial nationalism. The first wave was in the late eighteenth through the early nineteenth centuries in the Americas, and the second began around the turn of the twentieth century and proceeded after the World War II. With the exception of the Haitian slave revolt (which was a portent of the second wave later), the first wave was a settler-creole nationalism, exemplified in the American Revolution against England and the Latin American republican revolutions against Spain. These were very much successionist struggles. Led by whites or self-proclaimed whites, it did not fundamentally challenge empire as a form. The second wave was different. Its earliest stirrings lay in the founding of the Indian National Congress (1885), the Islamic revival movements in the Middle East (beginning in the late nineteenth century), and the Philippine Revolution against Spain (1896). It was not restricted to the Americas nor to white creoles. It was often led by nonwhite colonized groups. Therefore, the anti-colonial nationalist movements of this wave proclaimed the right to self-determination for all peoples regardless of race. Whether exemplified in the discourse of everyone from the Philippine Republic in 1896 (the first independent nation in colonial Asia) to Mahatma Gandhi in India later, this second wave of anti-colonial nationalism was a direct affront to the doxic principles of hierarchical differentiation in the colonial and imperial fields. Part of the doxa by which imperial hierarchies had been justified was racial: European colonizers were superior civilizationally and racially, and so the colonized must submit. This in turn had fed one of the "rules" or norms of competition in the inter-imperial field: competing states could justifiably take foreign territory and rule the presumably "inferior races" as colonial dependencies (Jackson, 1993: 114 ff.). But anti-colonial nationalism challenged these principles of hierarchial differentiation. Of course, the *illusio* remained in these movements. Anti-colonial nationalism assumed that there should be "nations" that map on to state boundaries. But anti-colonial nationalism nonetheless challenged the orthodoxy of the colonial and imperial fields and posited a radical heterodoxy – in other words, that all peoples around the world, regardless of race, were capable of nationhood, equal citizenship, and self-government.

The Indian National Congress (1885), the early work of W.E.B. DuBois, the Universal Races Congress of 1911, and various other activists represented some of the most vocal earliest expressions of this heterodoxy (DuBois, 1996). The Universal Races Congress in London brought "representatives of all races" from around the world to debate racial issues of the day. Though it included colonial officials and was politically conservative, it nonetheless helped to spread the monogenism thesis that rejected the dominant notion that the races of the world were of different species (Pennybacker, 2005). Later, writers in the French empire such as Aimé Césaire and Franz Fanon not only questioned racial orthodoxy but also the empires' claims to moral and cultural superiority (Césaire, 1955; Fanon, 1967 [1952]).

Anti-colonial nationalism was a subversion struggle rather than just a successionist one, but how did it lead to a transformation in global norms? The key lies in unprecedented pressures that were put upon the empires. These pressures were due to: a) challengers' *alliances* afforded by field homology that turned anti-colonialism into a palpable global movement; and b) the *intersection* of fields, and hence of field struggles, which put imperial metropoles under unprecedented pressure from all sides.

The colonial and the inter-imperial

While anti-colonial nationalism first emerged among a handful of educated elites within each colony, the movement was swiftly scaled upwards into a globally powerful movement. This was partly because of the intrinsic capacity of anti-colonial nationalism to mobilize disparate populations within colonial space. Because it proclaimed a universalism with its appeals to an abstract "nation", it was powerful political capital transcending tribal, ethnic, or religious difference. But the globalization of the anti-colonial movement was also due to the correspondence *within* and *between* colonial fields. First, *within* each colony, the corresponding colonial economic field enabled cross-class alliances with the local proto-bourgeoisie or comprador bourgeoisie who often competed with foreign capital. The rising middle-class elites and economic elites thereby formed a larger movement seeking more political representation, control over the state, and autonomy (Fanon, 1970). Second, homologies *between* colonial fields were crucial. Despite their many differences, colonies around the world shared a structure of colonizer-colonized and metropole-colony, which is why definitionally they are "colonies" in the first place (Osterhammel, 1999) – and which overlapped with a racialized binary of white-nonwhite. Colonized peoples around the world could thus find common cause.

In fact, elites from different colonies came to acknowledge and recognize each other as part of the same movement and became emboldened by each other's experiences (Ballantyne & Burton, 2014: 170 ff.). The Cuban revolution against Spain, the defeat of Russia by Japan in 1905, Gandhian populism in the 1920s – all of these events and more garnered global attention and mobilized colonized nonwhites around the world (Horne, 2003: 50). The response to Italy's invasion of Ethiopia in 1934 showed how far things had come. In this case, the reaction from anti-colonialists was global, sparking protests around the world, from Harlem to the Caribbean to Asia (DuBois, 1935; Grimal, 1978: 47; Furedi, 1994: 23).

Cross-national and cross-imperial organizing accompanied these glimmerings of recognition. The First Pan-African Congress in 1900, the Universal Races Congress of 1911, the First International Congress against Imperialism and Colonialism convened in Brussels in 1927, Bandung in 1955: at these and many other similar gatherings, anti-colonialists consecrated their new heterodox ideologies and set the basis for a truly global movement. In 1945, Kwame Nkrumah wrote and issued a *Declaration to the Colonial Peoples of the World* which was approved by a pan-African Congress held in Manchester in 1945. The Declaration set out the "rights of all people to govern themselves" and affirmed "the right of colonial peoples to control their own destiny". It continued: "All colonies must be free from foreign imperialist control, whether political or economic [. . .] we say to the peoples of the colonies that they must strive for these ends by all means at their disposal" (Boyce, 1999: 117).

As field homologies facilitated alliances across colonies, thus turning anti-colonial struggles into a transnational and cross-colonial movement, imperial powers felt new pressures. No longer just facing protests in one or another colony, they faced a global anti-colonial movement that increasingly became an unprecedented threat. In post-war England, the overwhelming tide of anti-colonial nationalism likely contributed to the Labour Party's anti-imperial stance, and also to various colonial reforms in British territories designed to appease anti-colonial sentiment. But the British state perceived new conditions too. A report prepared by the British Foreign Office in 1952 and subsequently circulated to the Colonial Office and throughout Whitehall was titled *The Problem of Nationalism*. The report's aim was to "suggest means by which we can safeguard our position as a world power, particularly in the economic and strategic fields, against the dangers inherent in the present upsurge of nationalism" (CO,[5] 1952).

Rising anti-colonial nationalism was also felt in the United States. Merriam's *Recent Tendencies in Political Thought* (1924), exemplary of the thought of the nascent American discipline of IR, declared that the rise of anti-colonial movements was one of the three main epoch-making processes around the globe (industrialization and feminism were the other two) (Merriam & Barnes, 1924). In the 1950s, Kohn (1958: 2) noted that, "until the end of the nineteenth century the words 'empire' and 'imperialism' were generally used in a laudatory and not a pejorative sense", but that "the meaning and implications of the word 'colonialism,' and of the closely connected terms 'empire' and 'imperialism' have undergone a profound transformation in recent decades." Reports of nearly all branches of the American government repeatedly worried over the threat of nationalism in the colonial world. In 1946, the former director of the Department of the Interior's Division of Territories and Island Possessions noted that the "time has passed when the peoples of the Indies, Indo-China, Burma and India would permit white men to dictate the tenor of their lives" (quoted in Go, 2011: 150).

Added to these pressures was inter-imperial competition. Besides their own colonial sub-fields, empires were also embedded in global imperial fields, wherein they allied or competed with each other for economic, security, and cultural capital (Go, 2008; Steinmetz, 2007) (see Figure 7.1). But the increasingly global reach of anti-colonialism added a new layer of complexity to the inter-imperial field. As early as 1916, Vladimir Lenin seized upon it, articulating anti-imperial rhetoric and calling for self-determination of all peoples around the world. Positioning Russia as a champion of subjugated peoples, Lenin here was trying to accrue political capital in the inter-imperial struggle and make new alliances. Lenin's move in turn compelled Woodrow Wilson to add pronouncements on self-determination in his Fourteen

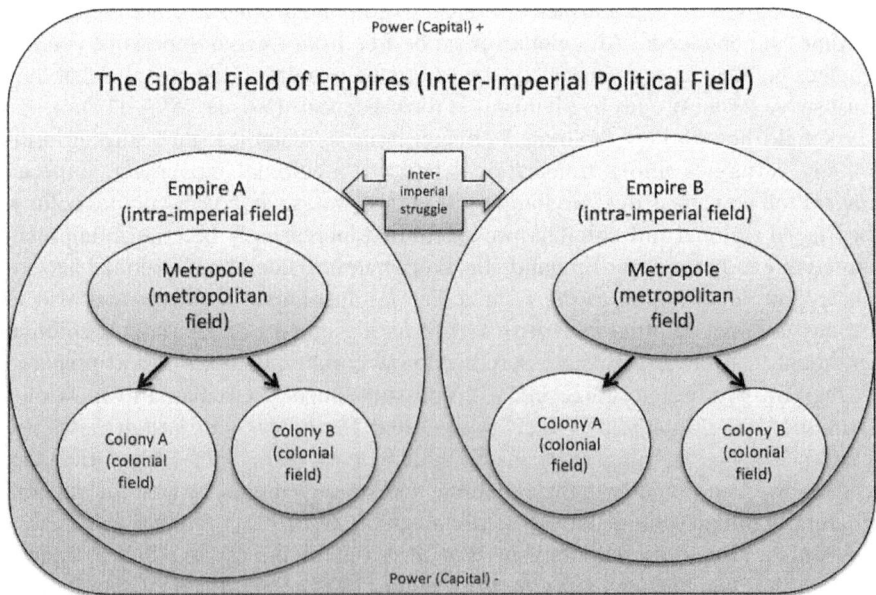

Figure 7.1 Imperial and colonial political fields

Points. Rather than the originator of anti-colonial nationalism, Wilson was just trying to keep up with Lenin (Manela, 2006: 40 f.). Before and during World War II,
Japan also seized upon anti-imperial rhetoric. Though itself a rising empire, it nonetheless claimed that the Western powers were the true enemy for suppressing anti-
colonial movements, and that anti-colonialists should join Japan – a discourse that
attracted African-American anti-imperialists like DuBois (Aydin, 2008: 21 ff.).

As the Cold War intensified beginning around 1947, inter-imperial competition
became more firmly structured around the issue of anti-colonialism. Officials in
Washington increasingly worried that the Soviet Union was playing upon anti-
colonial sentiment to their own advantage. They were especially concerned that
the Soviet Union would penetrate anti-colonial nationalist movements and use the
new powerful discourse to turn the world against the United States, Britain, and
their allies. A report from the Central Intelligence Agency (CIA) in 1948 noted
how "the colonial world is a ferment of nationalist activity" and that this had
been driven by a challenge to the preexisting racial order, as the "natives" were
revolting against "white superiority". It then warned that there was "widespread
support of colonial independence movements by a large group of recently liberated and other sympathetic states, particularly the USSR" and within the new
United Nations (CIA, 1948: 6). It especially worried over the fact that the USSR
was "exploiting" anti-colonial nationalism, and thereby recognized the pressures
from below and at the top.

> The colonial independence movement [. . .] is no longer purely a domes-
> tic issue between the European colonial powers and their dependencies. It
> has been injected into the larger arena of world politics and has become an
> element in the broader problems of relations between Orient and Occident,
> between industrialized and 'underdeveloped' nations, and between the West-
> ern Powers and the USSR.
>
> (CIA, 1948: 2)

A 1950 policy paper from the State Department assessed the situation in Africa
similarly:

> While Communism has made very little headway in most of Africa, Euro-
> pean nations and the United States have become alert to the danger of militant
> Communism penetrating the area. The U.S.S.R has sought [. . .] to play the
> role of the champion of the colonial peoples of the world [and] [. . .] gain the
> sympathy of nationalist elements.
>
> (USDS,[6] 1950: V, 1525)

Constraining empire, rethinking colonialism

Anti-colonial struggles thus articulated with inter-imperial competition to add
profound new challenges for imperial powers. Here, field theory's relational principles are paramount: even dominant players react and adjust in relation to others

in the field. They are in this sense not untouched by field dynamics. To be sure, due to the mounting pressures from below and, during the Cold War, from the side, the United States and Britain were forced to reconsider whether colonialism was a viable political form. Initial strategies by the British to manage anti-colonialism involved "modernizing colonialism": developmental projects aimed at appeasing dissatisfaction with colonialism (Cooper, 2005). But as nationalism continued to spread and as inter-imperial competition intensified, such efforts proved unsustainable. Colonialism in its entirety had to be rethought.

This rethinking is clear in London. In 1952, the Foreign Office and even the Colonial Office admitted:

> we have to-day no hope of maintaining our control of the Colonies in the pre-war political sense of the word 'control' [. . .]. Progress towards sovereign independence is both inevitable and desirable. We are bound to swim with the stream but we can hope to exert influence on the speed at which the current runs, both in general and in specific cases.
>
> (CO, 1952)

Views from Washington were the same, especially given competition from the USSR. "Further disintegration of the remaining colonial empires appears inevitable," wrote the CIA in 1948, and so colonial powers "must fully recognize the irresistible force of nationalism in their dependencies and take leadership in guiding these dependencies gradually toward eventual self-government or independence" (CIA, 1948: 14). This is exactly why the United States shifted its earlier support of colonialism. During the late 1940s and through the 1950s, the United States had spent billions to help France, England, Portugal, Belgium, and the Netherlands maintain their colonial control in strategically important areas. But it dropped this policy. The fear was that, if the United States continued to support colonialism, nationalist forces would ally with the Soviet Union. Supporting colonialism would damage America's "reputation". Secretary of State John Foster Dulles thus insisted that the United States should aid nationalist forces in Africa rather than suppress them, because America's "prestige" was at stake (USDS, 1955–1957: XVIII, 18–19). A State Department paper in 1952 identifying the "General Objectives of U.S. Policy Toward Colonial Areas" stated that America's main objective should now be to "favour the progressive development of all dependent peoples toward the goal of self-government," but only because doing so would make the United States appear as a champion of anti-colonialism and thereby enable it to counter the Soviet Union's competitive push.

> It is clearly in the interest of the U.S. to give appropriate encouragement to those [anti-colonial] movements which are non-communist and democratic in character. [This would] contribute toward the building of colonial areas into bulwarks against the spread of communism. [. . .] The importance of this

objective is clear in view of the Soviet Union's obvious bid for the sympathies of colonial peoples.

(USDS, 1952–1954: III, 1084–1085)

The United States thereby embarked upon a new campaign to sketch the Soviet Union as the true "imperialist", and to thereby counter the Soviets' claims to be the champion of the colonial world. One part of that campaign was the international distribution of hundreds of thousands of copies of the pamphlet *Who is the Imperialist?* The pamphlet listed all the territories that the USSR had annexed since 1939 and "described communist 'imperialism' in North Korea, Poland, North Vietnam, and Tibet" (Belmonte, 2013). The effort here was not just to portray the United States as the real champion of anti-colonialism but also the USSR as its enemy. In either case, the goal was calculated and precise: to use anti-colonial discourse as a means of winning hearts and minds.

In brief, while anti-colonial nationalism for colonized and postcolonial leaders was a powerful force that could enable them to mobilize populations across religious, ethnic, gender, and other lines, it also became a form of capital for imperial powers themselves. Symbolic competition among the great powers necessitated proving one's anti-colonial credentials: states adopted anti-colonial values as part of their effort to accumulate symbolic capital and convert it to political capital; that is, to legitimate their powerful position and win allies. As a result, colonialism became less an option than before. If anything, it had become a liability.

Suez, 1956 and the end of colonialism

To more clearly see how colonialism was excised from the imperial repertoire due to anti-colonial struggles and inter-imperial rivalry, let us consider one telling event: the Anglo-French military assault on Suez in 1956. In July of that year, Egyptian President Gamal Abdel Nasser announced plans to nationalize the Suez Canal Company, a British-French enterprise that had been initially founded to operate the Canal after its construction in 1869. Egypt had already achieved its official independence in 1922, but the Suez Canal Company still controlled the Canal and it was protected by British troops. The nationalization by Nasser therefore posed a serious threat to Britain's geopolitical and economic interests. Accordingly, the British orchestrated a military assault.

Why is this case of interest? In many ways, it marks the end of colonialism. Whereas in earlier years, Britain would have likely occupied the territory and perhaps turned it into a colony, this time it did not. Instead, after the invasion, the British cut and ran, leaving Egypt officially independent. In fact, Prime Minister Eden never entertained the idea of taking Egypt as a colony. The British-French ultimatum to Nasser, and released to the public, emphasized that troops would be used for "temporary" occupation. And in discussing the possible response to Nasser's nationalization of the Canal with President Eisenhower, Eden stated that the long-term goal was "the removal of Nasser, and the installation in Egypt of a regime less hostile to the West" (Boyle, 2012: 157). He later expressly stated to Eisenhower that the "old Colonial" approach was not their intention (Boyle, 2012: 181). This is in stark contrast with the British military intervention in 1882, which had led to a sustained occupation and the transformation of Egypt into a protectorate. Evidently such an action by 1956 could barely be entertained. This was a "pivotal" moment, representing a real turning point away from colonialism (Philpott, 2001: 183).

So why did Great Britain not use colonialism to realize its threatened interests in Egypt, as it had done multiple times in the past century or more? In their avowed version to the "old Colonial" approach, it is clear that London officials were concerned about the potentiality of anti-colonial protests and resistance. A few years earlier, the Foreign Office's report on nationalism worried about how

> there is always the danger that a particular blow [against Britain from nationalist forces] may set off a chain reaction with incalculable results, affecting not only Great Britain but other Western Powers and thus the stability and strength of the free world.
>
> (CO, 1952)

And a few months prior to that report, in January, Egyptians in Cairo had taken to the streets to violently cast out British troops who had remained stationed in the region. In his discussion with Eisenhower, Eden intimated that he understood the need to exercise restraint in whatever action would be taken by stating flatly: "I have not forgotten the riots and murders in Cairo in 1952" (Eden in Boyle, 2012: 164). Put simply, the anti-colonialists or "challengers" in the field were increasingly becoming recognized by the power-holders as a real threat. Field homologies generated the potential for anti-colonial movements to ally, and this upended the ability of Britain to do as it wished. The new anti-colonial movements, joining hands across colonial fields, made it harder for the British to colonize as before.

Of course, Great Britain at the time was already a weakened empire, so one might argue it makes perfect sense that it would refuse to embark upon another costly colonial intervention. But the United States did not colonize Egypt either. The United States *did* have the capacity to colonize the region. It also had the capacity to support the British, and had been doing so in other colonial areas. But in this case, it did neither. Why not?

The reason was exactly the articulation of intra-imperial pressures from below and the inter-imperial struggle: that is, due to field homologies and the intersection of fields. The Suez crisis had emerged just after the Bandung Conference – over which Dulles and many in Washington had fretted. It had also come after years of American concerns about rising nationalism in the region and, as noted, about the Soviet Union's attempts to portray itself as the champion of the colonized (Lucas, 2000: 14). The revolution in Egypt in 1952 had solidified these threats in the minds of American policymakers. Dulles noted in 1953 that the peoples of the Near East and South Asia are "suspicious of the colonial powers" and so "the day is past when [nationalist] aspirations can be ignored" (Lucas, 2000: 147). President Eisenhower told Winston Churchill in 1954 that "should we try to dam up [nationalism in the Middle East] completely, it would, like a mighty river, burst through the barriers and could create havoc" (Lucas, 2000: 147). And after the riots in Cairo against the British erupted in early 1953, Dulles reported to Eisenhower that the reputation of Britain, and its allies like the United States, was "deteriorating, probably to the point of non-repair". He continued: "The days when the Middle East used to relax under the presence of British protection are gone" (Lucas, 2000: 148).

Eisenhower's skepticism, concern, and eventual criticism of Eden and his interventionist policy followed. When Eisenhower read the ultimatum of the British and French governments noting "temporary" occupation, he was initially concerned that the meaning of "temporary" was too ambiguous to be a clear statement that Britain no longer had a colonial interest. He wrote to Eden that he was

> ignorant of our minimum objectives and what you expect to do after you attain them. But I am struck by the emphasis you placed in your announcement, as well as in your message to me, on the word 'temporary' in your occupation.
>
> (Eisenhower to Eden, November 1, 1956, PDE[7])

To this Eden responded in a way that discloses the concerns over anti-colonial sentiment that was on all their minds: "I can assure you that any action which we may have to take [. . .] is not part of a harking back to the old Colonial and occupational concepts. *We are most anxious to avoid this impression*" (Eden to Eisenhower, October 1, 1956, PDE, emphasis added). Later, concerned about the fact that others in the world might not be getting the signal, President Eisenhower wrote to Jawaharlal Nehru, in response to Nehru's letter of concern to him about Suez: "I can well understand that memories of colonialism linger in some countries, but we do have assurances from the Government of Britain that they have no intention of trying to revive this practice, regardless of appearances" (Eisenhower to Nehru, November 2, 1956, PDE).

As for America's own role, Eisenhower stated to Eden that he objected to the intervention on the grounds that the use of force would arouse anti-colonial sentiment, thereby not only prolonging an occupation but also pushing the region towards the USSR. He insisted that the British and French call for an immediate cease-fire, "clearly state the reasons why you entered the canal zone", and "state your intention to evacuate" immediately after the hostilities end. This would "diminish" the "almost universal resentment now" (Eisenhower to Eden, November 1, 1956, PDE). The Eisenhower administration also realized that, if the intervention were to continue, it would have to dissociate from it as much as possible. This was a reversal of policy from the previous years of supporting Europe in the colonial and postcolonial world. As noted, the previous strategy in the Suez had been to support the British in order to prevent it from going to the Soviets. Unless they tightened security, wrote Ambassador Caffery from Cairo to the State Department in 1951, "we must resign ourselves to the fact that the Canal Zone may, unless something foreseen turns up, explode with a loud bang at no distant date, an explosion with a potential chain reaction of occupation, revolution, eventual Commie domination" (USDS, 1951, V: 428). But anti-colonial sentiment had changed the terrain irrevocably, so the strategy now had to be disarticulation from the British.

The records of the National Security Council meetings on the matter more clearly reveal this line of thinking. The statements by Dulles are of particular interest, as his view ultimately won out. He first reminded everyone that, for the past decade or so, the United States had been walking a "tightrope" between supporting "our British and French allies on the one hand, and, on the other trying to assure ourselves of the friendship and understanding of the newly independent countries who have escaped from colonialism" on the other. But the Anglo-French assault on Suez now forced the Eisenhower administration to choose: would the United States continue to support the European powers as it had been doing, or would it do something different? The issue was that the Anglo-French assault appeared to the world to be "the straight old-fashioned variety of colonialism," and so in deciding whether to support the assault, the United States had "reached the point of deciding today whether we think the future lies with a policy of reasserting by force colonial control over the less developed nations, or whether we will oppose such a course of action by every appropriate means." They were choosing between the United States "following in the footsteps of Anglo-French colonialism in Asia and Africa, or splitting our course away from their course" (USDS, 1955–1957: XVI).

Dulles's own suggestion was that the United States should do all it could to avoid supporting European colonialism, once and for all. Why? If the United States supported the assault, "we will be looked upon as forever tied to British and French colonialist policies," and "all these newly independent countries will turn from us to the USSR." In short, "the United States would survive or go down on the basis of the fate of colonialism if the United States supports the French and the British on the colonial issues." And in Dulles's view, the world had changed too much. Given that "recent events are close to marking the death knell for Great Britain and France," the "British and French would not win" (USDS, 1955–1957: XVI). In other words, colonialism was over, and the United States was not about to go down with it. And if so, it was due to the threats posed by anti-colonial movements that had begun in local fields but had become a global force, not least due to field homologies and the intersection of fields.

Conclusion: anti-colonialism as the new doxa

The events of Suez are but one example showing that, in Bourdieu's terms, the "rules of the game" in the global political field had changed by the late 1950s. While power struggles between dominated and dominant – and among the dominant themselves – continued as ever, the terms or "rules" by which such struggles occurred were radically altered. Colonialism was no longer the way in dominant states could exert power over weaker societies. Nor was it the mode by which rival powers competed with each other, struggling to acquire more territory and hence resources. Quite the opposite: as seen, power struggles between the United States and the USSR during the mid-twentieth century took the form of *anti*-colonialism. Appealing to anti-colonial nationalism was a new form of symbolic capital, convertible to political capital: a way of winning support in wider fields of political struggle and thereby legitimating one's position.

This is the global political field that we have today. Anti-colonialism, once part of the challengers' subversive struggle, is now part of the orthodoxy and ultimately the new doxa: a new taken-for-granted norm. To be sure, because of the struggles noted above, anti-colonial nationalism has been institutionalized in the field, embedded in various resolutions of the United Nations and manifest in the fact that no great powers today seize new territories as they used to. The new "rule" is so institutionalized that it has become a part of the global discourse that pretenders to power – like India and China – try to manipulate or at least deploy anti-colonial discourse amidst their strategic positioning in the field (Miller, 2013). To this day, it seems, competition and struggle in the global field of political power cannot do without anti-colonial rhetoric as a form of capital. Of course, informal imperialism persists. Great powers can still intervene into the affairs of other countries, as long as they pay lip service to the principles of popular sovereignty. They can even use popular sovereignty as a *warrant* for neo-imperialism. When the United States invaded Iraq and Afghanistan, counterterrorism was one warrant, but the other legitimating discourse was that the people of Iraq and Afghanistan needed to be liberated from despotic rulers: colonialism as the means by which to realize anti-colonialism. The other legitimating discourse was that Iraq and Afghanistan needed to be rebuilt and strengthened precisely so that they could more properly exercise sovereignty; hence "nation-building". Informal imperialism, justified by reference to popular sovereignty, is but a contemporary extension of the discourse of anti-colonial nationalism, rather than its opposite.

Extending Bourdieusian field theory, this chapter has shown how and why this global transformation happened. For those familiar with the work of Bourdieu, it might not appear likely that Bourdieusian theory could help us apprehend global transformation; first, because Bourdieu's theories have been accused of emphasizing social reproduction rather than change; and second, because Bourdieu did not develop his conceptual apparatus to examine social relations on international, transnational, or global scales. Still, this chapter has shown that Bourdieu's field theory can indeed be scaled upwards to consider global matters, and it can be extended logically to capture social change. The key lies in recognizing the struggles and the different types of struggle among actors for capital, and the different relations between fields that shape the outcomes of those struggles. As seen, colonial fields generated what Bourdieu would call "subversive" struggles, prompting "challengers" (in this case, anti-colonial nationalists) to offer a new "heterodoxy" of national self-determination for all peoples against the prevailing "orthodoxy" and "rules of the game" in the existing global field of empires. Correspondences between colonial fields transformed this movement into a global movement, and articulated with the inter-imperial field of struggle. This in turn constrained the European empires and the United States. As part of their struggle to maintain their dominant positions in the field and ward off rivals (in this case, the Soviet Union), they were forced to adopt a new stance promoting anti-colonial nationalism as a form of capital. The inter-imperial field was thus transformed into one where colonialism was not only undesired as a political strategy of rule, it became a liability.

Notes

* For comments and suggestions on earlier versions of this paper, the author thanks Neta Crawford, Jeff Colgan, the participants of the workshop "End of Empires?" at Brown University, Srdjan Vucetic, Kevin McMillan, and the participants of the "International Theory Network" workshop at the University of Ottawa, George Lawson, Kirsten Ainley, Tarak Barkawi, and the participants of the "International Theory Workshop" at the London School of Economics, and the editors of this volume, Christian Schmidt-Wellenburg and Stefan Bernhard.
1 The work besides the present volume is growing; my own views on scaling up Bourdieu's field theory can be seen in Go and Krause (2016).
2 Most existing scholarship is primarily about decolonization rather than *non*-colonization (Strang, 1991; Crawford, 1993; Goerz, 1993; Jackson, 1993; Philpott, 2001; Wimmer & Min, 2006; Gartzke & Rohner, 2011; Reus-Smit, 2013: 153).
3 See Werron (2015) for a theorization of "competition". For purposes of this paper, I use the terms "competition" and "struggle" interchangeably.
4 Colonialism around the world in the modern era varied but this general pattern is evident (Anderson, 1983; Breuilly, 1982; Furedi, 1994; Goswami, 2004).
5 CO: Colonial Office, Public Records Office, Kew, UK.
6 USDS: United States Department of State.
7 PDE: Papers of Dwight D. Eisenhower.

References

Anderson, B. (1983). *Imagined Communities: Reflections on the Origins and Spread of Nationalism*. London: Verso.
Aydin, C. (2008). Japan's Pan-Asianism and the Legitimacy of Imperial World Order, 1931–1945. *The Asia-Pacific Journal, 6*(3), 1–44.
Ballantyne, T., & Burton, A. (2012). *Empires and the Reach of the Global 1870–1945*. Cambridge, MA: Belknap Press.
Belmonte, L. A. (2013). *Selling the American Way: US Propaganda and the Cold War*. Philadelphia, PA: University of Pennsylvania Press.
Bourdieu, P. (1977a). *Outline of a Theory of Practice*. Cambridge: Cambridge University Press.
Bourdieu, P. (1977b). Symbolic Power. In D. Gleeson (Ed.), *Identity and Structure* (pp. 112–119). Driffield: Nafferton Books.
Bourdieu, P. (1983). The Field of Cultural Production, or: The Economic World Reversed. *Poetics, 12*(4–5), 311–356.

Bourdieu, P. (1984). *Distinction: A Social Critique of the Judgement of Taste*. Cambridge, MA: Harvard University Press.

Bourdieu, P. (1985). The Social Space and the Genesis of Groups. *Theory and Society*, *15*(6), 723–744.

Bourdieu, P. (1988). *Homo Academicus*. Cambridge: Polity Press.

Bourdieu, P. (1989). Social Space and Symbolic Power. *Sociological Theory*, *7*(1), 14–25.

Bourdieu, P. (1991a). Epilogue: On the Possibility of a Field of World Sociology. In P. Bourdieu & J. Coleman (Eds.), *Social Change for a Changing Society*. Boulder, CO: Westview Press.

Bourdieu, P. (1991b). Genesis and Structure of the Religious Field. *Comparative Social Research*, *13*(1), 1–44.

Bourdieu, P. (1991c). *Language and Symbolic Power*. Cambridge, MA: Harvard University Press.

Bourdieu, P. (1992). *The Rules of Art*. Stanford, CA: Stanford University Press.

Bourdieu, P., & Wacquant, L. J. D. (1992). *An Invitation to Reflexive Sociology*. Chicago, IL: University of Chicago Press.

Boyce, D. G. (1999). *Decolonisation and the British Empire, 1775–1997*. New York, NY: St. Martin's Press.

Boyle, P. (Ed.). (2012). *The Eden-Eisenhower Correspondence, 1955–1957*. Chapel Hill, NC: University of North Carolina Press.

Breuilly, J. (1982). *Nationalism and the State*. Chicago, IL: University of Chicago Press.

Buchholz, L. (2016). What Is a Global Field? Rethinking Bourdieu's Field Theory Beyond the Nation-State. *Sociological Review*, *64*(2), 31–60.

Calhoun, C. (2006). Pierre Bourdieu and Social Transformation: Lessons from Algeria. *Development and Change*, *37*(6), 1403–1415.

Césaire, A. (1955). *Discours sur le colonialisme*. Paris: Présence Africaine.

CIA, Central Intelligence Agency. (1948). The Breakup of the Colonial Empires and Its Implications for US Security. Retrieved May 1, 2017, from www.cia.gov/library/readingroom/docs/DOC_0001166383.pdf

Cooper, F. (2005). Modernizing Colonialism and the Limits of Empire. In C. C. Calhoun & F. Cooper (Eds.), *Lessons of Empire* (pp. 63–72). New York, NY: The New Press.

Crawford, N. (1993). Decolonization as an International Norm: The Evolution of Practices, Arguments, and Beliefs. In L. W. Reed & C. Kaysen (Eds.), *Emerging Norms of Justified Intervention* (pp. 37–61). Cambridge: Committee on International Security Studies, American Academy of Arts and Sciences.

DuBois, W. E. B. (1935). *Black Reconstruction in America*. New York, NY: Russell & Russell.

DuBois, W. E. B. (1996). The Present Outlook for the Dark Races of Mankind. In Eric J. Sundquist (Ed.), *The Oxford W.E.B. Du Bois Reader* (pp. 47–54). New York, NY: Oxford University Press.

Fanon, F. (1967 [1952]). *Black Skin, White Masks*. New York, NY: Grove Press.

Fanon, F. (1970 [1967]). *Toward the African Revolution*. Harmondsworth: Penguin.

Furedi, F. (1994). *Colonial Wars and the Politics of Third World Nationalism*. London: I.B. Tauris.

Gartman, D. (2002). Bourdieu's Theory of Cultural Change: Explication, Application, Critique. *Sociological Theory*, *20*(2), 255–277.

Gartzke, E., & Rohner, D. (2011). The Political Economy of Imperialism, Decolonization and Development. *British Journal of Political Science*, *41*(3), 525–556.

Go, J. (2008). Global Fields and Imperial Forms: Field Theory and the British and American Empires. *Sociological Theory, 26*(3), 201–229.

Go, J. (2011). *Patterns of Empire: The British and American Empires, 1688–Present*. Cambridge: Cambridge University Press.

Go, J., & Krause, M. (2016). Fielding Transnationalism: An Introduction. In J. Go & M. Krause (Eds.), *Fielding Transnationalism*. Oxford: Wiley-Blackwell.

Goerz, G. (1993). *Contexts of International Politics*. Cambridge: Cambridge University Press.

Gorski, P. S. (2013). *Bourdieu and Historical Analysis*. Durham, NC: Duke University Press.

Goswami, M. (2004). *Producing India*. Chicago, IL: University of Chicago Press.

Grimal, H. (1978). *Decolonization: The British, French, Dutch, and Belgian Empires, 1919–1963*. Boulder, CO: Lynne Rienner.

Hilgers, M., & Mangez, E. (Eds.). (2015). *Bourdieu's Theory of Social Fields*. New York, NY: Routledge.

Horne, G. (2003). Race from Power: U.S. Foreign Policy and the General Crisis of White Supremacy. In B. G. Plummer (Ed.), *Window on Freedom* (pp. 45–66). Chapel Hill, NC: University of North Carolina Press.

Howe, S. (2002). *Empire: A Very Short Introduction*. Oxford: Oxford University Press.

Jackson, P. T., & Nexon, D. (1999). Relations Before States: Substance, Process and the Study of World Politics. *European Journal of International Relations, 5*(3), 291–332.

Jackson, R. H. (1993). The Weight of Ideas in Decolonization: Normative Change in International Relations. In J. Goldstein & R. O. Keohane (Eds.), *Ideas and Foreign Policy* (pp. 111–138). Ithaca, NY: Cornell University Press.

Kohn, H. (1958). Reflections on Colonialism. In R. Strausz-Hupé & H. W. Hazard (Eds.), *The Idea of Colonialism* (pp. 2–16). New York, NY: Frederick A. Praeger, Inc.

Krause, M. (2014). *The Good Project: Humanitarian Relief NGOs and the Fragmentation of Reason*. Chicago, IL: University of Chicago Press.

Lucas, S. (2000). The Limits of Ideology: US Foreign Policy and Arab Nationalism in the Early Cold War. In D. Ryan & V. Pungong (Eds.), *The United States and Decolonization* (pp. 140–167). London: Macmillan Press.

Manela, E. (2006). *The Wilsonian Moment: Self Determination and the International Origins of Anticolonial Nationalism*. Oxford: Oxford University Press.

Martin, J. L. (2003). What Is Field Theory? *American Journal of Sociology, 109*(1), 1–49.

Merriam, C., & Barnes, H. E. (1924). *A History of Political Theories: Recent Times*. New York, NY: Macmillan Company.

Meyer, J. W. (2010). World Society, Institutional Theories, and the Actor. *Annual Review of Sociology, 36*(1), 1–20.

Miller, M. C. (2013). *Wronged by Empire: Post-Imperial Ideology and Foreign Policy in India and China*. Palo Alto, CA: Stanford University Press.

Osterhammel, J. (1999). *Colonialism: A Theoretical Overview*. Princeton, NJ: Markus Wiener Publishers.

Pennybacker, S. (2005). The Universal Races Congress, London, Political Culture, and Imperial Dissent, 1900–1939. *Radical History Review, 92*(Spring), 103–117.

Philpott, D. (2001). *Revolutions in Sovereignty: How Ideas Shaped Modern International Relations*. Princeton, NJ: Princeton University Press.

Reus-Smit, C. (2013). *Individual Rights and the Making of the International System*. Cambridge: Cambridge University Press.

Sapiro, G. (2013). Le champ est-il national? *Actes de la Recherche en Sciences Sociales, 200*, 70–85.

Steinmetz, G. (2007). *The Devil's Handwriting: Precoloniality and the German Colonial State in Qingdao, Samoa, and Southwest Africa.* Chicago, IL: University of Chicago Press.

Strang, D. (1991). Global Patterns of Decolonization. *International Studies Quarterly, 35*(4), 429–454.

Swartz, D. (1997). *Culture & Power: The Sociology of Pierre Bourdieu.* Chicago, IL: University of Chicago Press.

Verter, B. (2003). Spiritual Capital: Theorizing Religion With Bourdieu Against Bourdieu. *Sociological Theory, 21*(2), 150–174.

Werron, T. (2015). Why Do We Believe in Competition? A Historical-Sociological View of Competition as an Institutionalized Modern Imaginary. *Distinktion: Journal of Social Theory, 16*(2), 186–210.

Wimmer, A., & Min, B. (2006). From Empire to Nation-State: Explaining Wars in the Modern World, 1816–2001. *American Sociological Review, 17*(6), 867–897.

Chapter 8

The double function of rankings

Consecration and dispositif in transnational academic fields

Julian Hamann and Christian Schmidt-Wellenburg

Introduction

One key question for the study of transnationalization and nationalization concerns the distribution of material and symbolic power: Who has the resources to unify, generalize, and guarantee the respective perception of the world as more or less transnational? Academia is a main source of authority to create perceptions of the world that define, chart, and explain why certain features of today's world appear as either national or transnational. At the same time, academically legitimated perceptions of the world can problematize certain aspects of the world, lead to the creation of policies, and finally mobilize political action that shapes national and transnational societization. Rankings play an important role for the distribution of resources that allow academic agents to assert perceptions of a more or less (trans)national world. Rankings act as both institutions of consecration that facilitate power shifts within the academic field, and as dispositifs that link the academic field to other fields and thus open it up for new modes of governance beyond the nation-state. In our contribution, we argue that both the success of rankings and the turmoil that they cause can be explained by this double function that rankings hold in the academic field and beyond.

Within the academic field, rankings function as consecratory institutions. As such, they do not merely depict but actively construct social order (Espeland & Sauder, 2007). When considering rankings as practices of worldmaking that define critical entities and qualities, determine the distribution of said qualities, and allow to derive a specific hierarchy of entities, we have to ask ourselves on which authority this capacity rests and how it constitutes legitimacy:

> Every power to exert symbolic violence, i.e. every power which manages to impose meanings and to impose them as legitimate by concealing the power relations which are at the basis of its force, adds its own specifically symbolic force to those power relations.
>
> (Bourdieu & Passeron, 1977: 4)

Yet, the symbolic violence that rankings exert as consecratory institutions goes even further than worldmaking. As we will propose in this chapter, rankings push – and are being pushed by – specific milieus, types of agents, paradigms, and strategies. It is these milieus, agents, paradigms, and strategies that can, amongst other things, assert perceptions of a more or less (trans)national world.

Rankings are efficacious in academia not only because the social order of academic fields is based just as much on symbolic recognition as it relies on material endowment. What is more, academic fields are highly transnational, yet anchored in national realms via higher education systems and institutions, national career paths, and labor markets (cf. Schmidt-Wellenburg, 2018). This "double bind" between the national and the transnational creates a situation in which consecration refers to both national and transnational orders of worth and authority. The boundaries of academic fields, their relation to other fields, and their symbolic and material hierarchies are simultaneously objects and results of symbolic valorization as performed by rankings. Against this backdrop, it is no surprise that rankings have played a considerable role in transnationalizing academic fields in recent decades (cf. Wedlin, 2010).

This is where the second function of rankings comes in: Academia has long developed from a field-specific specialist market for symbolic goods into a mass market for a lay public that spreads across fields and is interested in academic products like expert knowledge and degrees (Karpik, 2011). Rankings play an important role in opening up the academic field – to other social fields as well as to other nationally anchored academic fields (Brankovic, Ringel, & Werron, 2018). This is the constellation in which rankings function as dispositifs (Foucault, 1977), i.e., as heterogeneous ensembles of discourses, institutions, and regulations that convey field-specific legitimacies and hierarchies and, in turn, make field-specific products and operations intelligible to a wider public. As we will argue in this chapter, rankings as dispositifs open up the field by facilitating capital flows in two directions. Rankings organize a flow of academic capital that bypasses the nation-state and is redirected to international media, data, and educational corporations. Conversely, rankings organize a flow of political capital, allowing new modes of governance to enter the academic field, transcending nation-states (cf. Amsler & Bolsmann, 2012).

Highlighting the double function of rankings as consecratory institutions and as dispositifs, we join other scholars (e.g., Brankovic, Ringel, & Werron, 2018) who argue that rankings function both within and beyond specific fields. As they affect the overall social order and structuring of social space, rankings have to be considered as part of a bigger picture. While rankings are local tools of evaluation, they produce and reproduce political knowledge that has the potential to affect society at large. Therefore, we propose in this contribution that rankings are an expression of a more general change in the dominant modes of governance throughout society (Power, 1997; Heintz, 2016), and they both advance and benefit from processes of transnationalization.

Developing this argument, the following sections will give an empirical overview of the most important forms of rankings in the academic field, in order to derive from this a conceptual definition of rankings as consecratory institutions. Building on this, the final section is dedicated to the double function of rankings: as a particularly momentous consecratory institution, rankings propel power shifts in the academic field and beyond; as a dispositif, rankings operate at the intersection of different fields and advance processes of transnationalization by facilitating new modes of governance.

Main rankings in the academic field

Although evaluation systems, metrics, and indicators seem to have almost monopolized the symbolic valorization of academia and academics in the last few decades (cf. de Rijcke, Wouters, Rushforth, Franssen, & Hammarfelt, 2015), a thorough look at academic everyday life shows that there is a great variety of sites that perform consecration. Consecratory institutions in academia reach from peer review (Bakanic, McPhail, & Simon, 1987; Hirschauer, 2010) over obituaries (Hamann, 2016a) to book reviews (Riley & Spreitzer, 1970); from citations (Hargens, 2000) to acknowledgments in publications (Hollander, 2001); from academic titles and funding panels (Lamont, 2009) over professorial appointments (Hammarfelt, 2017); to letters of recommendation (Tsay, Lamont, Abbott, & Guetzkow, 2003) and funding systems (Hicks, 2012).

Although rankings are not entirely new consecratory institutions in the academic field, it was only in the 1980s that the mass media and therewith a wider public got involved in the production of rankings (cf. Hammarfelt, de Rijcke, & Wouters, 2017). According to our knowledge, the first case of a serial, regularly published ranking in the United States was the *U.S. News & World Report* (USN) college and university ranking that has been compiled since 1983 (Espeland & Sauder, 2016: 10; Usher, 2017). From then on, national and transnational rankings proliferated and spread across the globe – curiously, despite growing criticism from within the academic field. The proliferation of rankings occurred with an opening and marketization of the academic field for a lay audience in two instances. First, from the expansion of education of the 1960s and 1970s onwards, education has become a mass merchandise (Windolf, 1997). The academic field now attracts students that are not necessarily habitually prepared for traditional consecratory institutions, yet they still expect returns from their investment in university education. Second, cutbacks of public funding of university research and increased competition over funding in general in the 1980s have accelerated marketization and universities' accountability toward a lay public (Paradeise, Reale, Bleiklie, & Ferlie, 2009). It is the proliferation of rankings in the academic field that facilitates their double function as consecratory institutions and as dispositifs at the intersection of different fields.

We can distinguish different kinds of rankings in the academic field according to the entities they rank and the agencies they constitute in the process. The most prominent and well-researched rankings target the organizational level. *University rankings* create zero-sum comparisons of, for example, the research performance or studying conditions at universities (Brankovic, Ringel, & Werron, 2018). They attach numbers to these qualities and visualize the results publicly. Most university rankings focus on various indicators and measures of research performance (cf. Bekhradnia, 2016). For example, the *Times Higher Education World University Ranking* (THEWU), one of the most influential rankings when it comes to the global status order of universities (see Bowman & Bastedo, 2011), draws on no less than 12 measures that are weighed differently to determine the research performance of universities but leaves out teaching performance, only accounting for staff to student ratio. Hence, an order is produced, albeit a very specific one.

Some of the most momentous rankings do not target the organizational level but rather organizational units. *Department rankings* compare departments in specific research fields. They conduct zero-sum comparisons of the research performance, but sometimes also of the teaching environment of departments. They claim a comprehensive scope that includes all (relevant) departments in a respective research field. In 1988, the USN published the first ranking of Law Schools. The USN ranking has been published annually since and is an institution of consecration central to the field of US law schools (Espeland & Sauder, 2016). In the late 1990s, the German think tank Centrum für Hochschulentwicklung (CHE) produced a number of rankings of universities according to different subject areas that can be seen as European pilot projects. Meanwhile, the CHE rankings have offshoots in Austria, the Netherlands, and Switzerland. Published throughout a period of several years, the CHE rankings compared the studying conditions of degrees offered as well as research conducted in English studies, history, sociology, and education (CHE, 2009).

Far more sophisticated, and much better researched, are the department rankings conducted in the United Kingdom (UK): the Research Assessment Exercise (RAE) and, its successor since 2014, the Research Excellence Framework (REF). The assessment draws on peer review of individual research performance, the results of which are then aggregated to the department level. The REF not only (re)produces the symbolic order of UK higher education, but also informs the allocation of research funding (Hamann, 2016b). Remarkably, the actual rankings that compare departments in specific research fields are not produced by the REF itself but by media outlets that report about this main event in UK higher education and visualize the REF data for a broader audience. The REF has inspired assessments and rankings in many other national higher education systems, for example, in Australia (cf. Gläser & Laudel, 2007).

Whereas REF, CHE, and USN rankings are national in scope, the *Financial Times Ranking of Business Schools* is transnational. It was founded in 1998 as a ranking of European business schools, is published annually, and has evolved over the years from focusing on business schools from both sides of the Atlantic to an ever more international ranking, in which the much more recently established European business schools were integrated and assigned a position within a global status hierarchy (Wedlin, 2010: 204).

Whereas university and department rankings aim at the institutional organization of academia, *journal rankings* target knowledge production by assessing publication outputs. Journal rankings conduct zero-sum comparisons of citation rates for journals, which represents a redefinition of a quality – significance of a journal for a field – into a quantity. The result of the comparison is then presented to an imagined public of scholars, and their favor is distributed by the ranking as a public good to the ranked journals. There are crucial differences in the acceptance of journal rankings between research fields and disciplines. In the social sciences and humanities, there seems to be a fear that rankings might foster the tenets of the positivist-empiricist natural sciences (cf. Münch, 2010; Pontille & Torny, 2010). However, even within the social sciences, there are fields with a high affinity for journal rankings. In economics, the kind of competitive zero-sum comparison that is represented by journal rankings seems to be deeply ingrained in the disciplinary culture (Maeße, 2017; cf. Vogel, Hattke, & Petersen, 2017). Originally based on a qualitative consensus in mainstream economics about the top journals, journal rankings like the *Academic Journal Guide*, which is published by the Chartered Association of Business Schools, are now based on citations (i.e., a version of the Journal Impact Factor). Evaluating the obligatory publication outlets for faculty according to universal benchmarks, journal rankings have been found to condition research activity of individual academics – a form of reactivity – and even define the focus and trajectory of entire fields of research (Willmott, 2011). This might explain why, especially in economics, heterodox approaches seem to suffer from the broad and systematic application of rather uniform quality criteria (see Lee, Pham, & Gu, 2013).

Economists seem to be keen not only on ranking journals but even more on ranking each other: "It is worth noting that in no other social sciences can one find the extraordinary volume of data and research about rankings (journals, departments, and individuals) that economists produce" (Fourcade, Ollion, & Algan, 2014: 10). Bibliometric – and, increasingly, also altmetric – indicators are at the center of most *rankings of academics*, be they economists or not. Targeting neither the institutional level nor knowledge production, rankings of academics constitute agencies on the individual level. The best-known rankings of this kind are indeed rankings of economists conducted by newspapers such as *Handelsblatt* or *Frankfurter Allgemeine Zeitung* (Butz & Wohlrabe, 2016) in Germany or *The Economist* for an international audience. These rankings use bibliometric measures and combine them with mass media analysis to account for the academics' presence in public discourse, and they use surveys handed out to politicians in order to grasp economists' political influence (cf. Maeße, 2017). Although these rankings do not have a direct impact on how material and symbolic resources in the field are distributed, they all the same convey to a lay audience the field's hierarchy and its underlying principles. The same intention also seems to be at the basis of the rankings issued by the RePEc-network. RePEc is a bibliographical service for economic research. It is widely used to distribute papers and depends on economists uploading and classifying their own work. From this database, rankings are produced on research subjects, series and journals, institutions and authors. Individual economists are ranked monthly using information on where they publish and who cites them as indicators of their academic merits. Because RePEc is run and administered by academics, the monthly production of rankings does show the academic demand for such instruments of comparison and self-mirroring.

Academic rankings apply to universities, departments, journals, or academics. Whether they constitute agency on different organizational levels, for journals, or on the individual level, one overarching characteristic is that rankings have become more and more momentous in the academic field. They structure organizations in their missions and practices (Espeland & Sauder, 2007); they affect students, deans, and administrators as "engines of anxiety" (Espeland & Sauder, 2016); and they stratify national higher education systems (Hamann, 2016b). From a power analytical perspective, rankings regulate the value of knowledge as part of a new knowledge economy within and beyond higher education. This mode of operation is the foundation of rankings' double function. They are simultaneously *consecratory institutions* – which facilitate power shifts in the academic field by pushing (and being pushed by) specific academic milieus, types of agents, paradigms, and strategies – as well as *dispositifs* – which relate the academic field to other fields by opening it up for a broader public and transforming it into a source of symbolic power for new, transnational modes of governance.

Toward a conceptual definition of rankings

University, department, and journal rankings, as well as rankings of academics, constitute relational social orders in academic fields and produce inequality and equality, disunity and unity, or change and continuity (see Münch, 2008). After discussing the main rankings in the academic field, we are now able to provide a definition of rankings. In doing so, we draw on the important conceptual work by Jelena Brankovic, Leopold Ringel, and Tobias Werron (Werron & Ringel, 2017; Brankovic, Ringel, & Werron, 2018).

Rankings *subjectivize* the entities they rank by conceptualizing them not only as meaningful units but as units that are capable of engaging with the world in a rational way. Similarly, rankings subjectivize their audiences by creating expectations about the ranked entities' rational behavior. As we have seen in the section above, university rankings implicitly claim that universities are useful units of observation that, when compared, will disclose insights which can be used to rationally interact with universities. At the same time, ranked universities are depicted as agentic actors, as governable subjects who decide on their fate by the decisions they take in competitive situations (Meyer & Jepperson, 2000). In each ranking, the selection of subjectivized entities is simultaneously open and closed: Rankings are usually comprehensive in scope, and they claim to take into account all relevant entities in a given field; thereby they become a legitimate source of authority. At the same time, rankings are closed: they only account for a relatively limited number of dimensions of the ranked entities. This selectivity leads to normalization and exchangeability, as the quantifying scope concentrates on only a few qualities and relations of ranked entities (Simmel, 1900).

Rankings conduct *zero-sum comparisons* of the ranked entities by simultaneously attributing comparability and uniqueness (Werron & Ringel, 2017). Every rank can usually only be assigned once. Even when criteria of the comparison are not initially zero-sum, as in the case of, for example, publication output that is compared in department rankings, rankings transform these criteria into zero-sum criteria. At the same time, by only awarding each rank once, they establish an ordinal scale that transforms fractional into full differences (Bourdieu, 1988). Zero-sum comparisons are especially momentous because they reduce complexity and uncertainty (cf. Esposito & Stark, 2019). For example, most university rankings ignore the fact that quite some attraction of a university might be due to life-quality and reputation of the area in which it is located, and they rarely factor in the budget or tradition of the universities they rank. These factors play into the starting conditions for teaching and research performance of universities, but they are difficult to translate into comparative criteria. Thus, rankings tend to ignore them, invisibilizing a crucial aspect of domination and paving the way for an ideology of meritocracy.

As another aspect of complexity reduction, rankings transform the results of comparisons into numbers. Rankings either attach numbers to the qualities that they attribute to entities – for example, in the case of "research performance" – or they redefine existing quantities as qualities – for example, in the case of citation numbers. *Quantification* is an important aspect of zero-sum comparisons, because numbers allow for an introduction of small-scale, ordinal distinctions between entities that might not be all that easy to discern qualitatively (cf. Espeland & Stevens, 1998). One crucial effect of the introduction of small-scale differences through quantification is that otherness and gradual distinctions are transformed into absolute differences, which, in turn, informs the allocation of symbolic and material resources (cf. Werron & Ringel, 2017). Taking up the previous example of department rankings like the REF, rankings might not only disguise unequal starting conditions by neglecting the head start of a department at a traditionally prestigious university, but also transform the symbolic distinction between departments into definite rank inequalities.

Rankings make the results of comparisons public. *Publication* does not necessarily rely on a notion of "public" in terms of a concrete social group, for instance, "academics". Rather, rankings operate in front of an imagined public (cf. Werron, 2014), whose favor is distributed as a public good between the ranked entities. Here, the seriality of rankings is a particular function of the publication. Our overview on main rankings in the academic field conveys that many rankings provide comparisons not as a once-off snapshot of a symbolic order, but make a series of comparisons which opens up a diachronic comparative space. The effect is not only that ranked entities can take a trajectory across several rankings. More importantly, serial rankings can cement a hierarchy over time if the main rank order remains unchanged (see Hamann, 2016b on the REF). Another main function of the publication of comparisons is that rankings visualize the results of comparisons when they publish them (Brankovic, Ringel, & Werron, 2018). Visualization translates the clarity of quantified comparisons into a similarly clear visual operation. For example, rankings that sort academics in the form of a table simultaneously provide an overview and a hierarchization of the ranked entities.

Just like any other consecratory practice, rankings rest on a *doxical belief* in them. Usually even those agents that stand little chance in making it to the top of rankings not only believe in the rankings' valorization of entities, but also in the hierarchies created through them. Crucially, agents' doxical belief in rankings comprises the assumption that hierarchies produced by rankings rest on a set of given, natural, and legitimate qualities: "The legitimacy of power rests on its recognition, that means on the misrecognition of the arbitrariness which can be found at its base" (Bourdieu, 2011: 129, own translation). At the same time, the legitimacy of and beliefs in values and ensuing hierarchies is far from homogeneous. Different academic cultures are in favor of different consecratory institutions. The proliferation of rankings hence needs to be viewed as part of struggles between and about different consecratory institutions that are particularly momentous because certain forms of consecration will privilege certain fractions and, if accepted throughout the field, yield symbolic power (Bourdieu, 1985: 7).

The strategic double function of rankings

In light of the main rankings in the academic field and the main characteristics of rankings, we can now return to the double function of rankings as consecratory institutions and dispositifs. Both functions build on each other and are closely intertwined. They rely on the ability of rankings to present contingent appreciations of worth as just, rational, or natural. This invisibilization effect allows institutions of consecration to "back up and to enforce symbolically the objective relations associated with a solidarity of interests and habitual affinity due to closeness in social space" (Bourdieu, 2011: 128, own translation), thereby legitimizing relations of domination.

Rankings as consecratory institutions: shifts and changes in power in academia and beyond

As we propose in the previous section, the authority of rankings rests on their tendency to subjectivize ranked entities, treat the compared qualities as a given, quantify them, and create from the marked differences the foundation of a public competition between the ranked entities. In doing so, rankings a) showcase a comprehensive presentation of agents to everyone engaged in the field. Thereby, they b) establish a relational symbolic order of prestige that legitimizes the underlying material differences as legitimate, and, in doing so, c) glosses over differences that prevail all the same between the different agents. Crucially, these are *intended* consequences of rankings which are to be seen in addition to the *unintended* consequences that are usually emphasized by literature that is critical of rankings. Yet, the symbolic violence that rankings exert as consecratory institutions in the academic field goes even further: Rankings do not have the same intended and unintended consequences for all agents in the academic field. To convey this, we analytically distinguish *academic milieus, paradigms,* and *types of agents* (Table 8.1) and *strategies* (Table 8.2). Empirically, it is likely that specific milieus, paradigms, and types of agents are endowed with specific strategies according to their position in a field.

For a start, we propose that rankings consecrate certain *academic milieus* (Table 8.1). The milieus in question can be language-based, national, or related to specific disciplines. As a case in point, university rankings are fostering an existing hegemony of Western and English-language higher education systems (Ishikawa, 2009; Jöns & Hoyler, 2013). In a global competition between the providers of knowledge, rankings are tools to set strategic goals and bind actors in higher education to certain conceptions of what is desirable and valued (Kauppi, 2017) – not least, to international comparisons and a regulation of academic fields

Table 8.1 Milieus, paradigms, and agents that push and are being pushed by rankings in academic fields

Academic milieus	Milieus that are language-based, national, or related to specific disciplines, e.g., English language, Western higher education systems
Paradigms	Paradigms that have an affinity to markets and competition, e.g., rational choice and neoclassical economics
Agents	Agents that are new to a field and break into the domain of formerly dominant agents, e.g., European business schools

Table 8.2 Strategies that push and are being pushed by rankings in academic fields

Strategies of applicability	Producing outcomes that have value in their practical application. Influenced by corporate and business interests.
Strategies of governance	Managing academia and science for a specific purpose. Influenced by bureaucratic and political interests.
Strategies of marketing	Marketing knowledge and informing potential customers about market values. Influenced by reproductive interests of educational institutions.
Strategies of symbolic rebellion	Changing the prevailing order of consecration. Influenced by avant-garde and heretic interests in general.
Conservative strategies	Preserving current forms of consecration. Influenced by interests to maintain their own powerful position.

at a transnational level (Wedlin, 2010). It is no wonder that rankings also strike a note with neoliberal political agents' perception of governing as a polycentric task. This notion of governance instigates and monitors competition and relies on incentives and self-optimization.

Rankings are also consecratory institutions that prefer *paradigms* with a certain affinity to markets and competition (Table 8.1). As Alain Desrosières (2003) has pointed out, each form of governance not only has a body of governmental knowledge, expertise, and experts that it draws on and contributes to, but it is also connected to a unique form of statistical presentation of the world, making agents in this world accountable of rationally navigating themselves and others through this universe. Rankings fit perfectly with the main paradigm of rational choice and neoclassical economics that are gaining ground in many of the social sciences such as management and organization studies, economics, political science, and sociology.

We suggest that the affinity of rankings to markets and competition as well as governance agencies corresponds to two basic strategies that have been pushing their proliferation (Table 8.2). First, the strategy of producing outcomes that have value in their practical application. This *strategy of applicability* is closely connected to the world of business and influenced by corporate interests, for example, institutes of research in higher education and think tanks, as well as multimedia corporations. Second, a *strategy of governance* that puts the focus on managing academia and research either for the sake of a nation's or region's prestige and wealth, for global or mankind's development, or for the individual's well-being. The strategies of applicability and governance are likely to be linked to positions located at the heteronomous pole of the academic field, which are occupied by agents connected to the bureaucratic world and influenced by political interests – for example, scientific governance institutions, research councils, or the European Union. Importantly, such strategies are not necessarily conscious but also include the pre-reflexive sense for the social world that actors have because they are engaged in it (Bourdieu, 1998).

Rankings in the academic field also prefer specific groups of *agents* (Table 8.1). We argue that, by opening and restructuring fields, rankings particularly enable agents new to a field to break into the domain of formerly dominant agents. A good example is the transnational field of business schools structured by the *Financial Times* ranking, which managed to redefine what these schools are about, putting more emphasis on the traits of European business schools, thereby opening and altering the US-American field (Wedlin, 2010). At the same time, the example also highlights what dominant actors such as the top US business schools can gain from rearranging the field: they are now able to draw on resources on a global scale and have managed to proliferate their model, albeit slightly altered, worldwide.

In addition to the aforementioned strategies of applicability and governance, we find three more *strategies* that push rankings and are simultaneously pushed by them (Table 8.2). A third *strategy of marketing* pursues, for example, an interest in informing students and other potential customers about the value of their symbolic products and binding them to their educational institutions. This strategy is linked to positions that are rooted in the educational and hence reproductive practices of the academic field, occupied by agents like public and private institutions of higher education such as universities and business schools. A fourth *strategy of symbolic rebellion* is linked to aspiring agents in general that benefit from changes in the prevailing order of consecration. Among these agents are new disciplines and new generations of academics as well as heterodox, avant-garde, and heretic currents. Conversely, rankings are also pushed by *conservative strategies* associated with orthodox perceptions of the field in favor of preserving the existing order and linked to those positions in the field that profit from current, rankings-based forms of consecration. Remarkably, these positions in turn often benefit from other, more traditional forms of consecration as well, a circumstance that will convince some but not all of the traditional elites of the academic field to push rankings.

Rankings as dispositifs of transnationalization: advancing transnationalization by tapping new sources of symbolic power

Our overview on main rankings in the academic field highlights that their effects go beyond the boundaries of the field. Rankings have at their command a peculiar authority that allows them to relate different fields. In particular, as has been highlighted by other scholars (Maeße, 2017; Brankovic, Ringel, & Werron, 2018), rankings open up academia as a field-specific specialist market and make it intelligible for a general lay public across disciplinary and nation-state confinements. Interconnecting the academic field with media, economic, and political and other social fields, rankings fulfill the strategic function of dispositifs (cf. Maeße & Hamann, 2016; Maeße, 2017). In recent centuries, academics in most Western countries have relied on nation-state bureaucracies and their powers to generalize a stable (academic) world and unified perceptions of it. Academic certificates were issued by *state* universities, backed by *state* law and *national* legal systems, positions and research were financed by *nation-state* revenues, etc., as devices that also relate the academic field with other fields and facilitate capital flows across fields, drawing indirectly on nation-state legitimacy.

In recent times, one important capital flow that bypasses the nation-state and redirects academic capital has been the collecting, processing, and interpretation of vast amounts of data by international media and educational corporations. For example, Springer, Bertelsmann, and QS Quacquarelli Symonds publish academic products and sell teaching but also collect, connect, and analyze data on different academic practices (Münch, 2009). This amounts to an attempt at monopolizing academic capital that goes hand in hand with a different form of symbolic validation and subverts nation-state claims over academic capital. In many instances, such as the accreditation of degrees, the symbolic logic of academic fields has shifted away from state-bureaucratic backup and now relies on private or public-private for-profit organizations that are validated foremost by mechanisms of competition – for example, certification and audit agencies (Power, 1999). As Colin Crouch (2007) points out, the legitimacy for such arrangements no longer arises from the rule of law and democratic sovereignty that is basically accessible to all citizens, but instead from the efficiency in production, allocation, and quality control that market-competition entails and that is basically open to all consumers.

This subversive attempt at monopolizing academic capital also shows in the bibliometric databases that most rankings draw on, which, by monopolistic principle, need to be huge, and preferably exhaustive. These databases are provided by either Thomson Reuters's Web of Science or Elsevier's Scopus database (Hazelkorn, 2017: 273). Together with mass media outlets, such as *Financial Times*, THEWU, or USN, these corporations try to monopolize and monetize higher education data. Such alliances might also include state institutions aside from private actors, as is the case with the German research institute and think tank CHE. Founded in 1994, its shareholders are the Bertelsmann Foundation and the German Rectors' Conference (Kehm, 2017: 83). In collaboration with the weekly newspaper *Die Zeit*, CHE has published university rankings on different disciplines since 1998, making it one of the major trendsetters in German higher education policy in the last 20 years (Münch, 2009). A similarly strategic intervention, this time on the transnational level, can be seen in the creation of U-multirank, dedicated to creating Europe-wide rankings of departments. The ranking is operated by a consortium that also involves CHE and is funded by the European Commission (Kehm, 2017: 84).

As dispositifs located at the intersection of fields, rankings facilitate a second flow of capital across boundaries of fields and beyond the nation-state: rankings organize the flow of political capital into the academic field. This allows nation-states as well as transnational, state-like institutions to govern and steer national higher education systems and their institutions (Erkkilä, 2014). The hubs that state institutions, private corporations, media corporations, and data providers form around rankings testify the political interest in rankings (Amsler & Bolsmann, 2012). Rankings create prestige scales that are a major factor in restructuring markets of higher education which, in turn, are understood as markets of symbolic goods (cf. Bourdieu, 1985). Their symbolic potential makes rankings attractive as devices of "governing at a distance". For example, the OECD as well as the European Union attempt to "work around" nation-states (Marttila, 2014; Schmidt-Wellenburg, 2017; Baier & Gengnagel, 2018) in order to directly influence the behavior of academic agents. Nation-states are receptive to these strategies because they see their higher education and research policies as objects of national pride, and engage in an international competition for prestige (Jessop, Fairclough, & Wodak, 2008). Transnational institutions then become consultants and agents for the higher principles that moderate this competition (Meyer & Jepperson, 2000).

In sum, rankings' function as dispositifs facilitates different capital flows across the boundaries of fields and beyond the nation-state. One important factor for these capital flows is the multipositionality of agents that occupy speaker positions in different contexts. For example, economists engage in political fields as consultants and in media fields as experts, and thus their academic capital travels from the academic field into different spheres (cf. Maeße, 2018; Schmidt-Wellenburg, 2018). This development seems to lead to more autonomy from nation-state bureaucracy, and indeed promises to reduce clientelism and nepotism. However, simultaneously, economic rationales that give a premium to efficiency and usability gain influence in the academic field and result in a new heteronomous regime. Aiming for top ranks and at the same time pressured by rankings, universities and other educational institutions converge for-profit organizations. Those that already fit this template gain globally in market shares and reputation, and educational-cum-media corporations become close allies at the heteronomous pole of the field. Even on the individual level, scholars attempt to make their activities more visible and amenable to university management and marketing, giving in to an acceleration towards evaluation that is not least propelled by rankings (see the debate on accelerated academia, cf. Vostal, 2016).

Conclusion

In this chapter, we showed why rankings lend themselves to projects of transnationalization. As dispositifs, rankings open up academia as a field-specific specialist market and make it intelligible for a lay public across different fields and nation-state confinements. Facilitating flows of academic and political capital, rankings thereby interconnect the academic field with the media, economics, and the political and other social fields. As institutions of consecration, rankings establish a symbolic prestige order that legitimizes and simultaneously glosses over material differences between different agents. These symbolic effects do not affect all agents in a field alike, but push – and are pushed by – specific academic milieus, paradigms, types of agents, and strategies.

Both consecration and dispositif functions rely on some basic principles of the practical functioning of rankings. First, rankings are Janus-faced in their practical logic. They can be mobilized according to the autonomous logic of the academic field, i.e., scientific meritocracy, objectivity, and neutrality. Rankings can also be used according to heteronomous logics within the academic field. For example, as "political" projects, they lend themselves to transform universities into autonomous actors, to pitch different scientific cultures against each other, or to govern academic subjects. Lastly, rankings can also be mobilized for straightforward political purposes beyond the academic field – for example, to increase national prestige by emphasizing the performance of a national higher education system.

Second, the double function of rankings relies on the doxic belief of subjectivized actors: Academics and academic institutions are not only made calculable by rankings, they also become calculative, strategic, and governable agents. Rankings make ranked entities part of the field, instilling in them a belief in a meritocratic ideology according to which every university, department, or researcher can make it to the top of the ranking as long as they work hard enough and pursue the right strategies (cf. Kehm, 2017). The irony of a meritocratic belief in rankings that do not depict but recreate social orders (Espeland & Sauder, 2007) seems to escape the subjectivized actors the more they are engaged in the game. This equally holds true for all those that use rankings as means to orient and optimize their buying decisions in this symbolic market of degrees: students, graduates, and employers (Wedlin, 2010: 208; Espeland & Sauder, 2016: 40 ff.).

The consecration and dispositif functions of rankings rely on a third principle of practical functioning. Most rankings do not impose entirely new criteria of evaluation. Rather, they often rely on measurements and metrics that draw on traditional consecratory institutions of the academic field – for example, citations and publications, prizes and reputation, student numbers and funding. Buying into the traditional symbolic economy of the field increases the credibility of rankings as institutions of consecration and lends them authority to depict and change the symbolic order of the field. Simultaneously, rankings do not only take up traditional consecratory institutions but de-contextualize them via quantification, aggregation, and visualization. The result are rank orders that are essentially bereft of meaning and that can be recharged with meaning in different contexts, and thus, across fields and beyond national boundaries.

We propose in this chapter a power analytical take on academic rankings, highlighting how their double function as consecratory institutions and dispositifs make them a transnational(izing) phenomenon. Rankings play an important role for the distribution of resources that enable academic actors to define the world as more or less (trans)national. In particular, rankings endow specific academic milieus, paradigms, agents, and strategies with symbolic resources that allow them to make academic statements on a more or less (trans)national world. Simultaneously, rankings themselves contribute to the transnationalization of the academic field by lending specific milieus, paradigms, agents, and strategies symbolic authority from transnational sources, i.e., private corporations, media corporations, and data providers. At the same time, rankings devalue some nationally anchored resources, agents, and sources of legitimacy more than others. Rankings play a vital part in processes of transnationalization that are far from impartial and equitable, but rather advance a global circulation of expertise and knowledge that conforms to English-language, journal-based publication cultures; has value in its practical application; or corresponds to political and market interests. The resulting geographies of higher education display striking disparities between the economically prospering regions in North America, Europe, East Asia, and Australia, and large parts of South America, Africa, and Asia (Jöns & Hoyler, 2013). Academic rankings do not only accompany these processes by interconnecting fields, circumventing the authority of nation-states, and tapping transnational sources of authority. They also lend processes of transnationalization moral integrity by allowing for a clear conscience of meritocracy and transparency.

References

Amsler, S. S., & Bolsmann, C. (2012). University Ranking as Social Exclusion. *British Journal of Sociology of Education*, *33*(2), 283–301.

Baier, C., & Gengnagel, V. (2018). Academic Autonomy Beyond the Nation-State: The Social Sciences and Humanities in the European Research Council. *Österreichische Zeitschrift für Soziologie, 43*(1), 65–92.

Bakanic, V., McPhail, C., & Simon, R. J. (1987). The Manuscript Review and Decision-Making Process. *American Sociological Review, 52*(5), 631–642.

Bekhradnia, B. (2016). *International University Rankings: For Good or Ill?* Oxford: HEPI.

Bourdieu, P. (1985). The Market of Symbolic Goods. *Poetics, 14*(1–2), 13–44.

Bourdieu, P. (1988). *Homo Academicus*. Cambridge: Polity Press.

Bourdieu, P. (1998). *Practical Reason: On the Theory of Action*. Stanford, CA: Stanford University Press.

Bourdieu, P. (2011). Champ du pouvoir et division du travail de domination. *Actes de la recherche en science sociales, 5*(190), 125–139.

Bourdieu, P., & Passeron, J.-C. (1977). *Reproduction in Education, Society, and Culture*. London: Sage.

Bowman, N. A., & Bastedo, M. N. (2011). Anchoring Effects in World University Rankings: Exploring Biases in Reputation Scores. *Higher Education, 61*(4), 431–444.

Brankovic, J., Ringel, L., & Werron, T. (2018). How Rankings Produce Competition: The Case of Global University Rankings. *Zeitschrift für Soziologie, 47*(4), 270–288.

Butz, A., & Wohlrabe, K. (2016). Die Ökonomen-Rankings 2015 von Handelsblatt, FAZ und RePEc: Methodik, Ergebnisse, Kritik und Vergleich. *Ifo Working Paper No. 212*.

CHE, Centrum für Hochschulentwicklung. (2009). *Das CHE-Forschungsranking deutscher Universitäten 2009 – Methodik*. Gütersloh: CHE.

Crouch, C. (2007). Kommerzialisierung oder Staatsbürgerschaft. Bildungspolitik und die Zukunft des öffentlichen Dienstes. In J. Mackert & H.-P. Müller (Eds.), *Moderne (Staats)Bürgerschaft: Nationale Staatsbürgerschaft und die Debatten der Citizenship Studies* (pp. 167–212). Wiesbaden: VS.

de Rijcke, S., Wouters, P., Rushforth, A. D., Franssen, T. P., & Hammarfelt, B. (2015). Evaluation Practices and Effects of Indicator Use: A Literature Review. *Research Evaluation, 25*(2), 161–169.

Desrosières, A. (2003). Managing the Economy. In T. M. Porter & D. Ross (Eds.), *The Cambridge History of Science, Vol. 7: The Modern Social Sciences* (pp. 553–564). Cambridge: Cambridge University Press.

Erkkilä, T. (2014). Global University Rankings, Transnational Policy Discourse and Higher Education in Europe. *European Journal of Education, 49*(1), 91–101.

Espeland, W. N., & Sauder, M. (2007). Rankings and Reactivity: How Public Measures Recreate Social Worlds. *American Journal of Sociology, 113*(1), 1–40.

Espeland, W. N., & Sauder, M. (2016). *Engines of Anxiety: Academic Rankings, Reputation, and Accountability*. New York, NY: Russell Sage Foundation.

Espeland, W. N., & Stevens, M. L. (1998). Commensuration as a Social Process. *Annual Review of Sociology, 24*, 313–343.

Esposito, E., & Stark, D. (2019). What's Observed in a Rating? Rankings as Orientation in the Face of Uncertainty. *Theory, Culture & Society, 36*(4), 3–26.

Foucault, M. (1977). The Confession of the Flesh. In C. Gordon (Ed.), *Power/Knowledge: Selected Interviews & Other Writings, 1972–1977, by Michel Foucault* (pp. 194–228). New York, NY: Pantheon Books.

Foucault, M. (2009). *The Birth of Biopolitics: Lectures at the Collège de France, 1978–1979*. Houndmills, Basingstoke: Palgrave Macmillan.

Fourcade, M., Ollion, E., & Algan, Y. (2014). The Superiority of Economists. *MaxPo Discussion Paper, 14*(3).

Gläser, J., & Laudel, G. (2007). Evaluation Without Evaluators. In R. D. Whitley & J. Gläser (Eds.), *The Changing Governance of the Sciences: The Advent of Research Evaluation Systems* (pp. 127–151). Dordrecht: Springer.

Hamann, J. (2016a). 'Let Us Salute One of Our Kind': How Academic Obituaries Consecrate Research Biographies. *Poetics, 56*(3), 1–14.

Hamann, J. (2016b). The Visible Hand of Research Performance Assessment. *Higher Education, 72*(6), 761–779.

Hammarfelt, B. (2017). Recognition and Reward in the Academy: Valuing Publication Oeuvres in Biomedicine, Economics and History. *Aslib Journal of Information Management, 69*(5), 607–623.

Hammarfelt, B., de Rijcke, S., & Wouters, P. (2017). From Eminent Men to Excellent Universities: University Rankings as Calculative Devices. *Minerva, 55*(4), 391–411.

Hargens, L. L. (2000). Using the Literature: Reference Networks, Reference Contexts, and the Social Structure of Scholarship. *American Sociological Review, 65*(6), 846–865.

Hazelkorn, E. (2017). Globalization and the Continuing Influence of Rankings – Positive and Perverse – on Higher Education. In E. Hazelkorn (Ed.), *Global Rankings and the Geopolitics of Higher Education: Understanding the Influence and Impact of Rankings on Higher Education, Policy and Society* (pp. 267–293). London; New York, NY: Routledge.

Heintz, B. (2016). 'Wir leben im Zeitalter der Vergleichung': Perspektiven einer Soziologie des Vergleichs. *Zeitschrift für Soziologie, 45*(5), 305–323.

Hicks, D. (2012). Performance-Based University Research Funding Systems. *Research Policy, 41*(2), 251–261.

Hirschauer, S. (2010). Editorial Judgements: A Praxeology of 'Voting' in Peer Review. *Social Studies of Science, 40*(1), 71–103.

Hollander, P. (2001). Acknowledgments: An Academic Ritual. *Academic Questions, 15*(1), 63–76.

Ishikawa, M. (2009). University Rankings, Global Models, and Emerging Hegemony: Critical Analysis from Japan. *Journal of Studies in International Education, 13*(2), 159–173.

Jessop, B., Fairclough, N., & Wodak, R. (2008). *Education and the Knowledge-Based Economy in Europe*. London: Sense Publishers.

Jöns, H., & Hoyler, M. (2013). Global Geographies of Higher Education: The Perspective of World University Rankings. *Geoforum, 46*, 45–59.

Karpik, L. (2011). What Is the Price of a Scientific Paper? In J. Beckert & P. Aspers (Eds.), *The Worth of Goods: Valuation and Pricing in the Economy* (pp. 61–85). Oxford: Oxford University Press.

Kauppi, N. (2017). Ranking and Structuration of a Transnational Field of Higher Education. In R. Normand & J.-L. Derouet (Eds.), *A European Politics of Education: Perspectives from Sociology, Policy Studies and Politics* (pp. 92–103). London; New York, NY: Routledge.

Kehm, B. M. (2017). Embracing and Rejecting Rankings: Germany. In E. Hazelkorn (Ed.), *Global Rankings and the Geopolitics of Higher Education: Understanding the Influence and Impact of Rankings on Higher Education, Policy and Society* (pp. 79–96). London; New York, NY: Routledge.

Lamont, M. (2009). *How Professors Think: Inside the Curious World of Academic Judgment*. Cambridge, MA: Harvard University Press.

Lee, F. S., Pham, X., & Gu, G. (2013). The UK Research Assessment Exercise and the Narrowing of UK Economics. *Cambridge Journal of Economics, 37*(4), 693–717.

Maeße, J. (2017). The Elitism Dispositif: Hierarchization, Excellence Orientation and Organizational Change in Economics. *Higher Education, 73*(6), 909–927.

Maeße, J. (2018). Globalization Strategies and the Economics Dispositive: Insights from Germany and the UK. *Historical Social Research, 43*(3), 120–146.

Maeße, J., & Hamann, J. (2016). Die Universität als Dispositiv: Die gesellschaftliche Einbettung von Bildung und Wissenschaft aus diskurstheoretischer Perspektive. *Zeitschrift für Diskursforschung, 4*(1), 29–50.

Marttila, T. (2014). Die wissensbasierte Regierung der Bildung: Die Genese einer transnationalen Gouvernementalität in England und Schweden. *Berliner Journal für Soziologie, 24*(2), 257–287.

Meyer, J. W., & Jepperson, R. L. (2000). The 'Actors' of Modern Society: The Cultural Construction of Social Agency. *Sociological Theory, 18*(1), 10–120.

Münch, R. (2008). Stratifikation durch Evaluation: Mechanismen der Konstruktion und Reproduktion von Statushierarchien in der Forschung. *Zeitschrift für Soziologie, 37*(1), 60–80.

Münch, R. (2009). *Globale Eliten, lokale Autoritäten: Bildung und Wissenschaft unter dem Regime von PISA, McKinsey & Co.* Frankfurt am Main: Suhrkamp.

Münch, R. (2010). Der Monopolmechanismus in der Wissenschaft: Auf den Schultern von Robert K. Merton. *Berliner Journal für Soziologie, 20*(3), 341–370.

Paradeise, C., Reale, E., Bleiklie, I., & Ferlie, E. (Eds.). (2009). *University Governance: Western European Perspectives*. Dordrecht: Springer.

Pontille, D., & Torny, D. (2010). The Controversial Policies of Journal Ratings: Evaluating Social Sciences and Humanities. *Research Evaluation, 19*(5), 347–360.

Power, M. (1997). *The Audit Society: Rituals of Verification*. Oxford: Oxford University Press.

Raffnsøe, S., Gudmand-Høyer, M., & Thaning, M. S. (2014). Foucault's Dispositive: The Perspicacity of Dispositive Analytics in Organizational Research. *Organization, 23*(2), 272–298.

Riley, L. E., & Spreitzer, E. A. (1970). Book Reviewing in the Social Sciences. *The American Sociologist, 5*(4), 358–363.

Schmidt-Wellenburg, C. (2017). Europeanisation, Stateness, and Professions: What Role Do Economic Expertise and Economic Experts Play in European Political Integration? *European Journal of Cultural and Political Sociology, 4*(4), 430–456.

Schmidt-Wellenburg, C. (2018). German Economists' Discourse on European Crisis. *Historical Social Research, 43*(3), 147–188.

Simmel, G. (1900). *Philosophie des Geldes*. Leipzig: Duncker & Humblot.

Tsay, A., Lamont, M., Abbott, A., & Guetzkow, J. (2003). From Character to Intellect: Changing Conceptions of Merit in the Social Sciences and Humanities, 1951–1971. *Poetics, 31*(5–6), 23–49.

Usher, A. (2017). Short Global History of Rankings. In E. Hazelkorn (Ed.), *Global Rankings and the Geopolitics of Higher Education* (pp. 23–53). London; New York, NY: Routledge.

Vogel, R., Hattke, F., & Petersen, J. (2017). Journal Rankings in Management and Business Studies: What Rules Do We Play by? *Research Policy, 46*(10), 1707–1722.

Vostal, F. (2016). *Accelerating Academia: The Changing Structure of Academic Time*. Houndmills, Basingstoke: Palgrave Macmillan.

Wedlin, L. (2010). Going Global: Rankings as Rhetorical Devices to Construct an International Field of Management Education. *Organization, 42*(2), 199–218.

Werron, T. (2014). On Public Forms of Competition. *Cultural Studies ↔ Critical Methodologies, 14*(1), 62–76.

Werron, T., & Ringel, L. (2017). Rankings: Conceptual Remarks. In S. Lessenich (Ed.), *Geschlossene Gesellschaften: Verhandlungen des 38: Kongresses der Deutschen Gesellschaft für Soziologie in Bamberg 2016*. Retrieved October 3, 2019, from http://publikationen.soziologie.de/index.php/kongressband_2016/article/view/466

Willmott, H. (2011). Journal List Fetishism and the Perversion of Scholarship: Reactivity and the ABS List. *Organization, 18*(4), 429–442.

Windolf, P. (1997). *Expansion and Structural Change: Higher Education in Germany, United States and Japan 1870–1990*. Boulder, CO: Westview Press.

Chapter 9

A weak field of social policy?

A transnational perspective on the EEC's social policymaking (from the 1940s to the 1970s)

Karim Fertikh

Introduction

During the 2019 European election campaign, some party leaders on the left tried to mobilize the citizens with the promise of building a "Social Europe", in order to counterbalance what they described as a neoliberal and market-oriented European Union. The same calls have been issued at every European election since 1979. Hence, social Europe seems to be no more than an empty promise. When people say "social Europe failed", that "there is no social Europe", or even that "there will not be a social Europe" – *l'Europe sociale n'aura pas lieu*, as François Denord and Antoine Schwarz (2015) once put it – it implies a definition of what this social Europe would have to look like. Many studies on European social policies are in this sense normative: these policies are often implicitly compared to national social states, and miss the specificity of international arrangements in the social domain.

Social Europe cannot be seen as a European Welfare State (based on massive inter-individual and inter-state financial redistribution) in the making. In order to understand it, one must understand the specificity of international social policies and law. Far more than with financial redistribution, international social policies have dealt with the social effects of labor migrations and the standardization of national policies though international conventions on social matters – with progressive ambitions (led by a powerful transnational "reformist" coalition from the nineteenth century to the 1980s) (Cayet, 2011; Cayet & Rosental, 2013; Kott & Droux, 2013) or, more recently, neoliberal ones (Bernhard, 2010).

This research delves into a transnational field of social policy, populated with law professors, social reformers from political parties and trade unions, national officials in charge of social issues, and diverse professionals interested in some aspects of an international social policy. This field has been structured by international organizations (IOs) such as the European Economic Community (EEC)/ European Union (EU), the Organization for European Economic Co-operation (OECE) and the International Labour Organization (ILO). These institutions have provided venues, funding, legitimacy, opportunities for the publication and diffusion of ideas, but also contributed more generally to the creation of "gravitational" forces generating incentives for national actors such as interest groups, private companies, or academics to perceive these arenas and institutions as potentially profitable spaces in which to invest time and resources.

European social policy is embedded in the history of this transnational network of actors and IOs. "What is wrongly called the European project is de facto a sum of competing projects as well as forgotten drafts and attempts", as Didier Georgakakis (Georgakakis, 2018: 1085; see also: Bernhard, 2010: 13) deftly put it. Social Europe is definitely one of these attempted projects, and not the least important as it has long been promoted by major advocates of the European construction, such as the international trade-unions (Fertikh, 2017). Unknowingly using an expression, "social Europe", coined by legal specialists in the 1950s, specialists of Social Europe face a singular object. Social Europe is a sum of past projects, which have partly vanished – hence the tendency to deem social Europe a failure in terms of economic integration – and are partly nowadays taken for granted. One of the aims of this chapter is to describe some of these projects for orienting Europe toward more social policies, and to explain what the players had in mind when they called for a "social Europe" or a "Europe of workers" (a phrase trade-unionists have long preferred to use as a synonym for "social Europe"). How could sociology describe this part of the so-called European project and analyze the (apparent) scarcity of its achievements?

In order to describe the transnational dimension of social policy, this chapter relies on a sociohistorical approach, shedding light on the genesis of the European social policy from the 1940s to the 1970s – a period when its main institutions and categories (coordination, harmonization, non-discrimination) were forged. Relying on a prosopography of actors involved in the making of a European social law (Fertikh, 2016) and on a wide array of archives (ILO, EU, French Ministry of Labor, French social security administration) and documents, the analysis attempts to reflect the plurality of the players involved and focuses on the interrelations of many IOs and national administrations to explain the making of the European social law. Defined as a structured space of relations, the "field" concept does not confine these achievements to preexisting categories and strictly delineated institutions. I will first make a case for the value of the concept of weak field in exploring the making of the European social policies. Secondly, I will pinpoint the existence of an international space of relations related to the transnationalization of social rights, revolving around a few IOs. Thirdly, I will highlight the role of the "weak field" constituted by legal specialists and their transnational networks. Lastly, I will shed light on the making of a European social law, especially the "personalization" or "de-territorialization" of social security rights in the late 1950s.

The concept of "weak field"

The study of social policy is a potential source of worthwhile insights into policymaking in a transnational setting. On the one hand, it is often analyzed as a national policy only. Social scientists and historians have convincingly argued that social policy in Europe has fostered the legitimacy of states and contributed to the making of territorial nation-states (Raphael, 2013; Senghaas, 2015). As sociohistorians have shown, social benefits and entitlements contribute to creating subjective feelings of belonging to a national community amongst citizens. The French sociohistorian Gérard Noiriel (1998, 2006) has pointed out the importance of social policies when it comes to developing administrative instruments to identify individuals and to make the nation a "survival unit". Thus, the constructions of social (or welfare) states and national identities appear to be intertwined, as the social state is held as the backbone of European nation-states (Kaelble, 2000; Wagner, 2000). It is one of the reasons why the study of European social policies is shaped by this experience, and tends to suffer from what has come to be branded methodological nationalism (Wimmer & Glick Schiller, 2002). Indeed, the study of social Europe often implicitly relies on a comparison with national institutions. But if we are to grasp what exactly this social dimension of European integration actually was, we must acknowledge that the construction of European social policy cannot be understood as a process geared toward the replacement or the reproduction of national institutions, players, norms, and practices in the social domain. On the contrary, the process connects different systems and fosters their convergence. Players compare and harmonize social standards (social benefits, definitions of occupational diseases, required diplomas for certain occupations, definition of the extent of the "family" covered by a worker's social rights, and so on). While financial transfers between member states or between individuals hardly exist, European bureaucracies have been highly active in other domains of social policy, such as the coordination and the harmonization of national social systems forging other legal and administrative categories and techniques than the national ones.

Of course, other scholars have shed light on the transnational making of these social policies (Topalov, 1999b; Georgakakis & Vauchez, 2015). It has been a long time since historians and sociologists like Sandrine Kott, Madeleine Herren, Daniel Rodgers, and Christian Topalov (Herren, 1993; Rodgers, 2001; Lengwiler, 2009; Kott & Droux, 2013) have shown that even the most national social insurance schemes were framed and developed in a transnational context from the start (Sunil, 2006, 2017; Rosental, 2011; Béland & Peterson, 2015). Social policies were a collective invention that went beyond national borders. Researchers have noted the importance of reform networks (including philanthropists, politicians, scientists, trade-unionists, employees in national social administrations, and insurance companies), the organization of many international gatherings and conferences on a variety of sociopolitical issues as early as in the nineteenth century, and the precocity of the constitution of private or public international bodies. The precocity of transnational reformist networks in the domain of social policy should have led to a strong European social policy. On the contrary, some sociologists even think that there is no "social Europe" (Scharpf, 2009), that social Europe is still merely a possibility in a context where the national social states have lost their autonomy in the making of social policy but no genuine European social policy has emerged (Schildberg, 2010), or that social Europe could have existed but has come to a "dead end" (Lechevalier & Wielgohs, 2016). They argue that the "ordo" or "neoliberal" thrust of the Treaty of Rome and the focus on free trade (in the making of the single market) reduced the social dimension of European integration to a bare minimum. In the same vein, Pierre Bourdieu describes social Europe as no more than a "rhetorical illusion" (Bourdieu, 1999). Yet it is to some extent surprising that social Europe has so far failed, as there are strong, longstanding transnational networks of individuals and IOs in Europe that have successfully promoted international social policies. For a short period of time in the 1950s, social policy elites were seemingly much better off than many other sectorial elites, for example in agriculture and in international investment law.

This paradox between the early international integration of a European social policy field and the apparent scarcity of its achievements (the idea that there is no "Social Europe", nothing comparable with the market policy) may partly result from the inadequacy of the tools we use to analyze transnational social policies, and hence the use of national categories to conceive European social policy. A field theory approach, i.e., a conception relying on social spaces organized around different types of specific resources (or capitals) within which ideas, status, rules are produced and put in motion – is useful to untangle this conundrum.

More specifically, European social policy may be better explained by recourse to the concept of "weak field" to pinpoint the central role of legal arenas as spaces where "social Europe" was made (Vauchez, 2008). In the 1990s, the sociologist Christian Topalov first coined the notion to describe the transnational nebula of social reform in the nineteenth century: a field where the efficient forms of capital are produced in other (mainly national) fields and whose borders are porous (Topalov, 1999a). The field of European social law was encapsulated in other (bureaucratic, legal, political) fields. Legal specialists were of paramount importance in forging the categories of the European social law, and at the same time deeply involved and recognized in their national fields. Their international recognition depended on their national positions and resources. Hence, this field was weak and deprived of autonomy. Yet, it was not weak in its effects. As Antoine Vauchez (2008: 130, 2013) put it, "legal arenas stand out as the (main) forum of mediation between the dense interconnected array of sector-specific policy networks". Building law is building Europe, in the social domain as well.

Multi-sited transnational political processes

At the time of their creation in the 1950s, the European institutions were not singlehandedly specialized in the making of a single market. The European Coal and Steel Community (ECSC) and the EEC had extensive social competences, as Nicolas Verschueren (2012), a historian specialized in the ECSC, has shown. These organizations salaried numerous civil servants and experts to develop a European social policy, tackling issues like worker "readaptation" (social measures including retraining and redeployment for workers of declining industries, like Italian coal miners), social housing, social security, with the ECSC's International Convention for the Social Security of Migrant Workers and the EEC's

Regulations 3 and 4, and so forth. These achievements were at the time considered of significant importance.

In the infancy of the European Communities, in their courses and handbooks, law professors described the European Social Law to come as potentially the most important international legislation in the field. The EC enjoyed the symbolic prestige of Europe. The continent was seen, in the words of the ILO's associate director, as:

> the cradle of the world's social policy. Its contribution to the ILO is invaluable. Numerous ILO conventions are based on social legislations from European countries. (. . .) The continent remains, to a large extent, the soul and driving force of the International Labour Organization.
>
> (Conseil de l'Europe, 1961: 10)

A variety of elites, from international officials in charge of social affairs to academics and trade-unionists, considered the European Communities as a Mecca in the making for international social policy. Professors of international social law, which was at the time a developing academic discipline, prophesied the growing importance of these European institutions, giving them a central role in the construction of progressive international rights: "International social law at the European level is slated for a bright future due to the very organization of Europe, which seeks to become more and more coherent by virtue of an ineluctable sociological law", as the law professor Léon-Éli Troclet (1952) put it in the first handbook for international social law.

The European Communities were nevertheless newcomers in an already structured field: the production of international social policy was multi-sited, and the new European institutions were introduced to a structured field of cooperation and competition over what was called at the time "social prestige", the prestige derived from social achievements.[1]

A prosopographical approach of the individuals who populated the European institutions helps us understand in which sense there was a transnational field of social policy, that is: a system of interrelations between players who shared common views on the importance of social issues (even if they obviously often disagreed on what had to be done). From the beginning, the EEC's institutions had various departments and committees in charge of social affairs: they institutionalized a permanent international bureaucracy in charge of the making of social policy. My research focuses on two central institutions among them: the General Directorate for Social Affairs (GD 5) and the Social Commission of the European Parliament (EP). In the mid-1960s, the EEC GD 5 comprised 107 civil servants, which made it a mid-range Directorate (the General Directorate for Competition had 207 civil servants at the time) but not a neglected one. The social commission of the Common Assembly/European Parliament had 29 members in 1958 (86 in total during the 1953–1967 period under study here). The trajectories of the employees and members of these institutions show numerous interrelations as well as a circulation between national and international, private and public organizations. These individuals tend to share a pre-existing commitment to international cooperation in the social domain and international connections.

The players of this social policy field shared an international background. Their biographies showed, as Isabella Löhr put it, that they had "lives beyond borders" (Löhr, 2013). Social policy had long been internationally organized, and the field was polarized among various IOs. The players of the European social policy themselves participated in numerous international non-governmental organizations (NGOs), social movement organizations, and IOs before they shaped the EEC social policy. Indeed, the first Commissioners for Social Affairs and the first president of the EP's Social Commission took part in the organization of the "Social Conference" of the European Movement, held in Rome in July 1950.[2] The conference addressed many social issues that were relevant for the EEC – such as free movement of workers, vocational training, and social security – and called for an extensive social state as the basis for the free development of personality. More generally speaking, 30% of the members of the EP's social commission were members of deliberative assemblies of other IOs (European Council, West-European Union) or occupied a position in one of the Trade Unions' International Confederations.

Some of these most important players were companions of the most prestigious IO in the domain: the ILO. The ILO officials branded some of the experts of the European Communities or some of its officials as "friends" of their own organization. Léon-Éli Troclet (1902–1980), who presided over the EP's Social Committee in the 1960s, was one of these friends of the ILO. In the 1930s, the socialist politician and law professor already had an international scope of action and participated actively in the ILO from 1945 to 1980 (as Belgian delegate at the International Conference for Labor and as member of the Administrative Council of the International Labor Office from 1945 to 1951). The same could be said of officials from NGOs such as the International Confederation of Free Trade-Unions. The Belgian Walter Schevenels was the general secretary of the European Regional Organization of the International Confederation of Free Trade Unions (ICFTU) from 1950 to 1966, and played a major part in coordinating the trade-union position toward European integration. He was the general secretary of the ICFTU from 1930 to 1945. In an autobiographical document from the 1950s, he emphasized his role in the organization of international training curricula for young trade-unionists in his functions at the Centre d'éducation des métallurgistes (Centre for the Education of Steelworkers) in the 1920s. Between 1949 and 1959, he was the secretary of the Trade Union Advisory Committee to the Organisation for Economic Co-operation and Development (OECD).[3]

Their international background, a required capital for accessing the field, was part of the public identity they used when it came to justifying their recruitment in the EEC institutions. Many MEPs, for instance, highlighted their participation in the European Movement in their official biographies. The résumés of the players appointed in NGOs (the International Confederation of Free Trade Union, for instance) or in the GD 5 were centered on their international experience. The résumé of Lionello Levi Sandri (the second General Director in charge of Social Affairs at the EEC Commission in 1961), for instance, underlined his participation in various international negotiations, in the European Movement, and in the ILO's activities.[4] This could also be observed in other organizations: internationalization was a broader defining feature of this field of social policy. At the time, even national officials had an international profile, in the sense that they had connections and participated in numerous international conferences, for example in the domain of social security. In the 1940s, Pierre Laroque, who is often described as the father of French social security, spent several months every year traveling abroad, and noted how important international affairs were in his autobiography:

> In my arguments so far, I have reasoned as if the issues raised by the Social Security were restricted to the French territory. Of course, these kinds of problems were of paramount importance, especially when the Social Security scheme was developed and implemented. However, international concerns were never neglected and became increasingly important as the organization established itself and its routine.
>
> I always insisted on dealing personally with every international problem, and there were many, with which we were confronted. (. . .) The First Office of the Directorate General was in charge of international issues pertaining to social security, which came to be its main and ultimately exclusive activity.
>
> (Laroque, 1993: 211)

At the time, the French Ministry of Labor's directorate-general for social security established a department for European and international affairs, which soon became the most important of its departments.

The field of international social policy united many organizations, so that players were not only bound to the European Communities when it came to promoting an agenda for transnational social policy. Individuals and groups used the EEC institutions among other institutional settings. After World War II, social insurance was one of the most dynamic areas of international cooperation in the domain of social policy. Specialists of social insurances defended their view in multiple international arenas, from NGOs (International Social Security Association) to a wide array of IOs (European Council, EEC, ECSC, ILO). They drafted an International Convention for the Social Security of Migrant Workers (negotiated under the auspices of the ILO and the ECSC), which resulted in the 1958 EEC Regulations 3 and 4, the European Council's European Code for the Social Security, and numerous other bilateral and multilateral agreements. Between the 1940s and the late 1960s, some 400 international agreements on social security were concluded, mainly between European countries.

These (national and international) institutions worked as a *champ de force*, structured by power relations. The European Communities mobilized resources first gathered by other IOs and depended on other IOs, especially the ILO, which was the major player in the field (Guinand, 2003; Kott & Droux, 2013; Mechi, Migani, & Petrini, 2014). The ILO provided the European Communities with documents, information, and technical assistance, without which the EEC (the GD 5 or the Statistical Office) could not have achieved some of their goals (social security, harmonization of the definition of occupational diseases, international comparison of employment, salaries, etc.). The IOs cooperated, but were at the same time struggling to maintain or acquire dominance in the field of social policy. In confidential memos, ILO officials feared that the development of the ECSC and EEC social policy could result in the loss of what they called "social prestige", because these institutions would tend to silence the role of other IOs in the process of legitimizing their action:

> Faced with the criticisms constantly leveled at it, aware that only practical results in the social field will silence the critics, and convinced that in these circumstances the sharing of 'social prestige' with other organizations though joint venture is undesirable, the High Authority (of the ECSC) now tends to go it alone.[5]

They believed the ECSC was trying to "squeeze the ILO out of the picture in connection with activities undertaken jointly".[6] They deplored that it kept "the ILO 'in the dark' regarding certain initiatives in fields of close concern to the ILO". As a result, they condemned the High Authority's "separatist manoeuvers", and they asked for the ILO to be associated with the social programs carried out by the ECSC.[7] Embedded in this transnational setting, the European bureaucratic field did not monopolize power over the making of international social policy. It competed with other IOs as well as with national administrations, and mobilized external support to develop its social policy. Part of this support was provided by a group of internationalized law professors.

Brokers in the field: Law professors as transnational entrepreneurs

The EC's bureaucracy was at the crossroads of activist, political, and other bureaucratic and professional dynamics and endeavors. As the work of Antoine Vauchez has shown, the EU is at the same time a political and an academic construction, and legal specialists were brokers between fields of paramount importance. To gain power, EC officials mobilized diverse preexisting groups and the collective capital and authority these groups enjoyed. They extensively relied on legal specialists to gain an authority in the field of social policy.

An internationalized group of social law professors had a particularly crucial role in bridging the various IOs, forging the new categories of European and international social law. As brokers, social law professors contributed to defining the social rules of the game and the scope of possible international action; as Martti Koskienniemi argued, "there is no access to legal rules or the legal meaning of international behavior that is independent from the way competent lawyers see those things" (Koskenniemi, 2015: 569). Academics have always had an important role in shaping social states in Europe and beyond (Grimmer-Solem, 2005; Béland & Peterson, 2015). But research on the IOs has emphasized their paramount importance in bridging national administrative cultures, and establishing the authority of the elites of the European Communities and the self-fulfilling effects of their legal discourse (Georgakakis, 2018: 1087). Looking at the social law specialists and their academic capitals "emphasizes the social process of the construction of elites *as elites* by looking at the way they built their own authority" (Georgakakis & Rowell, 2013).

These law specialists were at the crossroads of national and international fields. They built the language and the scope of action of the Communities – in short, the "categories" (Zimmermann, 2001) of public policy. Social law professors acted as brokers between national and European institutions, and between IOs. The legal background of many officials and actors of the EC institutions explains the importance of legal categories in policymaking. In 1966, at GD 5, 44 civil servants held the highest rank (the so-called "A category"). Biographical data are occasionally spotty, but it transpires that one-fourth (11) were Ph.D. holders or French high civil servants who had graduated from the country's top schools – the Grandes Écoles. Likewise, 36% of MEPs had a legal academic background, and 19 out of 86 held a Ph.D. or were university professors.

The European institutions were not the only or main focus point of these academics at the time. These professionals had positions in national institutions, and were involved in national norm-making, as well as in transnational institutions. Additionally, some of them acted as governmental experts in international negotiations. It should be noted that social law specialists were already internationally organized as a profession before the constitution of the EEC. Their professional organization, the International Society for Labor and Social Security Law (ISLSSL), had been created step by step during the 1940s and the early 1950s. The ILO's resources and the mobilization of some ILO officials with a legal background were crucial in the development of the International Society. The contribution of these officials both to the structuring of social law as a discipline and to the establishment of an international expert authority is undeniable. The ILO provided the new organization with documentation, opportunities, and symbolic prestige; its directors were often in attendance at International Society congresses. ILO officials also played a role in enrolling professors into the International Society in countries where the ISLSSL had no representation.[8] The International Society played a capital role in structuring national associations of social law specialists, and in connecting these specialists. The French and Italian societies for labor law, for instance, were first created as national sections of the International Society. The national and international levels were not opposed, but combined in various ways.

The internationalization of social law specialists created a social milieu whose members had many opportunities to meet – expert committees, international conferences, and the biennial ISLSSL congresses – which was typical of the "scientific internationalism" described by Anne Rasmussen (1989). These were also moments for sociability, showing that these professors had more in common than scientific interest. Excursions or dinners were planned during the congress of the International Society, and even the wives of the overwhelmingly male professors partook in social activities while their husbands attended the sessions. The International Society made efforts to interconnect the many national institutes of labor, organizing exchanges of students and professors in the early 1960s.

When the European institutions were created by the Treaty of Rome, they relied on these preexisting legal resources. The ECSC and EEC enrolled some of the European social law experts of the ISLSSL in order to define the scope of their action in the social domain. In 1956, the ECSC High Authority – and later on, the EEC Commission – gathered a "group of social law specialists" to analyze the state of social legislation in the six member countries, and to steer the action of the Communities in the field. The French law professor Paul Durand, who was also president of ISLSSL and involved in various IOs, such as the ILO and the United Nations Educational, Scientific and Cultural Organization (UNESCO), presided over the group (see: Fertikh & Louis, 2019).

This situation shaped the EC's legal understanding in the social domain. The position of the law professors in the transnational field may go some way toward explaining their reluctance to embrace legal innovations (supranationality, a direct effect of European law) promoted by the EC officials. Social law specialists were at the time convinced that bilateral and multilateral international negotiations and a better understanding of foreign social legislations through "comparative social law" were the best ways to achieve the uncontroversial goal of "social harmonization". Their collective position, for example during the famous 1959 Milan-Stresa congress of the ECSC (Bailleux, 2010), defended an international social law, but refused to acknowledge the "supranationality" of European law, which most of the ECSC and EEC officials stood for (see for example, this paper by the General Director of the GD 5: Levi Sandri, 1967). In this way, they opened a path of dependency that was only altered by the European Court of Justice after the mid-1970s and the powerful transnational movement fostered by the United Nations in favor of women's equality (Wobbe & Biermann, 2009). While the international law specialists gave symbolic credit to the institutions of the Communities and contributed to forging the categories of European social law, they imposed a path of action on EC officials in the sociopolitical field.

Transnational category making: Categorizations and institutions

To address the output of these players' activities, I intend to propose a different outlook on the alleged scarcity of the results of efforts to establish a transnational social policy, and on the failure of the so-called "Social Europe". In this transnational field, new categories emerged, distinct from national ones: "occupational readaptation" (the subject of the EEC's first Social Fund of the EEC), deterritoralized social rights or "social harmonization", as well as coordination and convergence.

The EC officials were not the only ones to forge and use these categories. They were to a great extent dependent on the existing state of relations in the field of social policy. The production of these categories resulted from the endeavors of competing players in the transnational field of social policy. In the 1950s and 1960s, trade unionists, social democrats, Christian democrats, officials from IOs, and some national state servants and ministers – especially French – pushed an agenda for social harmonization in an attempt to frame the scope of European social policies. Harmonization was at the time a vague notion, which bureaucrats, jurists and trade-unionists struggled to define, trying to give it a progressive meaning: the EEC had to promote a convergence of the national social rights toward the better standards. A professor at the Sorbonne University in Paris, Paul Durand, who had been one of the founders of the ISLSSL, was active in the preparation of reports for various IOs. He helped the legal expert Jacques Doublet, the successor of Pierre Laroque as head of the Directorate General for Social Security at the French Labour Ministry, to develop the French position on "social harmonization" during the Messina Conference. The French Ministry was at the time eager to protect the extensive French social insurance system from market liberalization, and helped forge the watchword "social harmonization". GD 5 officials and socialist MEPs used the latter (which they tried to define performatively) to legitimate their action (Bernhard, 2010: 21), partly by commissioning numerous expert works on the topic. Many players outside the bureaucracy worked to push the agenda for social harmonization, such as the MEPs, whose Social Committee finalized a report on the subject. The rapporteur was the Dutch socialist Gerhard Nederhorst, who was the long-standing president of the Social Commission of the Common Assembly of the ECSC in the 1950s and a central figure of the scientific foundation of the Dutch trade union movement (Fertikh & Wieters, 2018). Hence, the report gave this transnational watchword a "progressive", worker-friendly character (meaning roughly "progressive social harmonization").

The EEC was not isolated in this domain: official reports from the ILO underlined the close cooperation between the organization in Geneva and the EEC Commission in the area of social harmonization, which was still in the 1970s part of the long-term action program of the ILO and of the Council of Europe.[9] The EC institutions were one of several arenas where the players tried to push their agenda on the protection of social systems from the effects of market liberalization (dumping) and on better labor protection in Europe. The internationalization of the social security rights may provide a good example of this embeddedness of the EEC institutions.

The European Convention for the Social Security of Migrant Workers (1957) was undoubtedly one of the most significant and lasting achievements in the field of European social policy (Ferrera, 2005). Concluded at first between the six ECSC member states, the treaty laid the basis for EEC Regulations 3 and 4

(1959) and promoted the idea of personalized or deterritorialized social rights. The negotiations were supervised by the ILO and took place in Geneva, the hub of international social policy, from 1954 to 1957. Negotiators were "governmental experts" from the administrations of social insurances; social law specialists such as Léon-Eli Troclet were also involved.

A legal revolution in the domain of social security, the deterritorialization of social rights – on a multilateral basis, not bilateral as was usually the case after World War II – was largely an assemblage of disparate national administrative categories, informed not only by administrative or insurance-related issues, but also by moral questions and populationist provisions, not to mention the imperial dimension of some of the member states (France and, later on, the United Kingdom in the 1970s) (Fertikh, 2019). The innovation thus featured contextual administrative and scientific provisions, such as the limitation of the payments outside the country of employment at a level compatible with the rules applied for Algerian Muslims working in the French *métropole* or the limitation of the payment of family benefits for non-national workers to a period of time devoted to finding proper housing for their children, serving two populationist aims at once: the quality of the population (though the adequacy of the housing conditions) and its quantity. Workers were prominent subjects of negotiation, considered with their families for mainly populationist reasons. There was no consideration of a broader "European citizenship" at the time. For the same populationist reasons, the nationality principle was far from abandoned: for instance, following the Convention, the children born in the worker's country of employment (not in the country of origin) did not make the parents eligible for a maternity allowance, on the grounds that they could claim the nationality of this country of employment in the *jus soli* countries. Emmanuel Comte points to other contextual considerations which shaped this social security policy, and hence what he calls the post– World War II open European "migration regime" – for example, the housing shortage in Germany and the Netherlands, leading these two countries to favor short-term migration and to defend the payment of family allowances outside their national territories in the negotiations (Comte, 2017: 68). This bricolage relied on various instruments forged in the field of social policy, which the Communities were lucky to benefit from at a time where the ILO or the Council of Europe could have taken over the leadership in the making of transnational social security law.

During the negotiations of the treaty, the debate on the internationalization of social insurance was embedded in the overall question of a social harmonization of its costs, with proposals for a European payroll tax and a European Clearance Agency or European Social Security Fund. These instruments would have lowered the risk of social dumping and preserved the social system within a context of market liberalization and international competition. Tensions ran high within the expert group; the French delegates threatened to cut the negotiations short if no supranational solution emerged. Deterritorialization created three groups of countries: immigration countries, such as France and Belgium, which would be contributing countries (two-thirds of all Italian migrants were at the time in these two countries); countries with low levels of European immigration, such as Germany or the Netherlands, for which the Convention had no major financial impact; and emigration countries, such as Italy, which would financially benefit from the treaty. Oppositions in the negotiation went along these lines. A purely materialist interpretation, emphasizing national interest, would not account for the fact that the delegates of the contributing countries agreed with the importance of the Convention, and thus did not refuse to play the game altogether, although they could have in light of the costs of deterritorialization. In the field, the internationalization of social security was largely acknowledged as a necessity. The delegates saw in this internationalization the opportunity to protect national achievements. At an individual level, these negotiations were a chance for some to embrace international careers. At an ideological level, the International Social Security Association, which was supported by the ILO and served as a venue for rank-and-file administrators of social insurance to meet, defended and publicized model forms for bilateral conventions, while social security administrations in Europe developed the first multilateral conventions (such as the Agreement concerning the social security of Rhine boatmen – short: the Rhine Agreement – in 1949), which the Association promoted and considered as important legal instruments at the time (Stephens & International Social Security Association, 1956).

This competition was not a competition between levels; it happened within a constellation of actors who shared the same professional conception of deterritorialization (which they all supported), but disagreed as to how to achieve it. On the one hand, the French delegates and experts tried to push a general, highly technical solution with both a new supranational administrative body (a clearance agency) and a modest supranational payroll tax to finance this body and part of the financial transfers. They received technical assistance from officials from both the ECSC and the ILO, who did the math and proposed scenarios to support their proposal. The supranational arrangement was an attempted compromise between diverse types of actors in the field, which was also pushed by the Italian delegation. The officials of IOs pushed for such a transnational solution, as it would reinforce the power of transnational regulation. On the other hand, the legal experts were far from being convinced by a supranational solution. The professor Paul Durand, who represented France in numerous international negotiations, opposed the concept of a supranational social law in the Milan-Stresa congress in 1956, as did the delegates of the low-contributing countries. Some of the latter were represented by experts with an academic affiliation, which could explain their general reluctance to agree to a supranational design, more than just an abstract "national interest".

This *intergovernmentalism* vs. *supranationalism* debate, to put it in simplified terms, was not a conflict between "levels", states versus IOs. The players shared the desire to achieve a degree of individualization of social rights. They expressed their position in categories that fit the field and the transnational milieu they addressed. French delegates did not argue that they supported a supranational arrangement for cost-sharing reasons, or because it would help protect the French social security from dumping by countries with less social protection.

They described their supranational arrangement as a "European" solution, which would pave the way for the constitution of a truly European social insurance. Furthermore, at the time when some of the greatest achievements in international social law were made, internationally protected rights, such as the "personal" social rights (receiving family or pension benefits outside of one's employment country, and health insurance in foreign countries) established by the 1957 Convention, remained solidly bound to states, and not only in the realm of social rights (Fertikh, 2019). In this sense, the fact that social policies have remained more of a "national" competence is not a given, something that would have been written in the Treaty of Rome itself, but the result of what Didier Georgakakis defines as the "battle for the definition of the situation inside the field which produces its self-fulfilling effect by giving symbolic resources to the winner of the day" (Georgakakis, 2018: 1090).

Conclusion

Thinking of the European social policy as a transnational field allows us to overcome the "historical mimicry" (Studer, 1995) that stems from analyzing EC/EU policy by focusing on their institutional borders. Here my research method has consisted in describing inter-individual relationships, and considering EC institutions as one arena and resource among others for individuals to deploy their strategies. The destiny of Social Europe has to do with these relationships and their structural transformations in time.

While the EC institutions were seen as attractive as a potential cradle for an international law, they were supported and challenged by many other powerful organizations with which they cooperated and competed. At the same time, some of their successes, and the professorial prophecies about European social law being the most important international law in the domain, paved the way for a shared belief in the inexorable development of *the Social Europe*. It may be that these high expectations for more social realizations still inform the depreciative tone of the literature on social Europe today.

The concept of field is helpful to analyze public policymaking without exclusively focusing on strictly delineated public administrations. Emphasis is placed on actors; the notion of "national interest" and the idea of an opposition between levels of government are reconsidered. In the field of transnational social policy, many of the valuable forms of capital (for instance: academic positions, governmental positions, and so on) are not produced in the field but rooted in other (mainly national) fields, even if the categories that were shaped in the field (harmonization, deterritorialization) are distinct from national categories. The concept of field ultimately provides us with another way of analyzing the alleged scarcity of European social achievements by focusing on topics that are not directly related to national welfare-stateness, putting the emphasis less on the redistributive character of the European institutions and more on the ways in which they have tried to make national traditions and institutions work together.

Notes

1 Geneva, ILO, box 197239: Brief for the Director General in connection with the forth-coming meeting with the president of the High Authority of the ECSC (End 1956, beginning 1957).
2 Florence, Historical Archive of the European Union (HAEU), ME 2213 and AHUE, ME 816.
3 Amsterdam, International Institute for Social History (IISH), ETUC, 89.
4 HAEU, CM2 1962–1162.
5 Geneva, ILO, box 197239: Brief for the Director General in connection with the forth-coming meeting with the president of the High Authority of the ECSC (End 1956, beginning 1957) (emphasis added).
6 ILO Archive, 197239, brief for the Director General in connection with his forthcoming meeting with the president of the High Authority of the ECSC, mid-1950s.
7 ILO Archive, 197239, brief for the Director General in connection with his forthcoming meeting with the president of the High Authority of the ECSC, mid-1950s.
8 Cf. for instance: ILO Archive 161277: Letter of Francis Wolf (legal adviser of the ILO) to Alexandre Berenstein (secretary of the ISLSSL), January 15, 1957.
9 In the 1970s, ILO officials worked together with the Council of Europe and the EEC to define a program of harmonization in the domain of social norms and social security. ILO, 199542: Beziehungen zwischen ILO und EWG, Minute Sheet (G. Perrin, October 5, 1971).

References

Bailleux, J. (2010). Comment l'Europe vint au droit: Le premier congrès international d'études de la CECA (Milan Stresa 1957). *Revue francaise de science politique, 60*(2), 227–266.

Béland, D., & Peterson, K. (2015). *Analysing Social Policy Concepts and Language: Comparative and Transnational Perspectives*. Bristol: Policy Press.

Bernhard, S. (2010). *Die Konstruktion von Inklusion: europäische Sozialpolitik aus soziologischer Perspektive*. Frankfurt am Main: Campus.

Bourdieu, P. (1999). Pour un mouvement social européen. *Le Monde diplomatique*, Juin 1 and 16–17, 1999.

Cayet, T. (2011). The ILO and the IMI: A Strategy of Influence on the Edges of the League of Nations, 1925–1934. In J. van Daele, M. Rodriguez Garcia, G. van Goethem & M. van der Linden (Eds.), *ILO Histories: Essays on the International Labour Organization and Its Impact on the World During the Twentieth Century* (pp. 251–269). Bern: Peter Lang.

Cayet, T., & Rosental, P.-A. (2013). Politiques sociales et marché(s): Filiations et variations d'un registre transnational d'action, du BIT des années 1920 à la construction européenne et à la Chine contemporaine. *Le Mouvement Social, 244*(3), 3–16.

Comte, E. (2017). *The History of the European Migration Regime: Germany's Strategic Hegemony*. London: Routledge.

Conseil de l'Europe. (1961). *L'Europe des travailleurs: La charte sociale européenne*. Stras-bourg: Conseil de l'Europe – direction de l'information.

Denord, F., & Schwartz, A. (2015). *L'Europe sociale n'aura pas lieu*. Paris: Raisons d'agir.

Ferrera, M. (2005). *The Boundaries of Welfare: European Integration and the New Spatial Politics of Social Protection*. Oxford: Oxford University Press.

Fertikh, K. (2016). La construction d'un droit social européen. *Politix, 115*(3), 201–224.

Fertikh, K. (2017). L'Europe sociale au ras du sol. *Raisons politiques*, *67*(3), 141–163.

Fertikh, K. (2019). From Territorialized Rights to Personalized International Social Rights? The Making of the European Convention on the Social Security of Migrant Workers (1957). In M. Baar & P. van Trigt (Eds.), *Marginalized Groups, Inequalities and the Post-War Welfare State: Whose Welfare?* (forthcoming). London: Routledge.

Fertikh, K., & Louis, J. (2019). Du droit international au droit européen: Une sociologie du droit social comme entreprise de cause. *Revue francaise de science politique*, *69*(1), 137–156.

Fertikh, K., & Wieters, H. (2018). Harmonisierung der Sozialpolitik in Europa: Sociohistoire einer sozialpolitischen Kategorie der EWG. In K. Fertikh, H. Wieters & B. Zimmermann (Eds.), *Ein Soziales Europa als Herausforderung* (pp. 47–84). Frankfurt am Main: Campus.

Georgakakis, D. (2018). European Integration. In W. Outhwaite & S. Turner (Eds.), *The Sage Handbook of Political Sociology* (pp. 1083–1103). London: Sage.

Georgakakis, D., & Rowell, J. (2013). Introduction : Studying Eurocracy as a Bureaucratic Field. In D. Georgakakis & J. Rowell (Eds.), *The Field of Eurocracy: Mapping EU Actors and Professionals* (pp. 1–15). Houndmills, Basingstoke: Palgrave Macmillan.

Georgakakis, D., & Vauchez, A. (2015). Le concept de champ à l'épreuve de l'Europe. In J. Siméant & B. Réau (Eds.), *Enquêtes globales en sciences sociales* (pp. 197–220). Paris: Editions du CNRS.

Grimmer-Solem, E. (2005). Social Science, Meiji Conservatism, and the Peculiarities of Japanese History. *Journal of World History*, *16*(2), 187–222.

Guinand, C. (2003). *Die Internationale Arbeitsorganisation (ILO) und die soziale Sicherheit in Europa (1942–1969)*. Bern: Peter Lang.

Herren, M. (1993). *Internationale Sozialpolitik vor dem Ersten Weltkrieg: die Anfänge europäischer Koorperation aus der Sicht Frankreichs*. Berlin: Duncker & Humblot.

Kaelble, H. (2000). Wie kam es zum Europäischen Sozialmodell? In A. Aust, S. Leitner & S. Lessenich (Eds.), *Sozialmodell Europa: Konturen eines Phänomens* (pp. 39–53). Opladen: Leske & Budrich.

Koskenniemi, M. (2015). *From Apology to Utopia: The Structure of International Legal Argument*. Cambridge: Cambridge University Press.

Kott, S., & Droux, J. (Eds.). (2013). *Globalizing Social Rights: The International Labour Organization and Beyond*. Houndmills, Basingstoke: Palgrave Macmillan.

Laroque, P. (1993). *Au service de l'homme et du droit: souvenirs et réflexions*. Paris: Assoc. pour l'Etude de l'Histoire de la Sécurité Sociale.

Lechevalier, A., & Wielgohs, J. (2016). *Social Europe: A Dead End: What the Eurozone Crisis Is Doing to Europe's Social Dimension*. Copenhagen: DJOF Publishing.

Lengwiler, M. (2009). Internationale Expertennetze und nationale Sozialstaatsgeschichte: Versicherung der Silikose in Deutschland und der Schweiz (1900–1945). *Journal of Modern European History*, *7*(2), 195–216.

Levi Sandri, L. (1967). Observation sur la notion de droit du travail, sa nature et ses limites. In L.-É. Troclet (Ed.), *Mélanges offerts à Léon-Eli Troclet* (pp. 195–203). Bruxelles: ULB.

Löhr, I. (2013). Lives Beyond Borders, or: How to Trace Global Biographies 1880–1950. *Comparativ: Zeitschrift für Globalgeschichte und Vergleichende Gesellschaftsforschung*, *6*(23), 7–21.

Mechi, L., Migani, G., & Petrini, F. (Eds.). (2014). *Networks of Global Governance: International Organisations and European Integration in a Historical Perspective*. Newcastle upon Tyne: Cambridge Scholars.

Noiriel, G. (1998). Surveiller les déplacements ou identifier les personnes ? Contribution à l'histoire du passeport en France de la Ie à la IIIe République. *Genèses: Sciences sociales et histoire, 30*, 77–100.

Noiriel, G. (2006). *Réfugiés et sans-papiers: la république face du droit d'asile; XIXe – XXe siecle*. Paris: Hachette.

Raphael, L. (2013). Grenzen von Inklusion und Exklusion: Sozialräumliche Regulierung von Armut und Fremdheit in Europa der Neuzeit. *Journal of Modern European History, 11*(1), 147–167.

Rasmussen, A. (1989). Les congrès internationaux liés aux expositions universelles de Paris (1867–1900). *Mil neuf cent: Revue d'histoire intellectuelle, 7*, 23–44.

Rodgers, D. (2001). *Atlantic Crossings: Social Politics in a Progressive Age*. Cambridge, MA: Harvard University Press.

Rosental, P.-A. (2011). Migrations, souveraineté, droits sociaux. *Annales: Histoire, Sciences Sociales, 66*(2), 335–373.

Scharpf, F. (2009). The Asymmetry of European Integration, or Why the EU Cannot Be a 'Social Market Economy'. *KFG Working Paper No. 6.*

Schildberg, C. (2010). *Politische Identität und Soziales Europa*. Wiesbaden: Springer VS.

Senghaas, M. (2015). *Die Territorialisierung sozialer Sicherung Raum, Identität und Sozialpolitik in der Habsburgermonarchie*. Wiesbaden: Springer VS.

Stephens, T. C., & International Social Security Association. (Eds.). (1956). *Reciprocity in Social Insurance: Report to the XII Meeting of the International Social Security Association, Mexico City, November-December 1955*. Geneva: Éditions Internationales.

Studer, B. (1995). Verschleierungstaktik als Herrschaftspraxis: Über den Prozeß historischer Erkenntnis am Beispiel des Kominterarchivs. *Jahrbuch für historische Kommunismusforschung, 3*, 306–321.

Sunil, A. (2006). *Decolonizing International Health: India and Southeast Asia, 1930–65*. Houndmills, Basingstoke: Palgrave Macmillan.

Sunil, A. (2017). Internationalizing Health in the Twentieth Century. In P. Clavin & B. Sluga (Eds.), *Internationalisms: A Twentieth Century History* (pp. 245–264). Cambridge: Cambridge University Press.

Topalov, C. (1999a). *Laboratoires du nouveau siècle: la nébuleuse réformatrice et ses réseaux en France, 1880–1914*. Paris: Ecole des hautes études en sciences sociales.

Topalov, C. (1999b). Le champ réformateur. In C. Topalov (Ed.), *Laboratoires du nouveau siècle* (pp. 461–474). Paris: Editions de l'EHESS.

Troclet, L. E. (1952). *Législation sociale internationale*. Bruxelles: Editions de la Librairie encyclopédique.

Vauchez, A. (2008). The Force of a Weak Field: Law and Lawyers in the Government of the European Union (for a Renewed Research Agenda). *International Political Sociology, 2*(2), 128–144.

Vauchez, A. (2013). *L'Union par le droit: L'invention d'un programme institutionnel pour l'Europe*. Paris: Presses de Sciences Po.

Verschueren, N. (2012). *Fermer les mines en construisant l'Europe: une histoire sociale de l'intégration européenne*. New York, NY: Peter Lang.

Wagner, P. (2000). Die Nation als Ressource für die Organisierung von Praktiken. In C. Didry, P. Wagner & B. Zimmermann (Eds.), *Arbeit und Nationalstaat: Frankreich und Deutschland in europäischer Perspektive* (pp. 23–26). Frankfurt am Main: Campus.

Wimmer, A., & Glick Schiller, N. (2002). Methodological Nationalism and Beyond: Nation-State Building, Migration and the Social Sciences. *Global Networks*, *2*(4), 301–334.

Wobbe, T., & Biermann, I. (2009). *Von Rom nach Amsterdam die Metamorphosen des Geschlechts in der Europäischen Union*. Wiesbaden: VS, Verl. für Sozialwiss.

Zimmermann, B. (2001). *La constitution du chômage en Allemagne: entre professions et territoires*. Paris: Maison des sciences de l'homme.

Chapter 10

The rise of a European field of evidence-based education

Tomas Marttila

Introduction

Ever since its beginnings after World War II, the political project of European integration has undergone various stages of development (Stone Sweet, Sandholtz, & Fligstein, 2001). Recent sociological research on European integration has interpreted these different stages as mirroring the influence exerted by varying constellations of European "knowledge-bearing elites" and visions of the overarching objectives of the European project they promote (Vauchez, 2008, 2015; Bigo & Madsen, 2011; Mudge & Vauchez, 2012; Schmidt-Wellenburg, 2017a). This chapter starts from Pierre Bourdieu's (1985: 22) theory of social fields and the assumption that expert groups' capacities to influence the European project correlate with their degree of "symbolic power" in the European political field.[1] Departing from this theoretical assumption, this contribution focuses on a more recent stage in European integration – the rise of a European field of education – and investigates how the rise of new symbolic elites in that field has paved the way for the official recognition of evidence-based education (EBE) as the cornerstone of the European Union's (EU) education policy agenda. The basic idea behind EBE is that educational policymaking must be emancipated from biased political interests and ideological dogma, and instead be based on empirical scientific evidence showing "whether a particular [policy] innovation works [. . .]" and "how much it improves outcomes and at what cost" (Fitz-Gibbon, 2002: 101). Moreover, the Organisation for Economic Co-operation and Development (OECD) (2007: 9) argues that political actors can better legitimize unpopular "educational policy decisions" when these are "based on the best evidence possible."

When looked at in retrospection, not only the fact that EBE has been added to the EU's official political agenda, but also the existence of any such agenda at all, may appear counterintuitive. It was only relatively recently that Anders J. Hingel (2001: 7) – the former Director General at the European Commission's (EC) division for education and culture – stated that "[t]he most optimal level of decision making in the field of education is at the national and/or the sub-national level." Hingel's statement epitomizes the political *illusio* – the unquestioned "fundamental belief" (Bourdieu, 2000: 11) – prevailing at that time, according to which the EU's initiatives in the area of education must respect the member states' "historical and cultural heritage" (Hingel, 2001: 7). Only few years later, the EU – and in particular the EC – had adopted a diametrical perspective stating that all EU member states must implement EBE in order to improve the performance of their national education systems. In 2007, the EC (2007: 6) stated that "systemic use of evidence" and "evaluation culture" based on scientific evidence constitute the future cornerstones of the European field of education.

Instead of acknowledging the EU's recognition of EBE as a result of objective necessities and dilemmas (functionalism) or compromises achieved between conflicting political interests (rationalism), Bourdieu's theory of social fields underlines that transnational processes in general, and the process of European integration in particular, bear witness to symbolic struggles between actors promoting their specific visions of an ideal transnational social order (Schmidt-Wellenburg, 2017a). Instead of referring "Europe" to a politically neutral and objective concept, research affiliated with Bourdieu's theory of social fields has proven that European integration has been driven by the competition between competing visions of Europe as a transnational social arena. Each of these visions has been linked to a distinctive set of ideas about the valid/invalid objectives and the legitimate/illegitimate strategies of European integration. Instead of assuming a rationalistic perspective that reduces these visions of Europe to a reflection of the explicit and strategic interests of different political groups, Mudge and Vauchez (2012) and Vauchez (2015: 3), amongst others, see the emergence of a "weak" transnational European political field characterized by its own logics of constituting symbolic elites as well as by the means and sources of assessing the validity of competing statements made about European integration.

Reflecting these ideas about European integration derived from Bourdieu's theory of social fields, this chapter departs from two hypotheses: *Firstly*, the notion of EBE has been embedded in a particular vision of Europe as a transnational social space. This sociospatial embedding has transformed EBE to a legitimate political strategy to develop and deepen European integration. *Secondly*, the conceived urgency to implement EBE in the European transnational social space underlines the social status of expert groups promoting it. Reflecting these hypotheses, this chapter is structured in two theoretical and empirical parts. The following part builds on the concept of the transnational social field originating from Bourdieu's theory of social fields and elaborates its general structural logics. It is argued that these structural logics provide a heuristic-analytic framework to detect and explain historical processes, events, and interactions behind the installment of EBE on the EU's official political agenda. The second part focuses on three historical stages of development toward a European field of education dominated by the notion of EBE.

Theoretical framework

In the recent past, sociologists have begun to study the social fields elaborated by Bourdieu in international and transnational contexts (e.g., Vauchez, 2008, 2014, 2015; Mudge & Vauchez, 2012; Georgakakis & Rowell, 2013; Schmidt-Wellenburg, 2017b). Drawing inspiration from this transnational turn in the empirical analysis of social fields, this chapter departs from the working hypothesis that the emergence of new transnationally disseminated political rationalities and strategies (e.g., EBE) is contingent on the establishment of transnational social fields (e.g., the European field of education). Bourdieu's theory of social fields serves above all as a heuristic "instrument that makes certain things visible while making other things automatically invisible", hence giving direction for empirical analysis (Bourdieu, 2011: 7 own translation; Medvetz, 2012: 35). Accordingly, Bourdieu's theory of social fields provides us with insightful information about the "invariant laws" and "universal mechanisms" characteristic of social fields, and how these characteristics become empirically observable in various social contexts (Swartz, 2013: 57). Even though all social fields resemble each other, recent research has witnessed the existence of different types of (primarily) national/transnational, weak/strong, and interstitial/self-enclosed social fields (e.g., Vauchez, 2008, 2014, 2015; Eyal & Buchholz, 2010). Of particular relevance for this chapter is Vauchez's observation that the EU's political agenda is shaped in the European transnational political field. With this intriguing insight in mind, the following section will characterize the general structural logics of transnational social fields as interstitial fields and elaborate how these logics allow us to grasp the processes resulting in the establishment of EBE on the EU's political agenda.[2]

Transnational social fields

According to Vauchez (2014: 204 f.), transnational social fields are structured by three logics of multipositionality, fungibility of symbolic power, and universalistic cultural frames. The *first* logic of *multipositionality* indicates that transnational social fields are inhabited by social actors whose affiliation with multiple other fields enhances their standing and symbolic power in this transnational field. The *second* logic – the *fungibility* (or transmissibility) of symbolic power – is closely related to the first logic and denotes that transnational symbolic elites do not only switch between positions in different social fields, but this switching actually increases their standing in transnational spaces (Georgakakis, 2013; Gram-Skjoldager & Knudsen, 2013; Vauchez, 2014). The *third* logic – the construction of *universalistic cultural frames* – highlights the cultural and social heterogeneity of transnational social fields. In order to exist as relatively autonomous social fields with their distinctive logics of authorization and delegation of symbolic authority, transnational social fields necessitate the presence of particular kinds of universalistic cultural frames that facilitate social actors' mutual understanding and recognition of each other as members of the same transnational social space. I shall now elucidate these three logics of structuration of transnational social fields in more detail and explain their heuristic function in the ensuing empirical analysis.

Multipositionality

Bourdieu (1993a: 72) referred social fields to "structured spaces of positions." Social positions describe distinctive sets of social roles, which social actors must assume and gain access to in order to be recognized and accepted by other actors of the field. Social positions are not objectively given. Instead, they result from past investments made to differentiate a social field from other social fields and define its internal structure (Medvetz, 2012: 35). Amongst other things, social fields differ with regard to the sets of criteria that social actors must fulfill in order to become legitimate contenders and holders of particular social positions. Access to a social position depends on the resources (i.e., *capitals*) that are available to social actors. On their part, social actors must take a particular interest in social positions and recognize sets of codes of conduct, perspectives, and interests affiliated with them, which they must adhere to in their actions in order to preserve their roles (Swartz, 2008: 48). In other words, social positions are socially embedded social roles linked to specific sets of social norms, standards, and reciprocal expectations. Therefore, Emirbayer and Johnson (2008: 15) argue that a "field of positions restricts the (actual and potential) position-takings available to specific actors within it", and that "the structure of the field of position-takings effectively permits only certain kinds of [. . .] [actors] to enter into the field."

Being interstitial social fields with "blurry" distinctions vis-à-vis other social fields (Eyal & Buchholz, 2010; Medvetz, 2012), the positions of transnational social fields can be entered without social actors having to distance themselves from their coeval positions in other fields. Hence, actors inhabiting certain transnational social fields must not "plunge from one world into another" (Eyal & Buchholz, 2010: 132). Therefore, Levitt and Glick Schiller (2004: 1011 f.) argue that transnational social fields are populated by social actors possessing "simultaneous" social positions in multiple social fields. Dezalay and Garth (2011: 277 f.) add that this multipositionality functions as symbolic capital because it shows that social actors are renowned and respected independent from any single sociostructural context. Hence, multipositionality gives evidence of social actors' sociospatially unrestricted status and reputation. In other words, multipositionality assumes the function of symbolic capital in two different regards: *Firstly*, social capital acquired from multiple social fields in the form of institutional affiliations and social ties is highly estimated in transnational social fields because it is considered to prove social actors' social and cultural independence from *any* single social context. *Secondly*, multiple affiliations with various types of (economic, political, academic, etc.) actors located on different sociospatial (e.g., supranational, national, subnational) levels is seen as proof of a cosmopolitan mindset expected from the legitimate representatives of socially and culturally heterogeneous transnational social spaces.

Fungibility of symbolic capital

In transnational social fields, social capital acquired from multiple social fields acts as symbolic capital and is the prerequisite for symbolic power. Bourdieu (1985: 731) referred symbolic power to social actors' capacities and legitimate right to participate in "the production of common sense" and therewith influence the "official [. . .] imposition of the legitimate vision of the social world" in a specific social field. Bourdieu

(1985: 731) also underlined that social actors' access to symbolic power depends on "symbolic capital", which social actors "have acquired in previous struggles" for symbolic power. Basically, symbolic capital refers to competences, qualifications, skills, and resources that figure as legitimate sources of establishment and retention of status differences in social fields. While international scientific reputation (e.g., citations, publications in scientific journals) constitutes symbolic capital in the academic field, the social standing in the economic field is based on past or expected future economic success (e.g., profit) (Bourdieu, 1989: 21; Swartz, 2013: 39). In contrast to more structurally bounded and demarcated social fields (mostly located in nation-state contexts), Mudge and Vauchez (2012: 455) and Vauchez (2014: 204) argue that transnational social fields and their definitions of the origins and forms of symbolic capital are subject to influence from other social fields. This relative structural openness of transnational social fields explains why transnational elites can transfer their social statuses in national fields into symbolic capital in transnational fields (Kauppi & Madsen, 2011: 327). Moreover, the fungibility of symbolic capital provides a possible explanation to why the "agents occupying the dominant positions in national and transnational spaces are the same people" (Dezalay & Garth, 2011: 278). In the European context, Mudge and Vauchez (2012: 451) have detected that positions equipped with symbolic power in the EU's transnational political field are shaped by actors originating from "multiple sorts of professional arenas." However, the fungibility of symbolic capital is always to some extent regulated by actors operating as transnational consecration instances. Bourdieu (1985: 13) names consecration instances as "gate keepers" possessing the legitimate right to control social actors' influence on the constitution of the legitimate worldview in a social field (cf. Bourdieu, 1993a: 75). The technocratic elites occupying high-rank positions in the EU's bureaucratic apparatus operate as consecration instances in the European political field (Botzem & Quack, 2008: 267; cf. Mudge & Vauchez, 2012; Vauchez, 2013, 2015; Schmidt-Wellenburg, 2017a). Despite being characterized as a weak social field, Georgakakis and Rowell (2013); Mudge and Vauchez (2012), and Vauchez (2015, 2008) have, amongst others, observed that the European political field and its specific consecration instances (e.g., European Court of Justice, EC) are becoming increasingly immune to influence exerted by nationally embedded political actors and expert communities. In this regard, Georgakakis and Rowell (2013: 8) observe that the fungibility of symbolic capital has been restricted by the "codification and institutionalization of the rules of interaction; the definition of specific rewards and specific bones of contention; the definition of specific resources necessary to be player in the [European political] field."

Universalistic cultural frames

It is a common practice to see social fields being structured by oppositions and conflicts between "dominant" actors yielding symbolic power and social groups "dominated" by their actions, interests, and perspectives (Swartz, 2013: 57). On the cultural level, this chiasmatic social structure correlates with the opposition between the "orthodox" worldview propagated by the symbolic elite and the "heterodox" worldview promoted by heretic groups (Emirbayer & Johnson, 2008: 11). Recurring on the afore-described multipositionality and fungibility of symbolic capital, this chiasmatic structure does not apply naturally to transnational social fields. Being characterized by a "high density" of inter-field social and symbolic relationships (Levitt & Glick Schiller, 2004: 1006), "dominant" symbolic elites cannot simply impose their worldviews upon "dominated" actors with deviating worldviews and interests. Instead, in transnational social fields the antagonistic division between "dominating" and "dominated" social groups must be sutured by universalistic cultural frames. Mudge and Vauchez (2012: 468) and Vauchez (2015: 17, 73, 103) argue that heterogeneous groups of actors populating the transnational social field are integrated by specific types of cultural frames which are (1) universalistic enough to apply to culturally diverse groups of actors; and (2) contentually indeterminate enough to remain open to diverging interpretations (cf. Eyal & Buchholz, 2010: 126; Medvetz, 2012: 25). In this regard, European integration legitimizing "visions of Europe" are cases of universalistic cultural frames (Mudge & Vauchez, 2012: 481). For instance, Vauchez (2008: 133) argues that the universalistic visions of Europe as a community of law and a common market have been essential for the formation of a transnational "European polity" because they have remained open for diverging national perspectives and political interests. Reflecting the pivotal role played by universalistic cultural frames, the distribution of symbolic power in transnational social fields depends on social actors' capacities to act as "spatial entrepreneurs" (Lawn & Normand, 2015: 4) that construct "hinges" between different social fields and their populations of actors (Abbott, 2005).[3] According to Lawn and Normand (2015: 4), such universalistic cultural frames have been essential for bridging the traditional social and cultural divisions between "national spaces and the European political arena."

Heuristic-analytic framework

The previously outlined three logics of transnational social fields constitute a heuristic-analytic framework that instructs particular types of historical processes and events to condition the establishment of EBE on the EU's political agenda. Moreover, even though these three logics are likely to have specific phenomenal contents in different sociospatial contexts, they can still serve as a heuristic theory that "map[s] out" our objects of analysis and "prepare[s] the ground for its empirical investigation by appropriate methods" (Nadel, 1962: 1). With regard to their heuristic function, multipositionality, fungibility of symbolic capital, and universalistic cultural frames instruct us to focus on the following phenomena when searching for possible explanations for the emergence of EBE in the European political field:

(1) The multiple social positions from which the meaningfulness of EBE was transferred to the European political field and was legitimized there;

(2) historical origins and sociospatial composition of the symbolic capital, which accredited the proponents of EBE as the new symbolic authority in the European political field;
(3) the historical origins and the contentual structure of the universalistic cultural frame that embedded the idea of EBE and equipped it with the status of a policy solution of relevance for the entire European context.

When searching for answers to these questions, it must be recognized that social fields are not objective and permanent social structures. They have been shaped and are transformed in ongoing social interactions. Reflecting the contingent relationship of transnational social fields with transnational social practices that structure them, this chapter will reconstruct how the relatively recent recognition of EBE was made possible by past historical stages and the interlinkage between education and European integration characteristic for each of these stages. These stages do not refer to mechanistic and objective stages of development, but they consist of and are characterized by specific articulations of education in the European transnational context. Reflecting this general methodological instruction, the following analysis retraces the recently emerging interest in EBE to developments having taken place during the past 20–30 years in the European political field. In particular, the following analysis is organized in three sections, each of which pays attention to a particular historical stage. *Stage I* describes the origins of the interest devoted to education in the European political field and explains the interlinkage between the general economization of education and the rising imaginary of a European space of education. *Stage II* elaborates how critique of the so called Open Method of Coordination (OMC) – a governance strategy to improve transnational policy learning in Europe – addressed by the EC and its expert groups changed the prevailing distribution of symbolic power between EC and EU member states. *Stage III* focuses on the increasing dominance of the EC as a consecration instance in the European political field and shows how it has utilized this role to install new groups of economic experts as new symbolic authorities in the area of education.

Stage I: the rise of a European space of education

Traditionally, issues related to education have played only a marginal role for European integration. Until the late 1970s, national and international education experts alike conceived of education as a matter of national governments. There was general consensus that practices and decisions linked to education are parts of "distinctive, historic systems" of education and that they are therefore "like apples and oranges: non-comparable" (Kamens, 2013: 120). In Europe, the official cooperation in the area of education started as late as in 1974, when the EU's Education Committee was created to coordinate the actions between EC and EU member states (Ertl, 2006: 7). This Committee originated from the report written by Henri Janne, which was the first official EU document to promote a transnational "European Dimension" in education (Janne, 1973: 26). In 1976, the Education Committee established an Action Program for Education, which was the first document of its kind to grant the EC the right to take initiatives in the field of projects related to transnational education. The Action Program also saw the establishment of several European initiatives – such as Community Programme for Education and Training in Technology (COMETT) and European Community Action Scheme for the Mobility of University Students (ERASMUS) – which were aimed at increasing education-related mobility between EU member countries (Ionnidou, 2007: 344). During the 1980s, the European dimension of education was expanded with initiatives taken to establish a European space for vocational qualifications and certificates (Ertl, 2006: 7). These initiatives were based on voluntary participation and served the purpose of mutual learning and exchange of information between EU member states.

It was only in the early 1990s that multilateral cooperation based on voluntary participation gave way to a multilevel governance regime within which national and supranational actors were assigned distinctive responsibilities. The Maastricht Treaty signed in 1992 established education as an official policy area on the European level and authorized the EU to take an own interest in national education policies (Ertl, 2006: 10). The reframing of education from a national to a transnational matter – dealt with by both national and non-national actors – was codified by the "Community logic of action" (Lee, Thayer, & Madyun, 2008). The Community approach to education, which was above all enforced by EC President Jacques Delors, encouraged the EU's education experts to make their own recommendations to "supplement" political decisions taken on the national level (Council of the European Communities, 1992: §126, 127). The Community approach was met with critique from EU member states, many of which insisted on the sustainment of the "subsidiarity principle" and hence the respect of national political sovereignty and local cultural and institutional differences (Ertl, 2006: 12; c.f. Field, 1997).[4] EU institutions – and in particular the EC – reacted to national critique of the Community approach by discovering for themselves the role of "policy clearinghouse[s]" specialized in "provid[ing] best practices, or models, found across the member states" (Lee et al., 2008: 454).

The policy documents, which were published by the EC in the 1990s, witnessed a radical reframing of education from a social and cultural matter to a primarily economic issue. Moreover, education policies were reconceptualized as strategic means used to maximize the quality of human capital required to sustain international economic competitiveness in the increasingly knowledge-based mode of production (Resnik, 2006; Lee et al., 2008; Romuald, 2010). Amongst other things, EU documents published on European structural adjustment strategies (e.g., European Regional Development Funds, European Social Fund) recognized the leveling of human capital production as the single most important precondition of economic cohesion in Europe (Jones, 2005: 249). Also, the EC's (1993) White Paper, which defined the EU's economic strategy for the rest of the decade, stated that EU member states' economic competitiveness would depend on their rapid transition to the knowledge-based mode of production, which again required drastic reforms of their education systems.

These empirical examples show that EU actors did not pay increasing attention to education because education was an objective in itself, but because the improved "investment in skills" constituted the "prime factor in competitiveness and employability" (EC, 1995: 50). In this context, the Knowledge Based Economy (KBE) constituted a universalistic cultural frame that provided a symbolic representation of EU member states as constituent parts of a common European transnational economic space. It was with reference to this transnational space that the EC positioned itself as a transnational symbolic authority which, in contrast to national actors, recognized the need to introduce the "European dimension in education and training" as a general strategy to improve education "in the face of internationalization and to avoid the risk of a watered-down European society" (ibid., 51). According to Resnik (2006), the network of concepts including knowledge-based production, human capital, economic competitiveness, and efficiency of policymaking in the educational sector figured as the cornerstones of the EU's "education-economic growth policy paradigm." This paradigm constituted the first truly transnational worldview on education in the European political field. The rise of this worldview is hardly surprising. After all, similar sets of ideas about education and its primarily economic meaning had already been adopted by international organizations including the OECD and the United Nations Educational, Scientific and Cultural Organization (UNESCO), but also by several EU member states, including France and Sweden (Field, 1997; Resnik, 2006: 182 ff.).

The "education-economic growth policy paradigm" gave rise to a vision of a transnational European space of education (EC, 1993, 1995, 1997). A special example in this regard was the EC's (1997: 5) statement that one of its key priorities was "the progressive creation of an open and dynamic European educational space, in which the learning and training will be implemented." Despite positioning itself as a symbolic authority responsible for the dissemination of the "education-economic growth policy paradigm", the EC's factual political influence was restricted by the Maastricht Treaty, according to which the Community level (i.e., EU institutions) should be restricted to making a contribution "to the development of quality education by encouraging co-operation between Member States" (Council of the European Communities, 1992: §149). At the same time, EU member states remained responsible "for the content of teaching and the organization of education systems and their cultural and linguistic diversity" (ibid.).

The Lisbon Strategy implemented in 2000 increased the relative autonomy of the European space of education vis-à-vis national political fields. *Firstly*, the Lisbon Strategy affirmed the importance of EU member states not only cooperating in the area of education, but also coordinating their education policies and education systems so as to strengthen the competitiveness of the European economic space. The agreement to bundle forces and converge national traditions of education was a reaction to the OECD's (e.g. 1996, 1997, 1998) recurrent critique of the disparate logics and qualities of human capital production in Europe (Ertl,

2006: 14). *Secondly*, Andreas J. Hingel – the Director General of the EC's division for education and culture – argued that the vision of a "European educational space" alone was not enough, but had to be institutionalized by developing a truly "European Model of Education" (Hingel, 2001: 7). The first step toward the institutionalization of the European model of education was taken in the Council of the European Union (CEU) (2001: 18) decision to develop "European guidelines" for education and translate these into concrete recommendations for "national and regional policies". *Thirdly*, the Lisbon Strategy institutionalized the European space of education also by authorizing a calculative logic of education policymaking unprecedented in the European context so far (Nordin, 2014: 145). Drawing inspiration from the OECD's system of indicators used in its international student achievement surveys (e.g., the Program for International Student Assessment [PISA]), EC and CEU agreed on the introduction of the Education and Training 2010 Working Program in 2001. The aim of this Working Program was to develop European benchmarks that capacitated political actors to compare the performance of national education systems across Europe (Lange & Alexiadou, 2007: 324; cf. CEU, 2001, 2002). These benchmarks were designed to make "the member countries to see their progress in relation to each other (benchmarking)," give rise to "peer learning", and motivate "the exchange of good practice" (Robertson, de Azevedo, & Dale, 2016: 32).

However, the mentioned task force exerted a formative impact on the European space of education not only because it developed a set of benchmarks, but also because it functioned as a consecration instance that qualified/disqualified particular expert groups as legitimate representatives of the European transnational polity. In particular, this task force – named the working group for "Measuring Lifelong Learning" – included a heterogeneous group of representatives from EU institutions (EC, EUROSTAT), national institutes for statistics, and international organizations (OECD, UNESCO, and the International Labour Organization) (EC, 2002, 2007). A notable feature with regard to the documents published by the task force is that these unmask the fulminant influence from a wider network of international education experts. According to Normand (2010), this network was composed of three subgroups:

(1) a group of education experts affiliated with the OECD's international student achievement surveys. The most prominent member of this group was Albert Tujnman, a former high-ranking official at OECD;
(2) an international group of education researchers sharing the worldviews and research interests of the school effectiveness research paradigm. Some members of this group had been sponsored by OECD in the 1980s;
(3) an international group of economists in the education sector that conducted statistical measurements of the relative efficiency and effectiveness of education policies. This group of highly renowned economists included the World Bank official Georges Psacharopoulos, Nobel Prize winner in economics James Heckman, leading US American economist of education Eric

Hanushek, and a group of German economists located at leading German research institutes in economics (e.g., Institute for Labor Economics IZA or Leibniz-Institut für Wirtschaftsforschung ifo).

The third group would appear a few years later as the vanguard behind the establishment of EBE on the EU's political agenda (cf. Biesta, 2006: 172; Resnik, 2006: 179; Lee et al., 2008: 446). To conclude, this first stage saw the emergence of a vision of a European space of education dominated by an economistic conceptualization of education as a means of human capital production. As a result of the Lisbon strategy and its implementation in the form of European benchmarks for education, the European space of education was institutionalized further. More importantly still, the development of the European benchmarks also saw the authorization of new groups of education experts as symbolic elites in the European political field.

Stage II: undermining subsidiarity

The articulation of the European space of education insinuated that national education systems belonged naturally to the same transnational social space. Here the European benchmarks for education were particularly important, because they made the European space of education and the associated national education systems empirically measurable and observable. However, the European benchmarks provided information only about the present differences/similarities and past trajectories of convergence/divergence between national education systems. Broadly speaking, these benchmarks were essential for national actors' capacities to learn about past political achievements and failures. The policy-learning itself was organized by the OMC. At its introduction, OMC was a mode of governance based upon voluntary learning and deliberation that was expected to result in development of "best practice and encourage[e] greater convergence towards the main EU goals" as defined in the Lisbon strategy from 2000 (EC, 2004b: 16). Despite its officially deliberative character, OMC had a disciplinary function because it facilitated the "monitoring and benchmarking of national progress" and put national actors under the pressure to implement the established best practice (Ionnidou, 2007: 341). Several scholars of European integration have referred OMC to all policy fields embracing a mode of meta-governance that facilitates the dissemination of EU's policy paradigms and political agendas on the national level (Haahr, 2004; Bernhard, 2006; Blatter, 2007).

In this regard, OMC played a pivotal role in the institutionalization of the European space of education because it assigned the EU the "mandate and an agenda for extending the reach of Europe's policy responsibility deeper into national territory" (Robertson et al., 2016: 30). Also, Maria João Rodrigues (2003: 37) – one of the architects behind the Lisbon strategy – saw in OMC the potential to raise national awareness for "a European dimension" in education and promote national actors to introduce "European guidelines" of education, and make them adopt a "management by objectives" type of political government of issues related to education. Moreover, as a result of its improved status within the European political field, the EC could carry on with the development of "certain objectives and a corresponding timeframe in a specific area (of social policy), which then become the basis for contracts with the member states" (Tuschling & Engemann, 2006: 453). The EC intervened even as a transnational moral authority in national policymaking by problematizing discrepancies between national education policies and the overarching goals defined in the Lisbon strategy.

The EC was one the most devoted supporters of European benchmarks in education. In 2001, the EC obliged all EU member states to "adopt European Benchmarks for education and training systems in areas which are central for the achievement of the strategic goal set in March 2000 by the Lisbon European Council" (EC, 2001: 2). Lacking any political power codified by EU statutes, the EC has asserted its symbolic authority within the European space of education by selecting expert groups and equipping them with the "power of definition" over the European political field. This logic of epistemic government – the government through the control of knowledge production – was a characteristic mode of governance in the EU of the early 2000s (Bernhard, 2006, 2010). For example, the EC exerted its authority vis-à-vis national governments by installing the so-called "Maastricht Consortium" – a group of national quality assurance agencies and research institutes[5] – to assess the extent to which national vocational education and training systems (VETs) had been adjusted to the policy goals defined in the Lisbon strategy (cf. EC, 2004a; Ertl, 2006: 19). The denomination of the so-called "High Level Group" is another tangible case of epistemic government. The High Level Group consisted of a group of economists, members of national parliaments, labor union officials, and global business leaders, and was assigned the responsibility to conduct "an independent review" of the development of national education systems since the implementation of the Lisbon strategy (EC, 2004b: 5). In its report, the High Level Group stated that the development of education systems achieved with the help of OMC had "fallen short of expectations" because member states had not "enter[ed] the spirit of mutual benchmarking" (EC, 2004b: 42). Furthermore, national actors' insufficient adoption of the logic of benchmark-based development of education had also prevented them from "act[ing] in a more concerted and determined way" (EC, 2004b: 7). The High Level Group recommended that the competitive comparison of education systems had to be combined with a morally charged exposition of good and bad performance (EC, 2004b: 17, 43). The High Level Group's recommendation to supplement the benchmarking with public critique of political mismanagement and underachievement conflicted clearly with the previous doxa of national political and cultural sovereignty codified by the subsidiarity principle, and which was also – at least officially – sustained by the OMC.

Subsequent documents from the EC (e.g. 2007), but also CEU (2006, 2007), not only confirmed the critique addressed by the High Level Group, but also problematized the lack of access to reliable knowledge of institutions, cultural factors, and education policies characteristic of high-achieving education systems. These documents constructed the lack of reliable and objective knowledge about the quality of education policies as the new major problem in the European space of education. To solve this problem, the EC created two new expert groups – the European Expert Network on Economics on Education (EENEE) and the Network of Experts on Social Sciences in Education (NESSE) – to elaborate possible strategies to improve the access to better and more reliable knowledge about the factors that characterize high-performing education systems. According to Lange and Alexiadou (2007: 326), it was these two groups, and in particular EENEE, which equipped the EC with the cultural capital required to legitimize the "pursuit of evidence-led policy making" in the European space of education.

Stage III: introducing EBE

EU documents published since the mid-1990s witness the surging official interest in increasing the statistical measurability of the quality of education in general and the economic value-add of public investments in education more in particular. Following the example of the OECD, the EU has taken the official stance that the performance of national education systems cannot be improved unless statistical data on education policies' contribution to student achievement has been improved substantially. In its first analytical report for the EC, EENEE (2006: 13) located the principal difference between the United States and the EU member states in the latter's insufficient access to statistically verified evidence about education policies' capacity to improve the production of human capital. Critique expressed by EENEE was based on a clearly economistic conception of education. *Firstly*, being intellectually embedded in the US-American economics of education tradition (e.g., Gary S. Becker, Jacob Mincer, Theodore W. Schultz), EENEE postulated that the quality of education must be determined by its factual capacity to increase economic growth (EENEE, 2006: 2). *Secondly*, EENEE also suggested that the quality of education should be measured by using statistical methods for impact evaluation developed in economics of education. In this regard, international comparisons of student achievement and, above all, the OECD's international student achievement surveys, are considered the showcase model for evaluation practices that had to be established in the European space of education. EENEE (2006: 31) justified the general evidence-turn in European education policymaking by postulating that EU member states will not be able to make "better-informed policies" unless they "design policy interventions in ways that are amenable to rigorous empirical evaluation, collect the necessary data on inputs and outcomes and implement independent evaluation studies that create knowledge on what works and what does not."

In a later analytical report, EENEE (2010: 6) drew on the standard repertoire of econometric impact measurement to define a toolbox of methods ensuring that "policies and practices can achieve their goals" and political actors can estimate whether "the difference in [policy] outcomes" stands in a statistically verified causal relationship to implemented education policies. In particular, EENEE

(2010: 6) stated that experimental designs for "counterfactual comparisons" used in econometrics constituted the ideal strategy to measure cause–effect relationships across several control groups. Due to practical and ethical concerns, EENEE argued also that, instead of artificial control groups, policymakers should induce scientific evidence about efficient education policies by means of conducting systemic reviews of existing empirical data. While the systemic review of data belonged to the standard governmental technologies used in the United Kingdom and the United States (Pirrie, 2001; Shavelson & Towne, 2004), it had not been recognized in the wider European context. Therefore, EENEE represented a heretic understanding of education policymaking that deviated clearly from existing governmental rationalities and technologies in the European space of education. In other words, EENEE had assumed the role of a contender that questioned the rationality of the existing legitimate worldview. In order to explain the underlying reasons for EENEE's rise to a new symbolic authority in the European political field, Bourdieu's theory of social fields advises us to focus on the symbolic capital that legitimized EENEE's heretic worldview.

Originating from the United Kingdom in the late 1990s, the notion of EBE entered the international scene of education as a result of its recognition by OECD. In its *Knowledge Management in the Learning Society* (2000), an edited volume featuring internationally renowned experts on policy evaluation, the OECD recognized EBE as the best strategy to optimize the efficiency of public investments in education. Reflecting its general interest in the use of scientific evidence in policymaking, the OECD organized four international conferences between 2004 and 2006, at which representatives of international organizations, national governments, and education researchers gathered to discuss the implementation of evidence-based policymaking (Burns & Schuller, 2007: 18). David-Pascal Dion – the Director General for Education and Culture at the EC – attended the concluding fourth conference held in London in July 2006. Dion (2006) identified EBE as the ideal instrument to implement the objectives defined in the EU's Education and Training 2010 work program. Moreover, Dion recognized two groups of economists, the Centre for Economic Policy Research (CEPR) in London and EENEE, which installed and founded by the EC, as the leading international experts on EBE.[6] Intriguing about the experts affiliated with the CEPR and EENEE was their close intellectual, institutional, and interpersonal relationship with the US-American economics of education tradition. The economics of education tradition was based on the commitment to use econometric methods to assess the economic value-add of public investments in education. EENEE's analytical reports made recurrent references to renowned representatives of the US-American economics of education tradition (e.g., Gary S. Becker, Eric A. Hanushek, James Heckman, Stephen Machin, Steve G. Rivkin). Moreover, a major part of the texts that EENEE referred to were articles published in high-ranked US-American scientific journals (*American Behavioral Scientist, American Economic Review, Education Economics*). EENEE was also interpersonally linked to the US-American field of the economics of education.[7] Several members of EENEE (e.g., Ludger Wößmann, Martin

Schlötter, Marc Piopiunik, Martina Viarengo, Marius Busemeyer) had attended the Program on Education Policy and Governance at the Harvard Kennedy School of Government that was established by Eric A. Hanushek[8] (Normand, 2010).

In its analytical reports, EENEE mobilized its intellectual and interpersonal affiliations with the economics of education to justify its policy recommendations. Moreover, EENEE enhanced its symbolic authority further by arguing that the econometric toolbox, which it recommended for the European space of education, had already been accepted and verified by the American Educational Research Association (EENEE, 2009: 1 f.). Another notable feature about EENEE is that its analytical reports[9] have been written by 38 authors, of whom 10 are included in IDEA's list of the world's leading economists on education.[10] Also, the majority of EENEE experts are located at internationally renowned research institutes in economics.[11] Recurring to these social, cultural, and symbolic resources held by EENEE, Jones (2010: 365) concludes that EENEE was "made up of some of the most high-profile and active economists on education from Europe and the United States, together with high-profile policy actors from the World Bank, the OECD and the European Investment Bank." Arguably, EENEE's social (e.g., interpersonal contacts), economic (e.g., economic value-add) and cultural capital (e.g., scientific credibility) can explain its sudden rise to the symbolic power in the European space of education (cf. Jones, 2010: 360). EENEE's analytical reports were of vital importance for the recognition and legitimation of EBE in the European context (Lange & Alexiadou, 2007: 326). The EC (2007: 8) verified EENEE's (2006) recommendation for a general evidence-turn in the European space of education and stated that the adoption of "evidence-based policy and practice" capacitates EU member states to "improve the quality and governance of education and training systems" (EENEE, 2006: 8). The political relevance of EBE was also recognized by the CEU (2006: no page), which in similarity to the EC recognized the need to "develop a culture of evaluation and [to take] a positive step towards the further development of evidence-based policy in education and training."

EENEE's policy recommendations, including its institution of EBE as the new legitimate worldview on education, were met with critique from EU member states. Above all, national governments criticized EENEE's reduction of education to an economic resource (Jones, 2010: 371 f.). Reacting to this critique, the EC (2007: 4) affirmed the validity of the subsidiarity principle and admitted that "there can be no simple prescriptions about what makes good policy or practice or about how transferable a policy might be." However, instead of abandoning the idea of EBE altogether, the EC sought alternative routes to promote EBE in the European space of education. Recurring to the traditional "program approach" to European integration that assigned the EC the legitimate right to coordinate political cooperation in Europe (Ertl, 2006: 12; Tuschling & Engemann, 2006: 453), the EC (2009) launched a call for proposals inviting European actors to initiate projects developing best practices for implementing EBE. Notably, this call for proposals was legitimized by the recommendations made by EENEE (Gough, Tripney, Kenny, & Buk-Berge, 2011: 7). Two out of the four accepted proposals were submitted by a group of education experts from England.[12] This group included David Gough, Ann Oakley, Philippa Cordingley, and Andrew Morris, all of whom had assisted the New Labour government in implementing EBE in England.[13] Moreover, the members had also worked for the OECD and had organized an OECD conference on EBE in London in 2006, which had featured the EC Director General for Education and Culture, David-Pascal Dion, as one of the keynote speakers (see previous).

While EENEE analytical reports had promoted EBE without taking into account different national education systems and diverging national political interests, the EC's call for proposals reflected the heterogeneity in the European space of education and was aimed at establishing transnational networks that cut across national boundaries and had the potential to change the political and public opinion in EU member states. In particular, the project Evidence Informed Policy and Practice in Education in Europe (EIPPEE), organized by Gough et al., succeeded in mobilizing political, academic, economic, and civil society actors from 23 European countries to discuss the use of scientific evidence in decision making (Normand, 2016: 38). The EIPPEE project has been perpetuated in the form of annual international conferences in which national education actors can participate irrespective of their official national political status in mutual learning processes. Moreover, EIPPEE conferences provide an alternative route to sediment the European space of education by providing national actors (e.g., teacher unions, universities, research institutes, and private companies) with the possibility to meet actors from non-European countries (e.g., Japan, New Zealand, the United States), representatives of the EU (e.g., EC, EUROSTAT) and international actors (e.g., Campbell Collaboration, OECD). It seems that the EIPPEE conferences provide a transnational venue to sediment the European space of education without violating the subsidiarity principle and opposing national governments' claims for political sovereignty over education.

Conclusion

Ever since its emergence in the late 1990s, the European space of education has developed into a transnational social field inhabited by education experts positing that their conceptions of education and rational education policymaking be applied to all EU member states. The EC acts as the dominant consecration instance in this transnational field of EBE. Amongst other things, the EC has shaped the European agenda for education by appointing expert groups (e.g., EENEE) to represent the official interests of the EU. However, reflecting its status of a weak social field, the European space of education has been subject to influence from both national and supranational academic and political actors. Moreover, it is apparent that the distribution of symbolic power in the European space of education witnesses the influences from the wider global field of power. While EBE was validated by its social and cultural links to the US-American economics on education tradition, the development of European benchmarks for education mirrors the OECD's influence. These multiple links to adjacent supranational and national social fields manifest that the European space of education has the character of an interstitial transnational social field. As is typically of an interstitial social field, symbolic elites located within the European space of education possess multiple positions on national and supranational levels. In particular, the case of EENEE shows that the formation of European symbolic elites has been based on the accumulation of transnational symbolic capital. Furthermore, EENEE also gives evidence of the increasing political influence that the US-American economic traditions and research institutes exert upon European policymaking (cf. Fourcade, 2006; Dezalay & Garth, 2011). Therefore, it is hardly surprising that it was a group of economists affiliated with the US-American economics of education tradition that succeeded in installing EBE on the EU's official political agenda.

However, EENEE's symbolic power would have been inconceivable without the prevalence of a transnational European space of education. The European space of education was the contingent outcome of universalistic cultural frames, which both the EU's technocratic elites and official representatives of EU member states could refer to. Above all, KBE worked as a universalistic cultural frame and encompassed European national economies within a transnational economic space qua "a master economic narrative" (Jessop, 2004: 168). Amongst other things, the development of European benchmarks for education was justified with reference to their capacity to improve the economic competitiveness of the European transnational economy. Besides KBE, the "education-economic growth policy paradigm" also provided a transnationally recognized framework to make sense of education as a production factor. In Abbott's (2005) terms, the reframing of education as a production factor constituted a cultural hinge that provided economic experts with privileged access to the European space of education.

The course of developments depicted in this chapter is not constrained to the European field of education. Numerous scholars of European affairs have shown how the general logic of European integration has transformed from voluntary and deliberative cooperation to a more calculative and disciplinary mode of governance, which relies on establishment of European expert groups, introduction of European benchmarks, and practices of naming and shaming (cf. Haahr, 2004; Bernhard, 2006, 2010; Heidenreich & Zeitlin, 2009). Reflecting these parallel developments in different European policy fields, it remains a pivotal task for future research to elucidate the reciprocal influences between the changing overall logics of European integration and transformation of the constellations of knowledge-bearing elites and political agendas in different policy fields.

Notes

1 Bourdieu (1985: 22) defines symbolic power as the legitimate right to install a particular perspective as the new "legitimate vision of the social world".
2 Emirbayer and Johnson (2008); Swartz (2008, 2013), and Vandenberghe (1999) include more detailed discussions about social fields' invariant phenomenal characteristics and general logics of structuration.

3　Abbott (2005) refers "hinge" to an issue or a group that interlinks two or more previously unrelated social arenas and their respective populations of actors.

4　According to Tuschling and Engemann (2006: 453), the subsidiary principle is based on the idea of European "uniformity" whilst maintaining respect to national "diversity".

5　This group included, amongst others, the Bundesinstitut für Berufsbildung (IBB) in Germany, the Centre for Innovation in Education (CINOP) in the Netherlands, the Institute for the Development of Vocational Training of Workers (ISFOL) in Italy, and the Quality and Certification Agency (QCA) in the UK (EC, 2004a).

6　CEPR was founded in 1983 by the economist Richard Portes at the London Business School. It serves as an independent research institute and consulting agency. CEPR has received funding from a wide range of public and private actors and organizations, including the European Central Bank and the European Investment Bank. In contrast to CEPR, EENEE was founded in 2005 to serve as a think tank that provides the European Commission with expert knowledge on economic issues. The European Commission appears also to be the primary source of funding for EENEE.

7　The original group of members included: Giorgio Brunello (University of Padua), Antonio Ciccone (University of Barcelona), Torberg Falch (University of Trondheim), Angel de la Fuente (University of Barcelona), Francis Kramarz (Centre de Recherche en Economie et Statistique, Paris), Stephen Malkin (London School of Economics), Daniel Münich (Economics Institute, Prague), Hassel Oosterbeek (University of Amsterdam), George Psacharopoulos (University of Athens), Ludger Wößmann (University of Munich).

8　Hanushek has held influential positions in the US field of education. Amongst other things, he worked for the U.S. Department of Education and the National Bureau of Economic Research (NBER), and has been a member of the Council of Economic Advisors and the National Academy of Education. In Europe, Hanushek is affiliated with leading European research institutes in economics (cf. www.hoover.org/profiles/eric-hanushek).

9　EENEE's analytical reports are listed on its official website (www.eenee.de/eenee-Home/EENEE/Analytical-Reports.html). Biographical data about EENEE members is gathered on their professional internet websites and profiles.

10　IDEAS is the largest bibliographic database dedicated to economics and available freely on the Internet. It is based on the Repository Research Papers in Economics (RePEC) that interlinks a vast amount of archives, is run by volunteers, and has over 55,000 registered authors.

11　These research institutes include the Centre for Economic Studies (CESifo) at the University of Munich, the IZA Institute of Labour Economics in Bonn, the Centre of European Economic Research (ZEW) in Mannheim, the London School of Economics, and the Hoover Institute in Stanford (US).

12　These projects are EBEP (applied by the City of Antwerp), Linked (applied by the European Schoolnet), and EIPEE and EIPPEE (both applied by David Gough).

13　David Gough was director of the EPPI Centre (Evidence for Policy and Practice Information and Co-ordinating Centre); Ann Oakley was Professor of Sociology and Social Policy at the Institute of Education at University College London; Philippa Cordingley was Chief Executive of CUREE (Centre for the Use of Research and Evidence in Education); Andrew Morris was Director of NERF (National Education Research Forum).

References

Abbott, A. (2005). Linked Ecologies: States and Universities as Environments for Professions. *Sociological Theory, 23*(3), 245–274.

Bernhard, S. (2006). The European Paradigm of Social Exclusion. *Journal of Contemporary European Research, 2*(1), 41–55.

Bernhard, S. (2010). *Die Konstruktion von Inklusion: Europäische Sozialpolitik aus soziologischer Perspektive.* Frankfurt am Main: Campus.

Biesta, G. (2006). What's the Point of Lifelong Learning if Lifelong Learning Has No Point? On the Democratic Deficit of Policies for Lifelong Learning. *European Educational Research Journal, 5*(3–4), 169–180.

Bigo, D., & Madsen, M. R. (2011). Introduction to Symposium 'A Different Reading of the International': Pierre Bourdieu and International Studies. *International Political Sociology, 5*(3), 219–224.

Blatter, J. (2007). Demokratie und Legitimation. In A. Benz, S. Lütz, U. Schimank & G. Simonis (Eds.), *Handbuch Governance: Theoretische Grundlagen und empirische Anwendungsfelder* (pp. 271–284). Wiesbaden: VS Verlag für Sozialwissenschaften.

Botzem, S., & Quack, S. (2008). Contested Rules and Shifting Boundaries: International Standard-Setting in Accounting. In M.-L. Djelic & K. Sahlin-Andersson (Eds.), *Transnational Governance: Institutional Dynamics of Regulation* (pp. 266–286). Cambridge: Cambridge University Press.

Bourdieu, P. (1985). Social Space and the Genesis of Groups. *Theory and Society, 14*(6), 723–744.

Bourdieu, P. (1987). What Makes a Social Class? On the Theoretical and Practical Existence of Groups. *Berkeley Journal of Sociology, 32*, 1–17.

Bourdieu, P. (1989). Social Space and Symbolic Power. *Sociological Theory, 7*(1), 14–25.

Bourdieu, P. (1993a). *The Field of Cultural Production.* New York, NY: Columbia University Press.

Bourdieu, P. (1993b). *Soziologische Fragen.* Frankfurt am Main: Suhrkamp.

Bourdieu, P. (1998). *Practical Reason.* Stanford, CA: Stanford University Press.

Bourdieu, P. (2000). *Pascalian Meditations.* Stanford, CA: Stanford University Press.

Bourdieu, P. (2011). *Kunst und Kultur: Zur Ökonomie symbolischer Güter: Schriften zu Kultursoziologie* (Vol. 4). Konstanz: UVK.

Burns, T., & Schuller, T. (2007). The Evidence Agenda. In OECD/CERI (Eds.), *Evidence in Education: Linking Research and Policy* (pp. 15–32). Paris: OECD/CERI.

CEU, Council of the European Union. (2001). *Report from the Education Council to the European Council: The Concrete Future Objectives of Education and Training Systems.* Brussels: European Commission. Retrieved March 2, 2016, from http://ec.europa.eu/education/policies/2010/doc/rep_fut_obj_en.pdf

CEU, Council of the European Union. (2002). *Detailed Work Program on the Follow-up of the Objective of the Education and Training Systems in Europe.* Brussels: Publications Office of the European Union. Retrieved June 3, 2018, from https://publications.europa.eu/en/publication-detail/-/publication/2d17e529-6c81-4b85-8d19-e9dbe65a93c0. Brussels: Official Journal of the European Union (2002/C142/01)

CEU, Council of the European Union. (2006). *Draft Conclusions of the Council of the Representatives of the Governments of the Member States, Meeting Within the Council, on Efficiency and Equity in Education and Training.* Brussels: Official Journal of the European Union (2006/C298/03).

CEU, Council of the European Union. (2007). *Presidency Conclusion: Brussels European Council 8/9 March 2007.* Retrieved September 2, 2019, from www.eea.europa.eu/policy-documents/presidency-conclusions-of-the-brussels

Council of the European Communities/Commission of the European Communities. (1992). *Treaty on European Union*. Luxembourg: Office for Official Publications of the European Communities.

Dezalay, Y., & Garth, B. G. (2011). Hegemonic Battles, Professional Rivalries, and the International Division of Labor in the Market for the Import and Export of State-Governing Expertise. *International Political Sociology, 5*(3), 276–295.

Dion, D.-P. (2006). Evidence-Based Policy in Education and Training. In OECD (Ed.), *Implementation, Scaling up, and Sustainability: Continuing Discussion on Evidence-Based Policy Research in Education*. OECD Conference held in London on July 6–7, 2006.

EC, European Commission. (1993). *Growth, Competitiveness, and Employment: The Challenges and Ways Forward Into the 21st Century: European Commission White Paper*. Brussels: European Commission. Retrieved September 3, 2019, from https://publications.europa.eu/en/publication-detail/-/publication/0d563bc1-f17e-48ab-bb2a-9dd9a31d5004

EC, European Commission. (1995). *Teaching and Learning: Towards the Learning Society*. Luxembourg: Office for Official Publications.

EC, European Commission. (1997). *Agenda 2000: For a Stronger and Wider Union*. Luxembourg: Office for Official Publications.

EC, European Commission. (2002). *European Report on Quality Indicators of Lifelong Learning: Fifteen Quality Indicators*. Brussels: European Commission.

EC, European Commission. (2003). Education and Training 2010: The Success of the Lisbon Strategy Hinges on Urgent Reforms. *Official Journal of the European Union, C 104, April 30, 2004*. Retrieved May 15, 2018, from https://publications.europa.eu/en/publication-detail/-/publication/59381b9f-3a72-4bca-9b8f-1f9029644152/language-en

EC, European Commission. (2004a). *Achieving the Lisbon Goal: The Contribution of VET: Draft Final Report to the European Commission*. London: QCA.

EC, European Commission. (2004b). *Facing the Challenge: The Lisbon Strategy for Growth and Employment*. Brussels: European Communities.

EC, European Commission. (2007). *Towards More Knowledge-Based Policy and Practice in Education and Training: Commission Staff Working Report*. Brussels: European Commission. Retrieved June 28, 2018, from https://publications.europa.eu/en/publication-detail/-/publication/962e3b89-c546-4680-ac84-777f8f10c590

EC, European Commission. (2009). *Call for Proposals EAC/26/2009: Evidence Based-Policy and Practice: Call for Proposals to Develop Networks of Knowledge Brokerage Initiatives*. Retrieved from https://euroalert.net/news/8879/grants-for-develop-networks-of-knowledge-brokerage-initiatives

EENEE, European Expert Network on Economics on Education. (2006). *Efficiency and Equity in European Education and Training Systems*. Brussels: European Commission. Retrieved July 13, 2016, from www.europarl.europa.eu/thinktank/en/document.html?reference=IPOL-CULT_ET(2007)389581

EENEE, European Expert Network on Economics on Education. (2009). *Methods for Causal Evaluation of Education Policies and Practices: An Econometric Toolbox*. Brussels: European Commission. Retrieved July 13, 2016, from www.ifo.de/en/node/12065

Emirbayer, M., & Johnson, V. (2008). Bourdieu and Organizational Analysis. *Theory and Society, 37*(1), 1–44.

Ertl, H. (2006). European Union Policies in Education and Training: The Lisbon Agenda as a Turning Point? *Comparative Education, 42*(1), 5–27.

Eyal, G., & Buchholz, L. (2010). From the Sociology of Intellectuals to the Sociology of Interventions. *Annual Review of Sociology*, 36, 117–137.

Field, J. (1997). The Learning Society and the European Union: A Critical Assessment of Supranational Policy Formation. *Journal of Studies in International Education*, 1(2), 73–92.

Fitz-Gibbon, C. T. (2002). Evidence-Based Policy and Management in Practice: Education in England, 1980s to 2002. *Public Policy and Administration*, 17(3), 95–105.

Fourcade, M. (2006). The Construction of a Global Profession: The Transnationalization of Economics. *American Journal of Sociology*, 112(1), 145–194.

Georgakakis, D. (2013). The Institutionalization of the European Administrative Corps as a Transnational Elite. In N. Kauppi & M. R. Madsen (Eds.), *Transnational Power Elites: The New Professionals of Governance, Law and Security* (pp. 36–60). London: Routledge.

Georgakakis, D., & Rowell, J. (Eds.). (2013). *The Field of Eurocracy*. Houndmills, Basingstoke: Palgrave Macmillan.

Gough, D., Tripney, J., Kenny, C., & Buk-Berge, E. (2011). *Evidence Informed Policymaking in Europe: EIPEE Final Project Report*. London: EPPI-Centre/University of London.

Gram-Skjoldager, K., & Knudsen, A.-C. (2013). Elite Transformations and Diffusion in Foreign Policy: A Socio-Historical Approach to the Emergence of European Power Elites. In N. Kauppi & M. R. Madsen (Eds.), *Transnational Power Elites: The New Professionals of Governance, Law and Security* (pp. 81–97). London: Routledge.

Haahr, J. H. (2004). Open Method of Coordination as Advanced Liberal Government. *Journal of European Public Policy*, 11(2), 209–230.

Heidenreich, M., & Zeitlin, J. (Eds.). (2009). *Changing European Employment and Welfare Regimes: The Influence of the Open Method of Coordination on National Reforms*. London: Routledge.

Hingel, A. (2001). Education Policies and European Governance: Contribution of the Interservice Groups on European Governance. *European Journal for Education Law and Policy*, 5(1–2), 7–16.

Ionnidou, A. (2007). A Comparative Analysis of New Governance Instruments in the Transnational Educational Space: A Shift to Knowledge-Based Instruments? *European Educational Research Journal*, 6(4), 336–347.

Janne, H. (1973). For a Community Policy in Education. *Bulletin of the European Communities, Supplement 10/73*. Brussels: European Communities Commission.

Jessop, B. (2004). Critical Semiotic Analysis and Cultural Political Economy. *Critical Discourse Analysis*, 1(1), 159–176.

Jones, H. C. (2005). Lifelong Learning in the European Union: Whither the Lisbon Strategy? *European Journal of Education*, 40(3), 247–260.

Jones, P. (2010). The Politics of the Economics of Education in the European Union. *European Educational Research Journal*, 9(3), 350–380.

Kamens, D. H. (2013). Globalization and the Emergence of an Audit Culture: PISA and the Search for 'Best Practices' and Magic Bullets. In H.-D. Meyer (Ed.), *PISA, Power and Policy: The Emergence of Global Educational Governance* (pp. 117–139). Oxford: Oxford Studies in Comparative Education.

Kauppi, N., & Madsen, M. R. (2013). Fields of Global Governance: How Transnational Power Elites Can Make Global Governance Intelligible. *International Political Sociology*, 8(3), 324–330.

Lange, B., & Alexiadou, N. (2007). New Forms of European Union Governance in the Education Sector? A Preliminary Analysis of the Open Method of Coordination. *European Educational Research Journal, 6*(4), 321–335.

Lawn, M., & Normand, R. (2015). Introduction. In M. Lawn & R. Normand (Eds.), *Shaping of European Education: Interdisciplinary Approaches* (pp. 1–13). London: Routledge.

Lee, M., Thayer, T., & Madyun, N. (2008). The Evolution of the European Unions' Lifelong Learning Policies: An Institutional Learning Perspective. *Comparative Education, 44*(4), 445–463.

Levitt, P., & Glick Schiller, N. (2004). Conceptualizing Simultaneity: A Transnational Social Field Perspective on Society. *The International Migration Review, 38*(145), 595–629.

Medvetz, T. (2012). *Think Tanks in America.* Chicago, IL: University of Chicago Press.

Mudge, S. L., & Vauchez, A. (2012). Building Europe on a Weak Field: Law, Economics, and Scholarly Avatars in Transnational Politics. *American Journal of Sociology, 118*(2), 449–492.

Nadel, S. F. (1962). *The Theory of Social Structure.* London: Cohen & West Ltd.

Nordin, A. (2014). Europeanisation in National Educational Reforms: Horizontal and Vertical Translations. In A. Nordin & D. Sundberg (Eds.), *Transnational Policy Flows in European Education the Making and Governing of Knowledge in the Education Policy Field* (pp. 141–158). Oxford: Oxford Studies in Comparative Education.

Normand, R. (2010). Expertise, Networks and Indicators: The Construction of the European Strategy in Education. *European Education Research Journal, 9*(10), 407–431.

Normand, R. (2016). What Works? From Health to Education, the Shaping of the European Policy of Evidence. In K. Trimmer (Ed.), *Political Pressures on Educational and Social Research* (pp. 24–40). London: Routledge.

OECD, Organization for Economic Cooperation and Development. (1996). *Lifelong Learning for All.* Paris: OECD/CERI.

OECD, Organization for Economic Cooperation and Development. (1997). *Education Policy Analysis.* Paris: OECD/CERI.

OECD, Organization for Economic Cooperation and Development. (1998). *Human Capital Investment: An International Comparison.* Paris: OECD/CERI.

OECD, Organization for Economic Cooperation and Development. (2000). *Social Sciences for Policy-Making.* Paris: OECD/CERI.

OECD, Organization for Economic Cooperation and Development. (2007). *Evidence in Education: Linking Research and Policy.* Paris: OECD/CERI.

Pirrie, A. (2001). Evidence-Based Practice in Education: The Best Medicine? *British Journal of Educational Studies, 49*(2), 124–136.

Resnik, J. (2006). International Organizations, the Education-Economic Growth Black Box, and the Development of World Education Culture. *Comparative Education Review, 50*(2), 173–195.

Robertson, S. L., de Azevedo, M. L. N., & Dale, R. (2016). Higher Education, the EU and the Cultural Political Economy of Regionalism. In S. L. Robertson, K. Olds, R. Dale & Q. A. Dang (Eds.), *Global Regionalisms and Higher Education* (pp. 24–48). Cheltenham: Edward Elgar.

Rodrigues, M. J. (2003). *European Policies for a Knowledge Economy.* Cheltenham: Edward Elgar.

Schmidt-Wellenburg, C. (2017a). Europeanisation, Stateness, and Professions: What Role Do Economic Expertise and Economic Experts Play in European Political Integration? *European Journal of Cultural and Political Sociology, 4*(4), 1–27.

Schmidt-Wellenburg, C. (2017b). Wissenschaft, Politik und Profession als Quellen diskursiver Autorität. In J. Hamann, J. Maeße, V. Gengnagel & A. Hirschfeld (Eds.), *Macht in Wissenschaft und Gesellschaft* (pp. 477–504). Wiesbaden: Springer VS.

Shavelson, R., & Towne, L. (2002). *Scientific Research in Education*. Washington, DC: National Academy Press.

Stone Sweet, A., Sandholtz, W., & Fligstein, N. (Eds.). (2001). *The Institutionalization of Europe*. Oxford: Oxford University Press.

Swartz, D. L. (2008). Bringing Bourdieu's Master Concepts into Organizational Analysis. *Theory and Society, 37*(1), 45–52.

Swartz, D. L. (2013). *Symbolic Power, Politics, and Intellectuals*. Chicago, IL: University of Chicago Press.

Tuschling, A., & Engemann, C. (2006). From Education to Lifelong Learning: The Emerging Regime of Learning in the European Union. *Educational Philosophy and Theory, 38*(4), 451–469.

Vandenberghe, F. (1999). 'The Real Is Relational': An Epistemological Analysis of Pierre Bourdieu's Generative Structuralism. *Sociological Theory, 17*(1), 32–67.

Vauchez, A. (2008). The Force of the Weak Field: Law and Lawyers in the Government of the European Union (for Renewed Research Agenda). *International Political Sociology, 2*(2), 128–144.

Vauchez, A. (2011). Interstitial Power in Fields of Limited Statehood: Introducing a 'Weak Field' Approach to the Study of Transnational Settings. *International Political Sociology, 5*(3), 340–345.

Vauchez, A. (2014). Transnationale Expertenfelder als schwache Felder: Der Entwurf des ersten Weltgerichtshofs und die Entstehung eines internationalen Expertentums. *Berliner Journal für Soziologie, 24*(2), 201–227.

Vauchez, A. (2015). *Brokering Europe: Euro-Lawyers and the Making of a Transnational Polity*. Cambridge: Cambridge University Press.

Chapter 11

The Euro crisis dispositif

Heterogeneous positioning strategies in polycentric fields

Jens Maesse

Introduction

The idea of transnational field analysis aims to understand the complex open-ings and translocal rearticulations of the social order beyond national autonomy and without fixed borders (Go & Krause, 2016). Transnational fields are trans-formative, dynamic, and open to ongoing conflicts over meaning and institution building (Bernhard & Schmidt-Wellenburg, 2014). My chapter will show why two aspects are central for understanding knowledge production in transnational fields: first, the *transepistemic* interconnectedness of different fields, which are open to each other as gradually fixed social structures (Bigo, 2011); and, second, the *complexity and multiplicity of meaning* that derives from discursive practices taking place in transepistemic fields. In order to develop this idea, my chapter draws on a discourse analytical reformulation of the field concept, which cumu-lates in a dispositif analytical approach.

Discourse analysts have criticized economic and institutional approaches in the social sciences for paying too little attention to interpretation processes, nego-tiations, conflicts, and controversies in the economy (Wullweber, 2015). Yet, many discourse approaches tend to reduce all aspects of the political economy to the semiotic level, thereby underestimating social hierarchies, routines, pro-cesses, and structures beyond the level of linguistic visibility (Diaz-Bone, 2017). In contrast, political-economic discourse approaches (Sum & Jessop, 2013) also emphasize structures, processes, and interdependencies that are not linguistically expressed. Here, "structures" are often presented in opposition to "discourse" as an extra-linguistic context.

My contribution follows a political-economic approach, as economic discourse cannot be reduced to mere linguistic representation. Yet, the opposition between discourse/language and structure/context must be overcome in order to grasp the full complexity of discursive practices in the political economy. I will use the dispositif concept (Foucault, 1980; Maesse & Hamann, 2016; Hamann, Maesse, Scholz, & Angermuller, 2019) to analyze discursive positioning strategies at both the *imaginary-symbolic* (language-related) and *institutional-sedimented* (field-related) levels of transnational discourse production. This idea draws on notions from Bourdieu's theory of social fields (Bourdieu, 1989) and Foucault's concept of the discursive utterance (Foucault, 1972). In sum, dispositif analysis reflects how the symbolic-imaginary visibility of social actors relates to complex institutionally sedimented modalities of existence in transepistemic conflict arenas. In order to illustrate this perspective, I will analyze heterogeneous positioning strategies in a European conflict arena.

To begin, I elaborate the shortcomings of conventional crisis interpretations and explain the method in more detail. I then outline the idea of various interlocking conflict arenas negotiating the Euro crisis discourse. Next, I analyze the struggle over economic policy ideas and concepts, and I demonstrate how a *critical-democratic positioning strategy* emerges. Then I examine the dispute over the institutional structure of European economic governance regimes; here I show how a *moderating positioning strategy* seems to replace or supplement the purely technocratic style of "Eurocracy".

Theory and methodology of dispositif analysis

My dispositif analysis of the Euro crisis argues for an approach to the political economy that respects the coexistence of different conflicts that cannot be reduced to one another. One single field does not form Europe; it is rather the result of a polycentric order where different discursive and institutional logics coexist and interact. The dispositif approach offers a heteroglossical perspective for analyzing how heterogeneous elements come together in a non-coherent socio-symbolic framework.

Shortcomings of conventional views on the European political economy

The Euro crisis is typically conceived, in public debates as well as in political and academic discourses, as either a "competition problem" or an "austerity failure" (Schmidt-Wellenburg, 2018a). In the first case, social and economic decline is considered to be the result of a lack of economic competitiveness of southern European countries, such as Greece, Italy, Spain, or Portugal. This is reflected by current account deficits of those economies and by a dysfunctional, indebted, and clientelistic state apparatus. The Euro crisis develops because financial markets lose confidence in those economies and set in motion a downward spiral affecting all sectors of the economy. In contrast, the second explanation focuses on the global interactions of financial markets and, in particular, the financial and structural imbalances between the European economies of the south and the north. The high indebtedness of the south is seen as an effect of too much saving in the north due to wage restraint, particularly in Germany. Accumulated surplus capital seeks reliable investment opportunities, but it does not find them due to demand shortfalls. The capital surpluses of the northern economies (especially Germany's) are only invested in speciously reliable opportunities, until bad investments collapse and the crisis turns into financial turmoil. Austerity measures function like pouring oil on the fire, because they further reduce demand and worsen investment opportunities dramatically.

Despite the fundamental contradictions that exist between these approaches, both perspectives have a tendency to reduce political-economic phenomena such as the Euro crisis to one singular conflict. This singular conflict is usually arranged around clearly defined actors, goals, and means. Many of these institutionalist and macroeconomic perspectives ignore the multipolar character of European socio-discursive relations. This makes them blind to the many grey zones in which Europeanized actors are involved, and to the interpretative dynamics, unintended results, and uncontrollable effects of negotiations. As a result of these shortcomings, a general pessimism about Europe as well as a reorientation towards the nation-state order arises (Streeck, 2014; Flassbeck & Steinhardt, 2018).

The logic of transnational fields

However, the nation-state order was never a fixed social terrain with autonomous social actors and the possibility of full democratic control. It was, rather, an imaginary concept used in politics and in the social sciences of the late nineteenth century and the first half of the twentieth century, for making a certain social terrain politically controllable and scientifically measurable (Desrosières, 1998). The nation-state concept is an ideological device and not an institutional reality (Go, 2017). A reorientation to the nation-state myth in transnational contexts seems scientifically questionable and politically problematic.

My dispositif analytical perspective on social fields provides a different view for the analysis of transnational phenomena, because in order to understand globalization and transnationalization, processes will not replicate the nation-state order on a higher geographical level. On the contrary, transnationalization means the dedifferentiation and rearrangement on the levels of *actors* and *field borders*: social actors become hybridized, and fixed borders of fields collapse and are transformed into a heterogeneous constellation of multi-layered and polycentric socio-discursive relations (Bigo, 2011).

Current theories of transnational fields have failed to grasp this heterogeneous character of transnationalization. For example, standard field analyses seek to explain every social action by actors' class positions fixed in clearly defined social fields (Lenger, 2018). Here, actors have a coherent habitus that regulates their logics of action, worldviews, and attitudes. The concepts of "closure", "border", and "autonomy" are of central importance. Social order emerges as an autonomous space of clarity and transparency, where each actor finds their singular position. This picture of regulated social order is replicated by transnational field theory. For instance, Larissa Buchholz (2016) highlights the importance of vertical autonomy in transnational fields when analyzing, e.g., the emergence of the global art field. According to Buchholz, a global social field arises as an autonomous social order above national as geographical fields. Yet, autonomy, clear boundaries, and coherent social identities are not features that characterize globalization in general, or Europeanization in particular.

Even critical approaches seem to apply the idea of a transnational field as a homogenous social space, based on clear boundaries of inclusion/exclusion, and producing coherent actors as "insiders" of the field. The authors of the Eurocracy thesis, for example, analyze Europe as a Brussels apparatus of technocrats and bureaucratic procedures (Georgakakis & Rowell, 2013). In the same vein as this approach, Frédéric Lebaron and Didier Georgakakis (2018: 16) analyze Yanis Varoufakis's intervention into the Euro crisis discourses "ending up as a shock", because Varoufakis acted as an "outsider" of the Brussels technocratic field and he was not familiar with the rules of the game. In this view, Europe is conceptualized as an autonomous social field where actors must become full members in order to act successfully in terms of the Eurocracy's relevance structures.

My critique of homogeneity-oriented and inclusion-oriented approaches is that Europe and the global/transnational cannot be reduced to exclusive and integrated institutional entities, such as Eurocracy or global-art auction markets, located at specific geographical sites – be it Brussels, or global cities such as New York. A transnational field is, rather, characterized by a combination of institutional, cognitive, and communicative realities, independent of their geographical locations and institutional autonomies (Delanty & Rumford, 2005; Eder, 2011). This includes genuine transnational (e.g., the European Commission) as well as national institutions (academic fields, regional/national parliaments, media debates) that relate to transnational instances in their communication and actors' cognitive orientations. The modalities that structure political, academic, or industrial (and many other) forms of communication and the cognitive orientations of their actors do not presuppose a certain exclusiveness and autonomy of global institutions (Robertson, 1992). On the contrary, the openness of field borders and the flexibility and hybridity of people's minds is a precondition for the possibility of transnational interconnectedness across field boundaries (Go & Krause, 2016). Transnationality is not possible without the dissolution of fixed social relations and a certain reconfiguration on levels "above" and "below" the nation-state imaginary. An autonomy as well as inclusion criterion for actors impedes the formation of proper transnational realities.

In contrast to autonomy-oriented and homogeneity-oriented approaches, "weak field" theories (Mudge & Vauchez, 2012) and discourse-field–oriented approaches (Maesse, 2018b; Schmidt-Wellenburg, 2018b; Hamann et al., 2019) highlight the polycentric and heterogeneous character of fields. These approaches share commonalities with the notion of dispositif. Both weak field approaches and discourse approaches focus on practices and structures of crossing field boundaries, translating knowledge from one context into other contexts, and getting involved in heterogeneous positioning games. These are the main characteristics of transnational fields. Europe is not formed as a closed social space; it is, rather, constructed by a multiplicity of interplays, exchanges, and rearticulations between European institutional settings, national polities, and different fields of expert knowledge production (Diez, 2001).

The logic of the field as a dispositif

I will use the notion of *dispositif theory* to analyze transnational fields as a) polycentric institutional structures and b) heterogeneous positioning arenas. The interplay of these two dimensions is of central importance. First, the institutional dimension is understood as transepistemic arenas, located at the intersection of different institutionalized sub-fields. This dimension relates to the fixed character of social relations with more or less open borders between the sub-fields. Positions are constructed on the basis of formal and fixed modalities (i.e., "professor", "director", "president"). Second, the discursive dimension is analyzed as a language-based practice, taking place in transepistemic arenas. Here, actors use symbols (language, pictures, gestures) to create images of themselves and others. These images are not imagined futures or fantasies (Beckert, 2016). Following a Lacanian understanding of subjectivity (Lacan, 1991), the imaginary relates to the split and dialogic character of identities of actors produced by enunciative processes. It is the image(s) that subjects produce in discourses about themselves vis-à-vis the many other voices in language games (Lyotard, 1989).

Taking both levels together, social actors always exist in dispositifs on two different but interrelated levels of *position* which are not homologous: one and the same actor has an institutional-sedimented position (i.e., "economics professor", "research director", "media star") as well as an imaginary-symbolic position (the "antagonist" in the enunciative logic of "me" and the "other" ruled by the moderation principle). We need at least two different methods to analyze this complex positioning game: one is based on classical sociological field analysis (statistics, interviews, etc.), and the other draws on linguistic methods of polyphony analysis.

The field dimension requires an *analysis of classical forms of capital*, such as university positions, public office, money, industrial innovation clusters, director positions, ministries, and so forth. Capital analysis shows how actors use different forms of sedimentation to take *institutional* positions. In contrast, the discourse analysis accounts for the ways in which actors (with high or low amounts of capital) take *imaginary-symbolic positions* through the use of language. This dimension is analyzed with *qualitative methodologies such as enunciative pragmatics* (Angermuller, 2014; Maesse, 2010; Zienkowski, 2016) and it accounts for the symbolic aspects of power and domination. As the analyses of text excerpts in the following sections will show, enunciative analysis will identify discursive markers such as deixis ("I", "me"), negation ("no", "not", "but", "un-"), boosters (all formulations that express solidarity and sympathy with content uttered to the speaker), hedges (all formulations that keep certain content uttered to the speaker at a distance), and other formal operators on the linguistic level (preconstructs, conventionalizers).

The results of the discourse analysis will be combined with the results of field analysis to understand how material-institutional positions relate to symbolic-discourse positions. The idea of a discourse analytical approach to (transnational) fields is *not* to presuppose a homology between the symbolic and the institutional. To conclude, the following ideas are central to this approach, and they will be explained and illustrated by the empirical examples in the final two sections:

*   First, positioning strategies are multi-dimensional processes; they are not directed towards a single, coherent subject. Positioning strategies operate through the interaction of different institutionalized and symbolic-imaginary discursive positions within heterogeneous, transepistemic fields.
*   Second, complex positionings are based on strategies and take place in a dispositif. This dispositif spans different social fields; it consists of symbolic-imaginary and institutionalized power structures; it contains various texts, practices, social hierarchies, and other elements of social life; and it negotiates different topics and issues in interlocking conflicts. A dispositif has no center.
*   Third, from an analytical viewpoint, the dispositif can be "sliced", as illustrated in the sections that follow. However, a dispositif does not resemble a geographical or structuralist space that can be categorized and measured. It operates rather like a rhizomatic tissue, the layers of which can be dissected piece by piece.
*   Fourth, a dispositif analysis implies both a linguistic-discourse analytical and a sociological-capital related view of different types of data (text and social context).

Interrelated fields of conflicts

In order to illustrate the dispositif approach, the following analysis will show how the Euro crisis discourse revolves around different interconnected field conflicts at different levels of the European political economy. As Figure 11.1 shows, different fields of conflict constitute the entire arena that is open to the inclusion of many more fields. This empirical analysis will only focus on two of them, in order to give an idea of how such an analysis operates.

The *first conflict* deals with different economic theories and economic policy concepts. An ordoliberal hegemony has been established since the end of World War II, especially in Germany, that is deeply influential within academia, media, and economic policy (Pühringer & Hirte, 2015). Furthermore, this ordoliberal policy paradigm was institutionalized on the European level by the European Union Treaties (Schmidt-Wellenburg, 2017). During the different phases of the Euro crisis, ordoliberalism became more and more challenged. The Greek drama in 2015 played an important role in the course of the Euro crisis. The third section will show how an ordoliberal *resolute* positioning strategy is replaced and

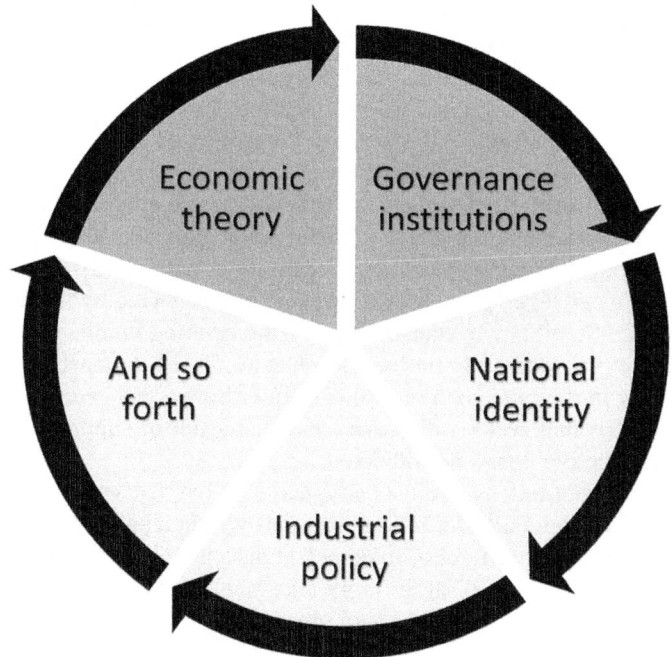

Figure 11.1 The open transepistemic conflict arena

challenged by a *critical-democratic* strategy. The conflict between these two discursive positioning logics, however, takes place against the background of certain transformations in the field of economics that support the construction of excellence and elite myths as new symbolic modalities of academic consecration. Greek rebels, such as Varoufakis, now "hijack" the symbolic capital that was constructed by those neoliberal elite myths, and they begin to speak of themselves as "star economists" in the name of academic excellence. Finally, the technocratic "there-is-no-alternative" (TINA) politics that is typical of neoliberal economic reform agendas in Europe is called into question by the establishment of a critical-democratic discourse logic (Maesse, 2018a).

The *second level of conflict* deals with the institutional framework of European economic policy. After the Euro crisis of 2008, it became obvious to many actors of the economic governance apparatus that the institutional fabric of the European Union, based on the Maastricht Stability Union and formal national autonomy in economic policy and financial supervision, was unable to withstand financial market distortions. As a consequence, the European Central Bank (ECB) introduced extraordinary measures, and for the first time in history, different

European governments launched coordinated investment programs (even if with small budgets). The situation in Greece was affected by this unstable governance structure as well. The initial strategy, launched by Alexis Tsipras and Varoufakis, was to play a game with blackmail and the possible collapse of the Euro zone. This political game was initiated to convince the Troika institutions (European Commission, ECB, International Monetary Fund) to stop austerity policies. The strategy failed because a so-called "firewall" was erected against the financial markets, which prevented "skipping" the Greek deficit to other economies (Lehndorff, 2014). Nevertheless, the Greek political poker game has helped to stimulate discussions about deepening institutional integration in the field of economic policy on the European level. This discussion process is reflected by the introduction of the European Stability Mechanism (ESM), the banking union, a blueprint, the Juncker plan, or the Macron initiative (Busch et al., 2016). Against this backdrop, I want to show in the final section of this chapter how a *moderating positioning strategy* develops that seeks a discursive balancing out of supposedly opposing interests of respective imaginary others.

This discursive attitude is not just "a typical case" of "EU-speech". It is rather a special linguistic modality for taking positions within a balanced conflict arena that makes a significant difference to other EU discourse logics (for the Bologna-Process, see Maesse, 2010). It is more like another "compromise", because compromises are not only made behind closed doors; compromise results from conflict, and each compromise becomes the starting point for many follow-up conflicts in an endless process of renegotiations (for the Stability and Growth Pact, see Costantini, 2017). Eurocracy theory seems to overemphasize compromise orientation and, therefore, underestimates conflict. It reduces Europe mostly to technocratic discourses in Brussels. But the technocratic Europe, which for a long time remained at a distance from the social, financial, and economic discourses of the respective European nation-states, becomes of secondary importance as European issues become more and more debated in the media and in national parliaments.

Now, a moderating discourse order emerges onto whom the regional politico-economic actors in almost all European countries are expected to project their hopes, opportunities, and fears. This general tendency can be interpreted as a further step toward a deeper democratization of Europe, because the critical democratic discourse order opens up the European discourse space for different possible political options. This goes hand in hand with a more comprehensive perception of singular problems in different nation-states as "European" problems, such as the Greek crisis in 2015, Italian populism in 2018, Brexit since 2016, Polish and Hungarian anti-Europeanism as a local power strategy, and Emmanuel Macron's commitment to Europe. Generally speaking, since the crisis of 2009, Europe has become more and more an overall projection screen for the big problems of our time, and solutions are always defined with respect to Europe (exit, deepening, transformation, etc.).

From Munich to Athens

The following empirical analysis[1] will show and illustrate how the dispositif of the Euro crisis spans and emerges from different regions. In a first step, I will show how the symbolic-imaginary and material-institutional positions in the academic region of the dispositif form a critical-democratic positioning strategy. Today's struggles over economic theories and policies developed during the twentieth century in the industrialized countries of the West and the East. Especially after World War II, a discursive order was established in Europe that was characterized by different forms of Keynesianism and economic liberalism (Hall, 1989). Germany, which took a leading role in European economic policy from the 1970s onwards (Huffschmid, 1994), was dominated by a well-established network of ordoliberal economists (Pühringer & Hirte, 2015). In contrast, Keynesian-style approaches became popular in the southern and southwestern countries of Europe (Hacker & Koch, 2017). While Europe's institutional integration in the field of economic policy (such as the foundation of the ECB and the introduction of the euro currency) has been pushed forward primarily by France since the 1980s, Germany and its economic policy allies in the northwest, and later in the east, have dominated the policy agendas within these institutions (especially the stability orientation in the Maastricht Treaty).

Sinn's position in the field of economics

Against this historical background, Hans Werner Sinn is regarded as one of the most influential advocates of a neoliberal, stability-oriented economic policy agenda with an outstanding media presence during the Euro crisis (Ötsch, Pühringer, & Hirte, 2017; Schmidt-Wellenburg, 2018b). Sinn took sides in favor of hard austerity measures, and he demanded the exit of Greece and other southern countries from the euro system. This claim was justified with micro-economic arguments, according to which southern economies could only become competitive by price reductions within an international comparative framework. Price reductions should be brought about, above all, by wage cuts and a devaluation of the national currency after exit from the euro system. Furthermore, these measures should be underpinned by cuts in the public sector. In the following analysis, I will show how Sinn's discourse position was formed by the interaction of *institutional* and *symbolic* positioning strategies.

In a first step, I will consider the *institutional level* of discourse production, i.e., the field dimension of the dispositif. Sinn's institutional discourse position is characterized by a strong embedding in the field of economic policy advice, as well as in the academic field. From a methodological viewpoint, both aspects can be measured and quantified. During the Euro crisis, Sinn's discourse production was backed by a strong institutional position as president of Munich-based ifo, one of the large German economic research institutes central to the German economic governance regime. This provides Sinn's discourse position with *political capital*. In addition, he was one of the few German-speaking economists who had already achieved a high international reputation in the academic world in the 1980s and 1990s. This accounts for a high level of *academic capital*. This is of particular importance because the role of academic capital in politico-economic positioning games changed in recent decades (Lebaron, 2008). The academic field of economics saw sustainable transformations in the 1990s to establish an academic excellence myth (Maesse, 2017b). The introduction of rankings and exclusive publishing in internationally recognized journals moved academic recognition towards discourses of excellence. Accordingly, symbolic capital and other forms of power can be accumulated if scientific success is reflected by A-journal publications and becomes measurable. This was also documented, in the public media, for a couple of years by *Handelsblatt*[2] rankings (Bräuninger, Haucap, & Muck, 2011; Maesse, 2015; Butz & Wohlrabe, 2016). Last but not least, Sinn is extraordinarily visible in the media, as the regular *Frankfurter Allgemeine Zeitung*[3] rankings show, which equips his discourse position with *popular capital*. To conclude, Sinn was in 2015 an institutional heavyweight in economic policy discourse on three different levels simultaneously: he was politically embedded, academically recognized, and prominent in the media.

Sinn's position in the ordoliberal discourse order

This institutional discourse strategy was completed by a *symbolic-imaginary* positioning strategy that can be described as a resolute positioning (for an in-depth analysis, see Maesse, 2018a). As the following discourse excerpt documents, Sinn takes a position as an advocate of austerity by adopting a *resolute strategy* through a moralizing attitude.

> Many European leaders have advocated **growth programmes** for Europe's **crisis-stricken countries**, meaning in fact **debt-financed expenditure** *programmes*. In this note, I will argue that such programmes are **not** the *right medicine*, since the Eurozone **suffers** from an *internal competitiveness problem* rather than a *temporary* **lack of demand**.
>
> (Sinn, 2014: 1, emphasis added)

Here, the speaker takes a symbolic-imaginary position through the construction of two images: the image of "me" and the image of the "other". The imaginary other is kept at a distance by strong valuations and sometimes drastically formulated hedges (marked in **bold**), while boosters like the "right medicine" should raise no doubts about the validity of Sinn's preferred economic policy measures, i.e., the "me" position. Through this strategy, the discourse divides the imaginary space into an area of proximity and distance, virtually demonizing the other. Thus, this resolute symbolic-imaginary positioning strategy aims to make "me" visible, someone who practically is in possession of the "right medicine", while the other appears as a "poisoner" of economic rationality.

Varoufakis's weak field position

When the Synaspismos Rizospastikis Aristeras (SYRIZA) party took hold in the Greek political scene step by step, starting in 2012 and being elected to the government for the first time in January 2015, opposition to the course advocated by economists such as Sinn and other economic politicians emerged at the European level. This pan-European positioning strategy of the SYRIZA discourse is underpinned, for example, by numerous examples of solidarization from a large number of politicians and economists with concern for Greek left-wing populists. Varoufakis is here regarded as a prominent example, but we find a similar discourse logic among his current and former political-economic allies. Therefore, speaking in the name of the SYRIZA movement was, on the symbolic-imaginary level, not restricted to actors with a Greek passport.

The SYRIZA movement not only emerged as a radical-democratic left-wing opposition. In addition, certain discursive protagonists entered the public media as a kind of "star economists". The most prominent among them was Varoufakis. Varoufakis studied and completed his doctorate at more left-wing, Keynesian-oriented institutions in the United Kingdom (Essex, Cambridge), before becoming professor of economics in Athens in 2000 and Greek Finance Minister in 2015 for a few weeks. At the same time, he was a visiting professor at the University of Texas. In terms of *institutional embeddings*, Varoufakis can be regarded as an ordinary economics professor with an international inclination and an interest in economic policy. Varoufakis has never achieved the highest consecration in economics, and he was not deeply anchored in the institutional structure of the political system. This accounts for his low *academic* and *political* capital. Therefore, the capital structure that makes up his institutional position was rather weak, compared to people like Sinn, even if Varoufakis possessed enough academic and political capital to enter the game. Nonetheless, people like Varoufakis increasingly switched to the role of "star economist" in the collective imaginary of the impending economic and political conflict in Europe. Furthermore, other international economists, who supported the Greek position, also contributed to this map of "stars" in the economics academic business (such as the son of the famous US economist Kenneth Galbraith, James Galbraith, who provided expertise to the SYRIZA government).

The imaginary positioning strategy that is put into practice in light of an academic excellence dispositif appears as a "takeover" of symbolic capital, mainly generated in the media realm. For the Greek rebels have been able to hijack the academic myths, mainly produced in more orthodox-conservative academic milieus of the economics discipline, to compensate for the deficits in institutional capital, as Varoufakis was "only" an ordinary professor and otherwise obtained hardly any institutional power position to increase his public visibility in the media. In this respect, it can be assumed that the Greek advocates were able to achieve high symbolic visibility for a certain time, not only in the media but also in the policy fields of other European nation-states. This was possible even though the institutional embedding remained rather weak.

The critical-democratic discourse logic

However, Varoufakis et al. have not only challenged the symbolic and institutional power relations in the European economic policy debate that was dominated by a certain German ordoliberalism at this point. As studies have shown, ordoliberalism, or neoliberalism, has never been the dominant theory and policy in most European countries (Hall, 1989). On the contrary, most countries feel more comfortable with demand-oriented policies, even today after years of ordoliberal practice of the Maastricht regime (Hacker & Koch, 2017). But speaking about this preference needs public support and official legitimacy. And this was achieved, primarily, because the *resolute positioning logic* of the liberal-conservative hegemony became more and more questioned and replaced by a new, *critical-democratic imaginary order* proposed by the Greek symbolic revolution. The following example taken from Robert Boyer, which is typical Keynesian discourse, illustrates how this critical-democratic discourse logic works (see also Maesse, 2018a: 22 f.):

> (1) The contemporary wide-scale austerity measures are likely to fail in most countries. (2) The first *fallacy* derives from the *false diagnosis* that the present crisis is the outcome of **lax public spending policy**, when it is *actually* the outcome of a **private credit-led speculative boom**.
> (Boyer, 2012, abstract, emphasis added by Jens Maesse)

What we can observe in this excerpt is a permanent dialogue between two antagonistic perspectives, evoked by discursive markers. On the one hand is the position of the opponent (the neoliberal other), which is kept at a distance from the speaker through hedges ("fallacy"). On the other hand, the discourse expresses the position of the speaker marked by a booster ("actually"). With both markers, certain macroeconomic labels are connected that help the reader identify the names of the political antagonists (marked in bold). This is how the discourse produces a symbolic-imaginary framework consisting of two antagonistic camps, and the public reader can follow the conflict between them. The democratic character of this discourse logic does not come from the possibility of the speaker not opting for both (and thus being "neutral"); rather, the speaker always expresses solidarity for one position. But the other position is not demonized or ignored, as in many neoliberal or technocratic discourses. Both positions, the speaker and the other, have a "legal" existence in this symbolic-imaginary order.

While the other in the conservative discourse is usually demonized, systematically devalued, and discursively excluded, now the (neoliberal) other of the critical-democratic camp is defined as a systematic alternative to the Keynesian program of "me". Thus, the other is *antagonized*. As Chantal Mouffe (2005) has pointed out, an antagonistic discourse order is democratic because it offers alternative thinking and behaving. A critical-democratic order, as I use this notion here, does not imply that people agree with Europe and that all problems are solved. And it does not mean that every utterance in economic policy discourses follows a post-technocratic, post-resolute logic. It rather implies open conflict, disagreement, and pessimism among the actors throughout Europe; but it also implies the possibility of evoking institutional transformations of European institutions, and it makes it easier for critics of neoliberalism and ordoliberalism to challenge established ideas and concepts in economic policy, such as a more moderate monetary policy (as represented by Mario Draghi), a greater sensibility to poverty and unemployment as economic problems (as in many debates and reports about the southern European countries), a discussion about the need for investment programs in Europe (such as the Juncker Plan), and many more.

This critical tendency takes many forms: the successful Portuguese economic policy of the center-left coalition government is only one significant example of this transformation of the imaginary order; the political chaos in Italy and the social and economic policies demanded by the Five Star Movement may be seen as part of this antagonistic tendency; the Polish right-wing government has also introduced social benefits for mothers; finally, Macron's European policy initiative, which (in contrast to his neoliberal domestic policies) finds support and sympathy among many Keynesians and other left-wing activists in Europe in particular, may also be seen as an effect of a new symbolic-imaginary order of interpretation and perception that would hardly be possible without the rise of SYRIZA.

From the 1990s until the Euro crisis, the neoliberal TINA logic and the resolute positioning style of neoliberal thinking were able to present their position as the only truth in town. This logic is now eroding. How does this relate to other regions of the dispositif, especially the political-institutional region of European economic governance?

Economic theory as a positioning metaphor

The field of European governance has a relatively long history. Since the foundation of the EU in 1992, the institutions of European economic policy have been strongly influenced by ordoliberal economic ideas, including budgetary discipline and price stability at the core. These governance measures were applied in European market places for goods, capital, and labor regulated by common standards. Budgetary discipline was provided through the Stability and Growth Pact, including balanced national budgets and a limitation on public debt. Price stability was the main task of the ECB, which was expected to keep European inflation at the 2% level. Further economic policies, such as wage policy, investments, infrastructure policy, industrial policy, or fiscal policy, were left to the nation-states' competencies. Yet, especially Keynesians always rejected this institutional logic as a one-sided supply-oriented structure that hinders economic growth, restricts innovations to a few areas, and stops social development.

The crisis as a driver of institutional transformation

After the spillover of the US real estate and financial crisis in 2007, this institutional network slipped into crisis, and crisis management practices were established (Heinrich & Kutter, 2014). In a first step, the ECB responded with extraordinary measures that were further developed in the following years: Money market intervention was accompanied by massive cuts in the general interest rate, which were later complemented by massive purchasing programs of government bonds and other assets. Through detailed interventions in financial markets, the ECB was able to stop the crisis, restrict sovereign debts in the countries of southern Europe, and bring Europe's economies back on a GDP growth path soon after 2009. With these measures, the ECB has not only exceeded its mandate, it has also defined new fields of intervention beyond its legislative competency. At the same time, there was a discussion about the introduction of Eurobonds intended to secure public funding in Europe. Finally, a crisis rescue mechanism was installed, initially through the European Financial Stability Facility (EFSF) and later through the ESM: States in need of funding could be refinanced by these institutions, and in turn had to accept reform measures that essentially amounted to austerity. This entire crisis management strategy was no longer compatible with the Maastricht logic (Bieling & Heinrich, 2015).

The Euro crisis and the subsequent takeover by SYRIZA can be considered the final act of this Euro crisis drama, and the takeover of SYRIZA had a significant impact on the institutional morphology of the dispositif. The conflicts in this crisis not only deal with economic policy theory, as explained in the previous section. They are furthermore an integral part of an ongoing conflict over institutional transformations in European economic governance. Underneath the surface of economic theory language, the introduction of new, and the transformation of established, institutions was negotiated simultaneously. The demands made in the name of the Greek crisis to "stop austerity" are therefore not only an economic policy positioning strategy. This discursive intervention relates rather to a second statement aiming at a transformation of precisely that field of European institutions in which legal positions are formed. Indeed, support for the Greek economy, as called for by SYRIZA and many other actors, would have meant suspension of the Stability and Growth Pact. While the ECB virtually singlehandedly broke off the dictum of price stability, the Greek crisis discourse is part of a discourse strategy undermining the Maastricht criteria. Both discourse strategies can be understood as attacks on a stability-oriented institutional framework in Europe, and both were gradually successful.

This gradual success is reflected by a number of new institutions that have been introduced (ESM, Banking Union). The new role of the ECB appears to be largely accepted. And alternative policy strategies are increasingly discussed, for example within the framework of the Five Presidents Report, the Juncker Plan, and the Macron initiative. Here, a couple of new elements of a future European institutional agenda become relevant, such as European investment initiatives, the introduction of a European economic government including a new budget, a European finance minister, joint debt management (Eurobonds), and a European social policy. The crisis has opened the EU governance structure to the introduction of new elements.

The discourse position of European officials

Gradual progress and institutional transformation are reflected by new institutional positioning strategies that can be described as *moderating strategies* of positioning. As the following example from the *Five Presidents Report* published in the midst of the Greek crisis in June 2015 shows, the speaker takes a mediating discourse position that tries to reconcile two paradigmatic alternatives:

> Europe's Economic and Monetary Union (EMU) today is like a **house that was built over decades** *but* only *partially finished*. When the storm hit, its **walls and roof** had to be stabilized quickly. It is *now high time to reinforce its foundations* and turn it into what EMU was meant to be: a place of prosperity based on *balanced economic growth and* **price stability**, a **competitive social market economy**, aiming at *full employment and social progress*. To achieve this, we will need to take further steps to complete EMU.
>
> (Juncker, Tusk, Dijsselbloem, Draghi, & Schulz, 2015: 4, emphasis added)

The discourse presents the speaker's moderating attitude by allowing two positions to emerge throughout the text excerpt that can be assigned to the neoliberal-stability–oriented camp and the Keynesian paradigm. While the markers for the stability camp are highlighted in **bold**, the markers for the Keynesian camp are *italicized*. These markers are used to identify academic-ideological affiliations and are not classical enunciative markers such as deixis, polyphony, or boosters/hedges. Rather, they are linguistic entities that are mainly used by field insiders as positioning markers. I suggest calling these discourse markers "conventionalizers", as they retrieve conventional insider knowledge about the political-ideological-social affiliation of certain types of language. While deixis/polyphony and boosters/hedges tend to be *universalistic* discourse markers, conventionalizers are *specific* discourse markers.

What we find is a moderating attitude of the speaker maneuvering through two camps and striving to put them in dialogue. This is done, in particular, by markers of negation (but) and time (now) and simple conjunctions (and). The economic terms (balanced economic growth/price stability/competitive social market economy/full employment and social progress) are by no means primarily used to negotiate economic policy theory. Rather, the language of theory is used as metaphor, negotiating an institutional conflict and moderating a situation of institutional transformation. As is typical for every metaphorical function, words are drained of their "original" content (economic theory) in order to be refilled with new meaning (institutional outlook). As such a metaphor, economic language is used to speak about governance possibilities within a governance structure; that is, by the very speech act itself, reflexively taken into question.

As we have already seen in the discrepancies between Sinn and Varoufakis/ SYRIZA, the institutional background plays an important role in discursive positioning strategies, because it accounts for complex meaning-making dynamics. In the case of the *Five Presidents* discourse, we can assume that economic policy phrases are not based on coherent institutional embeddings in an academic system. Rather, economic language serves as a positioning metaphor in an institutional discourse that deals with political-administrative responsibilities and related issues about economic governance and management. Economic governance is now discussed and exercised against the background of a moderating positioning strategy. It is neither a "strong state" nor "technocratic expertise" that controls the political and economic conditions. What we see is a discourse actor who moderates conflicting interests by dealing with different politico-economic questions. This speaker's position appears against the background of an ongoing transformation of the European institutional fabric. The institutional background of this moderating attitude is the situation of institutional transformation itself. However, the old governance order (Maastricht) is gradually suspended and can no longer sustain fixed speaker positions, while the new order does not yet exist, as it is about to be negotiated through discursive conflict. Therefore, a low degree of institutional coherence is combined with a moderating discourse strategy on the symbolic-imaginary level, while both aspects articulate and accelerate transformations of the EU economic governance system.

The rise of SYRIZA in the field of economic theory has contributed to shifting the symbolic-imaginary order of economic policy discourse towards a critical-democratic logic of interpretation. At the same time, it is part of a more complex conflict over transformation of the European institutional framework in the field of economic policy. This is how the Greek and the Euro crises bring together and constitute two regions of the dispositif. The positioning strategies in the first conflict have an indirect influence on the positioning strategies in the second field of conflict, connected through invisible threads. While in the early 2000s, neoliberal economic policies were often presented in a technocratic style against the background of the fixed institutional structure of the Maastricht Treaty (for example in the form of "reports" from the European Commission to the states about compliance with stability criteria following "petitions" from the "sinners" to postpone the timeframe and have non-enforcement of sanctions), a new wind now appears to blowing in the hallways of Brussels, while the institutional morphology is changing. Economic policies and ordoliberal institutions are both questioned, but the results in terms of positioning strategies differ, because they do not belong to the same area of the dispositif. Whereas the discourse on *economic theory* deals with different possibilities of economic management, the *institutional* discourse seeks to implement an incomplete symbolic order on the governance level.

Conclusion: complex positioning strategies in a heterogeneous dispositif

The aim of this chapter was to illustrate a dispositif analysis of transnational fields. Based on a discourse as well as field analysis of special actors of the Euro crisis discourse, the analysis has shown that Europe, understood as a dispositif, is currently in a state of transformation. This status of an institutional and discursive disequilibrium can be expressed as a movement from and struggle over different institutional and discursive position(ing)s, as illustrated in Table 11.1.

Whereas most analyses offer an interpretation of the EU crisis discourse that elaborates the structural conditions of the Brussels administration that seem to inhibit policy change and the implementation of a left-wing political program (e.g., Georgakakis & Lebaron, 2018), I prefer a different reading of the crisis discourse. My interpretation argues for higher sensibility for the new elements that emerged out of the crisis. We see, from my dispositif analytical perspective, the fissures in the Euro crisis discourse order, the transformative aspects on the level of governance institutions, and gaps in the fabric of Europe that open up space for future possibilities. In my view, Europe cannot be reduced to the Brussels apparatus. Europe is rather a framework of thinking, perceiving, and social action that penetrates all kinds of national institutions, debates, and policies. Today, the

Table 11.1 Institutional positions and discursive positionings

	Pre-crisis period (1990 until 2009)	Post-crisis period (after 2009)
Institutional positions	Much political, academic, and administrative capital (neoliberal economists); high degree of institutional coherence (EU-governance)	Little political, academic, and administrative capital (post-neoliberal economists); low degree of institutional coherence (EU governance)
Discursive positionings	resolute; predominantly technocratic (EU governance)	Critical-democratic (experts) and moderating logics (EU institutions)

politico-discursive logic of the Maastricht-EU is no longer at work. Europe is rather developing towards a post-neoliberal constitution whose structural elements will be established step by step.

The reason for this apparently "optimistic" picture is based on my analytical view of the crisis discourse. In my perspective, the critical discourses have by no means failed – Varoufakis's withdrawal in 2015 has neither put an end to his career as a European heretic nor to the SYRIZA project. The SYRIZA project is not only an alternative model for Greece; it is furthermore a name for a general alternative for the entire European economic governance, as the comeback of social programs in many European countries show. Through the Greece case (but also through the ongoing Brexit discourse) it became obvious for every nation-state in Europe that national autonomy does not exist anymore, at least in political priority fields (macroeconomic management, taxes, finances, industrial policy). The political economies of Europe are influenced by European dynamics that become visible in every little aspect, from industrial regulations to the common market and the customs union. Even national social policy is highly influenced by Europe due to budgetary restrictions and European citizenship (free movement of workers). Against this backdrop, figures such as Varoufakis or Thomas Piketty appear as European "innovators" not despite, but because of, the contradiction between a relative low amount of institutional capital and high symbolic visibility. New elements cannot emerge from a fixed social space; it rather results from the fissures of structural dissolutions.

Notes

1 Empirical data for field analysis as well as text excerpts of discourse analysis are selected on the basis of document studies, field studies, and ethnographic analyses carried out in the FED project (2011–2015, Universities of Mainz and Warwick, funded by the Volkswagenstiftung). The main selection criteria are their belonging to certain groups and actors and their relation to the economic crisis that culminated in the so-called Euro crisis that began in 2009 and became a political drama in 2015.
2 A leading German economic newspaper.
3 A leading German daily newspaper.

References

Angermuller, J. (2014). *Poststructuralist Discourse Analysis: Subjectivity in Enunciative Pragmatics*. London: Palgrave.
Beckert, J. (2016). *Imagined Futures: Fictional Representations and Capitalist Dynamics*. Cambridge, MA: Harvard University Press.
Bernhard, S., & Schmidt-Wellenburg, C. (Eds.). (2014). Politische Soziologie transnationaler Felder. *Schwerpunktheft Berliner Journal Für Soziologie, 24*. Wiesbaden: Springer VS.
Bieling, H.-J., & Heinrich, M. (2015). Central Banking in der Krise: Neue Rolle der Europäischen Zentralbank im Finanzkapitalismus. *Widerspruch 66, 34*(2), 25–36.
Bigo, D. (2011). Pierre Bourdieu and International Relations: Power of Practices, Practices of Power. *International Political Sociology, 5*(3), 225–258.

Bourdieu, P. (1989). *Distinction: A Social Critique of the Judgement of Taste*. London: Routledge.

Boyer, R. (2012). The Four Fallacies of Contemporary Austerity Policies: The Lost Keynesian Legacy. *Cambridge Journal of Economics, 36*(1), 283–312.

Bräuninger, M., Haucap, J., & Muck, J. (2011). Was lesen und schätzen Ökonomen im Jahr 2011? *DICE Ordnungspolitische Perspektiven, 18.*

Buchholz, L. (2016). What Is a Global Field? Theorizing Fields Beyond the Nation-State. *The Sociological Review Monographs, 64*(2), 31–60.

Busch, K., Troost, A., Schwan, G., Bsirske, F., Bischoff, J., Schrooten, M., & Wolf, H. (2016). *A Europe Built on Solidarity Is Possible! Pamphlet for Another European Union*. Hamburg: VSA.

Butz, A., & Wohlrabe, K. (2016). Die Ökonomen-Rankings 2015 von Handelsblatt, FAZ und RePEc: Methodik, Ergebnisse, Kritik und Vergleich. *Ifo Working Paper No. 212.*

Costantini, O. (2017). Political Economy of the Stability and Growth Pact. *European Journal of Economics and Economic Policies: Intervention, 14*(3), 333–350.

Delanty, G., & Rumford, C. (2005). *Rethinking Europe: Social Theory and the Implications of Europeanization*. London: Routledge.

Desrosières, A. (1998). *The Politics of Large Numbers: A History of Statistical Reasoning*. Cambridge; London: Oxford University Press.

Diaz-Bone, R. (2017). Classifications, Quantifications and Quality Conventions in Markets – Perspectives of the Economics of Convention. *Historical Social Research, 42*(1), 238–262.

Diez, T. (2001). Europe as a Discursive Battleground: Discourse Analysis and European Integration Studies. *Cooperation and Conflict, 36*(1), 5–38.

Eder, K. (2011). Europe as a Narrative Network. In S. Lucarelli, F. Cerutti & V. A. Schmidt (Eds.), *Debating Political Identity and Legitimacy in the European Union* (pp. 38–53). London; New York, NY: Routledge.

Flassbeck, H., & Steinhardt, P. (2018). *Gescheiterte Globalisierung: Ungleichheit, Geld und die Renaissance des Staates*. Berlin: Edition Suhrkamp.

Foucault, M. (1972). *The Archaeology of Knowledge*. New York, NY: Pantheon.

Foucault, M. (1980). *Power/Knowledge: Selected Interviews and Other Writings, 1972–1977*. New York, NY: Pantheon.

Georgakakis, D., & Lebaron, F. (2018). Yanis (Varoufakis), the Minotaur, and the Field of Eurocracy. *Historical Social Research, 43*(3), 216–247.

Georgakakis, D., & Rowell, J. (2013). *The Field of Eurocracy: Mapping EU Actors and Professionals*. London: Palgrave.

Go, J. (2017). Myths of Nation and Empire: The Logic of America's Liberal Empire-State. *Thesis Eleven, 139*(1), 69–83.

Go, J., & Krause, M. (2016). Fielding Transnationalism: An Introduction. *The Sociological Review Monographs, 64*(2), 6–30.

Hacker, B., & Koch, M. C. (2017). The Divided Eurozone: Mapping Conflicting Interests on the Reform of the Monetary Union. *FES Report.*

Hall, P. A. (Ed.). (1989). *The Political Power of Economic Ideas: Keynesianism Across Nations*. Princeton, NJ: Princeton University Press.

Hamann, J., Maesse, J., Scholz, R., & Angermuller, J. (2019). The Academic Dispositif: Towards a Context-Centred Discourse Analysis. In R. Scholz (Ed.), *Quantifying Approaches to Discourse for Social Scientists* (pp. 51–87). London; New York, NY: Palgrave.

Heinrich, M., & Kutter, A. (2014). A Critical Juncture in EU Integration? The Eurozone Crisis and Its Management 2010–2012. In F. Panizza & G. Philip (Eds.), *Moments of*

Truth: The Politics of Financial Crises in Comparative Perspective (pp. 120–139). London: Routledge.

Huffschmid, J. (1994). *Wem gehört Europa? Wirtschaftspolitik und Kapitalstrategien.* Heilbronn: Distel-Verlag.

Juncker, J. C., Tusk, D., Dijsselbloem, J., Draghi, M., & Schulz, M. (2015). *Completing Europe's Economic and Monetary Union.* Bruxelles: EU.

Lacan, J. (1991). *Das Seminar Buch 2: Das Ich in der Theorie Freuds und in der Technik der Psychoanalyse.* Weinheim: Quadriga.

Lebaron, F. (2008). Central Bankers in the Contemporary Global Field of Power: A 'Social Space' Approach. *The Sociological Review, 56*(1), 121–144.

Lehndorff, S. (2014). Die spaltende Integration Europas Ein Überblick. In S. Lehndorff (Ed.), *Der Triumph gescheiterter Ideen in Europa – Revisited Zehn Länderstudien* (pp. 7–39). Hamburg: VSA.

Lenger, A. (2018). Socialization in the Academic and Professional Field: Revealing the Homo Oeconomicus Academicus. *Historical Social Research, 43*(3), 39–62.

Lyotard, J.-F. (1989). *Der Widerstreit.* München: Fink.

Maesse, J. (2010). *Die vielen Stimmen des Bologna-Prozesses: Zur diskursiven Logik eines bildungspolitischen Programms.* Bielefeld: transcript.

Maesse, J. (2015). Economic Experts: A Discursive Political Economy of Economics. *Journal of Multicultural Discourses, 10*(3), 279–305.

Maesse, J. (2017). The Elitism Dispositif: Hierarchization, Discourses of Excellence and Organizational Change in European Economics. *Higher Education, 73*(6), 909–927.

Maesse, J. (2018a). Austerity Discourses in Europe: How Economic Experts Create Identity Projects. *Innovation: The European Journal of Social Science Research, 31*(1), 8–24.

Maesse, J. (2018b). Globalization Strategies and the Economics Dispositif: Insights from Germany and the UK. *Historical Social Research, 43*(3), 120–146.

Maesse, J., & Hamann, J. (2016). Die Universität als Dispositiv: Die gesellschaftliche Einbettung von Bildung und Wissenschaft aus diskurstheoretischer Perspektive. *Zeitschrift für Diskursforschung, 4*(1), 29–50.

Mouffe, C. (2005). *On the Political.* London: Routledge.

Mudge, S. L., & Vauchez, A. (2012). Building Europe on a Weak Field: Law, Economics, and Scholarly Avatars in Transnational Politics. *American Journal of Sociology, 118*(2), 449–492.

Ötsch, W. O., Pühringer, S., & Hirte, K. (2017). *Netzwerke des Marktes: Ordoliberalismus als Politische Ökonomie.* Wiesbaden: Springer.

Pühringer, S., & Hirte, K. (2015). The Financial Crisis as a Heart Attack: Discourse Profiles of Economists in the Financial Crisis. *Journal of Language and Politics, 14*(4), 599–625.

Robertson, R. (1992). *Globalization: Social Theory and Global Culture.* London: Sage.

Schmidt-Wellenburg, C. (2017). Europeanisation, Stateness, and Professions: What Role Do Economic Expertise and Economic Experts Play in European Political Integration? *European Journal of Cultural and Political Sociology, 4*(4), 430–456.

Schmidt-Wellenburg, C. (2018a). Europa und seine Krise als umkämpfte Objekte volkswirtschaftlicher Deutungen im Feld deutsch-sprachiger Volkswirt*innen. *Culture, Practice and Europeanisation, 3*(2), 30–55.

Schmidt-Wellenburg, C. (2018b). German Economists' Discourse on European Crisis. *Historical Social Research, 43*(3), 147–188.

Sinn, H.-W. (2014). Austerity, Growth and Inflation: Remarks on the Eurozone's Unresolved Competitiveness Problem. *The World Economy*, *37*(1), 1–13.

Streeck, W. (2014). *Buying Time: The Delayed Crisis of Democratic Capitalism*. London: Verso.

Sum, N.-L., & Jessop, B. (2013). *Towards a Cultural Political Economy: Putting Culture in Its Place in Political Economy*. Cheltenham: Edward Elgar.

Wullweber, J. (2015). Global Politics and Empty Signifiers: The Political Construction of High Technology. *Critical Policy Studies*, *9*(1), 78–96.

Zienkowski, J. (2016). *Articulations of Self and Politics in Activist Discourse: A Discourse Analysis of Critical Subjectivities in Minority Debates*. London: Palgrave.

Chapter 12

Tracing "the transnational" in the nationalization of school policy

The transformation of standards-based reform in the United States[*]

Sigrid Hartong

Introduction

A central theme in worldwide education policy transformation has been the emergence of standards-based reform, including curriculum and teaching standards, standardized assessments, and standardized monitoring and data collection procedures (e.g., Steiner-Khamsi, 2012; Landri, 2018; for Japan, see Takayama, 2013; for Spain, see Engel, 2015; for Australia, see Gorur & Wu, 2015; and for the United States and Germany, see Hartong, 2015, 2016a, 2018b). Various scholars have documented the promotion of this governmental toolkit (standards, assessments, data-based monitoring) by an array of international organizations (such as the Organisation for Economic Co-operation and Development, OECD), global expert networks, and think tanks, which together contribute to the growing adoption of common programs and values in countries across the world (Lingard & Grek, 2007; Alexiadou et al., 2016: 1 f.). As Gulson and colleagues (2017: 1) argue,

> the presence of new [e.g. global] policy networks and relationalities means that educational policymaking and governance are no longer simply occurring within the prefigured boundaries of the nation state but now involve a diverse cast of new actors and organizations across new policy spaces.

In line with this idea, scholars applying field theoretical perspectives have convincingly reconstructed the rise of an international (or global) education field (e.g., Münch, 2009; Hartong, 2012; Sellar & Lingard, 2013), which has gained increasing autonomy and power to affect national and local education contexts.

At the same time, however, scholars have documented that processes of transnationalization and the emergence of transnational fields – and this is also true for the enforcement of standards-based reform – neither equate with the rising power of international organizations or networks alone, nor with the concurrent diminishing relevance of nationalism (or localism). Instead, as Tröhler and Lenz (2015) remind us, on the one hand the contemporary world continues to be regularly imagined as made up of competing nation-states, a system which instruments such as standardized international large-scale assessments (e.g., the Programme for International Student Assessment, PISA) have helped to flourish (see also Waldow & Steiner-Khamsi, 2018). On the other hand, particularly when considering standards-based governance, it is also "the national" that has (re)gained growing importance as a (globally) accountable standard-setter and output-controller – ultimately, at least to some extent, enforcing container-like images of homogeneity within national boundaries. However, again one needs to be mindful not to confuse this imagination of national standardization with the intra-national networks, actors, and discursive formations that construct and stabilize it, and which have become simultaneously engaged in transnational relations. Hence, as Ball (2016) has shown, a key part of research on transnationalization (and transnational fields) is in fact understanding the manifold relations between international and intra-national policy flows, which together constitute particular policy spaces (such as "nationalized" standards-based governance), rather than trying to disentangle these spaces into distinct levels of governance (Piattoeva, 2018).

Building on this line of argumentation, this chapter provides selected examples of how standards-based reform in the United States from the 1960s onwards has emerged as a "fragmented, multi-scalar and multi-sectoral distribution of activity" (Dale & Robertson, 2012: 23), particularly around the collection of standardized school (performance) data,[1] while paying particular attention to the relation between shifting policy networks and shifting "representations" (Dale & Robertson, 2009: 1119) or "constitutions" (Savage & Lewis, 2017) of the national and transnational.

The United States provides an excellent case with which to trace the particular relevance of intra-national policy flows, given its federal, multilevel policy architecture in which power devolution (e.g., within standards-based reform) has been an issue of continuous political contestation and fragility (Wallner, Savage, Hartong, & Engel, 2020). Additionally, large cultural, social, and historic differences between states and regions have also played a key, yet widely under-researched role, not only in promoting standardization as a tool for equalizing school access and quality, but also in pushing one region in particular (the southern US states, institutionalized in the Southern Regional Education Board, SREB) to become a key advocate for nationalizing standards-based reform (see the third section in this chapter).

To better approach these intra-national policy flows, this chapter applies the dual lenses of policy network analysis (as the primary lens) and field theoretical thinking (as the secondary lens), which I explain in greater detail in the next section. In the third section, I then provide selected examples of the transformation of US standards-based reform between the 1960s and the 2010s, revealing its gradual transformation into an increasingly autonomous, nationalized field context, operating through topological and heterarchical policy relations. In this field, the national manifests itself as a heterogeneous, simultaneously fragile and stabilized assemblage of particular policy networks and practices, which nonetheless increasingly "reflect transnational traits and impulses" (Savage & Lewis, 2017: 1). I end with a discussion of the findings and implications for future research.

Engaging dual lenses of policy network analysis and field theoretical thinking

This chapter applies the dual lenses of policy network analysis and field theory thinking to examine shifting manifestations of nationalization and transnationalization in US standards-based reform, channeled in particular through the collection and relation-making of standardized data.

There has been a growing body of transnationalization studies that embrace field theoretical thinking (for an overview, see Schmidt-Wellenburg & Bernhard, Chapter 1) and identify new policy fields in which actors frequently operate across "traditional" field borders (see Fertikh, Chapter 9), such as national-international or education-economy, while contributing to the configuration of new ideas, structures, and material and symbolic orders (Marttila, 2014). Thus, such actors – who have exemplarily been described as "field hoppers" (Hartong, 2018a) – promote structural homogeneities between traditional fields, producing cross-field consolidation of particular field positions, and thus fostering the emergence of cross-field actor alliances within more intermediary (e.g., transnationalized) field structures. At the same time, however, approaching such structures both conceptually and methodologically has proved increasingly challenging, resulting in a continuous elaboration of field theory, including fruitful integrations of field and network analysis (e.g., Bernhard, 2010; Hennig & Kohl, 2011; Hartong & Schwabe, 2013; Fuhse, 2009).[2] Building on these developments, this chapter seeks to show how heterarchical and topological approaches of policy network analysis offer a fruitful (and simpler) way (than classical social policy network analysis, for example) to facilitate the empirical and methodological "tracing" of transforming field configurations in times of transnationalization.

Over the past few decades, a wide array of critical education policy research has explicitly addressed new dynamics associated with the ongoing globalization, standardization, and datafication of governance, thus also exploring the use of policy network analysis to "trace" growing global-local dynamics and complexities (e.g., Ong & Collier, 2005) as well as new patterns of policymaking across state, market, and private actors (Ball, 2016). In other words, scholars have been reconsidering how these processes of complex "rescalation" might be mapped, and how further elaborated scales of policy landscapes (beyond purely vertical, horizontal, or sectoral scalation) can be developed (see for example, Carney, 2009; Savage & Lewis, 2017; Staunæs, Brogger, & Krejsler, 2018). Thus, the past decade has witnessed a clear turn toward more open, relational policy approaches, which better capture (both conceptually and methodologically) the "piecemeal" (Ball, 2016: 1) character or "assemblage" (Savage & Lewis, 2017; Hartong, 2018b) of policies that (trans)form in concert with particular spaces of policymaking. This has also included a stronger focus on the constant (re)production of such spaces ("spatial turn") and the ways in which particular imaginations of space (such as "the national" or "the transnational") shape and are shaped by the educational phenomena, processes, and policy networks under examination (Gulson et al., 2017; Sobe & Kowalszyk, 2018: 198).

In line with this thinking, policy networks have been found to be increasingly characterized by *heterarchization* and *topologization:*[3] *heterarchical* policy relations (as applied i.a. by Ball, 2009; Olmedo, Bailey, & Ball, 2013; and Hartong, 2014) address new arrangements of policy actors operating, in particular, *between* levels (global to local) or sectors (e.g., private and public), while both new (e.g., international) or existent (e.g., domestic) actors become (re)assembled around particular (e.g., standardization) practices. One such example is international large-scale assessments that build on a complex network of international, national, and local actors, from governments and public agencies to private (test service) providers, who collectively enact assessments. The heterarchy-approach has hereby been found to be particularly useful for capturing the rising importance of intermediary actors such as think tanks, advocacy actors, philanthropists or – in the case of standards-based reform – data mediators that enforce and catalyse global-local or cross-sectoral policy flows (Steiner-Khamsi & Waldow, 2012; Ball, 2016; Hartong, 2016a).

At the same time, the heterarchy-approach pays particular attention to identifying forms of (sometimes hidden) "meta-governance" (Ball, 2009), which manage and often more indirectly control or align "collaborative" network constellations. For example, as Bloem (2016) has shown using the case of PISA, the OECD secretariat of education has been operating as one such powerful meta-governing agency, whose influence *within* the OECD has also often been underestimated. Meta-governance hereby not only refers to material asymmetries, but also to the distribution of symbolic power, often evoked through a particular flow of selective knowledge, such as particular forms of data. In this regard, "heterarchy assumes both a relative meaning of partnership within network structures and dominant sets of defined institutional practices to govern collaborative spaces" (Hartong, 2015: 16).

This specific consideration of symbolic power is also found in the characterization of policy network relations as increasingly *topological* (applied, e.g., by Allen, 2011; Lewis & Lingard, 2015; Ball, 2016; or Hartong, 2018b), which in the context of this contribution seems particularly relevant for exploring the important dimension of relating data in standards-based reform, one example being the implementation of monitoring infrastructures and performance comparisons. As defined by Rawolle and Lingard (2014: 608), topologization refers to "a new post-Euclidian geometry of spacial [network] relations, [integrated] [. . .] surface[s] created across the globe, helping to constitute a new culture through metrics, models, measures, and comparisons". In other words, Rawolle and Lingard point to a significant (technical) (re)construction of educational reality via numerical relation-making, comprising data which flow into standards, assessments, and monitoring practices, while also rearranging and empowering particular policy networks around data fabrication, mediation, and usage (Hartong, 2016a, 2018b).

As will be shown in the later sections of this chapter, an important mechanism in the gradual nationalization of standards-based reform in the United States after the 1960s[4] has been the fabrication of national data spaces for cross-state comparison, in which states are turned into equalized numerical units and benchmarked (thus topologically related) either against each other, against supra-state standards, or, later on, against international competitors, thus explicitly bridging territorial distance.[5] As argued by Lewis and Lingard (2015: 623), "territorial distance – as measured in kilometres or miles – becomes less reflective of near and far, of place and space, than does the topological notion of 'closeness' as expressed through relationality and connectedness". However, while topologization thus stresses ongoing processes of what could be described as governmental deterritorialization (which could actually be something different than transnationalization), this chapter addresses the as yet under-researched question of how this actually affects the (re)configuration of (intra-)national policy geographies such as territories, scales, or places (Hartong, 2016a).

In fact, while there has been a gradually increasing body of research adopting a critical orientation toward such shifting policy networks, the question of how different heterarchical and/or topological networks operate in (contesting or complementary) relation to each other remains unresolved. Addressing this question, a key argument of this contribution is that the transformation of US standards-based reform between the 1960s and 2010s has brought about not only a significant extension, but simultaneously and slightly paradoxically, a gradual reduction of (aligned) policy networks that manage and control the standardization of education, utilizing (the same) data. While early national standardization activities in the 1960s (including the standardized evaluation of federally funded schools and the implementation of the first national assessment of educational progress, NAEP) involved a wide range of new (partly contested) policy networks operating around these activities in an often uncoordinated way, later decades, and particularly the 2000s, witnessed increasing centralization, coordination, and alignment when implementing standardization, including the gradual dominance of particular (heterarchical/topological) policy networks. I argue that field theoretical thinking can offer a useful tool here to better capture this wider macro context of relations *between* policy networks, which, by competing for material and symbolic power (Bourdieu, 2001; Baier & Schmitz, 2012: 197), together evoke particular configurations of "the national" and "the transnational". At the same time, both conceptual lenses share an acknowledgement of the simultaneous existence of structural fragility and stabilization, which in field theory is also reflected in the question of field autonomy/heteronomy (Mangez & Hilgers, 2012). Thus, not only do the formation of heterarchies and the shift towards topologization appear as particular actor strategies to accumulate power and secure particular field positions, they also serve as a way to increase the autonomization of the field of standards-based reform against external influence (e.g., networks promoting a different way of governing education).

The (trans)nationalization of standards-based reform in US school policy between the 1960s and 2010s

The aim of the following section is to illuminate some examples[6] of how the emergence and transformation of US standards-based reform between the 1960s and the 2010s has been accompanied by shifting policy networks, particularly characterized by heterarchization and topologization, which resulted not only in the emergence of an increasingly autonomous field of standards-based reform, but also in shifting configurations of "the national" and "the transnational".

To understand the intra-national policy network transformations surrounding the rise of standards-based reform, it is important to take into consideration the regional and historically highly relevant distinction between the US states. Specifically, this distinction refers to (northern) states which prohibited slavery at an earlier date and played a rather significant national role in securing equal civil rights, versus (southern) states that for a long time defended slavery as a state right in opposition to national influence. While this historical distinction between northern and southern states became most prominent in the mid-nineteenth century during the Civil War (when there were two subnational "nations" fighting against each other), it continued to play a crucial role not only in the remaining resistance of southern states to providing equal educational access to different sections of the population, but also supported a strong conservatism in those states regarding the persistence of subnational education autonomy.

Despite this subnational divide, World War II did increase nationalism (and also a "national imaginary") as the United States defended itself as a union against international enemies, continuing after 1945 during the Cold War with Russia. In line with the idea of "catching up" with the East – further triggered by the famous Sputnik-shock in 1957 (Urban, 2010) – the federal government also implemented financial aid programs within education (the *National Defense Education Act*), all of which were nonetheless enacted on a voluntary basis without any significant monitoring procedures or standardization effects for the states. In the 1960s, however, this dramatically changed.

Precursors of topologization and heterarchization: Reforms in the 1960s and 1970s

Unlike any federal activity in US schooling until the 1950s, both the *Civil Rights Act* of 1964 and its according educational resolution, the *Elementary and Secondary Education Act* (ESEA) of 1965, clearly strengthened the national role in securing the equalization (and standardization) of school access and quality. The ESEA is of particularly significant relevance here, because it implemented a systematic, standardized federal funding scheme for supporting students in need (the so-called *Title 1 program*). Even though ESEA was organized as a voluntary funding scheme, it simultaneously and for the first time in US history, evoked the emergence of a multilevel policy network built around evaluation and monitoring – which was overseen, and thus meta-governed, by the Federal Department of Education (ED): "ESEA was not just a Federal handout to ease State and local educational budgets. It mandated a series of programs and priorities which involved a massive shift in the locus of policymaking power in American education" (Bailey & Mosher, 1968: 3). The amount of funding was thus calculated using a statistical formula, "computed on the basis of *nationally uniform* demographic and economic data" (Bailey & Mosher, 1968: 49, emphasis added) – data which had to be collected in a nationally standardized way, thus initiating the fabrication of the first topological space of nationally related and aligned calculation.

At the same time, states were obliged to have schools apply for Title 1 funding by using standardized indicators for evaluating not only their applications, but also the school projects that the money was used for. Evaluation data then had to be transmitted to the federal department, ensuring "that effective procedures, including provision for appropriate objective measurements of educational achievement, will be adopted for evaluating at least annually the effectiveness of the programs in meeting the special educational needs of educationally deprived children" (Bailey & Mosher, 1968: 51). To support the evaluation of projects, ESEA evoked the rise of a multiscale school effectiveness research network (Gomolla, 2013), as well as an empowerment of assessment providers around measuring and evaluating performance output, thus producing early forms of both heterarchical and topological relation-making across sectors and levels of policy.

A few years later, policy actors that had initially contributed to the empowerment of the federal department also started to promote the implementation of a nationally standardized, yet sample-based performance assessment, which then became the *National Assessment of Educational Progress* (NAEP). However, in order not to interfere with state educational authority and to prevent state resistance, the *Education Commission of the States* was founded as a new supra-state institution charged with overseeing the national assessment. In addition, NAEP was declared to not allow for cross-state performance comparisons (which, however, changed in the 1980s; see later) (Vinovskis, 2009: 17). While NAEP was initially funded by the Carnegie Foundation, after 1972 funding and coordination was taken over by the *National Center of Education Statistics* as the research arm of the federal department (Vinovskis, 1998: 8), which together with ESEA, now supervised two systems of national standardization, mediated through the relation-making of data.

In sum, the 1960s to 1970s saw several crucial policy network shifts related to the first-time implementation of (two different) nationalized topological spaces for standardized measurement: school evaluation (ESEA) and, later on, performance assessment (NAEP). At the same time, both programs covered only a small segment of schooling: ESEA evaluating one particular funding scheme for schools in need; NAEP using sample data from a selection of schools, age groups, and curricula without options for cross-state comparison. As a result, ESEA and NAEP clearly opened doors to further standardization and nationalization, particularly when regulations for federal funding became increasingly refined. Nevertheless, curriculum standards and standardized assessments for monitoring the performance of *all* US schools (as key elements of a nationalized field of standards-based reform) were not yet discussed by that time – although this was to change in the 1980s.

The southern push for "nationalizing" standards-based reform in the 1980s and 1990s

While the southern US states had historically opposed growing national influence over education, in the 1980s they turned into the key promoters of nationalizing standards-based reform, although this did include explicit limits on the federal capacity to hold states accountable for educational output. The Southern Regional Education Board (SREB), a non-profit organization founded as early as 1948, originally engaged in the implementation of data-based excellence standards for southern colleges and universities (SREB, 2013: 2–3). In 1981, the SREB, which by that time included 14 southern state members, turned toward K–12 education (SREB, 2013: 4), not only promoting cross-state education policy learning, but also evoking a stronger partnership between conservative governors and business actors, thus fostering and simultaneously meta-governing cross-sectoral relation-making. As powerful partners to the board, business actors strongly influenced the development of various reform initiatives in the southern region (Fuhrman, 2003: 8; Cuban, 2003), while simultaneously acting as "national" lobbyists for standards-based reform. The SREB adhered to the notion of preparing students for global competition, for example by developing standards to link school and higher education careers and by establishing standardized assessments that could be compared nationally (SREB, 2013: 4 f.).

When in 1983 the famous report *A Nation At Risk*[7] yet again painted a threatening picture of the United States lagging behind internationally, this played to the SREB's conservative interests, ultimately initiating a "national crusade" (Sacks, 2000) of education reform (see also Gordon, 2003; Mehta, 2013: 116), and the emergence of a national field of standards-based reform, initially ruled by SREB ideas and actors. Like the SREB, *A Nation At Risk* promoted stronger partnership between education and business interests, not only aiming for minimal standards (e.g., equal school access, as indirectly fostered in ESEA), but also for excellence as a national benchmark for every US student (Mehta, 2013: 42). This, as was argued by the SREB, demanded the development of a national curriculum and test standards (Ravitch, 2010: 22).

Building on this idea, it was again southern states which in the following years initiated corresponding reforms and further cross-state reform networks to share best practices, later partnering with the *National Governors Association*. In 1989, the reform alliance secured a further victory when President George H.W. Bush – a former SREB member – met with selected (southern) governors and business actors in Charlottesville, Virginia, to pass a catalogue of national education goals to improve the United States's global competitiveness, including the implementation of mandatory national curriculum standards. Corresponding federal laws in the 1990s included *America 2000* and *Goals 2000*, all of them (now declared national initiatives) promoted by former SREB members (Bill Clinton, Richard Riley, and Lamar Alexander) who in the 1990s served either as presidents or as education secretaries in the federal government. In this way, the SREB clearly operated as a heterarchy, building on cross-state, cross-sectoral, and cross-level policy relations (nonetheless embedded within one particular region of the country), while at the same time gradually filling powerful positions in the federal agencies with their own members. As a result, the SREB successfully provoked an increasingly stabilized imagination of "national" standards, assessments, and monitoring, based on the accumulation and reproduction of material and symbolic power.

Related to that transformation was a major change to the *National Assessment of Educational Progress* (NAEP, see last section), including a new test design which turned the assessment from "a passive thermometer to a much more aggressive posture" (Stake, 2007: 8). The new test design explicitly allowed for cross-state performance comparison, while it also significantly refined the (topological space of) NAEP data. Even though public access remained limited to aggregated data at that time, such data could now be customized to different student groups across the country:

> NAEP was redesigned in the early 1980s to cover four subject areas – reading, writing, math, and science – on a more frequent and regular schedule. In addition to the traditional assessments of 9-, 13-, and 17-year-olds, children in grades 3, 7, and 11 were to be examined. Improved matrix sampling of test items allowed for more rigorous analyses of the relationship between students' background information and their assessment scores. Finally, introduction of nonlinear scaling methods for data reporting allowed the clustering of related items.
>
> (Vinovskis, 1998: 13)

The transformation of NAEP was accompanied by the so-called wall chart-initiative (Stake, 2007: 8), which included the regular release by the federal department of individual state report cards summarizing educational performance. An evaluation report (the *Alexander-James Report*) was also included, authored by SREB member and reform promoter Lamar Alexander, who not only further advocated cross-state comparisons in NAEP, but also a turn from content-related curricular standards toward performance standards and a focus on literacy (Ravitch, 1983: 312). Consequently, the Education Commission of the States, which had formerly supervised the assessment, was replaced by the National Assessment Governing Board. Following Vinovskis (1998: 22),

> most board members were [. . .] selected because they appeared to agree with the general goals and orientation for NAEP as set forth in the Alexander-James report. When vacancies arose, either these individuals were reappointed or persons with similar views were selected.

In sum, the period from the 1980s until the 1990s marked the successful elaboration of a "national" constitution and imagination of standards-based reform that became gradually autonomized, with particular actors and policy networks achieving stabilized positions and articulating particular narratives within a now more clearly visible field context. Essentially, this nationalization of standards-based reform was supported by the heterarchical and topological relation-making triggered by the SREB. However, at the same time, the field remained fragile: even though the implementation of standards and standards-aligned assessments were now frequently discussed and successfully enforced at the state level, the idea of implementing national or supra-state curriculum standards failed to take hold – until the 2000s.

Establishing a (trans)nationalized field of heterarchies and topologies in the 2000s and 2010s

Responding to the failure to implement national curriculum standards, the federal government (not the reform alliance) increasingly focused on standardized performance monitoring *without* setting supra-state standards, as visible in the Elementary and Secondary Education Act (ESEA)'s reauthorization in 2001 of the *No Child Left Behind Act* (NCLB) (Anderson, 2007: 173; Payne, 2008: 10; Ravitch, 2010: 29). Thus, NCLB renounced the idea of national standards and instead relied on a standardized system of punishment and reward for state school performance, which was directly linked to the distribution of Title 1 funding (as the core element of ESEA). In this way, NCLB fabricated a new, nationally standardized, yet content-free tool – the *Adequate Yearly Progress* – for measuring the performance increase of diverse student subgroups, while obliging states to implement centralized standards and aligned assessments to measure such progress in their corresponding territories.

However, while the federal government renounced the idea of national (curriculum) standards, the heterarchically organized reform alliance continued to work on the development of (performance) standards, and therefore actively argued that global competition left "no alternative" (Munck, 2003). Thus, almost all members of this new policy network (including business actors, foundations, and think tanks) had significant international work experience or were part of international networking. Many acted as what could be described as "field hoppers" (Hartong, 2018a), becoming involved in various international, national, and cross-sectoral policy initiatives (e.g., economy, government, initiatives by international organizations), thus aligning reform ideas and creating cross-field homogeneities.

Consequently, with the growing involvement of such field hoppers in the promotion of K–12 performance standards, the transnational began to be conceptualized differently from the disparaging comparisons with the East seen in the past (as evident in the standardization initiatives of the 1960s or 1980s). Instead, standards-based reform was now constructed as part of a globalized context, thus requiring global-scale (instead of purely national or state-related) benchmarking procedures, which included the active participation of global actors (e.g., international organizations or global business leaders).

The alliance held two core summits in Palisades, New York, in 1996 and 1999, which ushered in supra-state performance standards (see www.achieve.org/ summits), and included the foundation of Achieve, Inc., a semi-governmental non-profit organization (led by a board of both governors *and* business actors), the establishment of which marked a crucial step toward the national rearrangement of governance through standards (for a more detailed description of the role of Achieve, see Hartong, 2016b). Following its formation, the reform-alliance assigned Achieve the task of benchmarking "world-class-standards" by comparing different standards from around the world with existing state standards, as well as organizing cross-state cooperation to expand nationally aligned standards-based governance. As a result, the reform initiative became anchored within a reconstituted global and business context, which was strategically initiated and supportively informed by Achieve. Thus, Achieve took on the role of meta-governance, building up a new multilevel yet simultaneously nationalized structure by topologically benchmarking, nationalizing, and also transnationalizing state standards (then named the *Common Core State Standards*). Practically, this was organized by establishing an *International Benchmarking Advisory Group* in 2008, which again mainly consisted of governors, business actors (such as Intel and Microsoft), and policy advocates, but also experts from international large-scale assessment projects, such as TIMSS (Trends in International Mathematics and Science Study) and PISA (Programme for International Student Assessment). This group was tasked with identifying indicators from so-called "world-best-performing" educational systems (e.g., Finland) that could be implemented within the United States in order to strengthen the standards framework. In 2008, the group released the report *Benchmarking for Success*, which once more scrutinized the weak performance of the United States in PISA rankings, while also promoting systematic international large-scale assessment benchmarking (as described previously) in standards-based governance. Additionally, the report addressed states more directly, urging them to take the lead in using studies like PISA for policymaking (instead of using NAEP), for example by encouraging them to participate in PISA individually (Engel & Frizzell, 2015; see also Niemann, Hartong, & Martens, 2018).

By 2010, almost every US state had adopted the Common Core State Standards and had begun implementing standards-aligned instruments. While Achieve continued to support state cooperation, its role now expanded to providing standards-aligned materials and digital resources for capacity-building, including standards training, advocacy, instructional support, and even standards-aligned classroom tasks.

A crucial push toward further national alignment (and thus the further stabilization of the field) was instigated by the federal *Race to the Top* program in 2009, which linked federal funding competition with a "recommendation" to adopt the new standards (Maranto & McShane, 2012). At the same time, Race to the Top provided funding for the development of supra-state assessment (aligned to the standards, and hence establishing a different structure than NAEP), using a scheme which nevertheless only allowed large consortia of states to apply for money. Consequently, two different yet competing state consortia were established after 2010 – the *Partnership for Assessment of Readiness in College and Career* (PARCC), and the *Smarter Balanced Consortia*. While both competed for state members within a now stronger nationalized market of standards-based assessments in the following years, the market was also opened up to global test providers who could partner with the consortia (today, PARCC is run by Pearson Education, the largest global provider of educational assessment), thus further stabilizing heterarchical structures around the autonomization of standards-based reform as a simultaneously nationalized *and* transnationalized field.

However, after 2015, the alliance around nationalized standards-based reform encountered another significant setback, when the Republican Party regained federal power and rolled back federal influence over state standards-based governance, supported by the newest reauthorization of the ESEA – the *Every Student Succeeds Act*. Consequently, both the standards and the new standardized assessments witnessed a notable opt-out movement, with decreasing numbers of states participating, instead returning to their individual standards and assessments. Thus, standards-based reform underwent a kind of reterritorialization in the form of state re-bordering, indicating a recurring fragility of the nationalized field. Conversely, however, the overall agenda of "challenging" standards, monitoring, and assessment has remained a core narrative in the new *Every Student Succeeds Act*, which now even more strongly encourages states to become successful meta-governors in standards-based reform. Additionally, with the new act, the federal Department of Education has expanded the scope of mandatory supra-state data collection to more than a hundred indicators, used by the federal department to constantly compare the performance of individual states, thus continuing to refine the nationalized topological space of (now more indirect) accountability.

Conclusion

This chapter has critically examined sociopolitical processes of transnationalization in US education policy, focusing on the transforming production, legitimization, and dissemination of knowledge (through data) by shifting policy networks over 50 years of standards-based reform. Furthermore, such shifting policy networks have been accompanied by changing constitutions of the national and transnational. Dual lenses of (heterarchical and topological) policy network analysis and field theoretical thinking were found to serve as useful tools for understanding

> space (a national space, in this case) no longer in terms of a priori coordinates – a fixed stage upon which events occur – but instead as something formed by relations between heterogeneous parts [. . .]. In this sense, space (and time) are decidedly more a posteriori in nature; that is, emergent, contingent and dynamic [. . .], and emerging out of material [and symbolic] relations.
>
> (Savage & Lewis, 2017: 20)

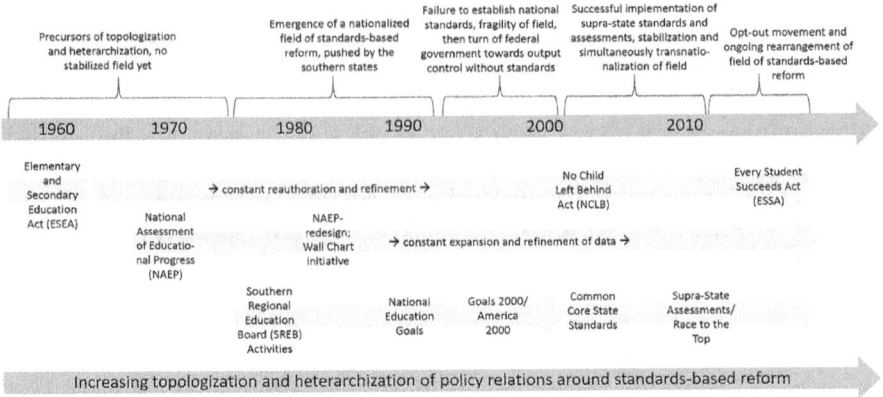

Figure 12.1 Topologization of heterarchization of standards-based school reform

In line with such reasoning, the findings presented in this chapter (which are further summarized in Figure 12.1) suggest a need for further study of the role of the "national" not (only) as opposing, but also as facilitating "representations" (Dale & Robertson, 2009) within powerful processes of transnationalization.

For example, until the late 1990s, transnational influence on US standards-based policy largely consisted of negative projection-making (shaming the United States as lagging behind international competitors such as Russia or China), without any significant policy borrowing (Steiner-Khamsi & Waldow, 2012) or benchmarking. This changed with the emergence of an alliance around the Common Core State Standards and the more systematic integration of these standards into a global frame of reference, for example by including developers of international large-scale assessments in the standards development process, as well as the benchmarking of "world-class standards". The analysis has thus illustrated how such shifting network constellations have fabricated particular forms of reform knowledge with which to imagine the transnational.

At the same time, intra-national (federal) policy dynamics and regional differences have been found to play key roles in the changing formations of standards-based reform as a nationalized field, particularly illuminated by the example of the SREB. However, as Savage and Lewis (2017: 20) argue, there is an "analytical difficulty inherent to researching national policies in federal systems", which accompanies the question of how the subnational can be properly taken into consideration when analyzing transnationalization, both conceptually and empirically. Policy network analysis and its integration with field theoretical thinking thus appears well suited to understanding not only the development, but also the residual fragility, of specific policies (such as standards-based reform), in addition to serving as a useful tool for embedding that development within the broader framework of federalism (see also Wallner et al., 2020).

Notes

* The presented research was funded by the Deutsche Forschungsgemeinschaft (DFG, German Research Foundation).
1 This does not mean, however, that school data was not collected before the 1960s. In fact, scholars have documented the governmental power of tests and educational statistics as early as the 1850s (Reese, 2013). Nonetheless, the period after the 1960s marks a crucial turn toward multilevel, nationalized school monitoring, which significantly differs from any earlier form.
2 For example, Bernhard (2008) and Hennig and Kohl (2011) have documented the importance of field theory for explaining *why* particular networks emerge in a particular way, according to social field positions.
3 For my earlier research applying and discussing these characteristics, see Hartong, 2015, 2016b, 2018a.
4 In this regard, heterarchization and topologization are in fact not "new" phenomena, but can be traced back at least several decades. Nevertheless, their scope has grown dramatically, particularly over recent years with the rise of digitalization and algorithmization.
5 See also Landri (2018: 39 ff.), who illustrates this transformation using the example of the European Education Space.
6 For a more detailed reconstruction, see Hartong, 2018a.
7 For a closer explanation of the relation between *A Nation at Risk* and US standards-based reform, see Hartong, 2018a: 128–132.

References

Alexiadou, N., Dovemark, M., Erixon-Arreman, I., Holm, A.-S., Lundahl, L., & Lundström, U. (2016). Managing Inclusion in Competitive School Systems: The Cases of Sweden and England. *Research in Comparative and International Education, 11*(1), 13–33.
Allen, J. (2011). Topological Twists: Power's Shifting Geographies. *Dialogues in Human Geography, 1*(3), 283–298.
Anderson, L. (2007). *Congress and the Classroom: From the Cold War to 'No Child Left Behind'*. Philadelphia, PA: University of Pennsylvania Press.
Baier, C., & Schmitz, A. (2012). Organisationen als Akteure in sozialen Feldern – Eine Modellierungsstrategie am Beispiel deutscher Hochschulen. In S. Bernhard & C. Schmidt-Wellenburg (Eds.), *Feldanalyse als Forschungsprogramm 1* (pp. 191–220). Wiesbaden: VS Verlag für Sozialwissenschaften.
Bailey, S. K., & Mosher, E. K. (1968). *ESEA: The Office of Education Administers a Law*. New York, NY: Syracuse University Press.
Ball, S. J. (2009). Academies in Context: Politics, Business and Philanthropy and Heterarchical Governance. *Management in Education, 23*(3), 100–103.
Ball, S. J. (2016). Following Policy: Networks, Network Ethnography and Education Policy Mobilities. *Journal of Education Policy, 31*(5), 549–566.
Ball, S. J., & Junemann, J. (2012). *Networks, New Governance and Education*. Bristol: Policy Press.
Bernhard, S. (2010). Netzwerkanalyse und Feldtheorie: Grundriss einer Integration im Rahmen von Bourdieus Sozialtheorie. In C. Stegbauer (Ed.), *Netzwerkanalyse und Netzwerktheorie* (pp. 121–130). Wiesbaden: VS Verlag für Sozialwissenschaften.
Bloem, S. (2016). *Die PISA-Strategie der OECD Zur Bildungspolitik eines globalen Akteurs*. Weinheim: Juventa.
Bourdieu, P. (2001). *Das politische Feld – Zur Kritik der politischen Vernunft*. Konstanz: UVK.

Carney, S. (2009). Negotiating Policy in an Age of Globalization: Exploring Educational 'Policyscapes' in Denmark, Nepal, and China. *Comparative Education Review*, *53*(1), 63–88.

Cuban, L. (2003). Business Influence on US Public Schools and Its Limits, 1880–2000. In M. Mangold & J. Oelkers (Eds.), *Demokratie, Bildung und Markt* (pp. 123–144). Bern: Peter Lang.

Dale, R., & Robertson, S. (2009). Beyond Methodological 'Isms' in Comparative Education in an Era of Globalisation. In R. Cowen & A. M. Kazamias (Eds.), *International Handbook of Comparative Education* (pp. 1113–1127). Dortrecht: Springer.

Dale, R., & Robertson, S. (2012). Towards a Critical Grammar of Education Policy Movements. In G. Steiner-Khamsi & F. Waldow (Eds.), *Policy Borrowing and Lending in Education: World Yearbook of Education* (pp. 21–40). London; New York, NY: Routledge.

Engel, L. C. (2015). Beyond the National: PISA's Influence in Education Policy Formation in the EU and Spain. *European Education*, *47*(2), 100–116.

Engel, L. C., & Frizzell, M. (2015). Competitive Comparison and PISA Bragging Rights: Sub-National Uses of the OECD's PISA in Canada and the US. *Discourse: Studies in the Cultural Politics of Education*, *36*(5), 665–682.

Fuhrman, S. H. (2003). Riding Waves, Trading Horses: The Twenty-Year Effort to Reform Education. In D. T. Gordon (Ed.), *A Nation Reformed? American Education 20 Years After a Nation at Risk* (pp. 7–22). Cambridge, MA: Harvard Education Press.

Fuhse, J. (2009). Lässt sich die Netzwerkforschung besser mit der Feldtheorie oder der Systemtheorie verknüpfen? In R. Häußling (Ed.), *Grenzen von Netzwerken* (pp. 55–80). Wiesbaden: VS Verlag für Sozialwissenschaften.

Gomolla, M. (2013). School Effectiveness and the Reframing of Discourses on Social Justice in Education. *Schweizer Zeitschrift für Soziologie*, *39*(2), 245–266.

Gordon, D. T. (Ed.). (2003). *A Nation Reformed? American Education 20 Years After a Nation at Risk*. Cambridge, MA: Harvard Education Press.

Gorur, R., & Wu, M. (2015). Leaning Too Far? PISA, Policy and Australia's 'Top Five' Ambitions. *Discourse: Studies in the Cultural Politics of Education*, *36*(5), 647–664.

Gulson, K. N., Lewis, S., Lingard, B., Lubienski, C., Takayama, K., & Taylor Webb, P. (2017). Policy Mobilities and Methodology: A Proposition for Inventive Methods in Education Policy Studies. *Critical Studies in Education*, *58*(2), 224–241.

Hartong, S. (2012). Overcoming Resistance to Change: PISA, School Reform in Germany and the Example of Lower Saxony. *Journal of Educational Policy*, *27*(6), 747–760.

Hartong, S. (2014). Neue Bildungsregulierung im Zeitalter der 'Governance by Numbers': Das Beispiel standardbasierter Bildungsreform in Deutschland und den USA. *Leviathan*, *42*(4), 1–29.

Hartong, S. (2015). Global Policy Convergence Through 'Distributed Governance?' The Emergence of 'National' Education Standards in the US and Germany. *Journal of International and Comparative Social Policy*, *31*(1), 10–33.

Hartong, S. (2016a). New Structures of Power and Regulation Within 'Distributed' Education Policy: The Example of the US Common Core State Standards Initiative. *Journal of Education Policy*, *31*(2), 213–225.

Hartong, S. (2016b). Between Assessments, Digital Technologies, and Big Data: The Growing Influence of 'Hidden' Data Mediators in Education. *European Education Research Journal*, *15*(5), 523–536.

Hartong, S. (2018a). *Standardbasierte Bildungsreformen in den USA: Vergessene Ursprünge und aktuelle Transformationen*. Weinheim: Juventa.

Hartong, S. (2018b). Towards a Topological Re-Assemblage of Education Policy? Observing the Implementation of Performance Data Infrastructures and 'Centers of Calculation' in Germany. *Globalisation, Societies and Education*, *16*(1), 134–150.

Hartong, S., & Schwabe, U. (2013). Wie 'Agenten des Wandels' deutsche Bildungspolitik transformier(t)en – Ein integratives Diffusionsmodell für die Prozesse PISA und Bologna. *Swiss Journal of Sociology, 39*(3), 493–515.

Hennig, M., & Kohl, S. (2011). *Rahmen und Spielräume sozialer Beziehungen: Zum Einfluss des Habitus auf die Herausbildung von Netzwerkstrukturen.* Wiesbaden: Springer-Verlag.

Landri, P. (2018). *Digital Governance of Education.* London: Bloomsbury Academic.

Lewis, S., & Lingard, B. (2015). The Multiple Effects of International Large-Scale Assessment on Education Policy and Research. *Discourse: Studies in the Cultural Politics of Education, 36*(5), 621–637.

Lingard, B., & Grek, S. (2007). *The OECD, Indicators and PISA: An Exploration of Events and Theoretical Perspectives.* Edinburgh: ESRC/ESF Research Project.

Mangez, E., & Hilgers, M. (2012). The Field of Knowledge and the Policy Field in Education: PISA and the Production of Knowledge for Policy. *European Educational Research Journal, 11*(2), 189–205.

Maranto, R., & McShane, M. Q. (2012). *President Obama and Education Reform.* New York, NY: Palgrave.

Marttila, T. (2014). Die wissensbasierte Regierung der Bildung – Die Genese einer transnationalen Gouvernementalität in England und Schweden. *Berliner Journal für Soziologie, 24*(2), 257–287.

Mehta, J. (2013). *The Allure of Order: High Hopes, Dashed Expectations, and the Troubled Quest to Remake American Schooling.* Oxford: Oxford University Press.

Münch, R. (2009). *Globale Eliten, lokale Autoritäten: Bildung und Wissenschaft unter dem Regime von PISA, McKinsey & Co.* Frankfurt am Main: Suhrkamp.

Munck, R. (2003). Neoliberalism, Necessitarianism and Alternatives in Latin America: There Is No Alternative (Tina)? *Third World Quarterly, 24*(3), 495–511.

Niemann, D., Hartong, S., & Martens, K. (2018). Observing Local Dynamics of ILSA Projections: A Comparison Between Germany and the U.S. *Globalisation, Societies and Education, 16*(1), 134–150.

Olmedo, A., Bailey, P. L., & Ball, S. J. (2013). To Infinity and Beyond . . .: Heterarchical Governance, the Teach for All Network in Europe and the Making of Profits and Minds. *European Educational Research Journal, 12*(4), 492–512.

Ong, A., & Collier, S. J. (2005). *Global Assemblages: Technology, Politics, and Ethics as Anthropological Problems.* London: Blackwell.

Payne, C. (2008). *So Much Reform, So Little Change: The Persistence of Failure in Urban Schools.* Cambridge, MA: Harvard Education Press.

Piattoeva, N. (2018). How Can Transnational Connection Hold? An Actor-Network Theory Inspired Approach to the Materiality of Transnational Education Governance. In A. Wilkins & A. Olmedo (Eds.), *Education Governance and Social Theory: Interdisciplinary Approaches to Research* (pp. 103–121). London: Bloomsbury.

Ravitch, D. (1983). *The Troubled Crusade: American Education, 1945–1980.* New York, NY: Basic Books.

Ravitch, D. (2010). *The Death and Life of the Great American School System: How Testing and Choice Are Undermining Education.* New York, NY: Basic Books.

Rawolle, S., & Lingard, B. (2014). Mediatization and Education: A Sociological Account. In K. Lundby (Ed.), *Mediatization of Communication* (pp. 595–614). Berlin: De Gruyter Mouton.

Reese, W. J. (2013). *Testing Wars in the Public Schools a Forgotten History.* Cambridge, MA: Harvard University Press.

Sacks, P. (2000). *Standardized Minds: The High Price of America's Testing Culture and What We Can Do to Change It*. Jackson, TN: Da Capo Press.

Savage, G. C., & Lewis, S. (2017). The Phantom National? Assembling National Teaching Standards in Australia's Federal System. *Journal of Education Policy*, *33*(1), 118–142.

Sellar, S., & Lingard, B. (2013). Looking East: Shanghai, PISA 2009 and the Reconstitution of Reference Societies in the Global Education Policy Field. *Comparative Education*, *49*(4), 464–485.

Sobe, N. W., & Kowalczyk, J. (2018). Context, Entanglement and Assemblage as Matters of Concern in Comparative Education Research. In J. McLeod, N. W. Sobe & T. Seddon (Eds.), *World Yearbook of Education 2018: Uneven Space-Times of Education: Historical Sociologies of Concepts, Methods and Practices* (pp. 197–204). London: Routledge.

SREB, Southern Regional Education Board. (2013). 65 Years Helping States to Improve Education. Retrieved June 19, 2017, from www.sreb.org/sites/main/files/file-attachments/13e04_65_years.pdf

Stake, R. E. (2007). NAEP, Report Cards and Education: A Review Essay. *Education Review*, *10*(1), 1–23.

Staunaes, D., Brogger, K., & Krejsler, J. B. (2018). How Reforms Morph as They Move: Performative Approaches to Education Reforms and Their Un/Intended Effects. *International Journal of Qualitative Studies in Education*, *31*(5), 345–352.

Steiner-Khamsi, G. (2012). Understanding Policy Borrowing and Lending: Building Comparative Policy Studies. In G. Steiner-Khamsi & F. Waldow (Eds.), *World Yearbook of Education 2012: Policy Borrowing and Lending in Education* (pp. 3–17). London; New York, NY: Routledge.

Steiner-Khamsi, G., & Waldow, F. (Eds.). (2012). *Policy Borrowing and Lending in Education: World Yearbook of Education*. London: Routledge.

Takayama, K. (2013). Untangling the Global-Distant-Local Knot: The Politics of National Academic Achievement Testing in Japan. *Journal of Education Policy*, *28*(5), 657–675.

Tröhler, D., & Lenz, T. (Eds.). (2015). *Trajectories in the Development of Modern School Systems: Between the National and the Global*. New York, NY: Routledge.

Urban, W. J. (2010). *More Than Science and Sputnik: The National Defense Education Act of 1958*. Tuscaloosa, AL: University of Alabama Press.

Vinovskis, M. A. (1998). *Overseeing the Nation's Report Card: The Creation and Evolution of the National Assessment Governing Board (NAGB)*. Washington, DC: NAGB.

Vinovskis, M. A. (2009). *From a Nation at Risk to No Child Left Behind: National Education Goals and the Creation of Federal Education Policy*. New York, NY: Teachers College Press.

Waldow, F., & Steiner-Khamsi, G. (2018). PISA for Scandalisation, PISA for Projection: The Use of International Large-Scale Assessments in Education Policy Making. *Globalisation, Societies and Education*, *16*(5), 557–565.

Wallner, J., Savage, G., Hartong, S., & Engel, L. (2020). Laboratories, Co-Producers and Venues: Illuminating the Varying Roles of Subnational Governments in the Formation of Standards-Based Assessments in Four Federations. *Comparative Education Review*, *63*(4), forthcoming.

Index